Brazil–Africa Relations

Brazil–Africa Relations

Historical Dimensions and Contemporary Engagements From the 1960s to the Present

Edited by
Gerhard Seibert and Paulo Fagundes Visentini

JAMES CURREY

James Currey
is an imprint of
Boydell & Brewer Ltd
PO Box 9, Woodbridge
Suffolk IP12 3DF (GB)
www.jamescurrey.com
and of
Boydell & Brewer Inc.
668 Mt Hope Avenue
Rochester, NY 14620–2731 (US)
www.boydellandbrewer.com

First published 2019

British Library Cataloguing in Publication Data
A catalogue record for this book is available on request from the British Library

ISBN 978-1-84701-195-4 (James Currey cloth)

This publication is printed on acid-free paper

Printed and bound in Great Britain by
TJ International Ltd, Padstow, Cornwall

MIX
Paper from responsible sources
FSC www.fsc.org FSC® C013056

Contents

Illustrations

Contributors

Analúcia Danilevicz Pereira is Professor of International Relations and of the Doctoral Programmes of International Strategic Studies and Political Science at Universidade Federal do Rio Grande do Sul (UFRGS); Professor of the Doctoral Programme of Military Science at the Escola de Comando e Estado Maior do Exército (ECEME); coordinator and researcher at the Centro Brasileiro de Estudos Africanos (CEBRÁFRICA) at UFRGS; and researcher at the Núcleo Brasileiro de Estratégia e Relações Internacionais (NERINT) at UFRGS. She is also editor of *Revista Brasileira de Estudos Africanos*.

Antonia Aparecida Quintão is Cultural Director at Instituto Histórico e Geográfico de São Paulo (IHGSP); Adjunct Professor at Universidade Presbiteriana Mackenzie in São Paulo. Researcher at the Núcleo de Estudos Interdisciplinares sobre o Negro Brasileiro at Universidade de São Paulo (NEINB-USP); and Núcleo de Diversidade e Liderança at Universidade Presbiteriana Mackenzie. She is the author of the books *Lá vem o meu parente: As irmandades de pretos e pardos no Rio de Janeiro e em Pernambuco (Século XVIII)* (São Paulo: Annablume, Fapesp, 2002) and *Irmandades Negras: Outro espaço de luta e resistência (São Paulo 1870–1890)* (São Paulo: Annablume, 2009).

Gerhard Seibert earned a PhD in Social Sciences at Leiden University, Netherlands, in 1999. Thereafter he was researcher at Instituto de Investigação Científica Tropical (IICT), Lisbon, Portugal. From 2008 to 2014 he was a researcher at the Centro de Estudos Africanos at ISCTE – Instituto Universitário de Lisboa (CEA / ISCTE-IUL). Since 2014 he has been Associate Professor at Universidade de Integração Internacional da Lusofonia Afro-Brasileira (UNILAB), São Francisco do Conde, Bahia, Brazil. He is the collaborator of two postgraduate programmes at the Centro de Estudos Afro-Orientais (CEAO), at Universidade Federal da Bahia (UFBA) and Universidade do Estado da Bahia (UNEB) respectively. He is the author of *Comrades, Clients and Cousins. Colonialism, Socialism and Democratization in São Tomé and Príncipe* (Leiden: Brill, 2006) and various articles in academic journals and book chapters.

Paulo Fagundes Visentini is a historian and Full Professor of International Relations at Universidade Federal do Rio Grande do Sul (UFRGS). He earned his PhD in History from the Universidade de São Paulo (USP) and a post-doctorate in International Relations from the London School of Economics. He held the Rio Barbosa Chair in Brazilian Studies at Leiden University, Netherlands, and the Rio Branco Chair in International Relations at the University of Oxford. He is also a researcher at the Conselho Nacional de Desenvolvimento Científico e Tecnológico (CNPq). The author of several books on contemporary world history and international relations, he is the founder of the Centro Brasileiro de Estudos Africanos (CEBÁFRICA) and editor of the journal *AUSTRAL: Brazilian Journal of Strategy and International Relations*.

Acknowledgements

This project would not have been possible without a research grant provided by the *Fundação para a Ciência e a Tecnologia* (FCT), the Portuguese public funding agency for science, research and technology (PTDC/AFR/110095/2009). The research project on Brazil – Africa relations was carried out by three of the authors at the former Centre of African Studies (CEA) at ISCTE – University Institute of Lisbon (ISCTE-IUL), Portugal, in the period from 2011–14. Several people have supported us during the research and in the process of publishing this book, which was mainly done in Brazil. We owe great thanks to Anna Cristina B. Pérez, project analyst at the Brazilian Cooperation Agency (ABC) in Brasília, who has provided lots of relevant information on Brazil's international development cooperation. We would also like to thank Carlos R.S. Milani at the Institute of Social and Political Studies (IESP) of Rio de Janeiro State University (UERJ) for having provided additional data on Brazil's technical cooperation. Several people have contributed to the writing of chapters. Pedro da Silva Alt, William Roberto, Livi Gerbase, and Ana Paula de Mattos Calich, research assistants at the Brazilian Centre for African Studies (CEBRAFRICA) of the Federal University of Rio Grande do Sul (UFRGS), have made contributions to Chapter 2. Isadora Caminha Coutinho of the International Strategic Studies Postgraduate Programme at the same university participated in writing Chapter 5. Maria Gabriela Vieira and Amabilly Bonacina, both students of International Relations at UFRGS, helped compiling the Chronology. They all deserve our gratitude. Further, we are particularly grateful to Rachel Evens in Lisbon, who has done the English language revisions of the entire manuscript with great accuracy. Without her excellent work, this book would not have been possible. We also would like to thank Daniel Metcalfe and Philip Havik, who provided the English language revisions of smaller sections of the book. Finally we are grateful for the useful recommendations and suggestions made by two anonymous reviewers, who read the entire initial book manuscript. However, the different authors of this book are solely responsible for the contents of their respective chapters.

Abbreviations

ABC	Agência Brasileira de Cooperação (Brazilian Development Agency)
ABI	Atlantic Basin Initiative
ABI	Associação Brasileira de Imprensa (Brazilian Press Association)
ACFI	Acordos de Cooperação e Facilitação de Investimentos (Agreements for Cooperation and Facilitation of Investments)
AFM	Apostolic Faith Mission
AFRICOM	United States Africa Command
AIDS	Acquired Immunodeficiency Syndrome
ANC	African National Congress
APEX-Brasil	Agência Brasileira de Promoção de Exportações e Investimentos (Brazilian Trade and Investment Promotion Agency)
ARM	African Rainbow Minerals
ARV	Antiretroviral
ASA	Africa–South America Summit
ASACOF	Africa–South America Cooperation Forum
ASQ	Agenda Social Quilombola (Social Agenda Maroons)
ASPA	Cúpula América do Sul-Países Árabes (Summit of South American–Arab Countries)
ATT	UN Arms Trade Treaty
AU	African Union
BIAO	Banque internationale pour l'Afrique occidentale (International Bank for Western Africa)
BNDES	Banco Nacional de Desenvolvimento (Brazilian Development Bank)
BRICS	Brazil, Russia, India, China and South Africa
BSGR	Beny Steinmetz Group Resources
CAMEX	Câmara de Comércio Exterior (Chamber of External Trade)

CAPES	Coordenação de Aperfeiçoamento de Pessoal de Nível Superior (Coordination for the Improvement of Higher Education Personnel)
CBERS	China–Brazil Earth Resources Satellite
CCB	Centro Cultural Brasileiro (Brazilian Cultural Centre)
CCS	Centro de Ciências de Saúde (Health Sciences Centre)
CEAA	Centro de Estudos Afro-Asiáticos (Centre for Afro-Asian Studies)
CEAO	Centro de Estudos Afro-Orientais (Centre for Afro-Oriental Studies)
CECA	Centro de Estudos de Cultura Africana (Centre for Studies of African Culture)
CELPE-Bras	Certificado de Proficiência em Língua Portuguesa para Estrangeiros (Brazilian Certificate of Proficiency in Portuguese for Foreigners)
CENTCOM	United States Central Command
CNPq	Conselho Nacional de Desenvolvimento Científico e Tecnológico (National Council for Scientific and Technological Development)
CONAPIR	Conferência Nacional de Promoção da Igualdade Racial (National Conference for the Promotion of Racial Equality)
COPAL	Alliance of Cocoa Producing Countries
CPLP	Comunidade de Países de Língua Portuguesa (Community of Portuguese-speaking Countries)
CRESMAC	Centre Régional de Sécurité Maritime de l'Afrique Central (Regional Centre for Maritime Security in Central Africa)
CsF	Ciência sem Fronteiras (Science Without Borders)
DAC	Development Assistance Committee
DAF	Divisão da África (Africa Division, Foreign Ministry)
DIEESE	Departamento Intersindical de Estatística e Estudos Socioeconômicos (Intersindical Department of Statistics and Socioeconomic Studies)
DRC	Democratic Republic of the Congo
EAD	Ensino à Distância (Distance Education)
ECCAS	Economic Community of Central African States
ECOWAS	Economic Community of West African States
EEZ	Exclusive Economic Zone
EMBRAPA	Empresa Brasileira de Pesquisa Agropecuária (Brazilian Agricultural Research Corporation)

EMGEPRON	Empresa Gerencial de Projetos Navais (Management Company for Naval Projects)
ENEM	Exame Nacional do Ensino Médio (National High School Exam)
ENH	Empresa Nacional de Hidrocarbonetos (National Hydrocarbons Company, Mozambique)
EU	European Union
EUCOM	United States European Command
FAO	United Nations Food and Agriculture Organization
FCP	Fundação Cultural Palmares (Palmares Cultural Foundation)
FHC	Fernando Henrique Cardoso, Brazilian President (1995-2002)
FIFA	Fédération Internationale de Football Association (International Federation of Association Football)
Fiocruz	Fundação Oswaldo Cruz (Oswaldo Cruz Foundation)
FFLCH	Faculdade de Filosofia, Letras e Ciências Humanas (Faculty of Philosophy, Arts and Human Sciences)
FNLA	Frente Nacional de Libertação de Angola (National Liberation Front of Angola)
Frelimo	Frente de Libertação de Moçambique (Mozambique Liberation Front)
FTAA	Free Trade Agreement of the Americas
G77	Group of 77
GEO	Group on Earth Observations
GDP	Gross Domestic Product
GGC	Gulf of Guinea Commission
GHFSI	Global Hunger and Food Security Initiative
GPRA	Gouvernement provisoire de la République algérienne (Provisional Government of the Algerian Republic)
HIV	Human Immunodeficiency Virus
IBA	Instituto Brasileiro de Algodão (Brazilian Cotton Institute)
IBEAA	Instituto Brasileiro de Estudos Afro-Asiáticos (Brazilian Institute for Afro-Asian Studies)
IBGE	Instituto Brasileiro de Geografia e Estatística (Brazilian Institute of Geography and Statistics)
IBSA	India–Brazil–South Africa Dialogue Forum
IBSAMAR	India–Brazil–South Africa Maritime
IFES	Instituções Federais de Ensino Superior (Federal Institutions of Higher Education)

IIAM	Instituto de Investigação Agrícola de Moçambique (Agricultural Research Institute of Mozambique)
IILP	Instituto Internacional de Língua Portuguesa (International Portuguese Language Institute)
ILO	International Labour Organization
IMO	International Maritime Organization
INCRA	Instituto Nacional de Colonização e Reforma Agrária (National Institute of Colonisation and Agrarian Reform)
INESC	Instituto de Estudos Socioeconômicos (Institute of Socioeconomic Studies)
IOR-ARC	Indian Ocean Rim Association for Regional Cooperation
IPEA	Instituto de Pesquisa Econômica Aplicada (Institute of Applied Economic Research)
IURD	Igreja Universal do Reino de Deus (Universal Church of the Kingdom of God)
JICA	Japan International Cooperation Agency
LAM	Linhas Aéreas de Moçambique (Mozambique Airlines)
LAS	League of Arab States
MABLA	Movimento Afro-Brasileiro Pró-Libertação de Angola (Afro-Brazilian Movement for the Liberation of Angola)
MCTI	Ministério da Ciência, Tecnologia e Inovações (Ministry of Science, Technology and Innovation)
MDB	Movimento Democrático Brasileiro (Brazilian Democratic Movement)
MDIC	Ministério da Indústria, Comércio Exterior e Serviços (Ministry of Industry, External Trade and Services)
MEC	Ministério da Educação (Ministry of Education)
Mercosur	Mercado Común del Sur (Southern Common Market)
MINURCAT	Mission des Nations Unies en République centrafricaine et au Tchad (United Nations Mission in the Central African Republic and Chad)
MINURSO	Mission des Nations Unies pour l'Organisation d'un Référendum au Sahara Occidental (United Nations Mission for the Referendum in Western Sahara)
MINUSCA	Mission multidimensionnelle intégrée des Nations Unies pour la stabilisation en Centrafrique (United Nations Multidimensional Integrated Stabilization Mission in the Central African Republic)

MINUSTAH	Mission des Nations Unies pour la Stabilisation en Haïti (United Nations Stabilization Mission in Haiti)
MNUCDR	Movimento Negro Unificado Contra a Discriminação Racial (United Black Movement Against Racial Discrimination)
MONUSCO	Mission de l'Organisation des Nations Unies pour la stabilisation en République démocratique du Congo (United Nations Organization Stabilization Mission in the Democratic Republic of the Congo)
MPLA	Movimento Popular de Libertação de Angola (People's Movement for the Liberation of Angola)
NATO	North Atlantic Treaty Organization
NEPAD	New Partnership for Africa's Development
NGO	Non-governmental Organisation
OAB	Ordem dos Advogados do Brasil (Brazilian Bar Association)
OAF	Odebrecht Africa Fund
OAS	Organization of American States
OAU	Organisation of African Unity
ODA	Official Development Assistance
OECD	Organisation for Economic Cooperation and Development
ONUMOZ	United Nations Operation in Mozambique
OPEC	Organization of Petroleum Exporting Countries
Palop	Países Africanos de Língua Oficial Portuguesa (Officially Portuguese-speaking African Countries)
PBC-GB	UN Peacebuilding Commission Guinea-Bissau Configuration
PBQ	Programa Brasil Quilombola (Brazil Maroons Programme)
PCB	Partido Comunista Brasileiro (Brazilian Communist Party)
PEC-G	Programa de Estudantes-Convênio de Graduação (Exchange Programme for Undergraduate Students)
PEC-PG	Programa de Estudantes-Convênio de Pós-Graduação (Exchange Programme for Postgraduate Students)
PEI	Política Externa Independente (Independent Foreign Policy)
PLANAPIR	Plano Nacional da Promoção da Igualdade Racial (National Plan of the Promotion of Racial Equality).
PNAD	Pesquisa Nacional por Amostra de Domicílios (National Household Sample Survey)

PNPIR	Política Nacional da Promoção da Igualdade Racial (National Policy for the Promotion of Racial Equality)
PROEX	Programa de Financiamento às Exportações (Export Financing Programme)
ProSAVANA	Programa de Cooperaçao Tripartida para o Desenvolvimento da Agricultura da Savana Tropical em Moçambique (Trilateral Agriculture Development Cooperation Programme in Mozambique's Tropical Savannah)
ProUni	Programa Universidade para Todos (University for All Programme)
PSDB	Partido da Social Democracia Brasileira (Brazilian Social Democracy Party)
PST	Partido Social Trabalhador (Social Labour Party)
PT	Partido dos Trabalhadores (Workers' Party)
PTA	Preferential Trade Agreement
PUC-MG	Pontifícia Universidade Católica de Minas Gerais (Pontifical Catholic University of Minas Gerais)
SACU	Southern African Customs Union
SADC	Southern African Development Community
SADCC	Southern African Development Coordination Conference
SATO	South Atlantic Treaty Organization (as was proposed)
SEADE	Fundação Sistema Estadual de Análise de Dados (Foundation State System of Data Analysis)
SECAD	Secretaria de Educação Continuada, Alfabetização e Diversidade (Secretariat of Further Education, Literacy and Diversity)
SENAC	Serviço Nacional de Aprendizagem Comercial (National Service of Commercial Training)
SENAI	Serviço Nacional de Aprendizagem Industrial (National Service for Industrial Training)
SEPPIR	Secretaria Nacional de Políticas de Promoção da Igualdade Racial (National Secretariat for Policies to Promote Racial Equality)
SERPRO	Serviço Federal de Processamento de Dados (Federal Service for Data Processing)
SMM	Sociedade Moçambicana de Medicamentos (Mozambican Medical Drugs Society)
SOUTHCOM	United States Southern Command
SUS	Sistema Único de Saúde (Single Health System)
SWAPO	South West African People's Organisation

UEMOA	Union Economique et Monétaire Ouest Africaine (West African Economic and Monetary Union)
UERJ	Universidade do Estado do Rio de Janeiro (Rio de Janeiro State University)
UFBA	Universidade Federal da Bahia (Bahia Federal University)
UFG	Universidade Federal de Goiás (Goiás Federal University)
UFJF	Universidade Federal de Juiz de Fora (Juiz de Fora Federal University)
UFMG	Universidade Federal de Minas Gerais (Minas Gerais Federal University)
UFPA	Universidade Federal do Pará (Pará Federal University)
UFRGS	Universidade Federal do Rio Grande do Sul (Rio Grande do Sul Federal University)
UFRJ	Universidade Federal do Rio de Janeiro (Rio de Janeiro Federal University)
UFSCar	Universidade Federal de São Carlos (São Carlos Federal University)
UK	United Kingdom
UN	United Nations
UNAMID	United Nations African Union Mission in Darfur
UNASUR	Unión de Naciones Suramericanas (Union of South American Nations)
UNAVEM	United Nations Angola Verification Mission
UnB	Universidade de Brasília (University of Brasília)
UNCLOS	United Nations Convention on Law of the Sea
UNCTAD	United Nations Conference on Trade and Development
UNDP	United Nations Development Programme
UNEF	United Nations Emergency Force
UNESCO	United Nations Educational, Scientific and Cultural Organization
Unicamp	Universidade Estadual de Campinas (Campinas State University)
UNICEF	United Nations Children's Fund
UNIFSA	United Nations Interim Security Force for Abyei (Sudan)
UNILAB	Universidade da Integração Internacional da Lusofonia Afro-Brasileira (University of International Integration of Afro-Brazilian Lusophony)

UNIOGBIS	United Nations Integrated Peacebuilding Office in Guinea-Bissau
UNITA	União Nacional para a Independência Total de Angola (National Union for the Total Independence of Angola)
UNMIS	United Nations Mission in Sudan
UNMISS	United Nations Mission in South Sudan
UNOC	United Nations Operation in the Congo
UNOCI	United Nations Operation in Côte d'Ivoire
UNOMOZ	United Nations Operation in Mozambique
UNSOA	United Nations Support Office for the African Union Mission in Somalia
US	United States
USAID	United States Agency for International Development
USP	Universidade de São Paulo
WFP	World Food Programme
WTO	World Trade Organization
ZOPACAS	Zona de Paz e Cooperação do Atlântico Sul (South Atlantic Peace and Cooperation Zone)

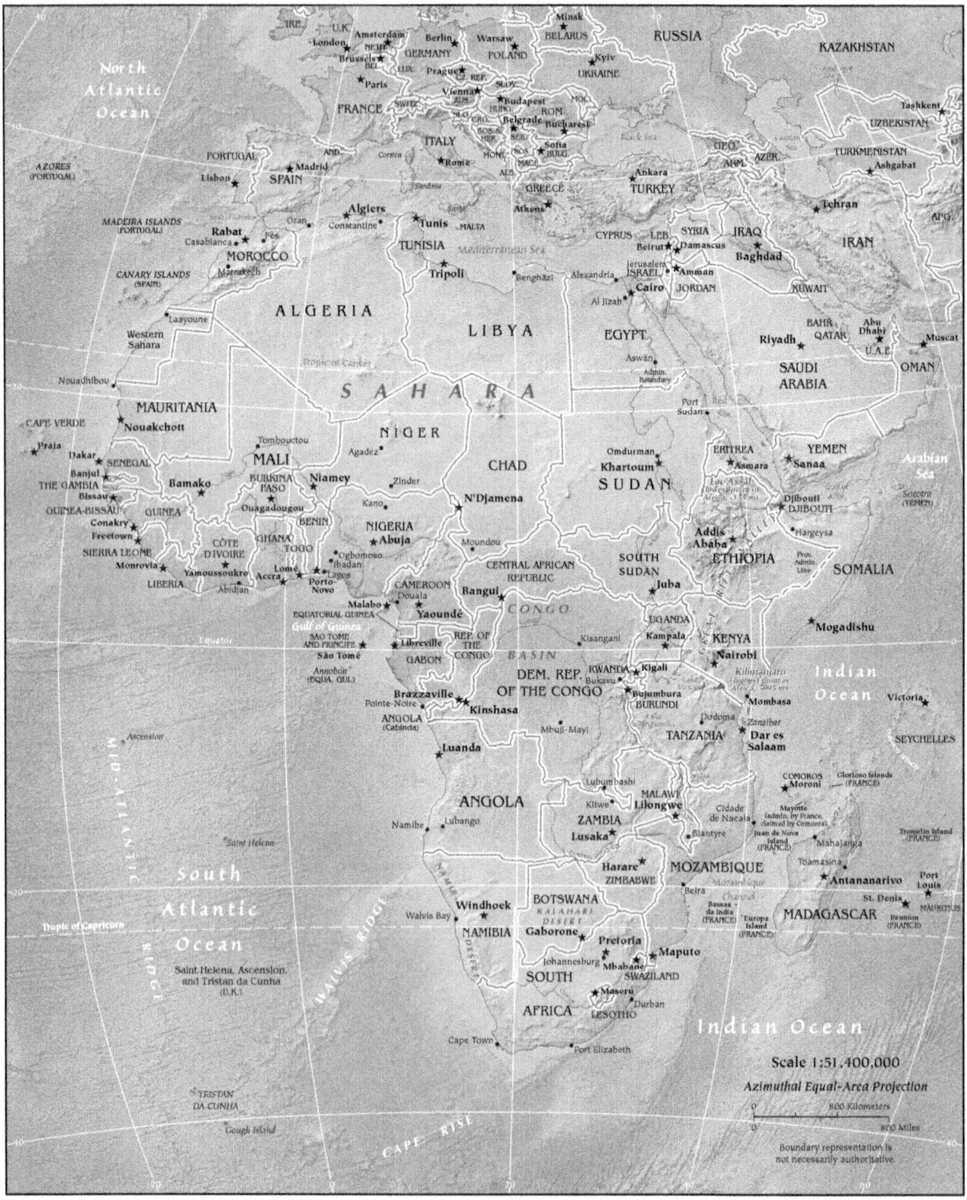

Political map of Africa. Courtesy of the University of Texas Libraries, The University of Texas at Austin

Introduction: Brazil–Africa Relations – Historical Dimensions and Contemporary Engagements from the 1960s to the Present[1]

Gerhard Seibert

In the 2000s, together with China and India, Brazil was one of the emerging powers that significantly strengthened relations with Africa and challenged the dominance of former European colonial powers and the United States on the continent. At the same time, they offered new opportunities of trade and development cooperation for African countries, and improved their bargaining position vis-à-vis foreign partners. Compared with China and India Brazil's engagement in Africa has been considerably smaller in terms of trade and investments, as well as development cooperation. However, Brazil's relations with the continent do not only differ in scope, but also with regard to historical, cultural, economic and geo-strategic aspects. Brazil's relations with Africa go back to the early 16th century when the then-Portuguese colony began to receive regular shipments of African slaves. As a result of the forced migration of some four million Africans during more than three hundred years, currently roughly half of Brazil's population is at least partly of African descent. Consequently, Brazil claims historical and cultural affinities with Africa, particularly with the continent's five Portuguese-speaking countries, with which it shares a common language and the same colonial power, albeit a colonialism in a different historical and geopolitical context. Moreover, unlike China and India, Brazil is less dependent on raw materials from Africa, since it is a resource-rich country itself and a major commodity exporter. In addition, Brazil has regional geo-strategic interests in the South Atlantic that is bordered by several Western and Southern African countries.

[1] This book brings together the results of a research project on Brazil–Africa relations that three of the authors carried out at the former Centre of African Studies (CEA) at ISCTE – University Institute of Lisbon (ISCTE-IUL) from 2011 to 2014. The project (PTDC/AFR/110095/2009) was financed by a research grant of the Fundação para a Ciência e a Tecnologia (FCT), the Portuguese national funding agency for science, research and technology.

Lyal White points out that, since the Second World War, Brazil's foreign policy has been guided by two opposing broad strands of thinking, which also have shaped its relations with Africa. The first strand of thought privileges relations with the United States and other developed countries to achieve international recognition and Brazil's own socioeconomic development. The second line of thinking underlines Brazil's identity as a developing country, where it seeks closer relations with other developing nations in the South to achieve those objectives.[2] According to their ideological orientation, consecutive Brazilian governments have pursued one of the two different stands of foreign policy thought, which in academic discourse are also known as the Americanism paradigm and the Globalism paradigm.[3] President Luiz Inácio Lula da Silva (2003–10), adopted the second strand of foreign policy thinking. Immediately after having assumed power he declared Africa a priority as part of his country's ambitious global foreign policy aimed at playing a greater role in a multipolar system that had replaced the bipolarity of the Cold War period. The rhetoric in Lula's approach to Africa frequently referred to Brazil's historical and emotional debts with Africa due to the slave trade and slavery. This discourse was not completely new, but unlike most of his predecessors Lula also recognised the existence of racism in Brazil. When, during a trip to Senegal in 2005, he visited Gorée Island, a former slave port, he asked for forgiveness for what Brazil had done to Africans.[4] Such statements were also directed to the Afro-Brazilian population, which formed a significant part of his and his party's domestic constituency. To satisfy the demands of his Afro-Brazilian constituents, immediately after taking office in 2003 his government passed a law that introduced teaching in African and Afro-Brazilian history and culture into Brazil's public and private schools and created the National Secretariat for Policies to Promote Racial Equality (SEPPIR) to combat racial discrimination.[5] In fact, Lula's foreign policy towards Africa was explicitly articulated with his policies of social inclusion and the struggle

[2] Lyal White, 'Understanding Brazil's new drive for Africa', *South African Journal of International Affairs*, 17:2 (2010), 223.

[3] Letícia Pinheiro, *Política externa brasileira (1889–2002)* (Rio de Janeiro: Zahar, 2004).

[4] Eduardo Scolese, 'Lula pede perdão por negros que foram escravos no Brasil', *Folha de São Paulo*, 15 April 2015, http://www1.folha.uol.com.br/fsp/brasil/fc1504200508.htm.

[5] Gladys Lechini, 'O Brasil na África ou a África no Brasil? A construção da política africana pelo Itamaraty', *Nueva Sociedad* (2008), 67.

against racism and against racial discrimination at home.[6] Lechini concludes accordingly that 'emphasis was placed on ensuring coherence between domestic and foreign policies, responding to the growing domestic demand of the Afro-descendant population'.[7]

Brazil's foreign policy strategy was to diversify the country's bilateral relations by strengthening ties in the Global South to gain greater autonomy from, and reduce dependence on, the United States and other Western countries. A concrete objective of this ambitious foreign policy was a permanent seat as the representative of South America on the UN Security Council. In this context, the votes of fifty-three (since 2011 fifty-four) African countries were crucial, especially as Brazilian ambitions to become a permanent member of a reformed UN Security Council were contested by its own Latin American neighbours. Stolte perceives the Lula government's engagement in Africa as a fundamental part of a foreign policy strategy to achieve international prestige and credibility in its quest for great power status.[8] However, the priority given to Africa was also driven by economic considerations, particularly as an export market for manufactured goods and engineering projects. In the 2000s, high economic growth rates in several African countries as a result of high commodity prices, which in turn were a result of increasing demand by emerging economies, particularly China, made the continent increasingly attractive for Brazilian investments and trade. To emphasise Africa's priority in Brazil's foreign policy President Lula made twelve official visits to twenty-three different African countries, more visits to the continent than all his predecessors combined. From 1983 to 2000 four of his predecessors made altogether five trips to Africa and visited ten different countries.[9] Lula became the personification of Brazil's new African policy and, thanks to his charisma and solidarity discourse, gained considerable personal prestige in Africa. However, it was not for the first time that Brazil strengthened bilateral relations with African countries. Two earlier attempts were made in the second half

[6] Irene Vida Gala, 'A Política Externa do Governo Lula para a África. A política externa como instrumento da ação afirmativa ... e ainda que não só' (dissertation, Brasília: Instituto Rio Branco, 2007), 54; Patrícia Soares Leite, *O Brasil e a Cooperação Sul-Sul em três momentos de política externa: os governos Jânio Quadros/João Goulart, Ernesto Geisel e Luiz Inácio Lula da Silva* (Brasília: Fundação Alexandre Gusmão, 2011), 201.

[7] Gladys Lechini, 'BRICS e África: a grande incógnita', *Boletim de Economia e Política Internacional*, 9 (2012), 141.

[8] Christina Stolte, *Brazil's Africa Strategy: Role Conception and the Drive for International Status* (New York: Palgrave Macmillan, 2015), 83.

[9] Gala, 'A Política Externa', 44.

of the 20th century under different domestic and international political and economic circumstances. However, they also had in common a claim for greater independence from the United States, the strengthening of South–South relations, the bid for a greater role for Brazil in international politics, and the desire to expand its foreign trade partners. Lechini corroborates that 'the rapprochement with African states had a political nature in the context of South-South relations, and a pragmatic commercial nature due to the interest in diversifying trading partners.'[10]

As already pointed out, Brazil and Africa maintained close relations during the Atlantic slave trade when over four million African slaves were deported to its territory. After Brazil's abolition of the slave trade in 1850 and the colonisation of the continent by European powers in the late 19th century the country's relations with Africa practically ceased to exist. A first attempt to re-establish Brazil's relations with several newly independent African countries was made in the early 1960s, as part of the Independent Foreign Policy pursued by the presidents Jânio Quadros (1961) and João Goulart (1961–64). They sought greater political autonomy vis-à-vis the United States and the Salazar dictatorship in Portugal, which resisted decolonisation, while they also expected new economic opportunities for Brazil in the newly independent African states. However, this first short-lived rapprochement with Africa was terminated by the military coup in 1964, because the ruling right-wing military realigned their foreign policy with Washington and Lisbon. A second rapprochement with Africa was made by the last military rulers Ernesto Geisel (1974–79) and João Figueiredo (1979–85) to guarantee Brazil's oil supplies, open new export markets for the country's increasing industrial output, and play a greater role within the group of developing countries. In economic terms this period was quite successful, since Africa reached the largest share of Brazil's foreign trade ever, while Brazilian companies operated direct maritime and air connections with African countries, and Brazilian commercial banks established branch offices on the continent. At the end of the Figueiredo presidency Africa accounted for approximately 10% of Brazil's foreign trade, which was larger than its combined trade with the neighbouring South American

[10] Gladys Lechini, 'Is South-South Co-operation still Possible? The case of Brazil's strategy and Argentine's impulses towards the new South Africa and Africa', in *Politics and Social Movements in an Hegemonic World: Lessons from Africa, Asia and Latin America*, edited by Atilio A. Boron and Gladys Lechini (Buenos Aires: CLACSO, 2005).

countries.[11] However, from the mid-1980s Brazils relations with Africa suffered a serious setback in all sectors as a result of its debt crisis and the economic and financial problems that affected African countries at the same time. Consequently, Brazil's relations with Africa dropped to levels of the 1960s, while it prioritised relations with Latin America, Western countries and the emerging economies like China and India.

It was not until 2003 when Lula came to power that Brazil initiated its third rapprochement with Africa. During his eight-year presidency Brazil successfully strengthened ties with Africa on all levels, both bilaterally and multilaterally.[12] From 2003 to 2008, Brazilian trade with Africa increased significantly from $6.2 billion to $25.9 billion; however, proportionally it never reached the share of 1985. Besides, the trade with the entire continent was considerably less than Brazil's trade with single countries like China, the United States or Argentina.[13] Nevertheless, compared with other BRICS countries, Brazil registered the second-highest growth of trade with Africa after China.[14] Backed by government loans provided by the Brazilian National Development Bank (BNDES), large Brazilian companies in the construction, mining and energy sectors considerably increased investments in a few African countries, particularly in Angola, Mozambique and South Africa. In addition, another state-owned financial institution provided export credits to help increase Brazilian exports to several African countries. However, despite increasing investments and trade with the continent, during the Lula presidency Brazil failed to establish regular air connections or maritime traffic with African countries, which has hampered the expansion of Brazilian exports to the continent. Only in October 2016 did a Brazilian airline inaugurate regular flights from São Paulo to Johannesburg, while Brazil's few other direct air connections with the neighbouring continent are all operated by African companies.

During the Lula government, Brazil considerably increased its involvement in South–South development cooperation as a foreign policy tool, particularly in Africa, while it continued to be a development assistance recipient itself. Brazil has claimed that its development cooperation is a horizontal relationship between equal partners in search of mutual

[11] José Flávio Sombra Saraiva, *África parceira do Brasil atlântico. Relações internacionais do Brasil e da África no início do século XXI* (Belo Horizonte: Fino Traço Editora, 2012), 21.

[12] Ibid., 97.

[13] Stolte, *Brazil's Africa Strategy*, 135.

[14] Ian Taylor, Africa Rising? *BRICS – diversifying dependency* (Woodbridge: James Currey, 2014), 35.

benefits, based on its own successful programmes to overcome poverty and underdevelopment and without any economic or political conditions for partner countries. Of course, despite such claims of unselfishness, in several cases it has become difficult to consider Brazil's cooperation as an instrument dissociated from its own economic interests, as Hirst rightly observes.[15] Brazil has provided technical cooperation projects for more than forty African countries; however, about half of the projects were conducted in the five Portuguese-speaking African countries. Moreover, the country doubled its embassies in African countries from seventeen to thirty-four and additionally opened two consulates, while several multilateral organisations involving African countries were either revived or newly established on Brazilian initiative. Brasília revitalised the South Atlantic Peace and Cooperation Zone (ZOPACAS), established in 1986, and strengthened its engagement with the Community of Portuguese-speaking Countries (CPLP), founded in 1996. In 2003, together with India and South Africa, Brazil created the trilateral IBSA Dialogue Forum to claim greater involvement in international politics, and in 2006 it was co-founder of the Africa–South America Summit (ASA), comprising twelve Latin American and fifty-four African countries. Unlike China, India, France, the United States and other countries, Brazil has not held regular summits with African leaders, but instead has strengthened ties with Africa bilaterally and through those multilateral initiatives. While the scope of Brazil's trade, investments and development cooperation with Africa is considerably less than that of China, India and several Western countries, its policy makers believe that Brazil has a comparative advantage in its relations with Africa, since, due to colonialism and the slave trade, it has a shared history with Africa, while its soils and climate are akin to those of the continent across the Atlantic. Local critics have criticised the discrepancy of the political elite's official discourse of Brazil's African-ness and proximity with Africa and the persistence of racial inequality and racial discrimination within its own society. For example, only in December 2010 Brazil promoted the first of the very few black career diplomats as ambassador. From 2002 to 2012, despite affirmative actions, only nineteen (2.9%) of the 741 students enrolled at the country's diplomatic academy Rio Branco were black.[16] However,

[15] Mónica Hirst, *Aspectos Conceituais e Práticos da Atuação do Brasil em Cooperação Sul-Sul: os Casos de Haiti, Bolívia e Guiné-Bissau*. Texto para Discussão (Brasília: Instituto de Pesquisa Econômica Aplicada – IPEA, 2012), 16.

[16] João Fellet, 'Apesar de ação afirmativa, só 2.6% dos novos diplomatas são negros', *BBC Brasil*, 21 November 2012, www.bbc.com/portuguese/noticias/2012/11/121120_itamaraty_acoes_afirmativas_jf.shtml.

both Lula and his successor Dilma Rousseff (2011–16) publicly admitted the existence of racial discrimination in the country and took various measures to improve the social inclusion and mobility of the country's black population.

Officially President Dilma declared the continuation of Lula's African policy when she took over in 2011. However, in fact, she focused more on domestic affairs, and had a more utilitarian approach to foreign policy. Stolte argues that although Dilma maintained his predecessor's discourse of solidarity and cultural affinities with Africa, 'she moved Brazil away from Lula's strong development profile.'[17] While Lula's presidency benefited from high commodity prices and considerable annual economic growth, Dilma's government was soon affected by social unrest and a serious economic crisis, which contributed to her early departure by a controversial impeachment process initiated in May 2016. During her presidency, Brazil's trade with Africa still increased from $20.6 billion in 2011 to $28.5 billion in 2013, but then dropped to $17 billion in 2015 and only $12.4 billion in 2016. In 2017 the downward trend was stopped thanks to a 20% growth of Brazilian exports to the continent. Consequently, trade with Africa recovered to $14.9 billion. Nevertheless, due to economic constraints and falling commodity prices, in recent years Brazil's engagement in Africa has diminished on all fronts. Since 2014, additionally hit by corruption investigations of the *Lava Jato* operation by the Federal Police, the major Brazilian companies present on the continent have all disinvested, while the country's expenditures for development cooperation with African countries have been significantly reduced. Several of the multilateral initiatives involving Africa have lost vigour, and their scheduled summits have been repeatedly delayed. When President Michel Temer succeeded Dilma Rousseff, his neoliberal government immediately questioned the utility of the country's many embassies in Africa and announced prioritisation of relations with industrialised countries. His government has returned to the first strand of foreign policy thinking and replaced the rapprochement with the Global South with a greater alignment with the United States and other industrialised countries. The election of the right-wing President Jair Bolsonaro in October 2018 further reinforced this foreign policy change, since he has advocated Brazil's return to close relations with the United States and other developed countries and a shift away from what he considers to be ideologically biased foreign policy. It seems that Brazil's third attempt to strengthen relations with Africa has definitively

[17] Stolte, *Brazil's Africa Strategy*, 158.

come to a close, since it was not sustainable in the long term due to both economic and political reasons. Like in the 1960s and in the 1980s, also this time Brazil will certainly maintain political and economic relations with African countries, but they are likely to remain reduced and side-lined, as happened after the end of the two previous periods of its rapprochement with Africa.

The various contributions to this volume largely reflect a Brazilian perspective, since three of the four authors are Brazilian scholars. Chapter 1 provides an overview of Brazil's changing relations with Africa from the country's early colonial period under Portuguese domination in the 16th century until 1990 when the country's second rapprochement with Africa since the 1960s had failed due to the financial and economic crisis at the end of the military dictatorship (1964–85). The chapter contextualises Brazil's relations with Africa historically within the perspective of two opposite foreign policy paradigms known as *americanismo* and *globalismo*, which in turn were the result of different domestic and international political and economic circumstances. Chapter 2 examines Brazil's Africa policy under several presidents in the period 1990–2016. The chapter's focus is on the eight-year presidency of Lula da Silva when Africa became a priority as part of the country's ambitious global foreign policy. It analyses the motivations and instruments of Brazil's African policy under President Lula and the changes occurred under his successors Dilma and Temer. Chapter 3 deals with the role and relevance of international organisations and multilateral initiatives for Brazil's relations with the African continent. It shows that, besides strengthening bilateral ties with African countries, under President Lula Brazilian diplomacy especially used multilateral organisations to increase the country's political weight both regionally and globally. Several regional organisations were newly established for this purpose, while others were revived. Chapter 4 analyses the role and impact of Brazil's international development cooperation in Africa during the Lula and Dilma governments. The focus is on technical cooperation coordinated by the Brazilian Cooperation Agency (ABC), but the overview also includes educational, financial and security cooperation. Since 2003 Brazil has increasingly used development cooperation, rhetorically characterised as a horizontal relationship between equal partners in search of mutual benefits, as a foreign policy tool to strengthen political and economic relations with African countries. The focus is on the particularities, scope, ambitions and realities of Brazil's international development cooperation. Chapter 5 looks at the South Atlantic as part of Brazil–Africa relations from a geo-strategic and historical perspective, and the growing importance of regional multilateral organisations for peace and security. It demonstrates how the South Atlantic region has become increasingly important for Brazil's security concerns and claims for a higher status within the international political system, and to enhance its national political and economic interests in Africa and beyond. Chapter 6 critically examines the issues of racism and racial inequality in Brazilian society, including recent political efforts to address these severe challenges for the country's future and credibility abroad. Under President Lula, Brazil's African policy has explicitly been associated with his government's domestic policies to fight racial discrimination and promote racial equality at home, at least rhetorically. From a historical perspective, this chapter examines the deplorable socioeconomic situation of Brazil's large population of African origin and the changes brought under the policies of racial equality since 2003. Chapter 7, the final chapter, analyses Brazil–Africa relations in the post-Lula period when they suffered a decline on virtually all levels as a result of the economic and political crisis that has hit Brazil in recent years. In fact, the reduction of Brazil's relations with Africa in the 2010s has been due to both an economic crisis and a change of the foreign policy paradigm. In addition to the economic recession, investments by large Brazilian companies in Africa were also affected by the *Lava Jato* anti-corruption operation. The chapter reveals how the status of Brazil's African policy has been subject to the interrelated factors of changing paradigms of domestic foreign policy thinking and the country's economic performance and priorities.

1

Brazil–Africa Relations from the 16th Century to the 20th Century

Gerhard Seibert

Introduction

From the early 16th to the mid-19th century, Brazil maintained close relations with Africa that were dominated by the slave trade. During this period more than five million Africans were deported to Brazil, making it by far the largest destination of the transatlantic slave trade. Brazil's colonial economy was based on three main pillars: external dependency, large landownership and slavery.[1] The African slaves shaped Brazilian society and culture. Following the end of the slave trade in 1850 and the colonisation of Africa by European powers from the late 19th century, Brazil's relations with Africa ceased for more than a century and were only re-established in the early 1960s when the presidents Jânio Quadros and João Goulart pursued an independent foreign policy that rejected automatic alignment with the United States and Portugal, and sought to expand the country's bilateral relations with socialist countries and newly independent countries in the Afro-Asian world. Brazil was portrayed as an anti-colonial and anti-racist country that shared many similarities with other Third World countries. However, the Independent Foreign Policy was fiercely counteracted by the anti-communist opposition and the influential Portuguese immigrant communities that supported the Salazar regime's colonial policy. In addition, the foreign policy remained ambiguous and inconsistent as, despite the rhetoric, Quadros and Goulart never dared to put Brazil's close relations with Salazarist Portugal or South Africa's apartheid regime at risk.

The military coup in 1964 ended Brazil's first rapprochement with African countries due to the anti-communist military leaders' realignment of the country's foreign policy with Washington and Lisbon. Africa only reappeared as a target of Brazil's foreign policy when the country's

[1] Paulo Fagundes Visentini, *A Relação Brasil-África. Prestígio, cooperação ou negócios?* (Rio de Janeiro: Alta Books, 2016), 6.

economic growth was threatened by the Arab oil embargo in 1973. Brazil's pragmatic foreign policy offensive towards Africa under the Ernesto Geisel presidency in 1974 was facilitated by the military coup that overthrew the Portuguese dictatorship in April that year. Under Geisel and João Figueiredo, the last two military rulers, Brazil successfully strengthened political and commercial relations with African countries. However, this second rapprochement with Africa also proved unsustainable due to Brazil's financial crisis in the mid-1980s and Africa's economic decline in the same period, when the diplomatic and trade relations between Brazil and African countries dropped to the levels of the early 1960s. It was not until President Lula da Silva took office in 2003 that Brazil embarked on a third attempt to strengthen ties with Africa as part of an ambitious global external policy. The chapter focuses on Brazil – Africa relations in the second half of the 20th century.

Africa in Brazil; Brazil in Africa

As a result of the slave trade, 51% of Brazil's population of 191 million is at least partly of African descent, according to the most recent population census in 2010. Africans have not only contributed to the physical appearance of Brazilians, but have also influenced the country's culture, language, religious life and cuisine. In the early 20th century, the first scholarly publications appeared on the contributions of Africans to Brazilian social life and culture. The pioneer of Afro-Brazilian studies was the psychiatrist and physical anthropologist, Raimundo Nina Rodrigues (1862–1906), whose best-known book *Os Africanos no Brasil* was published posthumously in 1932.[2] Although representative of the racist concepts of the time, his work covers many details about the social, cultural and religious life of Africans in Brazil. In the 1930s, Arthur Ramos (1903–49), a psychiatrist and anthropologist, published several books on Afro-Brazilian life and culture. However, the most influential was Gilberto Freyre's (1900–87) book *Casa-Grande & Senzala*, first published in 1933, in which he acknowledged the contributions of Africans to the country's history and culture.[3] His approach was exceptional at a time when racist thought was still influential in academia. However, his affirmations of comparatively harmonious relations between white

[2] Raimundo Nina Rodrigues, *Os Africanos no Brasil* (São Paulo: Madras Editora, 2008 [1932]).

[3] Gilberto Freyre, *Casa-Grande & Senzala* (Lisbon: Livros do Brasil, 2003 [1933]). The English translation of the book titled *The Masters and the Slaves* was published in 1946.

masters and black slaves in colonial Brazil later served to substantiate the supposed existence of racial democracy in the country (see next section). All the studies published at the time focused on African heritage and influences in Brazil, but did not deal with the country's relations with the African continent that had been cut off since the mid-19th century.

Brazil's relations with Africa date back to the mid-16th century when the regular slave trade began which, until its abolition in 1850, gave rise to the deportation of about 5.5 million Africans to Brazil, of whom an estimated 4.8 million survived the middle passage. This is almost half of the estimated 10.7 million African slaves who arrived alive in the Americas.[4] Sugar cane production in Bahia and Pernambuco in the 16th and 17th centuries, gold and diamond mining in Minas Gerais, Goiás and Mato Grosso in the 18th century, and coffee cultivation in São Paulo and Rio de Janeiro in the 19th century provided a steady demand for African slave labour. Initially, plantation owners in Brazil enslaved local Indians to work on the sugar plantations. Indian plantation slaves dominated until 1600 but, thereafter, were quickly replaced by African slaves who were considered less vulnerable to disease and more suited to agricultural work and forced labour.[5] Until the end of the 19th century, slave labour was used in all sectors of Brazil's economy and throughout the entire country. Between 20% and 30% of all Brazilian households possessed slaves. Masters with five or less slaves represented half of the total slave owners and they possessed a quarter of all slaves. Until 1850, the average squad in most of the country varied between five and eight slaves and was rarely larger than this.[6] When slavery was finally abolished in Brazil in 1888, only 5% of the total population were slaves.[7]

The principal homelands of the slaves varied during the three centuries of the slave trade and differed in the various regions in Brazil. Throughout the entire period, by far the most slaves came from the Congo-Angola region (70%), the Gulf of Benin (18%), Mozambique (5.7%), the Gulf of Biafra (2.4%), Senegambia (2.2%), and the Gold Coast (1.3%).[8] Until Brazil's independence from Portugal in 1822, Brazilians served in the military and as civil servants in the Portuguese territories in Africa. In addition, until the end of the slave trade in 1850 Brazilians engaged in

[4] Francisco Vidal Luna and Herbert S. Klein, *Escravismo no Brasil* (São Paulo: Imprensa Oficial do Estado de São Paulo & Editora da Universidade de São Paulo, 2010), 168.

[5] Ibid., 39.

[6] Ibid., 155.

[7] Alberto da Costa e Silva, *Um Rio Chamado Atlântico. A África no Brasil e o Brasil na África* (Rio de Janeiro: Editora Nova Fronteira, 2003), 22.

[8] Luna and Klein, *Escravismo*, 169.

the slave trade in Angola and the Slave Coast of West Africa. The former territory traded predominantly with Rio de Janeiro and the latter with Salvador da Bahia. The most famous Brazilian slave trader was Francisco Felix de Souza in Quidah, where the king of Dahomey appointed him as Cháchá, a local chief. He reached the Slave Coast in the late 18th century to engage in the slave trade. When he died in 1849 he had become a wealthy local slave trader with considerable political influence.

As the number of slaves already indicates, colonial Brazil maintained particularly close relations with Angola. This slave trade was not triangular, but bilateral and went directly between Luanda, Benguela and Brazilian ports. Until 1822, Angola was a major supplier of slave labour and a Brazilian sub-colony since it was more closely linked to Brazil, especially Rio de Janeiro, than to Portugal.[9] In this period, three Brazilians served as governors of Angola.[10] During Brazil's colonial period, diplomatic missions of the rulers of Abomey, Porto Novo (Benin) and Onim (Lagos) were received in Salvador, Recife and Rio de Janeiro because the Portuguese government's relations with African states were maintained through Brazil.[11] When Brazil unilaterally declared its independence from Portugal in 1822, groups in Angola, Cabo Verde and Mozambique agitated in favour of the separation of these colonies from Portugal and for a union with Brazil. Therefore, when Portugal finally recognised Brazil's independence in the Treaty of Peace and Alliance in 1825, mediated by the United Kingdom, Brazil's Emperor Pedro I promised not to accept proposals from any of the Portuguese colonies to unite with the Brazilian Empire. The United Kingdom was also interested in ending Brazil's trade relations with Africa since it wanted to establish its commercial and maritime hegemony in the South Atlantic.[12] Twice, in 1835 and 1850, Brazil asked the Portuguese government to sell them land in Angola to establish a settlement for former slaves, as the British and Americans had done this in Sierra Leone and Liberia respectively, but Portugal rejected the request.[13]

[9] Alberto da Costa e Silva, 'O Brasil na África Atlântica', *Revista do Património Histórico e Artístico Nacional*, 34 (2012), 361.

[10] Samuel Yaw Boadi-Siaw, 'Development of Relations between Brazil and African States, 1950–1973' (PhD dissertation, Los Angeles: University of California, 1975), 12.

[11] Alberto da Costa e Silva, *As relações entre o Brasil e a África Negra, de 1822 à 1ª Guerra Mundial* (Luanda: Museu Nacional da Escravatura, 1996), 8.

[12] Eli Alves Penha, *Relações Brasil-África e Geopolítica do Atlântico Sul* (Salvador: EDUFBA, 2011), 47.

[13] Gilberto da Silva Guizelin, 'Relações Brasil – África: A Missão Niterói à Libéria'. *Cadernos do Centro de História e Documentação Diplomática – CHDD*, 15:28 (2016), 550.

During the monarchy (1822–89), Brazil maintained a modest diplomatic representation in Africa. Shortly after the recognition of its independence, in 1826, Brazil appointed a consul to Luanda. The Portuguese governor in Luanda accepted the Brazilian diplomat for a period of eight months while waiting for Lisbon to authorise his appointment. This, however, was denied as Lisbon was opposed to foreigners residing in the Portuguese colonies. In fact, Portugal feared that the Brazilian consul could support a political movement in favour of Angola's independence or union with Brazil and encourage maritime trade with Brazil at a time when Lisbon was trying to redirect Angolan trade to Portugal. Consequently, the Brazilian consul had to leave Luanda in 1827. It was only after the abolition of the slave trade in Brazil that Lisbon accepted the establishment of a Brazilian consulate in Luanda, in 1854. At the time, Brazil also had consular offices in the Cape of Good Hope and St. Helena, where the British had established mixed commission courts to adjudicate cases of captured slave ships. The Brazilian consuls in the two ports used to submit protests when captains of captured Brazilian slave vessels were condemned. In 1863, Brazil appointed an honorary consul in Mauritius. In 1868 and 1871, Brazil established vice-consulates in São Tomé and in Príncipe respectively. Already in 1850, Hermenegildo Frederico Niterói became Brazil's first diplomatic representative in an independent African country when he was appointed consul general and chargé d'affaires in Liberia, which had achieved independence in 1847.[14] In 1853 Niterói returned to Brazil after his mission failed to negotiate the settlement of former Brazilian slaves successfully with the Liberian government; Brazil had refused to agree to the Liberian government's requirement to maintain the black settlers during the first six months after their arrival.[15] In neighbouring Sierra Leone, Freetown hosted the Anglo-Brazilian Mixed Commission that operated from 1830 to 1845 to judge cases of illegal slave trafficking. However, during this period Brazil was frequently without a representative in this bilateral court, the counterpart of which was based in Rio de Janeiro.[16]

In the course of the 19th century, about eight thousand former Brazilian slaves were relocated to West Africa. Their remigration was largely a result of Brazil's most significant slave revolt, the Malê Rebellion in Salvador in 1835, and the repressive measures against the free African population taken in its aftermath by the local authorities to prevent other uprisings. In September 1835, about two hundred Africans accused of

[14] Costa e Silva, *As Relações*, 18–19.
[15] Guizelin, 'Relações Brasil – África', 564.
[16] Costa e Silva, *Um Rio Chamado Atlântico*, 29.

being involved in the Malê Revolt were deported to West Africa; over the following decades hundreds of former slaves left Brazil voluntarily for Africa, frequently to avoid the discriminating measures against the black population.[17] These returnees settled in cities like Accra (Ghana), Lomé (Togo), Quidah, Porto Novo, and Agoué (Benin) and Lagos (Nigeria), where they created distinctive Afro-Brazilian communities in their own separate neighbourhoods. The Afro-Brazilian community in Accra is locally known as Tabom, derived from the Portuguese *está bom* (all right), while communities in Togo and Benin are known as Agudás and in Lagos as Amarôs. Their collective identity was marked by the Portuguese language and names, Catholicism, Brazilian architecture, cuisine and folklore. Until the First World War, many returnees still maintained social and commercial ties with Brazil, particularly with Bahia. Then the United Kingdom and France discouraged their West African colonies from having relations with Brazil.[18]

Still under European colonial rule, many members of the Afro-Brazilian communities played prominent roles in local political, economic and cultural life. Sylvanus Olympio, a descendent of a prominent Brazilian immigrant of mixed Portuguese, African and Amerindian ancestry from Bahia, was Togo's first independent President from 1960 until his assassination during a military coup in 1963.[19] Since the 1960s, Brazil has re-established ties with the Tabom and other still traceable communities of former slaves in West Africa. In May 1963, the cultural attaché at the embassy in Lagos, Antônio Olinto, organised the visit of Romana da Conceição, a member of the local 'Brazilian' community, to Brazil. She had left Recife in 1900 for Lagos, where she had since lived.[20] When Brazil established an embassy in Ghana in 1961, Raymondo Souza Dantas, a black journalist, was appointed ambassador. Shortly after his arrival in Accra, Souza Dantas and his wife and son were honoured during a formal reception by more than three hundred Tabons.[21] On the official visit of President Lula da Silva (2003–10) to Ghana in 2005 more than forty years later, he and his delegation were welcomed by over two

[17] Lisa Earl Castillo, 'Mapping the nineteenth-century Brazilian returnee movements: Demographics, life stories and the question of slavery'. *Atlantic Studies*, 13:1 (2016), 30.

[18] Costa e Silva, 'O Brasil na África Atlântica', 369.

[19] Raymundo Souza Dantas, *África Difícil* (Rio de Janeiro: Editora Leitura, 1965), 44; Alcione Meira Amos, *Os Que Voltaram. A história dos retornados afro-brasileiros na África Ocidental no século XIX* (Belo Horizonte: Tradição Planalto, 2007), 147.

[20] Boadi-Siaw, 'Development of Relations', 150.

[21] Amos, *Os Que Voltaram*, 81.

hundred Tabons and their leaders in the Brazilian embassy in Accra. During the welcome celebration, Lula was symbolically enthroned as Tabom chief. In his address, Lula declared that he made a family-like visit to Ghana and felt at home, as if he was in Bahia.[22]

Brazil's withdrawal from Africa

Between 1550 and 1850 African slaves represented 86% of the immigrants in Brazil, while the other 14% were Portuguese. After the end of the slave trade, the abolition of slavery and the beginning of Africa's effective occupation by European colonial powers following the Berlin Conference of 1884/85, Brazil's relations with the African continent practically came to a standstill. The country prohibited the immigration of Africans and encouraged the immigration of Europeans from Italy, Portugal, Spain, Germany and Poland, but also accepted Lebanese and Japanese immigrants. From 1884 to 1893, 883,668 European immigrants entered Brazil, 510,533 of whom were Italians. In 1890, Brazil's population was composed of 6,302,198 whites, 5,934,291 mixed-race, and 2,097,426 blacks. Between 1884 and 1940, Brazil received 4,177,286 immigrants, predominantly Italians, Portuguese and Spanish. Consequently, the proportion of the population of European descent increased considerably. According to the 1940 census, the total population was 41,236,315, and it was made up of 26,171,778 whites, 6,035,869 blacks, 8,744,365 mixed-race, 242,320 Asians and 41,893 people who did not declare their skin colour.[23] Africa and the Africans became increasingly unknown and alienated, distant geographically and culturally: 'The image of Africa became a geographic and human unit, just as distant and away as the poles.'[24] At the same time, influential racial theories of whitening predicted that the African element in the Brazilian population would disappear within a few generations as a result of massive white immigration and miscegenation.[25]

In the first half of the 20th century, Brazil only maintained full diplomatic relations with Egypt and South Africa, and trade with the latter accounted for 90% of its modest external trade with the continent. In 1943, South Africa opened a consulate in Rio de Janeiro, while in

[22] Ibid., 89.

[23] José Honório Rodrigues, *Brasil e África: outro horizonte*, 1st ed. (Rio de Janeiro: Editora Civilização Brasileira, 1961), 71.

[24] Rodrigues, *Brasil e África*, 7.

[25] Visentini, *A Relação*, 15.

1948 Brazil established a legation in Pretoria.[26] In 1942, Africa represented 3% Brazil's foreign trade, while continental America accounted for 70.2%, Europe 26.0% and Asia 0.2%.[27] In the same year, Brazil entered the Second World War with a 25,000-man expeditionary force that fought alongside the Allied Forces in Italy. Brazil's participation in the Allied Forces provided the country with international prestige and resources to finance industrial development based on import substitution.[28] At the same time, Brazil cautiously began to demonstrate greater concern for international issues beyond its own hemisphere. In 1955, the diplomat Bezerra de Menezes participated as Brazilian observer in the Bandung Conference. Back home he published the book *Brazil and the Afro-Asian World* where he advocated solidarity with the Afro-Asian countries and the development of an independent foreign policy. He believed that Brazil's supposed racial equality was its main political and diplomatic weapon to strengthen relations with these countries.[29] In 1957, Itamaraty, the Foreign Ministry, produced the first memorandum on the emerging Afro-Asian world and its implications for Brazil. However, the proposed fact-finding mission to various African and Asian countries did not materialise.[30] The Brazilian elite's traditionally 'strong self-identification as a member of the Western ethnic, cultural, and political community' impeded closer relations with the Afro-Asian world and facilitated the country's 'acceptance of the ideological pro-Western interpretation of its role in the Cold War.'[31] After the war, Brazil remained a close ally of the United States, the country's principal creditor. In addition, this uncompromising alignment with that major power was considered a way of strengthening Brazil's own bargaining power.[32] Defenders of Brazil's pro-American policy believed that the country's national security relied on Washington's deterrent power and ability to contain communism.[33] In 1958, President Juscelino Kubitschek

[26] Ibid., 11.

[27] Rodrigues, *Brasil e África*, 204.

[28] Penha, *Relações Brasil-África*, 152.

[29] Jerry Dávila, *Hotel Trópico. Brazil and the Challenge of African Decolonization, 1950–1980* (Durham and London: Duke University Press, 2010), 9.

[30] Pio Penna Filho and António Carlos Moraes Lessa, 'O Itamaraty e a África: as origens da política africana do Brasil'. *Estudos Históricos*, 39 (2007), 63.

[31] Wayne A. Selcher, *The Afro-Asian Dimension of Brazilian Foreign Policy 1956–1972* (Gainesville: The University of Florida, 1974), 225.

[32] Christina Stolte, *Brazil's Africa Strategy: Role conception and the drive for international status* (New York: Palgrave Macmillan, 2015), 61.

[33] Selcher, *The Afro-Asian Dimension*, 14.

(1956–61) launched the Pan-American Operation, which restricted the focus of Brazil's foreign policy primarily to the Americas.[34]

Brazil also maintained close relations with the Salazar dictatorship in Portugal. In 1953, during the second presidency of Getúlio Vargas (1951–54), the two countries signed a Treaty of Friendship and Consultation. The obligation to consult each other on international issues of common interest conditioned Brazil's foreign policy options in relation to Salazar's colonial policy, which was fiercely opposed to decolonisation. Already in 1951, Portugal had renamed its colonies in Africa and Asia as overseas provinces, and in so doing denied being a colonial power. As overseas provinces, the territories were beyond the jurisdiction of the United Nations. In 1957, the Brazilian representative at the United Nations supported the Portuguese claim that its African territories were not colonies, but overseas provinces.[35] There was an influential Portuguese immigrant and business community in Brazil that lobbied in favour of Salazar's position by stressing historical and cultural commonalities between the two countries. The lusophile Brazilian elite cherished cultural and emotional affinities with Portugal, while anti-colonialism was predominantly viewed from a Cold War perspective as suspicious of communist sympathies. Besides, any position that condemned Portuguese colonialism was viewed as a negation of Brazil's Lusitanian heritage. In 1963, former President Juscelino Kubitschek allegedly confessed during a visit to Portugal that 'even when I was President of the Republic I never made a distinction between Brazil's foreign policy and Portugal's foreign policy'.[36]

The inauguration of Kubitschek in 1956 was attended by representatives from both Ethiopia and South Africa, and the following year his government sent representatives to attend Ghana's independence celebration. Brazil formally created embassies in Tunisia and Morocco in late 1959 but they were only staffed after 1960.[37] In April 1960, Kubitschek recalled Brazil's diplomatic representative in South Africa in protest against the Sharpeville massacre.[38] In December that year, Emperor Haile Selassie of Ethiopia became the first African head of state to pay an official visit to Brazil. However, due to a coup attempt

[34] Ibid., 14; Visentini, *A Relação*, 12.

[35] Boadi-Siaw. 'Development of Relations', 59.

[36] José Honório Rodrigues, *Brasil e África: outro horizonte*. 2nd ed. (Rio de Janeiro: Editora Civilização Brasileira, 1964), 396.

[37] Boadi-Siaw, 'Development of Relations', 78–79.

[38] Irene Vida Gala, 'A Política Externa do Governo Lula para a África. A política externa como instrumento da ação afirmativa ...e ainda que não só' (dissertation, Brasília: Instituto Rio Branco, 2007), 32.

at home, he was forced to cut short his visit and make a hasty return to Addis Ababa. Twenty-one African countries gained independence during Kubitschek's presidency, a development that Brazil could not disregard. 1960 became known as the Year of Africa because seventeen African countries achieved independence in that year alone. Brazil sent delegations to the independence celebrations of a few of these countries, including the Republic of Congo, Madagascar, Nigeria and Togo.[39] As the newly independent countries joined the United Nations, African affairs increasingly became part of the organisation's political agenda. Consequently, it was at this multilateral level that Brazil gradually came into closer contact with African countries.[40] While Brazil had regularly sided with European colonial powers on matters related to colonial issues at the United Nations before 1960, on 14 December of that year it voted in favour of a resolution that called for the speedy and unconditional end of colonialism. However, although Brazil supported decolonisation in general terms, it still sided with the colonial powers on concrete issues. Already the next day, Brazil objected to another resolution that directly named the territories about which Portugal had to report to the United Nations under article 73 of its Charter. Later that month, Brazil abstained from the vote on a resolution in favour of Algeria's independence.[41]

Independent Foreign Policy: Brazil's return to Africa

There was a shift in Brazil's foreign policy in 1961 when the newly elected President Jânio Quadros and Vice-President João Goulart launched the Independent Foreign Policy (PEI) that rejected automatic alignment with the United States and Portugal, sought closer relations with the then-socialist countries and the independent developing countries in Asia and Africa, and conceived Brazil as an emerging world power. For the first time, Brazil attributed an African dimension to its foreign policy.[42] To confirm this change in foreign policy, the Foreign Ministry created a separate Africa Division.[43] In the context of the construction of Brazil as an emerging world power, the continent was considered a space in

[39] Boadi-Siaw, 'Development of Relations', 84.

[40] Ibid., 51.

[41] Ibid., 62.

[42] José Flávio Sombra Saraiva, *África parceira do Brasil atlântico. Relações internacionais do Brasil e da África no início do século XXI* (Belo Horizonte: Fino Traço Editora, 2012), 18.

[43] Patrícia Soares Leite, *O Brasil e a Cooperação Sul-Sul em três momentos de política externa:os governos Jânio Quadros/João Goulart, Ernesto Geisel e Luiz*

the South Atlantic region where Brazil could gain influence.[44] Africa was considered Brazil's natural sphere of influence due to history and geographic proximity, and racial democracy was expected to be a comparative advantage when dealing with African countries.[45] These ideas had been conceived by developmental nationalists from the political left since the mid-1950s but were only implemented under Quadros and Goulart. The so-called *americanistas* were opposed to these ideas; for both political and economic reasons, they advocated the traditional idea of Pan-Americanism and a special relationship with the United States to promote Brazil's socioeconomic development and industrialisation.[46]

Quadros had visited Cuba during the election campaign, and a few weeks after his election in October 1960 he made a world tour of almost three months that took him to the Soviet Union, Egypt, Yugoslavia, India and Japan. Impressed by his observations during the trip, he wanted to make Afro-Asian relations a principal element of his Independent Foreign Policy approach.[47] Once in power, Quadros declared that, although ideologically tied to the West, Brazil would not participate in the Cold War, rather advocating only its own national interests. He portrayed Brazil as an anti-colonialist and anti-racist country that shared many similarities with other developing countries in the Third World. Quadros stressed that Brazil shared common cultural and ethnic roots with Africa. He declared that Brazil's efforts in Africa could only constitute a modest repayment of the immense debt it had with the African peoples due to their sufferings during slavery and their contribution to the formation of the Brazilian nation.[48] In February 1961, Quadros annoyed Salazar when he granted political asylum to a former Portuguese colonial officer, Henrique Galvão, and his supporters after they had hijacked the Portuguese ship *Santa Maria* off the coast of South America in January in an attempt to take it to Luanda to provoke a rebellion against the Salazar dictatorship.[49] Moreover, Quadros established relations with Fidel Castro's Cuba – which formally approached the Soviet bloc in 1961. Quadros opposed all sanctions against Cuba and even decorated Che Guevara, Cuba's Economy Minister at the time,

Inácio Lula da Silva (Brasília: Fundação Alexandre Gusmão, 2011), 98; Visentini, *A Relação*, 24.

44 Penha, *Relações Brasil-África*, 151.

45 Dávila, *Hotel Trópico*, 51.

46 Leite, *O Brasil*, 80.

47 Selcher, *The Afro-Asian Dimension*, 82.

48 Rodrigues, *Brasil e África* (2nd ed.), 385; Selcher, *The Afro-Asian Dimension*, 82.

49 Dávila, *Hotel Trópico*, 34; Visentini, *A Relação*, 28.

with Brazil's second-highest award for foreign statesmen in recognition of his desire to strengthen cultural and economic ties with Brazil.[50] In 1961 and 1962, Brazil participated as an observer in the conferences of the non-aligned countries in Belgrade and Cairo but it never joined the Non-Aligned Movement, since Brazil was unlikely to be able to play a leadership role in the organisation and hence preferred to avoid risking any further deterioration of the relations with the United States.[51]

The new foreign policy was supported by the main parties, and many writers and scholars; these included the historian, José Honório Rodrigues (1913–87), who published an authoritative book in 1961 on Brazil's relations with Africa. Rodrigues believed that, given geographic proximity and the historical ties with Africa, Brazil should privilege close relations with African countries. The Independent Foreign Policy was also supported by those who wanted Brazil to play a major role in international politics. In 1963, the geographer Delgado de Carvalho advocated that Brazil deserved a permanent seat in the UN Security Council due to the size of its population, territory and economy, as well as its diplomatic prestige.[52] However, the Independent Foreign Policy of Quadros and Goulart inevitably displeased Washington and Lisbon and the conservative opposition at home, although in practice the policy was less radical than its political rhetoric. Many of their conservative opponents viewed the establishment of relations with Afro-Asian developing countries and the Eastern bloc as almost synonymous with communism.

When Quadros resigned in August 1961 after only seven months in office, it was said that his unexpected decision resulted in part from the fierce opposition to his foreign policy. He was succeeded by Vice-President João Goulart, who announced the continuation of the Independent Foreign Policy. Initially, the military had been opposed to Goulart who was suspected of communist sympathies. To appease the military, the National Congress adopted a parliamentarian regime with a prime minister, who assumed some of Goulart's presidential competences. Concerning Africa, Goulart merely continued the bilateral relations established under Quadros, but he did not develop many new bilateral initiatives. His government opened only one embassy with a resident ambassador, in Algeria in 1962. In the same year, Goulart announced his intention to visit several African countries, including Ghana, Nigeria, Senegal and Tunisia; however, the trip never materialised as he was heavily involved

[50] Leite, *O Brasil*, 95.
[51] Visentini, *A Relação*, 30.
[52] Penha, *Relações Brasil-África*, 160.

with domestic politics.[53] At a meeting of the Organization of American States (OAS) in June 1962, Brazil abstained in the vote on the expulsion of Cuba from the organisation. The decision created outrage within the conservative opposition and the military.[54] In October, during the Cuban missile crisis, Brazil voted in the OAS in favour of the blockade of Cuba but against military invention. In November that year, Goulart re-established diplomatic relations with the Soviet Union that had been broken in 1947. In January 1963, a popular referendum adopted the return to the presidential system. During Goulart's presidency, which was marked by increasing public debt, economic crisis and social conflicts, the opposition to and criticisms of the foreign policy approach further increased. The ongoing crisis and pressure from the opposition resulted in considerable weakening within Itamaraty, which was headed by five different Foreign Ministers from 1961 to 1964.[55]

Already, before his election, Quadros argued that Brazil should maintain diplomatic relations with all countries provided that it was in the national interest, and that extending Brazil's foreign relations with Asia and Africa and the resulting advantages for its foreign trade would increase Brazil's international authority beyond the South American region. He believed that Brazil had an important role to play in the Afro-Asian world given the characteristics of its economy, its racial origins, and the feelings of its people.[56] It was part of a culturalist discourse that stressed Brazil's cultural, ethnic and historical ties with Africa. Quadros' Foreign Minister, Afonso Arinos de Melo Franco, shared these ideas. When he took office in February 1961, Arinos declared that:

> Brazil was in a particularly favourable position to serve as a link between the Afro-Asian world and the great Western powers. A democratic and Christian people, whose Latin culture was enriched with the presence of autochthones, African and Asian influences, we are ethnically mestizos and culturally mixed of elements from the vast geographic and demographic areas, which in this century blossom to international life. Further, the processes of miscegenation, with which the Portuguese metropolis shaped us and facilitated our racial democracy, which, though not as perfect as we would wish, is, however, the most advanced one in the world. We do

[53] Boadi-Siaw, 'Development of Relations', 142, 151.

[54] Cláudio Oliveira Ribeiro, 'Imprensa e política africana no Brasil: uma análise dos governos Jânio Quadros e João Goulart', *África. Revista do Centro de Estudos Africanos. USP, São Paulo* 24-25-26 (2002–05), 55.

[55] San Tiago Dantas (September 1961 to July 1962), Afonso Arinos (July to September 1962), Hermes Lima (September 1962 to June 1963), Lins e Silva (June to August 1963), Araújo Castro (August 1963 to March 1964).

[56] Rodrigues, *Brasil e África* (2nd ed.), 373–4.

> not have prejudices against coloured races, as occurs in so many white or predominantly white people, or prejudices against whites, as happens with predominantly coloured people. Therefore, the legitimate exercise of our sovereignty will take us in international politics to sincerely support the efforts of the Afro-Asian world for democracy and freedom.[57]

White left-wing politicians and intellectuals believed that, unlike the United States, Brazil's absence of racial discrimination and process of miscegenation had allowed it to achieve a 'racial democracy'. The concept has been attributed to the sociologist Gilberto Freyre, who argued that racial democracy had been the outcome of the unique Portuguese capability to adapt Western culture to tropical environments by acculturation and miscegenation. Freyre advocated that, regardless of their colour, all Brazilians possessed a common African heritage. Consequently, this made Brazil uniquely suited to approach newly independent African and Asian nations, whereas white Europeans and Americans were conditioned by their colonial past and racist ideas and would therefore be unable to avoid racial conflicts with these countries. Although blacks were almost absent in high government positions and in the National Congress, Brazilian politicians and intellectuals seriously believed that the supposed racial harmony was a key political instrument in the pursuit of an effective foreign policy in the Afro-Asian world.[58] According to this culturalist approach, it was also believed that, as a successfully industrialising tropical country, Brazil was able to resolve the technical problems of other tropical nations. Brazil was portrayed as the largest black nation outside Africa and, itself a former colony, thus free of any neo-colonial aspirations. As Brazil was lacking political and economic policy instruments, the country pursued a culturally reasoned policy approach to strengthen relations with Afro-Asian countries and increase its international prestige.[59]

Closer relations with developing countries were also motivated by the quest for new export markets for manufactured goods that the domestic market could not absorb due to a lack of purchasing power. Until the 1950s, Brazil's economy had essentially been agrarian and geared to the export of primary products to industrialised countries. Subsequently, consecutive governments promoted a development policy based on import substitution industrialisation, which resulted in high economic growth for a considerable period. However, this development policy also increased the country's need to import capital goods and technology

[57] Ibid., 375–6.
[58] Selcher, *The Afro-Asian Dimension*, 56.
[59] Ibid., 61.

from industrialised countries, resulting in increasing external debts. Brazilian products were believed to be better suited for other developing countries than products from Western countries. In an attempt to promote Brazil and its exports, Quadros sent the navy vessel *Custódio de Melo* on a goodwill tour to various African ports. Carrying 178 navy cadets and official representatives of Itamaraty, the National Confederation of Industry and the Coffee Institute, the ship left Brazil in September 1961 and returned in February the following year. During the voyage, the Brazilians organised cultural exhibitions and trade fairs and stressed Brazil's historical ties with Africa.[60]

In February 1961, Quadros asked Itamaraty to draw up Brazil's new African policy. At the same time, he ordered the creation of scholarships for Africa and a 20% reduction in diplomatic service salaries, equal or superior to $400 a month; half of the savings resulting from this cut was to be used to finance the scholarships for African students. The following month, Quadros approved Minister Arinos' Africa policy project that included cultural agreements with Morocco, Senegal, Ghana, Tunisia and Nigeria, and the number of scholarships for Africans was set at twenty for 1961, forty for 1962, eighty in 1963 and one hundred each for 1964 and 1965; initially, it was limited to students of medicine, pharmacy, odontology, architecture, agronomy and veterinary medicine. The project proved to be a failure. In 1961 and 1962, twenty-two students from Cabo Verde, Cameroon, Ghana, Nigeria, Portuguese Guinea, Senegal and Sierra Leone did Portuguese language courses in Salvador before being distributed to various universities around the country, but the modest initiative was then discontinued due to a lack of funds.[61]

Quadros also sent a diplomatic mission to Sierra Leone, Ghana, Togo, Dahomey (now Benin), Nigeria, Cameroon, Côte d'Ivoire and Guinea-Conakry headed by José Pereira Coelho de Souza – a member of the Chamber of Deputies and the ambassador to the above-mentioned countries – with the aim of gathering information on trade opportunities, including oil exports to Brazil. In Conakry, the mission met with representatives of the People's Liberation Movement of Angola (MPLA), who asked for student scholarships for Angolan students and Brazil's diplomatic support for the struggle for independence. A second mission headed by Foreign Minister Afonso Arinos in Dakar negotiated a cultural agreement with Senegal that later proved to be largely unproductive.[62]

[60] Boadi-Siaw, 'Development of Relations', 148.
[61] Ibid., 147.
[62] Visentini, *A Relação*, 29.

Besides the establishment of new embassies in Ethiopia, Ghana, Côte d'Ivoire, Nigeria and Senegal, and the staffing of those in Tunisia and Morocco, the Africa policy project in the economic sector paved the way for the conclusion of agreements with African coffee and cocoa producers to mitigate the competition in these cash crops, prevent major fluctuations in the world market and stabilise the level of exports.[63] The first negotiations with other leading producers had started in the late 1950s. At the time, coffee was still Brazil's principal export product. Brazil, Ghana, Nigeria, Côte d'Ivoire and Cameroon together represented 80% of world cocoa production and, at a meeting in Abidjan in January 1962, they founded the Alliance of Cocoa Producing Countries (COPAL). In September 1962, the first International Coffee Agreement was signed establishing an export quota for the principal South American and African producers to maintain stable coffee prices. The successful negotiations of the two producer agreements meant that Brazil had defended common economic interests with African countries for the first time. Henceforward, African producers were no longer seen as rivals but as fellows within the international marketing system. In an attempt to increase Brazilian trade with Africa, the Goulart government approved a proposal made by Quadros in June 1962 for the Brazilian Lloyd Lines to establish a direct sea route to Lagos to replace the transhipment of Brazilian exports in New Orleans and Durban.[64] However, the regular bimonthly merchant shipping connection with West Africa was discontinued after a few voyages due to insufficient cargo.[65]

In 1961, Accra became the first site of the new Brazilian embassies in West Africa.[66]At the time, Brazil viewed Ghana as the most developed Black Country and its first President Kwame Nkrumah (1960–66), a prominent advocate of Pan-Africanism, was considered the leading spokesman of independent Africa. Quadros appointed the Afro-Brazilian journalist, Raymundo Souza Dantas, who was an official in his presidential office, to the position of ambassador in Ghana; he was Brazil's first black ambassador and the only one until 2010 when the black career diplomat Benedicto Fonseca Filho was promoted to ambassador. Nkrumah is reported to have said that Brazil should also send black

[63] Rodrigues, *Brasil e África* (2nd ed.) 377–8. Selcher, *The Afro-Asian Dimension*, 84.

[64] Rodrigues, *Brasil e África* (2nd ed.), 281.

[65] Selcher, *The Afro-Asian Dimension*, 86.

[66] Already in 1960 Brazil had established a legation in Accra. One of the reasons Brazil was interested in relations with Ghana, was that it was the world's largest cocoa producer.

diplomats to important Western countries if it really wanted to prove the existence of racial harmony.[67] On one occasion, a Ghanaian politician commented that Dantas must feel at home as he was of African descent. Reflecting on this, Dantas came to the conclusion that for various reasons he could not feel at home, even though he was black and considered a descendant of Africans. He noted: 'My world is different, as well as my civilisation, despite all contact points and existing familiarities between the two universes.'[68] In late 1963, close to his resignation, Dantas was disappointed with his government's lack of support for his embassy. He declared:

> It is my duty to note that that our embassy was never properly equipped to function effectively ... I cannot help alluding to what our action in Ghana could have been, if we had actually been in a position to accomplish all that was planned.[69]

After Dantas' return to Brazil in 1963, Itamaraty did not appoint another ambassador in Ghana until 1968.[70] Other embassies in Africa suffered from a similar lack of interest and support from Itamaraty. Brazil's ambassador in Rabat also complained about the neglect of his embassy.[71] Nevertheless, Quadros' diplomatic offensive in Africa received positive reactions from the other side. In 1961, consecutive delegations visited Brazil from Cameroon, Nigeria and Gabon to hold talks on bilateral political and commercial relations. Official delegations from the Republic of Congo, Nigeria and Kenya followed over the next two years.[72] In 1962, Ghana and Senegal opened embassies in Brazil; Egypt had previously been the only African country with an embassy.[73] However, Quadros' foreign policy was inconsistent since he simultaneously strengthened relations with white-ruled Southern Africa and Portuguese colonies. He established a consulate in Salisbury, Southern Rhodesia (now Zimbabwe), where a white minority claimed power, and in March 1961 received a South African trade mission when possible joint naval exercises with South Africa were discussed. He also opened a consulate in Bissau, Portuguese Guinea, and upgraded Brazil's honorary consulate in Lourenço Marques (now Maputo), Mozambique, to consulate

[67] Selcher, *The Afro-Asian Dimension*, 57.

[68] Raymundo Souza Dantas, *África Díficil* (Rio de Janeiro: Editora Leitura, 1965), 35.

[69] Ibid., 96; Selcher, *The Afro-Asian Dimension*, 87.

[70] Dávila, *Hotel Trópico*, 48.

[71] Boadi-Siaw, 'Development of Relations', 143.

[72] Ibid., 113–14, 144.

[73] Ibid. 143.

general. He even approved the establishment of a consulate in Oran, Algeria, during the territory's liberation war against France.[74]

Quadros' Independent Foreign Policy was formally in favour of decolonisation, and condemned apartheid. However, there were still divisions within Itamaraty between opponents of Portuguese colonialism and those who remained committed to Brazil's special relationship with Portugal. Moreover, the influential Portuguese immigrant organisations concentrated in Rio de Janeiro and São Paulo were fiercely opposed to any anti-colonial policy. Consequently, the government's position was often ambiguous in practice, as can be seen by the way it voted in the United Nations. Brazil abstained when the General Assembly voted Resolution 1603 in April 1961 that set up a committee to investigate the events in Angola following the start of the liberation struggle there. The official justification was that Brazil could not vote against Angola because of its anti-colonial policy, but it could not vote in favour either due to the friendship with Portugal.[75] However, in December 1961, when Tiago Dantas was Foreign Minister, Brazil voted in favour of the United Nations Resolution 1699 that condemned Portugal's refusal to provide the information requested on the territories under its administration. Dantas declared that Brazil's firm anti-colonial position had for the first time resulted in an affirmative vote on the Angolan question, but he also made it clear that cordiality and respect would always preside over relations with Portugal.[76]

But in the same month Brazil abstained in the vote on Resolution 1724 that called upon France and the Provisional Government of the Algerian Republic (GPRA) to resume negotiations on Algeria's independence. A GPRA delegation to Brazil in 1960 to sensitise Itamaraty to the Algerian cause had been in vain. Brazil was not willing to jeopardise its traditionally close relations with France, whose considerable investments were indispensable for the country's economic development.[77] In January 1962, Brazil voted in favour of Resolution 1742 that defended Angola's right to independence. The Brazilian UN representative and former Foreign Minister, Afonso Arinos, declared that Angola's independence would serve Portugal's own long-term interests. In December that year, Brazil again abstained in the vote on Resolution 1807 that

[74] Daniel P. Aragon, 'Chancellery Sepulchers. Jânio Quadros, João Goulart and the Forging of Brazilian Foreign Policy in Angola, Mozambique, and South Africa, 1961–1964'. *Luso-Brazilian Review*, 47:1 (2010), 126.

[75] Ribeiro, 'Imprensa e política africana', 24.

[76] Ibid., 52.

[77] Filho and Lessa, 'O Itamaraty', 61–62.

reaffirmed the right of the peoples of the territories under Portuguese administration to independence, and on Resolution 1819 that condemned the colonial war in Angola. In December 1963, Brazil again abstained in the vote on Resolution 1913 on the self-determination of the Portuguese territories.[78]

Brazil's position remained ambiguous and inconsistent as it abstained on resolutions in the General Assembly but voted against Portugal in the Security Council. Still, in July 1963, Brazil's representative in the UN Security Council declared his support for the independence of the Portuguese territories and offered his country's assistance to a peaceful decolonisation process. At the same time, Brazil voted in favour of Resolution S/5380, which condemned Portuguese colonialism as a threat to peace and security in Africa, and called upon Portugal to end the colonial wars and grant independence to its territories.[79] The Security Council vote, however, was criticised by a delegation of parliamentarian observers of the Senate to the Eighteenth Session of the UN General Assembly as harmful to Brazil's national interest and founded on dubious political considerations that failed to take into account the special relationship with Portugal, Portuguese Africa's role in national security and the potential advantage of expanding Brazilian exports to Europe through Portugal.[80]

Brazil's voting behaviour in the United Nations was equally inconsistent on South Africa's apartheid regime. Brazil tended to support resolutions that condemned the apartheid regime's racist policy but abstained when voting on resolutions demanding concrete sanctions. In contrast to that with other African countries, Brazil's trade with South Africa was significant. Quadros and Goulart were aware of South Africa's commercial potential, which outweighed that of all black African countries in the 1960s. In 1961, South Africa accounted for half of Brazil's trade with Africa that, as a whole, represented less than 1% of the country's total external trade. From 1962 to 1964, South Africa's share in Brazil's trade with Africa increased to 70%.[81] In November 1961, Brazil voted in favour of a resolution that asked the South African government to abandon the racial policy of apartheid. In November the following year, Brazil abstained in the vote on another resolution that asked for a trade boycott and breaking diplomatic relations with South Africa. Brazil's position at the Security Council was similarly inconsistent. In

[78] Dávila, *Hotel Trópico*, 97.
[79] Selcher, *The Afro-Asian Dimension*, 162.
[80] Ibid., 165.
[81] Aragon, 'Chancellery Sepulchers',138–9.

August 1963, the Brazilian delegation supported a resolution that called on South Africa to abandon apartheid and asked the member states to cease selling armaments to the country. At the same time, however, Brazil voted against a paragraph in the same resolution that called for a trade boycott of the apartheid regime.[82] Despite the condemnation of apartheid, Itamaraty made no comment on the Rivonia Trial in 1963/64 involving Nelson Mandela, Walter Sisulu and eight other defendants. In fact, during the period from 1961 to 1964, there was no significant breach in Brazil's relations with the apartheid regime.

The increasing relevance of the Afro-Asian world and Brazil's ambitions to strengthen economic and political relations with the newly independent countries also resulted in the establishment of a few Afro-Asian study centres, some of which still exist today. Already before the election of Quadros, in September 1959, the Centre for Afro-Oriental Studies (CEAO) was founded by the Portuguese exile, George Agostinho da Silva, at the Federal University of Bahia (UFBA) in Salvador. This interdisciplinary centre owes its location to the significant African cultural heritage present in Bahia. The CEAO organised Brazil's first exchange programmes with African students and professors and was visited regularly by African diplomats. However, in later years its research and courses focused mainly on Afro-Brazilian studies. In April 1961, the Quadros government established the Brazilian Institute for Afro-Asian Studies (IBEAA), a policy advisory body initially subordinated to the presidency, which aimed at strengthening relations with the Afro-Asian world. The IBEAA focused on Africa and held seminars, exhibitions and debates, with the frequent participation of representatives from Africa. Its director and members of the board were academics and others who shared African positions on colonialism and racism. In March 1962, the IBEAA was transferred to the Itamaraty. Due to its anti-colonial positions, it became extinct after the military takeover in 1964.

In 1973, Candido Mendes de Almeida, political advisor to Quadros and former IBEAA founder set up the Centre for Afro-Asian Studies (CEAA) at the University Candido Mendes, a private higher education institution in Rio de Janeiro. In 1965, the Centre for Studies of African Culture (CECA) was formed at the Faculty of Philosophy, Sciences and Arts of the University of São Paulo (USP), which hosted the biggest programme in Afro-Asian studies. In 1969 it was renamed Centre for African Studies (CEA). In addition to academic studies on Africa being fostered in the early 1960s, anti-colonial political activism was

[82] Boadi-Siaw, 'Development of Relations', 140.

also permitted in Brazil. From 1961 to March 1964, a group of exiled Angolan students in São Paulo, organised as the Afro-Brazilian Movement for the Liberation of Angola (MABLA), tried to influence public opinion against Portuguese colonialism, but without a great deal of success.[83] In 1963, the Mozambique Liberation Front (Frelimo), formed the previous year in Dar es Salaam, Tanzania, opened a representation in Rio de Janeiro.[84]

Military rule: Brazil realigns with Washington and Lisbon

The military coup of 31 March 1964 ended Brazil's political rapprochement with Africa as the new right-wing military ruler Castelo Branco (1964–67) immediately returned to former alignments. Brazil broke relations with Cuba and Guevara's award was retroactively rescinded to please Washington. Brazil re-established close relations with the United States and Portugal's dictatorial regime, which categorically rejected international demands for the decolonisation of its African territories. Castelo Branco assured Salazar that his government wanted to strengthen 'the union between our two peoples in the fight for the preservation of the great moral principles and common ideals of justice and peace'. At the same time, his government strengthened the collaboration with South Africa's apartheid regime that was viewed as an ally in the fight against communism.[85] In contrast, the new military government clearly considered other African countries as less relevant. Consequently, the military regime largely ignored African positions on colonialism and racism. The Brazilian secret service detained MABLA activists and other African students because of their support for the liberation struggles. The Frelimo office was searched by the police and its representatives were imprisoned, only being released after the intervention of Senegalese President Léopold Senghor and African diplomats in Brazil.[86]

At the earlier invitation of the Goulart government, Senghor paid a one-week visit to Brazil in September 1964. He visited several cities, universities and industrial centres, and gave public lectures and news conferences. In addition, Senghor signed commercial and agricultural agreements with Brazil, which were the first of the kind with a Sub-Saharan African country. In fact, the visit represented the end of closer relations

[83] Selcher, *The Afro-Asian Dimension*, 164.
[84] Ovídio de Andrade Melo. 'O reconhecimento de Angola pelo Brasil em 1975'. *Comunicação & Política*, 7:2 (2000), 100.
[85] Boadi-Siaw, 'Development of Relations', 160.
[86] Ibid., 163.

with Africa as it was the last high-level political-diplomatic exchange with an African country until 1972.[87] It is illustrative of the military regime's political relations with Africa that, in August 1968, 44.5% of Brazil's diplomatic and consular personnel in Sub-Saharan Africa were located in South Africa and Portuguese Africa. At the same time, Brazil's total diplomatic personnel in Portugal were 2.3 times that of Sub-Saharan Africa, including South Africa and the Portuguese territories.[88] While the expansion of Brazil's diplomatic network in Africa had almost come to an end, in 1966 Nigeria opened an embassy in Brasília. Primarily commercial motives prompted the Costa e Silva government (1967–69) to open embassies in Addis Ababa and Nairobi in 1967. Ethiopia and Kenya were Africa's principal coffee-producing countries, and Addis Ababa hosted the Organisation of African Unity (OAU) and the UN Economic Commission for Africa, where Brazil expected to gather information on new markets.[89] Again prompted predominantly by economic interests, in 1968 Brazil established diplomatic relations with the Republic of Congo, Côte d'Ivoire and Sudan, and the following year with Uganda and Zambia.[90] All in all, relations with African countries were not a priority for Brazil's foreign policy. The same applies to African countries with regard to Brazil. From 1966 to 1973, the number of Sub-Saharan countries with embassies in Brasília only increased from three to five.[91]

Indeed, Brazil was the only developing country that did not vote in favour of the UN resolutions that condemned the Portuguese colonial policy. During the military dictatorship, Brazil sided explicitly with Portugal in General Assembly votes on Portuguese colonialism. In December 1965, Brazil abstained in the vote on a resolution that recommended setting a deadline for independence of colonial territories and calling on the international community to boycott Portugal and South Africa. In the same month, Brazil opposed a resolution that condemned Portugal's colonial policies and recommended breaking diplomatic and trade relations with Lisbon. In December 1966, Brazil joined fourteen Western countries that voted against a resolution calling on Portugal to immediately apply the right of self-determination to the peoples of its colonies and requesting all states to deny Portugal any support which enabled it to continue colonial repression. When the government announced the visit of a navy vessel to Angola in February 1967, perceived as a gesture

[87] Ibid., 207.
[88] Selcher, *The Afro-Asian Dimension*, 105.
[89] Ibid., 93
[90] Boadi-Siaw, 'Development of Relations', 209.
[91] Ibid., 275.

of support for Portugal, the ambassadors of Algeria, Egypt, Ghana and Senegal protested and asked Itamaraty to clarify its position on Lisbon's colonial policy. In a joint statement to the press, the diplomats cautioned that the naval visit impaired Brazil's relations with Africa. Brazil's Foreign Minister considered the joint statement as impropriate and denied any harm to relations with African countries.[92] In December 1968, Brazil opposed another resolution that supported the principles of self-determination and independence of Portugal's colonies.

The military regime was also careful not to harm Brazil's economic interests in South Africa, albeit inconsistently. Brazil's trade with South Africa accounted for 90% of trade with Sub-Saharan Africa and had increased steadily since 1962.[93] In June 1964, Brazil's delegate abstained in the vote on a Security Council resolution that called on Pretoria to end political trials of apartheid opponents and release political prisoners. However, only a few days later, the same delegate supported another resolution that condemned apartheid policies and called on Pretoria to renounce the execution of condemned opponents and to grant amnesty to political prisoners. At the General Assembly in December 1965, Brazil's representative supported resolutions condemning apartheid as a threat to international peace and security and asking for sanctions against South Africa and the establishment of a UN Trust Fund to help victims of apartheid. However, he declared that his government was against sanctions and abstained on the respective paragraph of this resolution. Nonetheless, around the same time Brazil agreed to hold an international anti-apartheid conference scheduled for August 1966. A few weeks before the conference, Brazil cordially welcomed South Africa's Foreign Minister, who on arrival asked that the internal problems of his country be respected. In response, his Brazilian counterpart assured him that 'Brazil respects the national sovereignty of other countries of the world, though she would desire that the problem of racism did not exist there'. At the General Assembly in December 1966, apparently as a result of the conference, Brazil supported two resolutions condemning apartheid and asking for support for its victims. In 1968, Brazil continued condemning apartheid, but refused to support resolutions that asked for sanctions against South Africa. Despite UN protests, in 1969 Brazil allowed South African Airways to include a stopover in Rio de Janeiro in their new flight from Johannesburg to New York.[94]

[92] Ibid., 167–70.
[93] Ibid., 184.
[94] Ibid., 184–8.

However, the military rulers were interested in maintaining commercial relations with Afro-Asian countries. In 1965, the Castelo Branco government sent a twenty-two-member trade-promotion mission lasting six weeks to Senegal, Liberia, Ghana, Nigeria, Cameroon and Côte d'Ivoire. The mission was met with great interest for the purchase of Brazilian shoes, clothing, tinned foods, pharmaceutical products and electric instruments. At the same time, the Brazilians analysed the possibilities for the import of oil, coal, bauxite, phosphates, gum arabic, and natural rubber. The trip resulted in the beginning of oil imports from Nigeria and increased phosphate imports from Senegal. In 1966, a second mission visited South Africa, Angola, Mozambique, Ghana and the Côte d'Ivoire to analyse the potential consequences of increased trade with Portuguese Africa and South Africa for Brazil's relations with Black Africa. The mission considered the prospects of trade with Southern Africa to be promising, while the trade potential with West African countries was assessed as only modest.[95] In 1967, Brazil's exports to Sub-Saharan Africa totalled only $13 million, about one third of the country's exports to Belgium and Luxembourg.[96] The Brazilian Lloyd Lines reopened a monthly sea route to West Africa in February 1968 to facilitate exports; this included the ports of Dakar, Monrovia, Tema, Takoradi, Lagos, Luanda and Lobito.[97] Already, in October 1967, Lloyd had inaugurated Brazil's first regular sea route to Asia, including stops in Durban and Lourenço Marques (now Maputo).[98] Apart from South Africa, Brazil was particularly interested in economic opportunities in Portuguese Africa. In March 1968, the government of Costa e Silva ratified agreements negotiated with Portugal in 1966 giving Brazil access to trade and investments in Portuguese colonies. In 1970, the Brazilian airline Varig started weekly flights to Luanda.

During the presidency of Emílio Médici (1969–74), annual average economic growth of 11% created the need to open new markets for Brazilian products.[99] Brazil also required African diplomatic support for its claim to an extension of its territorial waters to 320 km (200 miles), endorsed in 1970.[100] An attempt to expand exports to Africa was made in October and November 1972, when Foreign Minister Mário Gibson Barboza made a trip to Côte d'Ivoire, Ghana, Togo, Dahomey, Zaire

[95] Selcher, *The Afro-Asian Dimension*, 92; Boadi-Siaw, 'Development of Relations', 210.
[96] Selcher, *The Afro-Asian Dimension*, 125.
[97] Ibid., 120.
[98] Ibid., 121.
[99] Dávila, *Hotel Trópico*, 37.
[100] Leite, *O Brasil*, 157; Visentini, *A Relação*, 36.

(now the Democratic Republic of the Congo), Gabon, Cameroon, Nigeria and Senegal. It was the first official visit of a Brazilian Foreign Minister to Africa. The delegation comprised thirty-two members, including eleven diplomats and six reporters. The trip started in Abidjan on 25 October and ended in Dakar on 23 November, during which time Barboza signed several bilateral cultural, commercial and technical cooperation agreements. In his meetings, he tried to avoid direct discussions of Brazil's position on Portuguese colonial rule, while at the same time signalling to the Portuguese government the need to change its colonial policy. In Ghana and Nigeria, the local press criticised Brazil's close relations with Portugal, and President Ahidjo of Cameroon refused to meet with Barboza for the same reason. In Senegal, Senghor supported Barboza's idea of Brazilian mediation in Portugal's colonial conflict but this was rejected by the Portuguese government.[101]

In early 1973, Barboza visited Egypt and Kenya where he signed bilateral cultural and commercial agreements. In the same year, Brazil established diplomatic relations with Gabon, Guinea-Conakry and Sierra Leone, and opened an embassy in Libya.[102] In addition, Brasília received several official delegations from Zaire, Nigeria, Côte d'Ivoire, Tanzania, Uganda and Ghana. In September and October 1973 Adalberto Camargo, president of the Afro-Brazilian Chamber of Commerce (AfroChamber), headed a mission of forty-five businessmen representing seventy Brazilian companies to Senegal, Côte d'Ivoire, Ghana, Togo, Benin, Nigeria, Cameroon, Zaire and Libya, where more than two hundred Brazilian products were presented. In 1968, Camargo, an Afro-Brazilian businessman and federal deputy, founded the (still existing) AfroChamber in São Paulo. Camargo, born in a poor rural family, had migrated to São Paulo at the age of sixteen where he made a fortune from car rentals. In 1966, aged forty-three, he was elected to the Chamber of Deputies for São Paulo state and remained as a deputy until 1978. He always advocated the participation of Afro-Brazilians in a commercial and political rapprochement with Africa. Concerned that none of the initial forty-five businessmen in his trade mission was black, Camargo persuaded eleven white businessmen to have their companies represented by Afro-Brazilians. The trade mission, which was locally supported by Brazilian diplomats, was well received by the African partners.[103] In December 1973, a hundred Brazilian companies

[101] Dávila, *Hotel Trópico*, 155–66.

[102] Visentini, *A Relação*, 40.

[103] Ivo de Santana, 'Relações económicas Brasil–África: a Câmara de Comércio Afro-Brasileira e a intermediação de negócios no mercado brasileiro'. *Estudos Afro-Asiáticos*, 25:3 (2003), 529.

participated in a trade fair organised by Itamaraty in Lagos.[104] Brazil's total trade with Sub-Saharan Africa apart from South Africa and the Portuguese colonies increased from $33.3 million in 1968 to $101.9 million in 1972.[105] From 1972 to 1974, Brazilian exports to Africa went up by 481% from $90.4 million to $435.3 million, while in the same period imports from Africa rose by 445% from $153 million to $680 million.[106]

Although Brazil successfully strengthened trade relations with Africa, the Médici government continued supporting Portugal's colonial policy. At the UN General Assembly in November 1969, Brasília abstained in the vote on a resolution reaffirming the inalienable right of the peoples of the Portuguese colonies to self-determination and independence and condemning Portugal's colonial wars. In December that year, Brazil again abstained on a resolution reaffirming the legitimacy of the struggles against apartheid and Portuguese colonial rule in Southern Africa. One year later, Brazil voted against another resolution that condemned Portuguese collaboration with South Africa and Rhodesia, and called on Portugal to end the colonial wars.[107] In December 1971, Brasília voted against a further resolution that condemned Portugal's colonial wars in Africa. In the following two years Brazil's position did not change. In November 1972, Brazil opposed a resolution that asked Lisbon to enter into direct negotiations with the liberation movements in her colonies. In November 1973, Brazil did not support UN Resolution 3061 which recognised the unilateral declaration of independence of Guinea-Bissau on 24 September of that year.[108] As for the apartheid regime, under the Médici government Brazil continued separating economics from politics. The country maintained its trade relations with South Africa but, in the period from 1969 to 1973, to appease African states, Brazil supported several UN resolutions that condemned apartheid policies.[109]

In search of oil and export markets: Strengthening relations with Africa

However, the 1973 oil crisis triggered by the Arab oil embargo threatened Brazil's energy security and economic growth, and prompted the military regime to change its African policy. The threat became even

[104] Boadi-Siaw, 'Development of Relations', 274.
[105] Ibid., 263.
[106] Santana, 'Relações económicas', 531.
[107] Boadi-Siaw, 'Development of Relations', 233.
[108] Ibid., 235.
[109] Ibid., 239–42.

more imminent in November 1973 when seventeen African oil-exporting countries included Brazil in a list of six countries to be targeted by an oil embargo in retaliation for their intransigent positions in questions related to Southern Africa, especially with regard to Portugal's colonial policies in Angola and Mozambique.[110] In early 1974, President Médici and the National Security Council approved Foreign Minister Barboza's proposal to confront Portugal with an ultimatum to either decolonise or face Brazil's explicit rejection of its colonial policy.[111] In the late 1960s and early 1970s, the average annual growth of Brazil's economy was 10% for seven consecutive years, a boom that the military rulers did not wish to jeopardise. At the time, Brazil was the eighth-largest economy in GDP terms.[112] Due to the rise in oil prices following the Arab oil embargo, the cost of Brazil's oil imports skyrocketed from $710 million in 1973 to $2.8 billion in 1974.[113] The threat to economic growth and the quest for raw materials and new export markets motivated the military regime of Ernesto Geisel (1974–79) to embark on a new foreign policy called 'Responsible and Ecumenical Pragmatism'. It prioritised economic interests over ideological affinities in its quest for new export markets and energy security. This foreign policy made diversifying foreign partners a priority and rejected the idea of a special relationship and an unconditional alignment with the United States.[114] Geisel had been head of the petroleum company Petrobras and was aware of the importance of Brazil's energy supply. Consequently, Brazil changed its attitude with regard to Pretoria and publicly condemned the apartheid regime. The fall of the Portuguese dictatorship on 25 April 1974, about six weeks after Geisel's inauguration, facilitated the change in relation to Portugal's colonies. Brazil was the first country to recognise the new regime in Lisbon, but soon distanced itself from the leftist rulers when they radicalised.[115] To demonstrate its new African policy, in July 1974 Brazil formally recognised the independence of Guinea-Bissau, deliberately before the recognition by Portugal's new government in September that year. Brazil only gave the Portuguese government 24 hours' notice before announcing the recognition. Coming eight months after Brazil had refused to recognise Guinea-Bissau's independence in the United Nations, this recognition marked the turn of Brazil's Africa policy. In

[110] Leite, *O Brasil*, 147.
[111] Dávila, *Hotel Trópico*, 169.
[112] Visentini, *A Relação*, 43.
[113] Dávila, *Hotel Trópico*, 170.
[114] Leite, *O Brasil*, 129; Stolte, *Brazil's Africa Strategy*, 63.
[115] Dávila, *Hotel Trópico*, 176.

the same year, it established an embassy in Bissau to demonstrate this change of policy.[116] At the same time, Itamaraty proposed to increase the embassies in Sub-Saharan Africa from six to eleven and to serve another twenty-one countries from these embassies.[117]

Meanwhile a diplomatic mission, composed of Ítalo Zappa, head of Itamaraty's Africa Division, and the councillor Sérgio Weguelin Vieira, was formed to establish direct contacts with the liberation movements of Mozambique and Angola. The mission's main objective was to propose the creation of special representations in Luanda and Lourenço Marques to perform diplomatic functions during the transition government. Portugal's foreign minister, Mário Soares, had been notified of Brazil's intentions.[118] In December 1974, the Brazilian diplomats held talks with a Frelimo delegation headed by Samora Machel in Dar es Salaam in Tanzania. The Brazilians stressed that their country's foreign policy was guided by an anti-colonialist stance and the principle of non-interference in other countries' affairs. However, Machel fiercely criticised Brazil's complicity with Portuguese colonialism and its disdain for the liberation movements. He said that Brazil was no priority for Mozambique and rejected the establishment of a special representation.[119] In January 1975, the diplomat Ovídio de Andrade Melo, hitherto consul in London and meanwhile appointed to negotiate the establishment of the special representatives, spoke in Dar es Salaam to Frelimo's vice-president Marcelino dos Santos about the proposal. Dos Santos replied that such a decision could only be taken collectively by Frelimo's Political Bureau. In February, Dos Santos told Melo during a second meeting in Dar es Salaam that Frelimo could not accept the proposal as Brazil had supported Portugal during the liberation war.[120] He explained that as Brazil could not be considered a friendly country it had to wait until after independence to establish diplomatic relations with Mozambique. He reminded Melo that in 1964 the Brazilian government had closed the Frelimo representation in Rio de Janeiro and had even threatened to deport its staff to Portugal.[121] Brazil was also not invited to Mozambique's independence celebrations on 25 June 1975; instead, Frelimo chose to invite two representatives from the Brazilian left, Luís Carlos

[116] Filho and Lessa, 'O Itamaraty', 70.
[117] Dávila, *Hotel Trópico*, 172.
[118] Ovídio de Andrade Melo. *Recordações de um Removedor de mofo no Itamaraty. Relatos de política externa de 1948 à atualidade* (Brasília: Fundação Alexandre Gusmão, 2009), 97.
[119] Filho and Lessa, 'O Itamaraty', 72.
[120] Melo, 'O reconhecimento', 90, 99.
[121] Melo, *Recordações*, 111–12.

Prestes of the Communist Party of Brazil (PCB) and Miguel Arraes of the Socialist Labour Party (PST).[122] At the same time, the new Frelimo government expelled the Brazilian consul. Brazil's first ambassador in Mozambique did not take office until 1976.

Brazilian diplomacy was more successful in the case of Angola where there was fighting between three rival liberation movements – People's Liberation Movement of Angola (MPLA), National Liberation Front of Angola (FNLA) and National Union for the Total Independence of Angola (UNITA). In January 1975, Melo spoke to MPLA leader Agostinho Neto during a flight from Dar es Salaam to Nairobi, Kenya. Neto agreed to the creation of a special representation in Luanda and praised the potential of cooperation on all levels between Angola and Brazil, 'two countries fraternised by culture, by ethnicities and miscegenation.' Melo was delighted by Neto's courtesy and his culturalist argument that sounded familiar to him.[123] That same month, Melo talked to the UNITA leader, Jonas Savimbi, in South Angola and FNLA leader, Holden Roberto, in Kinshasa, Zaire, who both approved the idea of a special representation. Unlike Frelimo, a consolidated movement without any internal competition which could easily reject Brazilian aid, the three rival Angolan movements could not afford to discard support from an external ally.[124] Melo, however, was clearly less impressed by the two leaders than he had been by Neto.[125]

In March 1975, Melo returned to Luanda to head Brazil's special representation, accommodated in the *Hotel Trópico*. Officially, he maintained equidistance with the three liberation movements, but he soon considered the MPLA to be the most competent to rule the country. Although the three movements had signed the Alvor Agreement on their participation in a transitional government in January 1975, they were unwilling to share power and soon started fighting each other. By August, the MPLA controlled Luanda after expelling the two rival movements from the city. This coincided with the arrival of the first Cubans to support MPLA troops. Finally, Melo came to the conclusion that the MPLA was already the *de facto* ruler of Angola and advised Itamaraty to immediately recognise the country's independence. In contrast, there was active opposition to the socialist MPLA from the United States and South Africa, which feared Soviet influence in the region and therefore

[122] At the time, they were political exiles in Algeria and the ex-Soviet Union respectively.

[123] Melo, 'O reconhecimento', 92; Melo, *Recordações*, 103.

[124] Dávila, *Hotel Trópico*, 194.

[125] Melo, 'O reconhecimento', 94, 98.

supported FNLA and UNITA. Even the OAU was divided on the question of Angola's legitimate government as only half of the member states were in favour of the MPLA.[126]

On 11 November 1975, Brazil became the first country to grant the People's Republic of Angola diplomatic recognition, ignoring Washington's explicit request not to do so. Melo represented his country during the independence celebrations and left Luanda forever in January 1976. Later, Melo opined that the fact that President Geisel was of German descent and Ítalo Zappo of Italian origin had contributed to Brazil's changing stance on Portuguese colonialism since neither of them were lusophiles.[127] However, there were fierce criticisms of the recognition of the MPLA government among conservative segments in Brazil at the time, as a result of Cuban and Soviet support for the MPLA. Due to the political pressures, Brazil's embassy in Luanda was only officially established on 31 December and the first ambassador was not sent until March 1976.[128] Melo's own diplomatic career was damaged by his role in the MPLA's recognition and he was only promoted to ambassador in 1986, the first promotion of a diplomat after Brazil's re-democratisation.[129] However, Brazil was rewarded in 1976 when Petrobras became the first foreign oil company invited by Angolan President Agostinho Neto (1975–79) to explore for oil in his country.[130] The MPLA government also helped Brazil improve its difficult relationship with Frelimo in Mozambique.[131]

In Southern Africa, Brazil assumed a position against colonialism, white-minority rule and racism. In May 1976, Brazil recognised the South West African People's Organisation (SWAPO) as the legitimate representation of the people of Namibia. In 1977, Brazil participated in the International Conference in Maputo in Support of the Peoples of Zimbabwe and Namibia and in the World Conference for Action against Apartheid held in Lagos, Nigeria. In the same year, Brasília implemented the UN arms embargo against South Africa and closed its consulate in Cape Town. This led to a decline in the relevance of Brazil's economic relations with South Africa; whereas it had been Brazil's only relevant

[126] David Fig, 'The Political Economy of South-South Relations: The case of South Africa and Latin America' (PhD dissertation, London: Dep. of International Relations, London School of Economics, 1992), 208.
[127] Melo, 'O reconhecimento', 81; Melo, *Recordações*, 91.
[128] Dávila, *Hotel Trópico*, 211.
[129] Melo, 'O reconhecimento', 131; Filho and Lessa, 'O Itamaraty', 79; Melo, *Recordações*, 92.
[130] Fig, 'The Political Economy', 204.
[131] Visentini, *A Relação*, 45.

trading partner in Africa in the early 1970s, only 5% of its exports to Africa went to South Africa at the end of the decade.[132]

In the years that followed, Brazil strengthened its ties with African countries; this also resulted in a considerable increase in bilateral trade as well as large Brazilian enterprises, such as Petrobras and the construction company Norberto Odebrecht, doing business in Africa. In 1975, Volkswagen of Brazil established a car assembly plant in Kaduna, Nigeria, while Mercedes-Benz of Brazil and Marco Polo exported trucks and buses to Nigeria.[133] In 1977, the Brazilian airline Varig inaugurated a regular flight from Rio de Janeiro to Lagos. The Brazilian government provided a wide range of subsidies and incentives to promote exports to African countries. The state-owned *Banco do Brasil* maintained branch offices in Abidjan, Lagos, Cairo, Casablanca, Dakar, Libreville and Tunis to support Brazilian companies and finance African import of Brazilian products. In addition, *Banco do Brasil* acquired 40% of the Paris-based International Bank for Western Africa (BIAO), with more than a hundred branch offices in the region. Brazil established credit lines to finance imports of goods and services to Angola, Mozambique, Senegal, Côte d'Ivoire, Gabon, Guinea-Bissau, Niger, Mali and Togo.[134] Despite this financial support network, it became increasingly difficult to access the international funds necessary to finance large projects as these funds refused to provide credit for Brazilian projects in Third World countries. This problem was tackled by means of counter-trade, which enabled the partial or complete payment of goods with goods. This payment method was particularly important for oil imports from Nigeria, which became Brazil's major African trading partner in the 1980s. From 1972 to 1981, Brazil's exports to Nigeria increased from $1 million to $770 million.[135] Under the counter-trade agreement, Brazil imported about 100,000 barrels of oil per day and exported the equivalent of 40,000 barrels of oil per day in vehicles, spare parts and other products. In November 1984, another counter-trade agreement was signed with Angola and provided for the partial payment in Angolan oil of the $650 million construction of the Capanda hydroelectric dam by Norberto Odebrecht.[136]

[132] Leite, *O Brasil*, 151.
[133] Dávila, *Hotel Trópico*, 227–8.
[134] Leite, *O Brasil*, 144.
[135] Dávila, *Hotel Trópico*, 226.
[136] Ivo de Santana, 'Notas e comentários sobre a dinâmica do comércio Brasil-África nas décadas de 1970 a 1990'. *Revista brasileira da política internacional*, 46: 2 (2003), 120–22.

Apart from Odebrecht, several other Brazilian construction companies built roads, airports and other infrastructure projects in various African countries in the early 1980s. Exports were also promoted through the establishment of trading companies. The trading company Interbrás, a subsidiary of Petrobras, established an association with twenty-one Brazilian companies in Nigeria to commercialise about a hundred manufactured products under the exclusive trade mark, Tama. In April 1978, Brazilian soccer star Pelé made a twelve-day tour of Nigeria promoting Tama products.[137] Apart from Nigeria and Angola, other Brazilian trading partners in Africa included Mozambique, Zaire, Tanzania, Senegal, Mauritania, Liberia and Côte d'Ivoire.[138] In the 1980s, arms sales accounted for a considerable share of Brazilian exports to Africa. At the time, Brazil was one of the six major arms exporting countries.[139] The main importers of Brazilian armaments included Gabon, Morocco, Sudan, Togo, Burkina Faso and Zimbabwe. In 1988, the United States intervened to stop Brazilian military supplies to Libya worth $1 billion. During this period, Brazil's role in Africa was as another developing country and a member of the G77, the group of developing countries established in 1964. The Itamaraty perceived Brazil as an intermediary country, which together with other Third World countries took action to foster peace, reduce the gap between rich and poor countries and promote international cooperation by serving as a bridge between different cultures and civilisations.[140]

The last military ruler, João Figueiredo (1979–85) was the first Brazilian and Latin American president to make an official trip to Africa, when he visited Nigeria, Senegal, Guinea-Bissau, Cabo Verde and Algeria in November 1983. By strengthening its ties with African countries, Brazil sought to increase its importance in the international arena. From 1974 to 1984, Brazil's embassies in Africa increased from twelve to twenty-one.[141] In addition, six African heads of state and several foreign ministers, ministers and government delegations paid visits to Brazil during the Figueiredo government. At the United Nations, Brazil condemned South Africa's apartheid regime and the illegal occupation of South West Africa (now Namibia) by Pretoria. Under the Figueiredo presidency,

[137] Dávila, *Hotel Trópico*, 239.

[138] Santana, 'Notas e comentários', 123.

[139] José Nunes Pereira, 'Brasil-África no Governo Figueiredo: um balanço'. *Contexto Internacional*, 2 (1985), 94.

[140] Ibid., 85.

[141] Bruno Gonçalves Rosi, 'As Relações Brasil-África no Regime Militar e na Atualidade'. *Revista Conjuntura Austral*, 2: 3–4 (2011), 37.

Brazil's trade with Africa reached its peak. Between 1972 and 1981, Brazilian exports to Africa increased by 2,170% from $90.4 million to $1,963.3 million. In the same period, imports from the continent rose by 1,290% from $152.9 million to $1,982.2 million. In 1981, Brazilian trade with Africa reached about 9% of its total external trade, the highest percentage ever.[142] Not even during the Lula da Silva government, when Brazilian exports to Africa again rose significantly in absolute terms, did they ever equal the share of total exports of the early 1980s. From 1979 to 1984, Brazil's trade with Africa increased by 170.6%, considerably more than its trade with the United States (61.9%), East Europe (46.4%), Asia (40.3%), the Middle East (14.8%), and the European Community (1.3%). The five main African trading partners were Nigeria, Algeria, South Africa, Angola and Egypt. In 1984, manufactured goods accounted for 88.6% of Brazilian exports to Africa, while oil represented 94.0% of its imports from Africa. However, Brazil's trade with Africa represented only 2% of the continent's total foreign trade at the time.[143] Moreover, cultural cooperation with Africa was limited to the broadcast of Brazilian soap opera series (*telenovelas*) in Angola and Cabo Verde; and on the other hand, technical cooperation came in the form of professional training for participants from twelve African countries provided by the National Service for Industrial Training (SENAI) and the National Service of Commercial Training (SENAC).[144]

In the mid-1980s, there was a setback in Brazil's political and economic relations with Africa due both to the economic crisis in Brazil caused by the unsustainable external debts left by the military regime, and also Africa's economic predicaments at the time. Brazil's foreign debt increased from $25 billion in 1975 to $105 billion in 1985. In the 1980s and 1990s, Brazil's average annual growth in gross domestic product (GDP) declined to just 2.2% and 1.8%, respectively. The policy of state incentives for export substitution went from being a growth factor to an obstacle for economic growth. Consequently, Brazil replaced state intervention to promote exports through subsidies and incentives, which had dominated during the industrialisation period, with a trade liberalisation policy.[145]After 1985, Brazil's foreign policy prioritised bilateral relations with neighbouring countries in South America, the

[142] Pereira, 'Brasil-África', 84.

[143] Ibid., 89.

[144] Sucupira and Roque Santeiro, the names of informal markets in Praia and Luanda stem from Brazilian *telenovelas*. The former still exists, while the latter was closed in 2010.

[145] Santana, 'Notas e comentários', 119.

United States, the European Community, and subsequently with emerging powers like Russia, China and India. Consequently, during the government of José Sarney (1985–90), Africa's share of Brazilian exports declined from 7.9% to 3.3%, while its share of imports slumped from 13.2% to 2.8%. Due to its own economic problems, Brazil was no longer able to grant import credit to African countries, many of which were also hit by economic crises in the 1980s. Direct weekly flights from Brazil to Abidjan, Lagos, Luanda and Maputo came to an end.[146] In 1994, the AfroChamber ceased to publish its magazine, the circulation of which had reached 20,000 copies in the early 1980s. The number of its affiliated companies also fell from more than three hundred to about fifty.[147] Only a few larger companies, including Petrobras and Odebrecht, continued to invest in Africa.

Brazil's economic problems resulted in the closure of the Brazilian embassies in Ethiopia, Tanzania, Cameroon, the DRC, Togo and Zambia. Consequently, Brazil's relations with Africa became largely restricted to the *Países Africanos de Língua Oficial Portuguesa* (Palop – Officially Portuguese-speaking African Countries) and Nigeria, an important oil supplier. Only twenty-four of the thirty-four Brazilian diplomats based in Africa in 1983 remained in their posts in 1993, while the number of diplomats in Europe and South and North America rose from 362 to 418.[148] Despite this decline in Brazil's bilateral relations with Africa, the Sarney government developed two multilateral initiatives involving Africa. Following Brazil's proposal at the United Nations in 1986, the Zona de Paz e Cooperação do Atlântico Sul (South Atlantic Peace and Cooperation Zone – ZOPACAS) was established to prevent the proliferation of nuclear arms and the establishment of naval bases by foreign powers in the region. In addition, ZOPACAS was expected to strengthen economic, political and cultural relations between the member states, which initially included Argentina, Brazil, Uruguay and nineteen coastal African countries. In addition, at a meeting in São Luís, Maranhão, of the governments of Brazil, Portugal and the five Palop countries in 1989, it was agreed to set up the International Portuguese Language Institute (IILP) headquartered in Praia, Cabo Verde; approval was also given to the project to create a community of Portuguese-speaking countries and this finally came into effect in 1996 in Lisbon when the Comunidade de Países de Língua Portuguesa (CPLP) was formally constituted by the seven countries.

[146] Ibid., 130.
[147] Santana, 'Relações económicas', 537.
[148] Dávila, *Hotel Trópico*, 247.

Conclusions

The abolition of the slave trade in 1850 and the colonisation of Africa by European powers from the late 19th century ended more than three hundred years of Brazilian involvement in Africa, which had been dominated by the slave trade. The resulting forced immigration of more than four million Africans shaped Brazil's demography, society and culture. Between the 1960s and the mid-1970s when the independence of most former African colonies offered political and economic opportunities to extend external relations, Brazil experienced two periods of rapprochements with the neighbouring continent. The first, rather short-lived, rapprochement occurred from 1961 to 1964 during the governments of Jânio Quadros and João Goulart as part of their Independent Foreign Policy, while the second rapprochement took place from 1974 to 1985 during the presidencies of Ernesto Geisel and João Figueiredo, the last two military dictators. Although the two attempts to re-establish closer ties with Africa occurred in different political and economic contexts, they also had several things in common. They both represented a change in Brazil's foreign policy, which during most of the 20th century was dominated by *americanismo*, a strategy to achieve Brazil's development primarily through regional cooperation and a close partnership with the United States and other industrialised Western countries. In contrast, the two rapprochements with Africa were part of the foreign policy paradigm of *globalismo*, marked by a greater autonomy from the United States and an extension of external relationships with developing countries in the Global South in an attempt to gain more political influence internationally.[149] Both periods of rapprochement were conditioned by the bipolarisation of international politics during the Cold War. Although the presidencies of Quadros/Goulart and Geisel/Figueiredo were antithetical ideologically, they used the same culturalist discourse of Brazil's African-ness, the country's claimed proximity to Africa thanks to its black heritage in society and culture. They believed and tried to make their African partners believe that there was racial democracy in Brazil that would provide the country with a comparative advantage in its relations with other developing countries.

However, at the same time there were significant differences between the four presidencies. In the early 1960s, Brazil was still a predominantly agrarian country and mainly a coffee exporter, with industrialisation still in its initial stages. Quadros and Goulart were democratically elected

[149] See Letícia Pinheiro, *Política externa brasileira (1889–2002)* (Rio de Janeiro: Zahar, 2004).

presidents, whose PEI was frequently suspected by their many political opponents as a sign of communist sympathies. They re-established Brazil's relations with African countries, but predominately in the political and cultural domains, while the external trade with Africa remained almost non-existent during the three-year period. Their short-lived rapprochement was ended mainly due to political reasons by a military coup, whose leaders immediately resumed their former close ties with the United States and Portugal, which at the time exercised considerable influence on Brazil's foreign policy through a powerful immigrant community. Until 1974 the military governments did not completely abandon Africa, but they realigned themselves with Salazar's colonial policy and, politically, Africa ceased to be a priority. Nevertheless Brazil's external trade with Africa increased slightly during the period.

Principally motivated by economic concerns, and afraid of a possible oil boycott by African and Arab countries, President Geisel initiated another rapprochement with Africa. Meanwhile, Brazil had now become an industrialised country with high economic growth rates thanks to a successful state-driven policy of import substitution. Geisel's change in Brazil's African policy was facilitated by the fall of the dictatorship in Lisbon, which paved the way for the independence of the five former Portuguese territories in Africa. The recognition of Angola's left-wing MPLA government by Geisel's right-wing military dictatorship in November 1975 was a proof of the ideological pragmatism of his African policy. Subsequently Geisel successfully strengthened Brazil's relations with African countries, particularly as far as investments and foreign trade was concerned. With the support of credit and other incentives provided by the state, his successor Figueiredo succeeded in further increasing Brazil's foreign trade with Africa at levels that were thereafter never reached again. However, the second rapprochement under Geisel and Figueiredo proved to be equally unsustainable, since it came to an end due to Brazil's financial crisis that coincided with Africa's own debt crisis. As a consequence, Brazil's relations with Africa retreated significantly on virtually all levels. After 1985, Brazil's democratic governments that were confronted with mainly financial and other domestic problems returned largely to the *americanismo* paradigm, which privileged economic and political relations with the United States and other industrialised and emerging countries, while Africa was side-lined for the rest of the 20th century.

2

Brazil–Africa Relations under Globalisation: From Adaption to Consolidation

Paulo Fagundes Visentini

Introduction

During President Lula's government, Brazilian diplomacy gave a privileged place to Africa, and relations intensified. A strategic vision and a coherent perspective were the new basis of the Brazil–Africa relations, which became the principal focus of the so-called South–South cooperation. While many believe the relations with Africa proved the solidarity dimension of President Lula's social programme, others consider them as no more than prestige diplomacy, a 'waste of time and money'. Moreover, some regard these relations primarily as business diplomacy, a kind of 'soft imperialism', which was only to be different from China's presence in Africa in its form and intensity.

Lula's successor, Dilma Rousseff, exercised a diplomacy considered 'continuity without priority', especially in the case of Africa. Nevertheless, relations between the two sides of the South Atlantic Ocean followed their course. But after Rousseff's impeachment in 2016, the Michel Temer government followed a diplomatic path without a clear African policy strategy. Although Africa is no longer at the top of Brazil's international agenda, the connections already established are working at many levels.

Historical background

Following the end of the Cold War and the creation of Mercosur in 1991, Africa was considered a secondary arena within a diplomacy based on a neoliberal view of globalisation and favouring Organisation for Economic Cooperation and Development (OECD) countries. Fernando Collor de Mello (March 1990 to September 1992) was the first president to be elected by direct vote since Jânio Quadros, back in 1961. After he took office in 1990, his neoliberal economic policies opened a new phase of relative distancing from Africa. The Washington Consensus, whereby vertical North–South relations were given priority over horizontal South–South relations, started to govern the strategic vision of the Brazilian elite. The decline of trade between Africa and Brazil that followed was the result of the adjustment plans on both sides of the Atlantic Ocean, the withdrawal of state financing of exports and many other branches of the economy, and the need to buy oil from Argentina to balance trade relations within the Mercosur, the South American common market. Nevertheless, President Collor visited the region in 1991 after Nelson Mandela's release from prison and the independence of Namibia, which received Brazilian help to structure its navy. Meanwhile, not only did the number of Brazilian diplomats in Africa decline steadily but, like the Middle East, Africa lost political and administrative status within the Foreign Ministry structure. A short-term cost-benefit view determined all actions, reversing the strategic policies pursued by previous governments.

The fall of the Berlin Wall in 1989, the disastrous reforms of Mikhail Gorbachev in the Soviet Union that ultimately led to its collapse in 1991, and the rise of the United States and its neoliberal ideas provided a strong base for globalisation. Collor de Mello took office at a time of intense change on the international stage. Like many other peripheral countries, Brazil had been affected by a decade of serious economic instability and urgently needed to find a solution to its difficult financial situation. To that end, the Collor government adhered to the Washington Consensus, which was a set of reforms proposed by the International Monetary Fund, the World Bank and the US Treasury for crisis countries like Brazil. Collor and his ministers explicitly defended these recommendations. They included the liberalisation of foreign trade and this was advanced in 1991 with the creation of Mercosur, which aimed at the future creation of a common market of Brazil, Argentina, Uruguay and Paraguay. Domestically, the privatisation of state-owned enterprises that began under Collor and continued during the two terms of Fernando Henrique Cardoso (1995–2002) were the most visible signs of the liberal discourse. The very foundations of the economic model underpinning the global projection of the Brazilian diplomacy were shaken.

The country no longer had its own project but tended to follow the agenda set by the North. In this context, Collor deepened the regionalisation process of Brazilian foreign policy that had started in the 1980s, and concentrated on dialogue with South American neighbours while pleading with the US for better treatment of Brazil's foreign debt. Collor followed both drivers of that policy, but changed the nature of the latter; he established a close relationship with Washington with a 'real sense of a partnership founded on common values, aspirations and endeavours'.[1] In addition, Collor sought to 'redesign Brazil's Third World profile' through a modernising discourse that, in theory, would provide Brazil with greater opportunities in the aftermath of the Cold War. These positions would involve a *reduction* of Brazil–Africa relations, as outlined by Sarney at the end of his administration.

The Collor administration did not entirely distanced itself from Africa. Collor retained a positive rhetoric in relation to the African continent, even though this was not translated into concrete diplomatic, commercial or political advances. Africa was only mentioned by Collor and his Foreign Ministers, Francisco Rezek (1990–92) and Celso Lafer (1992), in speeches related to the Brazilian government's support for the Zona de Paz e Cooperação do Atlântico Sul (South Atlantic Peace and Cooperation Zone – ZOPACAS); this remained one of Brazil's priorities, according to Collor in his speech at the UN General Assembly in 1990. Other reasons included the firm stand against apartheid (an easy discourse given that the regime was near its end) and the desire for an economic partnership with the SADCC (forerunner of SADC), the economic community of Southern Africa.

The interest in ZOPACAS meant that Collor's only visit to Africa, in September 1991, was precisely to the southern part of the continent. The seven-day visit began in Angola where he met with President José Eduardo dos Santos and expressed his wish to work with African countries, highlighting the investments Petrobras made in that country. Previously, in May 1991, a high-level Brazilian delegation had met the UNITA leader Jonas Savimbi in Brussels amid negotiations of the ceasefire agreement. The attention given to Namibia should also be noted; Brazil promptly established diplomatic relations following its independence and Collor also visited the country in September 1991. Angola and Namibia are the two African countries in ZOPACAS with the longest Atlantic coast. Mozambique and Zimbabwe were the other two countries included in Collor's trip to Southern Africa. A month before the trip, Nelson Mandela had visited to Brazil, about a year and a half after his release; he was awarded with the Grand Cross of the Order of Rio Branco, a Brazilian distinction for diplomats and foreigners.

Collor was also able to take advantage of past initiatives such as agreements signed with African countries during the Figueiredo and

[1] Fernando Collor, 'Presidente Fernando Collor é recebido na Casa Branca. Resposta à saudação do Presidente George Bush na cerimónia oficial de chegada, na Casa Branca, em 18 de junho de 1991', *Resenha de Política Exterior do Brasil*, 17:68 (1991), 165.

Sarney administrations. Notably, these past initiatives included trade agreements with Cabo Verde (1986) and Zimbabwe (1988); an economic cooperation agreement with Algeria (1987); and an agreement for scientific, technical and technological cooperation with Morocco (1984). In addition, a joint committee was set up at Collor's initiative to promote trade between Brazil and Tunisia in 1990. However, the commercial effect of the agreements was almost nil and Africa's share in Brazil's foreign trade averaged only 3.2% during Collor's term.[2]

Moreover, Collor's external priorities and the difficulties facing the country meant no concrete progress came out of the firm rhetoric in favour of a rapprochement with Africa. Cuts were made to the staff of diplomatic missions and during Celso Lafer's short administration of the Foreign Ministry, Brazil removed diplomats from Libya in compliance with international sanctions. Cultural, educational (the PEC foreign scholarship programme was reduced) and technical cooperation also decreased, high-level visits in both directions declined and the culturalist discourse began to be deconstructed. The 'Collorful' Brazil wanted to be white. Only the internationalised enterprises such as the state oil company, Petrobras, the construction company, Norberto Odebrecht, and the mining company, Vale (formerly Vale do Rio Doce), continued to operate in Africa.

After Collor's impeachment and removal on charges of corruption, he was replaced by Itamar Franco in late 1992; the climate was one of political instability. A nationalist, Franco defended the principle of national sovereignty and put a stop to new privatisation initiatives, although previously planned privatisations went ahead. Externally, the new President prioritised upgrading Brazil's presence on the world stage, compared with the setbacks during Collor's government. Brazil's foreign policy goals also included a multilateral system, at both economic and political levels, and the consolidation of Brazilian action within international bodies like the UN and the WTO. Itamar appointed Fernando Henrique Cardoso (FHC) to the Foreign Ministry, where he remained in office until May 1993. During his short administration, Cardoso transformed the Foreign Ministry, which, even after suffering an increasing turnover, still defended the previous government policies. By promoting various international seminars, FHC managed to convince most diplomats that they should foster Brazil's insertion in the neoliberal globalisation.

Cardoso took a low profile in Brazil's international discourse and was quite timid in the defence of a more favourable institutional framework

[2] Cláudio Oliveira Ribeiro, 'Relações Político-Comerciais Brasil-África' (PhD dissertation, Universidade de São Paulo, São Paulo, 2007), 107.

for developing countries or the proposals for new multilateral initiatives.[3] As Foreign Minister, FHC gave priority to the economic issues facing Brazil, and little emphasis was placed on the country's interests due to changes in the international political order. In early 1993, the Minister confirmed the Collor administration's priorities for Brazil's partnerships, namely, with newly industrialised countries and with the 'First World'. These priorities excluded Africa as a relevant area of commercial interests for Brazil. The Minister even stated that the Africa policy had been a mistake and that it only served for the Brazilian military to claim an alleged hegemony in the South Atlantic. This statement sparked controversy among those criticising Africa's reduced importance in Brazil's foreign policy. Cardoso reconciled them by saying that the relations with the African continent should flourish due to a ripening Africa policy, despite the difficulties on both sides of the Atlantic.[4]

Celso Amorim, who would later also be Foreign Minister of Lula, was Cardoso's successor at the Foreign Ministry from May 1993 to the end of 1994. There was a return to a somewhat articulated vision of an Africa policy. More importantly, bilateral and multilateral support (via the UN) was given to the peace and reconstruction process in some African countries, especially Angola and Mozambique. However, these actions were due also to Brazil's candidacy for a permanent seat in the UN Security Council. Amorim's appointment was a clear indication of the foreign policy the government wanted to pursue. The Foreign Minister's administration was marked by an autonomist and purposeful stance in the new environment, and diplomacy was used to recover concepts that neoliberals believed were no longer of any use. Amorim claimed: 'It is imperative that we do not limit ourselves by adopting a merely reactive attitude towards an agenda set out externally, we must be able to define our own foreign agenda instead'.[5] At the opening of the 48th UN General Assembly, Amorim said that 'Brazil believes that the sovereign national state is the basis of international law and politics' and that 'a relativisation of the principle of sovereignty – which would never be argued in relation to the powerful countries – would lead to setbacks in the democratisation of international relations'.[6]

[3] See Ney Canani, *Política Externa no Governo Itamar Franco (1992–1994): continuidade e renovação de paradigma nos anos 90* (Porto Alegre: Editora UFRGS, 2004).

[4] See Eli Alves Penha, *Relações Brasil-África e geopolítica do Atlântico Sul* (Salvador: EDUFBA, 2011).

[5] Canani, *Política externa.*

[6] Celso Amorim, 'O Brasil na 48ª Sessão da Assembleia Geral da ONU', *Resenha de Política Exterior do Brasil*, 19:73 (1993), 59–68.

There was a process of selective options for the development of relations with Africa; some key countries were prioritised and the limited efforts were concentrated in these countries. Consequently, South Africa, Angola and Nigeria were the focus of the Brazilian foreign policy in the continent. At the multilateral level, ZOPACAS was reactivated and the relations with the five Países Africanos de Língua Oficial Portuguesa (Officially Portuguese-speaking African Countries – Palop) countries were strengthened at a meeting of foreign ministers of Portuguese-speaking countries in Brasília. Concerning ZOPACAS, in September 1994, Brazil hosted the third ZOPACAS ministerial meeting, when South Africa became a member after having established majority-rule democracy. The Declaration on the Denuclearisation of the South Atlantic was also signed at this meeting. The Brazilian Foreign Ministry saw the project of a community of Portuguese-speaking countries as a mechanism to bring nations together on specific or general topics, thus favouring common goals. Furthermore, it began seeing such a community as a possible junction for various processes of economic integration in progress in the South Atlantic, which could benefit trade between blocs at a time of US-led offensive with its FTAA (Free Trade Area of the Americas).

Brazil also took advantage of the articulation with the Portuguese-speaking countries to contribute to the deployment of troops in UN peacekeeping missions in Mozambique (1994) and Angola (1995). Another line of action in Brazil's Africa policy was also concentrated in Southern Africa, related to the re-emergence of South Africa as an important bilateral trading partner. This new stage was marked by the visit of Brazil's Foreign Minister in May 1994. According to Celso Amorim, Brazil and South Africa represented two 'elephants' in their respective regions. Amorim argued that the problem of asymmetries in existing regional integration processes in both continents could be offset by the expansion of cooperation between the two regional blocs. This in fact happened only in 2003 when the trilateral India–Brazil–South Africa Dialogue Forum (IBSA) was established.

The proposal of a community of Portuguese-speaking countries and the reaffirmation of ZOPACAS coincided with the decline in trade relations between Brazil and African countries. These initiatives therefore emerged as attempts to maintain a bridge with the other side of the Atlantic, in order to produce results for Brazil in the future. In short, the discourse and practice on Africa policy were contradictory during Itamar Franco's administration given that trade and diplomatic relations with Africa declined in the 1990s. The reduction in the number of Brazilian embassies in Africa at the end of 1993 reflects this downward trend: Brazil had twenty-four diplomats in Africa, compared to 161 in Europe, fifty-two in North America and seventy-seven in South America.[7] In view of this situation, there is no doubt that the Brazilian presence in Africa became concentrated on a few countries and specific initiatives.

The foreign policy of the government of FHC, known as 'presidential diplomacy', attempted to enter actively into globalisation in the belief that this entailed increasing Brazil's presence in international and regional forums, using the latter to promote cohesion in the discussions held in the former. In addition, the government prioritised relations with the developed countries, mainly the United States and European countries, so as to foster technology transfer and increase bilateral trade. It was also a time of budget constraint at the Foreign Ministry (with large cuts in staff), and as a result it became necessary to select specific and limited foreign policy guidelines.

The setting in Brazil was one of strong optimism due to the recent economic and political stabilisation (Real Plan), although the more limited production (Brazil had become an importer rather than exporter) that was already visible in Cardoso's first year in office hampered the government's efforts. Cardoso came to power in an international scenario of neoliberal policies and the strengthening of issues such as human rights, the environment, disarmament and economic liberalisation. It was an era of increased importance for international organisations and regional forums, which fostered globalisation. The political focus was to generate confidence for foreign investors who benefited from purchasing already installed facilities at a low cost, namely the powerful Brazilian state-owned enterprises. The foreign exchange inflows stemming from the privatisation process kept the *real*, the Brazilian currency, strong, and offset the deficits in the balance of payments caused by massive imports. Brazil stopped manufacturing many products to focus on goods that, under the new rules, might be competitive. Everything else could be imported. And only the OECD markets were considered. There was, in fact, a new appraisal of a deeply ideological political reality, but now in the context of post-Cold War.

Africa went through a decade of economic downturn and adaptation to economic stabilisation programmes dictated by international financial institutions, and there was general pessimism about the continent's development potential. These negative factors added to the dominant political instability, which, in the words of José Pimentel, resulted in a high 'Africa cost'.[8] In spite of that, FHC's Foreign Minister, Luiz

[7] See Ribeiro, 'Relações político-comerciais'.

[8] José Vicente de Sá Pimentel, 'Relações entre o Brasil e a África subsaárica', *Revista Brasileira de Política Internacional*, 43 (2000), 9.

Felipe Lampreia, stated: 'We no longer have the material conditions that allowed us, in the 1970s, to make the qualitative leap of Africa diplomacy of the late Foreign Minister Azeredo da Silveira, nor the aid capacity to let us give priority attention to African countries that are among the poorest in the world'.[9] A clear example of this was the closure of six diplomatic posts in the African continent.

Although Africa's place in Brazil's international relations remained modest under the two FHC administrations, there were some important initiatives and a slight change during the second term which would be qualitatively deepened by the Lula government. The Brazilian Army actively participated in UN peacekeeping missions in Angola and some other countries from 1995. Cardoso visited Angola and South Africa in 1996 when he signed agreements covering various areas, and in 1998 President Mandela visited Brazil. The new South Africa emerged as an important partner for Brazil. In 2000, the country signed a Framework Agreement with Mercosur. Similarly, cooperation in the field of public policies grew, especially when Brazil began its struggle to break the international patent rights of medicines against AIDS, the epidemic ravaging Southern Africa.

When President Cardoso began to criticise the 'asymmetric globalisation' in the context of the *real* currency crisis, greater convergence emerged between Brazil and the African states in world diplomacy and its multilateral forums, especially on economic issues. The foreign policy for Africa therefore sought to prioritise bilateral relations with selected countries in Southern Africa and the South Atlantic – South Africa, Namibia, Angola and other Palop countries. Most of Africa was left out of foreign policy, with the government saying that the relations with specific cores would be a 'springboard' for the development of the rest of the continent[10] as those countries had experienced recent successes in political and economic terms: 'after Namibia's independence, the end of apartheid in South Africa and the election of Nelson Mandela, the consolidation of peace and democracy in Angola will be the next sign

[9] Luiz Felipe Lampreia, 'Palavras do Ministro das Relações Exteriores, Embaixador Luiz Felipe Lampreia, por ocasião da solenidade de encerramento do Seminário sobre Zumbi e as Relações Afro-Brasileiras', *Resenha de Política Externa do Brasil*, 22:77 (1995), 201.

[10] Luiz Felipe Lampreia, 'Palavras do Senhor Ministro das Relações Exteriores, Embaixador Luiz Felipe Lampreia, por ocasião da abertura da Reunião Ministerial da Comunidade de Países de Língua Portuguesa, Salvados, Bahia, 17 de julho de 1997', *Resenha de Política Exterior do Brasil*, 24:81 (1997), 15–18.

that this region is destined to occupy a prominent place in the developing world'.[11]

Foreign Minister Lampreia explicitly declared:

> We should not look at Africa only as the largest number of votes in the UN, being able to help our country get a permanent seat in the Security Council. [...] *Opening embassies in all African countries makes no sense*, in my opinion, since, besides being a huge expense to the taxpayer, it is impossible to meet the expectations created by this gesture. Brazil ends up being a disappointment to them. A large number of African countries have deep ties with their former colonial powers, which are embodied in trade preferences, financing, educational support and even military cooperation. *We cannot hope to compete with France, Britain or the European Union in these fields.* The alternative has to be more limited, mainly focused on cultural cooperation, which is our best tie, on technical cooperation and on financing Brazilian companies; it is imperative to set priorities. Our priorities under FHC were the Portuguese-speaking countries and South Africa.[12] (Emphasis added)

That is, Brazil should only seek the available vacant spaces, without disputing with any nation, especially those former colonial powers whose markets the country naively longed for. Even the African support for the Brazilian bid for permanent membership of the UN Security Council was undesired. The apparent paradox can, however, be explained: Brazil did not want the support of small players to win political space; rather, it expected to be invited by the powerful countries due to its good behaviour. Analysing the Brazilian policy for Africa in this period, Brazil's participation in the UN peacekeeping missions in Angola (UNAVEM III, to which Brazil sent more than eleven hundred men) and Mozambique (ONUMOZ) demonstrates the Brazilian ideal of linking Africa foreign policy with international organisations. If we look at the three countries that received Brazilian attention in this period, relations with South Africa became the over-riding priority, as expressed in a presidential speech on the Brazilian desire to 'build a bridge over the Atlantic'.[13]

[11] Fernando Henrique Cardoso, 'Discurso do Presidente da República por ocasião da sessão solene de abertura da reunião de Cúpula da Comunidade dos Países de Língua Portuguesa, Lisboa, 17 de julho de 1996', *Resenha de Política Externa do Brasil*, 23:79 (1996), 29–32.

[12] Luiz Felipe Lampreia, *O Brasil e os ventos do mundo*. Memórias de cinco décadas na cena internacional (São Paulo: Objetiva, 2010), 283.

[13] Fernando Henrique Cardoso, 'Discurso do Presidente Fernando Henrique Cardoso, por ocasião do banquete oferecido pelo Presidente da República da África do Sul, Nelson Mandela. Pretória, 27 de novembro de 1996', *Resenha de Política Externa do Brasil*, 23:79 (1996), 169.

From this bridge, the Brazilian Government aimed to strengthen ties between Mercosur and SADC to liberalise trade between both regions.

In the context of globalisation, it is also worth mentioning that the penetration of Brazilian television (especially soap operas) in Africa grew from the late 1980s as well as the establishment of networks for smuggling, drug and weapons trafficking, and money laundering (in a two-way flow). Cultural and security issues were therefore often common in the relations between the two sides of the South Atlantic. Brazil also began to receive refugees and immigrants from Africa. At a certain point, economic relations between Brazil and Angola declined significantly, but a new agreement was signed between the two countries when Angola's debt was rescheduled in 1995. In addition, the reciprocal visits of heads of states indicated they both wanted to maintain relations.[14] Finally, the visit by Namibia's President, Sam Nujoma, to Brazil in 1995 showed the interest in strengthening relations between the two countries. Two initiatives also signalled this interest: the project of agricultural development of northern Namibia with direct participation of Brazilian technicians, and naval cooperation. Brazil trained Namibian officers and soldiers and was ready to provide the goods and services Namibia needed for its future navy.

Another important project was the CPLP, founded under Cardoso in 1996, but built on initiatives by the Presidents José Sarney and Itamar Franco. In his opening speech to the CPLP Summit in Lisbon in 1996, FHC stated that the community was built on three pillars: political cooperation for the defence and promotion of common interests, development cooperation and promotion and defence of the Portuguese language. In the early years, the CPLP encountered difficulties; the lack of political and economic content in CPLP formulations and practices was a major concern among the community's less favoured countries.[15] By focusing on the cultural and linguistic aspect and on diplomatic and solidarity ties, the CPLP failed to present projects of great importance that entailed heavy investments by the Brazilian Government.

Despite progress in the relations with specific African countries, the Brazilian policy during Cardoso's first term maintained its basic guidelines, which implied the exclusion of Africa from any major international projection of Brazilian politics. In his second term (1999–2002), FHC's foreign policy was led first by Foreign Minister Luiz Felipe Lampreia

[14] Kamilla Rizzi, *O Grande Brasil e os pequenos PALOP. Relações do Brasil com Cabo Verde, Guiné Bissau e São Tomé e Príncipe* (Porto Alegre: Leitura XXI/CEBRAFRICA-UFRGS, 2014), 76–81.

[15] Ribeiro, 'Relações Político-Comerciais', 145.

(1999–2000) and later by Celso Lafer (2001–02); similar to domestic policy, it continued to be characterised by neoliberalism. According to Amado Cervo and Clodoaldo Bueno, the drivers of the President's diplomatic policies were based on the disposal of assets of Brazilian companies for sale, submission to political consensus and increasing external debt, in short performing a dependent position in the international system.[16] By complying with these provisions, the administration favoured relations with First World countries (or economies seen as stable), to the detriment of South–South relations, exemplified by the negotiations with the FTAA and international financial institutions.

On the other hand, it is worth noting that there was a slight change in the second period of FHC's government, marked by criticism of 'asymmetric globalisation', due in part to the *real* crisis (1999). Throughout the period, however, relations with Africa were marked more by cultural and historical proximity than by commercial partnerships or political rapprochement. In the words of Cardoso:

> Our perception of Africa is an almost immemorial perception, given the black presence in Brazil. Not exactly the political Africa, but rather religion, slavery, the colour of our skin. [...] Today's Africa is something else. The information on Africa is very scarce in Brazil. I would point out two exceptions only: Angola, because of greater economic interests of Brazilians there and because Brazil supported the MPLA; and South Africa, which is a new fact, and also due to the extraordinary presence of Nelson Mandela. The rest of Africa is very little spoken of, there is very little information.[17]

This excerpt also reveals the clear policy focus on certain African countries, mainly in Southern Africa, notably South Africa and Angola, but also to a lesser extent the other Portuguese-speaking countries and Nigeria. It thus becomes apparent that there was not a foreign policy for the continent as a whole, but a clear selectivity based on a short-term cost-benefit logic. Regarding South Africa, it is remarkable that an agreement was signed with Mercosur at this stage to establish a free trade area, seeking greater economic integration. With Angola, joint actions were held in the areas of public safety and education. There was also a certain rapprochement with Nigeria due to the purchase of oil. In addition, Brazil was engaged in the consolidation of the CPLP and bilateral cooperation was established with some countries to fight AIDS.

[16] See Amado Cervo e Clodoaldo Bueno, *História da Política Exterior do Brasil* (Brasília: Ed. UnB, 2010).

[17] Fernando Henrique Cardoso e Mario Soares, *O mundo em português: um diálogo* (Rio de Janeiro: Paz e Terra, 1998), 87.

Finally, it is important to note that the African participation in Brazil's imports increased from 3% in Cordoso's first term to 5.5% in the second.[18] This was the result of economic growth in Africa due to cooperation with emerging powers such as China and India since the turn of the century, which his government had overlooked as it was focusing on the North. Still, despite these positive data and the aforementioned slight change, Brazil continued the trend set by earlier governments of closing embassies in African countries. Cardoso's second term therefore maintained its extra-regional policy focused on the developed countries and, despite specific actions and particular bilateral relations, its policy towards Africa was quite limited.

The 21st century and the emergence of a multidimensional Africa policy

In 2003, Luiz Inácio 'Lula' da Silva, who had a metalworking and unionist background, was elected President through a coalition led by his Workers' Party. It was the first time since independence that the government was headed by someone from outside the traditional elite. And this made a remarkable internal and external difference. Even with his poor schooling, the President had great sensitivity to social and global issues – and a considerable talent for politics and negotiations. Celso Amorim was appointed Foreign Minister with Samuel Guimarães as his Deputy Minister, while the history professor Marco Aurélio Garcia was chosen as the Special Advisor to the Presidency on international affairs.[19]

From the start of the Lula administration in 2003, Brazilian diplomacy paid special attention to Africa by increasing ties with the continent, and Brazil developed an 'active, affirmative and propositional diplomacy'. Brazil–Africa relations were then based on a strategic vision and a coherent perspective (both quite optimistic) and they became the focus of the so-called South–South or horizontal cooperation. Bilateral and multilateral relations developed, notably in the areas of trade and investment (mainly in the oil, mining and infrastructure sectors), health, science and technology, social programmes, technical cooperation, diplomacy, and even security and defence.

At home, the government adopted effective programmes to fight poverty such as 'Zero Hunger', while affirmative policies sought to integrate the disadvantaged people of African descent into Brazilian mainstream

[18] Ribeiro, 'Relações político-comerciais'.

[19] He remained in office until May 2016 when he was dismissed by the new President Michel Temer.

society. As early as March 2003, one initiative promoted the entry of more black people in the diplomatic cadres by offering scholarships to prepare for the Rio Branco Institute[20] examinations. In education, the PEC-G and PEC-PG programmes (scholarships for foreign students to take undergraduate courses and postgraduate studies in Brazil) were expanded with the inclusion of more Brazilian universities (with an increase in the number of places and scholarships) and greater emphasis was placed on cooperation in scientific research as well university teacher exchanges.

Courses and events were offered in Africa and seminars were promoted on both sides of the Atlantic to deepen mutual understanding. Africa thus came to be seen as the most important field of action in the framework of South–South cooperation, accompanied by an increase in bilateral trade and Brazilian technical cooperation activities on the continent.

For many, relations with Africa were proof of the solidarity dimension of President Lula's social programme through the international extension of national actions, while others regarded these relations only as 'prestige diplomacy' which wasted time and money. Others (especially critics on the left) also considered them from the perspective of 'business diplomacy', a kind of *soft imperialism*, which differed from the Chinese presence in Africa only by its form and intensity. However, the strategic and economic pillars of this recent rapprochement have been more important: although the African continent shows marked levels of poverty, there had been no economic stagnation in the region, a relevant fact that constituted an important role for Brazil's global ambitions.

Brazil, China and India were the new players in African international politics. After a long period of detachment, Brazilian society and its inter-state relations with Africa went beyond the rhetoric stage or simple continuity of previous actions, and gained greater incentive from the Lula government. From the Brazilian perspective, the historical bonds, the large number of African descendants in the country and the internal debate on racial equality were all part of the need for a closer and cooperative relationship with African partners.

Although opposition parties accused the Lula government of 'wasting money on a continent without a future', Brazilian enterprises gained ground and reinforced their presence, mainly Petrobras, Odebrecht and Vale, among other transnational public and private Brazilian companies. Whereas initiatives from China, and more recently India, were guided

[20] Brazil's national diplomatic academy.

by economic objectives – despite their aid in infrastructure – and the US presence was focused on security issues and geopolitics, the Brazilian strategy of cooperation brought new elements.

The diplomatic discourse and practices under Lula led to the formation of priority alliances with partners within the South–South sphere. In this regard, the African continent became one of the most important areas of influence in Brazilian diplomatic plans, second only to South America. One of the first actions was to modify the Foreign Ministry's internal structure for Africa: besides Africa Division I and II, the government separated the Department of Africa and the Middle East to make way for another department just for the African continent. Consequently, Africa Division III (DAF-III) was established.

There was a substantial change in Brazil's foreign policy from 2003, which thereafter aimed to establish alliances with partners in the South–South axis and emphasised the importance of the African continent in the Brazilian strategy for international insertion. A clear sign of this was the high level of diplomatic investment in the continent that led to several visits to African nations (and by African leaders to Brazil) and a number of cooperation agreements in various areas: by the end of his second term, President Lula had been to Africa twelve times and had visited twenty-three different countries, some of which more than once (totalling twenty-nine state visits to African nations). In the same period, forty-seven African leaders from twenty-seven countries visited Brazil. President Lula made far more official visits than all his predecessors together.[21]

This change in Brazilian foreign policy was justified first by the government's greater understanding of the importance Africa played in boosting Brazil's projection internationally and in its strategy of global insertion to fulfil its aspiration as an emerging middle power. On the

[21] For the purposes of this study, the methodology considered was that of the Foreign Ministry (2011) to classify visits as bilateral and multilateral. Multilateral visits are 'the visits without any registered appointment with local authorities; when there are bilateral and multilateral appointments on the same occasion, the visit is considered bilateral' (MRE, *Balanço de Política Externa 2003–2010 – África – Defesa*, Brasília, 2011, 6, our translation). Under Lula, therefore, the multilateral visits to Africa were: São Tomé and Príncipe for the CPLP Fifth Conference of Heads of State and Government (2004); Nigeria at the First Africa–South America (ASA) Summit (2006); South Africa to attend the India–Brazil–South Africa Summit (2007); Ghana for the Twelfth United Nations Conference on Trade and Development (UNCTAD) (2008); Cabo Verde for the Brazil–Community of West African States (ECOWAS) Economic Summit; and South Africa to launch the 2014 FIFA World Cup (2010).

other hand, the new policy was also explained by the African Renaissance following international recognition of its status in large part due to the appreciation of its commodity exports and China's growing investment in the region.

Like former President Jânio Quadros, President Lula even stated: 'Brazil has a moral and ethical commitment to the African continent.' Another relevant point in this Africa policy is the opening/reopening of Brazilian diplomatic posts on the continent; seventeen new Brazilian embassies were opened in Africa, bringing the total to thirty-six embassies and two general consulates (fourth position in the world after the US, France and China). Unlike the nations with which Brazil already had established relations, the presence of an embassy was considered essential to enable the advancement of new initiatives. Africa's diplomatic presence in Brazil also intensified: from 2003 to 2010, the number of African diplomatic missions accredited in Brasília rose from sixteen to twenty-nine, a high number considering the financial difficulties of many countries in Africa.

Brazil's decision to forgive the foreign debt of some African countries (legally required to allow new financing) should also be interpreted through this new Brazilian position.[22] According to the United Nations Development Programme (UNDP), the Brazilian Government forgave African countries approximately $1 billion in debt in order to fulfil some of the Millennium Development Goals, which included technical support to the South with technology and knowledge transfer. About $815 million targeted heavily indebted poor countries while $116.6 million concerned other African countries. Nigeria stands out from these countries with relieved debt, with a cancellation of 67% of its debt (pending since the 1980s, totalling approximately $162 million); Mozambique is another noteworthy example as Brazil agreed to forgive 95% of its bilateral debt worth $351 million.

It would not be an exaggeration to call Brazil's Africa policy under Lula a revolution. During the Football World Cup in South Africa in July 2010, Lula made his penultimate and eleventh trip to Africa as President. He visited Cabo Verde, where he attended the Brazil–ECOWAS Summit to promote cooperation with West African countries. He then travelled to Guinea-Bissau, Equatorial Guinea, Kenya, Tanzania, Zambia and South Africa. Agreements were signed with Vale and Petrobras in Kenya and Tanzania. Although Africa was also considered a priority under Lula's successor, President Dilma Rousseff (2011–16), she sought

[22] Such forgiveness depended on the following two conditions: (i) return for investment in education, and (ii) consideration for the purchase of Brazilian products.

to maintain his Africa policy in a less favourable environment. Lula's commitment to Africa was also demonstrated by the focus given to it by the Lula Institute, which he created after leaving the Presidency.

The rise of Dilma Rousseff to power symbolised the continuity of Brazil's international insertion project started during Lula's government. With regard to Brazil's Africa policy, both the President and her first Foreign Minister, Antônio Patriota, indicated they would maintain, and even intensify, the pattern of relations with the continent. Yet this was not what happened since there was *continuity without* priority and, in the case of Africa, even regression. President Dilma, who had a more technical character, had to address the challenges of the international economic crisis and renew the lagging national infrastructure for the 2014 Football World Cup; she depended on a sluggish state apparatus, stuck because of the 1988 Constitution, and regulatory rules established by the neoliberal governments. In addition, she was more sensitive to issues of human rights (which she had been deprived of under the military regime when she was a political prisoner). Thus, given the progress made under Lula in foreign policy, she lowered its priority and gave Antônio Patriota, the Foreign Minister, great autonomy; however, after a number of problems, he was replaced in August 2013 by Foreign Minister Luiz Alberto Figueiredo, but foreign policy remained unchanged.

The importance of Africa in Brazil,s international insertion strategy can also be perceived through the number of high-level visits between Brazilian and African authorities. Dilma Rousseff (who 'does not like travelling'), made her first trip to Africa in October 2011, visiting three countries: South Africa (where she attended the Fifth IBSA Summit), Angola and Mozambique. In her second trip to Africa, in February 2013, Dilma Rousseff attended the Third ASA (Africa–South America) Summit in Equatorial Guinea. During the same trip, she visited Nigeria and she returned to South Africa in March that year for the Fifth BRICS (Brazil, Russia, India, China and South Africa) Summit of Heads of State and Government. Two months later, she participated in the Fiftieth Anniversary of the African Union (formerly the Organisation of African Unity) in the Ethiopian capital, Addis Ababa. In December 2013, Dilma returned to South Africa to attend the funeral of Nelson Mandela, accompanied by her four predecessors Lula da Silva, Henrique Fernando Cardoso, Fernando Collor and José Sarney. However, due to increasing domestic political and economic concerns, this was her last visit to an African country before leaving office in May 2016.

Several heads of state visited Brazil for the World Cup, notably Jacob Zuma of South Africa, Denis Sassou Nguesso of the Republic of the Congo, and Joseph Kabila of the Democratic Republic of the Congo.

The World Cup was followed by the BRICS Summit in the city of Fortaleza, where the establishment of the BRICS Bank was announced. This was an extremely important step for South–South cooperation at the global level and for the early formation of a new international financial order, which may benefit predominantly African countries.

The intensification of high-level political and diplomatic contacts between Brazil and Africa resulted in the opening of negotiations and even the signature of several agreements in various areas such as technical cooperation and defence. In the defence area alone, agreements were signed with Angola, Nigeria, Senegal, South Africa, Namibia, Equatorial Guinea and Mozambique. Another important issue was Brazil's role in peace processes and in political and humanitarian crises in Africa. One of the most consistent examples has been the Brazilian presidency of the UN Peacebuilding Commission Guinea-Bissau Configuration (PBC-GB) since 2014, an effort to promote peace and political stability in that country. In addition, multilateral mechanisms of relations with African countries developed under Lula from 2003 have continued, at least formally. These include the ASA, IBSA and the revitalised ZOPACAS.

However, for political and economic reasons, these multilateral initiatives have also lost dynamics and vigour in recent years. Soon after the widespread social protests in June 2013, Brazil began to pay considerable attention to the internal demands raised by the demonstrators. The Foreign Ministry lost considerable political and financial strength during Dilma's administration especially with regard to South–South cooperation. This was particularly marked in relation to Africa where personnel and resources were cut and several joint initiatives were stopped.

Economic diplomacy: Trade and investment

Since the 1980s, internationalised companies have been the major promoters of Brazilian private investment in Africa and they have conducted infrastructure, energy and mining works across the continent. Investments in the energy industry were not restricted to oil; there was also support for sustainable energy sources such as biofuels; this enabled plantations belonging to small farmers and family farms, which would otherwise have had a small market, become viable. The transnational Brazilian companies also played an important role under Lula as they strengthened ties with African countries and were therefore substantially favoured by the President's political diplomacy. The increase in trade missions during the Lula administration was a significant sign of this and resulted in a growing number of Brazilian companies (especially service exporters) in Africa: Vale, Petrobras, the bus manufacturer Marcopolo, and the construction companies Odebrecht, Camargo Corrêa, Queiroz Galvão, OAS and Andrade Gutierrez were among the large companies with an active presence in the continent.

Vale, the world's second-largest mining company, gained the right to exploit the Moatize coal reserves in northern Mozambique: in early 2009, the company launched a project for a coal-mining complex with an estimated value of $1.3 billion, which was expected to produce 11 million tons of coal per year for export to Brazil, Europe, Asia and the Middle East. In total, the project should generate 8.5 million tons of metallurgical coal (used to make steel) and 2.5 million tons of thermal coal (used in power generation). Vale relies on the support of twenty other Brazilian companies for the project, expanding the project's dimension in terms of bilateral relations. The initiative was forecast to transform Mozambique into Africa's second-largest coal producer, after South Africa. In addition to generating 3,000 jobs for the local community in the construction stage and another 1,500 upon opening, it was also expected to improve the country's situation in world trade as Mozambique's economy has traditionally been dominated by subsistence agriculture. This was not Vale's only investment in Africa. In March 2009, the company announced the creation of a joint venture with African Rainbow Minerals Limited (ARM) in Zambia, aimed at increasing the strategic options of the copper belt in Africa. Furthermore, Vale was also present in Malawi through investments in the railway sector to ensure the outflow of production. In recent years, the company has disinvested from four African countries.

On the other hand, Petrobras – the world leader in deep-water oil extraction technology – has been operating in Africa since the 1970s: in Angola, the oldest African branch of the company, there are six active extraction and production blocks and eleven new wells are planned; in Nigeria, where Petrobras has worked since 1998, various investments were made in 2008 to increase the company's participation in the country as one of the world's largest oil producers. It is worth noting that, under Lula, Petrobras expanded its actions and investments to four other countries: Tanzania (2004), Libya (2005), Mozambique (2006) and Senegal (2007). By 2016 Petrobras was engaged in oil production only in Angola and Nigeria, while in Gabon and Tanzania the company participated in oil exploration. Reference should also be made to Petrobras' agreement with Mozambique's National Hydrocarbons Company (ENH),[23] a state-owned enterprise, which included research

[23] In the context of renewable energy, other initiatives include the signature of a Memorandum of Understanding between Brazil and the West African Economic

into biofuels production – an initiative that the Brazilian Government has fully encouraged to promote the 'biofuel revolution'. More recently, the company has ceased operations in Libya, Benin and Namibia.

Major Brazilian construction companies have also been present on African soil. Odebrecht, for example, has operated in Africa since the 1980s. Over the years, it established a strong partnership with Angola after the construction of Capanda Dam began in 1984. Mozambique has been another important market, where the company has worked for example on the infrastructure development of the Moatize coal complex, operated by Vale. Odebrecht's businesses in Africa have not been limited to infrastructures. Through its Africa Fund, established in 2012 to manage its business interests in the continent, it began operating within retail trade, film and mining industries. Camargo Corrêa, another construction company, has also had projects in Mozambique and Angola since 2006, operating in the areas of energy, mining, transport and sanitation. About 16% of the economic growth in Angola's GDP ($91 billion) originated from Brazilian companies, especially in the service sector.

It is also noteworthy that Brazilian exports to Angola went from just $235 million in 2003 to $1.9 billion in 2008, surpassing the export flow to South Africa and Nigeria, previously Brazil's largest trading partners in Africa. In 2008, the main Brazilian companies operating in Angola other than Odebrecht were Petrobras, Costa Negócios e Tecnologia and Brazil's Volvo – each of which exports to the value of over $50 million to the country. As a result of the recent economic crises in both countries, from 2014 to 2015 Brazilian exports to Angola fell by 48.6% from $1.26 billion to $648 million and Angolan imports to Brazil fell drastically by 97.1% from $1.1 billion to only $31.8 million. In 2016, Brazilian exports to Angola dropped further to $540 million, while imports from Angola into Brazil increased slightly to $72 million.

The initial growth of Brazilian exports was also stimulated by the increase in funding allocated by the Banco Nacional de Desenvolvimento (Brazilian Development Bank – BNDES). This included the opening of credit lines for African countries to purchase Brazilian products. This had become a very common practice with Angola, which negotiated a new line of credit with Brazil in early 2012, based on the guarantee of 20,000 barrels of oil per day. Similar models were applied in other

---

and Monetary Union (UEMOA, in its French acronym) (2007), Brazil–European Union–African countries trilateral cooperation (2009) and the Structured Programme for the Support of Other Developing Countries in the area of Renewable Energy (2009).

countries, including Ghana and Mozambique. The BNDES also acted to facilitate the internationalisation of Brazilian companies in Africa; this included stimulating investment in areas such as telecommunications and banks with the aim of expanding the spectrum of Brazilian investments beyond sectors like infrastructure and energy.[24]

Lula's period was marked by a sharp expansion of trade between Brazil and Africa. Although trade flows increased almost continuously over the 1990s, this became particularly visible after 2003. Indeed, during the period 2003 to 2012, it increased from just over $ 6 billion to more than $10 billion, compared with $5 billion to $6 billion between 2002 and 2003.[25] These figures resulted from two important – yet certainly not exclusive – factors. Brazil was not only a traditional exporter of primary products, services and manufacturing but had also become an exporter of capital and technology. This phenomenon has also been observed in other developing economies like India, South Africa and China. Despite unstable regimes, armed conflicts and other forms of violence, health problems and immense poverty in Africa, it was considered a suitable territory for investment by Brazilian companies. At the same time, it has been one of the few natural frontiers still open for business expansion in industries such as oil, gas and mining and a stage of global competition for access to increasingly scarce raw materials in great demand. Nevertheless, it should be noted that Brazil has also been an exporter of these goods and thus does not need to obtain them from Africa.

A deeper analysis of figures suggests that Brazil took advantage of the opportunities offered by the African continent. As pointed out by Claudio Ribeiro, from 1996 to 2006, Brazilian exports to Africa grew by 487%, while imports grew 478%. Under the Lula administration and at the start of Dilma's government, the growth continued; for example, exports reached $12 billion in 2011, nearly five times the 2003 figure of $2.4 billion. Another important aspect is the composition of the export

[24] In order to expand the supporting network for Brazilian companies in Africa, BNDES signed two memoranda of understanding with African institutions in 2012. The first was signed with the African Development Bank during the Rio+20 conference and covers cooperation possibilities in project financing, reducing credit risk and social and economic development in Africa, among other areas. The second memorandum was signed with the Development Bank of Ethiopia (BNDES, BNDES e bancos africanos de desenvolvimento assinam Memorandos de Entendimento', 21 June 2012, accessed 26 December 2018, www.bndes.gov.br/wps/portal/site/home/imprensa/noticias/conteudo/20120621_mou).

[25] Ministério do Desenvolvimento, Indústria e Comércio Exterior (MDIC), *Balança Comercial Brasileira: Dados Consolidados 2012* (Brasília, 2013).

basket, most of which consists of industrial products and services. Figure 1 below shows these trade patterns.

The figure clearly reveals the effect of Africa's rapprochement policy on trade relations between Brazil and the continent. The upward trend is interrupted in 2009, when it fell to $17 billion due to the global economic crisis. In 2010, however, flows increased again to over $20 billion before peaking in 2011 at $27.6 billion. This was followed by a decline in 2012 to about $26.5 billion. In 2013 Brazil's trade with Africa peaked at $28.5 billion, but then dropped considerably to only $17 billion in 2016 as a result of Brazil's economic crisis and economic decline in African oil-producing countries. The dynamics of exports and imports suggests that these positive results were due to the expansion of commodity and capital exports.

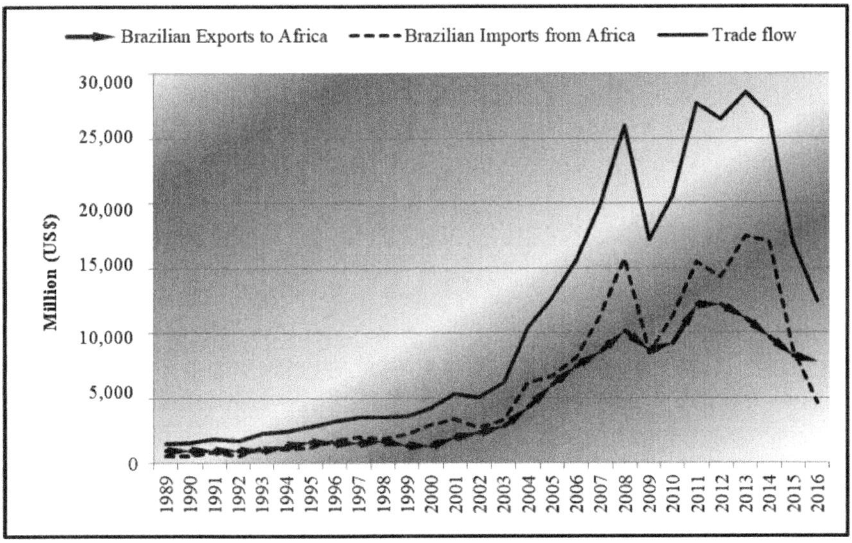

Figure 1 Brazilian trade with Africa 1989–2016 (US$)

The expansion of trade between Brazil and Africa was driven by business missions to Africa, organised by the Ministry of Development, Industry and Foreign Trade (MDIC) in partnership with the Brazilian Trade and Investment Promotion Agency (APEX-Brasil) and the Foreign Ministry. They involved meetings with government representatives, seminars and business meetings, in which Brazilian companies sought to increase the international insertion of their products, particularly in markets regarded as non-traditional. Investments by Brazilian entrepreneurs were also encouraged by APEX-Brasil through its Business Centre in Luanda, established in 2010. The strategy for strengthening

Brazil–Africa economic relations also entailed signing multilateral agreements, notably the Mercosur-Southern African Customs Union (SACU) Preferential Trade Agreement, signed in 2008. The main purpose of the accord was to facilitate access to the markets of both blocs in order to increase the two-way flow of trade and investment. In 2015, Brazilian exports to the SACU countries South Africa, Namibia, Botswana, Swaziland and Lesotho accounted for $1.38 billion, with a Brazilian trade surplus of about $720 million.

Technical, educational and social cooperation

Brazil has grasped technical cooperation as an essential tool of its external action. Its South–South cooperation fosters knowledge transfer, training, employment of local labour, and designing projects that recognise the circumstances of each nation by identifying their demands. Social protection has been one of these, and several countries have requested support to implement Brazilian social protection and poverty reduction programmes. The process is very advanced in Angola, Kenya and Senegal, which have consolidated such programmes. South–South cooperation has also had a political dimension as both Africa and Brazil have been interested in contributing to the construction of a multipolar world system and developing more-balanced multilateral mechanisms. The reform of the UN has been a particularly decisive element. More than obtaining a seat for Brazil as a Permanent Member of the Security Council, it is also about including other developing countries, giving more power to the General Assembly (so that the less powerful members are represented) and, fundamentally, transforming the Economic and Social Council into the most important organ within the UN for the promotion of development. The United Nations should no longer be just a 'police station' and discussion forum with some specific programmes; it should be the leader of world development. However, this would not be achieved simply through a 'fair' project; there should be a *balance of forces* capable of inducing change. And cooperation among developing countries was expected to make a difference.

Thus, active cooperation in the development of Africa and Latin America was at the heart of the government's social programmes and the interests of the Brazilian state. Many critics lacked historical and strategic vision. It was not just out of charity that Brazil transferred know-how, technology and public policies. Africa has been an important aspect of Brazil's definition of its identity as a Third World nation, in an attempt to overcome the country's dominant elitist perspective of a 'Western' nation. Approximately one half of the Brazilian population is of African descent. By defining Brazil's priority external partners, the country was also defining its *national identity*, which has been crucial to consolidate a *national project*. After all, Brazil is a mixed-race and developing nation.

Until 2011, Brazil stepped up its international cooperation efforts for the development of Southern countries. While this took shape in various forms, technical cooperation was the most important. For the Brazilian Government,

> The focus of [technical] cooperation [...] is the transfer of knowledge and experience through training, consulting, institutional capacity-building and implementation of pilot projects. Thus, two main objectives are met: to improve the living conditions in the supported locations and to generate technical capacities that allow the results of cooperation to be internalised. (Authors' translation)[26]

This was part of what is conventionally called solidarity diplomacy, in which the ultimate goal was to promote development in recipient countries. The Agência Brasileira de Cooperação (Brazilian Development Agency – ABC), part of the Foreign Ministry and responsible for enabling and monitoring Brazil's technical cooperation, has been one of the main agents of this cooperation. The ABC was established in 1987, but its growing importance was demonstrated by the increase in its executed budget and the number of countries covered; its budget for the African continent grew by 15.8% between 2005 and 2009.[27] Its initiatives in Africa (where it applied, in 2014, 71.5% of its resources), approximately 161 cooperation actions – encompassing projects and isolated activities – were carried out with African countries in various areas: education, agriculture, livestock, health, environment, public administration, information technology, e-government, culture, energy, urban development, vocational training and sports. The front line of Brazilian cooperation in African countries involved the Palop countries. The Brazilian cooperation provided to Angola, Mozambique, Guinea-Bissau, São Tomé and

[26] Luiz Inácio Lula da Silva, 'Discurso do Presidente da República, Luiz Inácio Lula da Silva, por ocasião da abertura de Encontro Empresarial, durante visita à República do Congo, Brazzaville, 16 de outubro de 2007', *Resenha de Política Exterior do Brasil*, 34:101 (2007), 133–4.

[27] Moreover, under Lula, framework agreements were signed for technical cooperation with several countries, including Equatorial Guinea, Gambia, Sierra Leone and Rwanda, in addition to negotiations opened with Ethiopia, Mauritania, Chad, among others. Nonetheless, more than half of the funds invested in Africa are still earmarked for Portuguese-speaking countries (ABC, África – Execução Financeira 2000–2014', 2010).

Príncipe and Cabo Verde corresponded in 2008 to 74% of the resources allocated to technical cooperation projects in Africa.

The official visits made by President Lula, usually accompanied by business groups, also gave great impetus to important cooperation initiatives. These included the creation of Brazilian technical education centres for vocational training through cooperation between the ABC and the Serviço Nacional de Aprendizagem Industrial (National Service for Industrial Training – SENAI). Vocational training centres are already operating in Angola, Cabo Verde, Guinea-Bissau, and São Tomé and Príncipe, and another one was expected to be installed in Mozambique as soon as some financial constraints were overcome. The Brazil–Angola Vocational Training Centre in Luanda is an instructive example. Founded in 2000, it was the result of several years of planning and technical coordination following the identification of a number of local difficulties, such as the lack of qualified workforce. Thus, the project has supported the training of qualified staff in the areas of engine mechanics, construction, electricity, clothing and computers, contributing to the effort of social reintegration and national reconstruction. In 2005, the Brazilian Government transferred the management to its Angolan counterpart.

Agriculture has been a key feature in the context of technical cooperation. For instance, the establishment of a Regional Office of EMBRAPA (the Brazilian Agricultural Research Corporation) in Accra (Ghana) in 2006 was in response to demand from African countries; the goal of this agency was to act as a facilitator in the transfer process of agricultural and forestry technologies. EMBRAPA's technical cooperation in support of the Cotton Initiative for the benefit of the Cotton-4 member countries (Benin, Burkina Faso, Chad and Mali, which were joined by Togo in 2014) was noteworthy and is one of ABC's structural projects. Approved through the Complementary Agreement to the African Union-Brazil Technical Cooperation Agreement, the project provides for the establishment of partnerships to promote technical cooperation for the sustainable development of the cotton chain. In Senegal, EMBRAPA offered technical cooperation for the development of rice growing; in Mozambique, the triangular cooperation initiative with Japan known as ProSavana has helped develop agriculture in savannah regions. In addition, ABC projects in health care, prevention and treatment programmes of diseases like HIV/AIDS, malaria and sickle cell anaemia have been implemented with Zambia, Benin and the Republic of the Congo, among others.

In the area of governance, Brazil has cooperated with Angola, Cabo Verde and São Tomé and Príncipe, through SERPRO (Brazil's Federal Data Processing Service), for the installation of Tele-Centres, including digital inclusion activities; these centres opened in Cabo Verde and São Tomé and Príncipe in 2004, and in Angola in 2009. Brazilian cooperation in the health areas has focused mainly on supporting the fight against malaria, HIV/AIDS and sickle cell anaemia. It is worth noting the important Brazilian support for actions to combat HIV/AIDS in Mozambique, namely through the economic feasibility study for the implementation of an antiretroviral drugs factory in the country. The initiative provides for training by the Brazilian Government of Mozambican professionals to work in the factory, which was inaugurated in 2012, as well as for support to strengthen the public agency responsible for regulating health activities.

The following cooperation projects in education deserve special note: the Adult and Youth Literacy Projects in São Tomé and Príncipe, and Mozambique, and the transfer of the *Bolsa Escola* ('School Grant') programme methodology in Mozambique and São Tomé and Príncipe; and in Angola, the 'Capacity-Building for Preparing a Curriculum Proposal' project. There have also been other Brazilian initiatives in different sectorial areas; the country has lent electronic voting machines for elections in Guinea-Bissau.

In November 2007, the Brazilian delegation at the fourth meeting of the Group on Earth Observations (GEO) in Cape Town announced that Brazil and China would grant free distribution of images from the China–Brazil Earth Resources Satellite (CBERS) for the African continent, The aim was to facilitate the monitoring of natural disasters, deforestation, drought, desertification, threats to agricultural production and food safety, and public health by African governments and organisations. In addition to supplying high-quality images, Brazil has also committed to providing the necessary software for image processing and other interpretation instruments, as well as training for African users.

In November 2013, the Sotuba Experimental Station of the Cotton-4 Project was inaugurated in Mali; serving as a regional centre for agricultural research to neighbouring countries, it was coordinated by the Brazilian Cooperation Agency and implemented by EMBRAPA. The First Session of the Brazil–Nigeria Mechanism of Strategic Dialogue also took place. Later that month, Defence Minister Celso Amorim travelled to Cabo Verde to discuss the strengthening of security conditions in that region of the Atlantic, and to inaugurate Brazil's permanent naval mission in Praia in support of the modernisation of Cabo Verde's Coast Guard.

In August 2014, Brazil provided funds to combat the Ebola epidemic in West Africa. In humanitarian cooperation with Guinea, Liberia and

Sierra Leone, the Brazilian health and the foreign ministries joined forces to donate basic disaster supply kits to support local activities. In October, a further $13.5 million worth of supplies was donated. In the following month, Fortaleza hosted the Second Brazil–Africa Forum, an initiative of the Brazil–Africa Institute together with the Lula Institute.

September 2014 was marked by two major developments in the area of defence cooperation between Brazil and Africa. The first was the agreement to sell seven Brazilian patrol vessels to the Angolan Navy. The second was the announcement of joint defence studies and military technological research by Brazil and South Africa, in order to acquire new markets and become strong enough to compete with more developed countries in the sector.

Finally, South–South cooperation brings mutual benefits. According to the 2010 UNCTAD Report, *Economic Development in Africa*,

South-South Cooperation is also attractive to African countries because it promises an alternative to the problems encountered with the current foreign aid mechanisms and represents a new dimension of economic, financial and commercial international systems, on which African countries can effectively exercise their influence.[28]

Grants for foreign students to study in Brazilian higher education institutions, as well as the promotion of Brazilian culture abroad are also important features of the Brazilian strategy to promote international development. Internally, Law 10.639 (2003) seeks to revitalise the importance of Africans' contribution to the formation of Brazil. With regard to cultural promotion, Brazil has nine lectureships in Africa in which professors are to further knowledge of Brazilian culture and the Portuguese language. In addition, there are six Brazilian cultural centres (CCBs) on the African continent.[29]

Brazil–South Africa Partnership

The role played by the new South Africa in Brazil's Africa policy should also be highlighted. It was one of Brazil's traditional trading partners, the latter having concentrated 90% of its annual exports to the continent

[28] UNCTAD, *Economic Development in Africa Report 2010* (Geneva, 2010).

[29] The Brazilian lectureships in Africa are based in the following countries: Cabo Verde, Cameroon, Ghana, Guinea-Bissau, Benin, Gabon, Nigeria, São Tomé and Príncipe, and Kenya. The cultural centres are distributed as follows: Angola, South Africa, Mozambique, Guinea-Bissau, São Tomé and Príncipe, and Cabo Verde. (Information collected from the online depositary of the Ministry of Foreign Affairs of Brazil for the years 2003 to 2013.)

there until the mid-20th century. Besides the political rapprochement after the end of the apartheid regime, South Africa's economic growth and its position as an emerging regional power further increased bilateral relations. South Africa is not only the largest African economy in terms of size, but also the main gateway for the distribution of goods to the interior of the continent, and is therefore an important potential market for Brazilian exports and a privileged connection with the continent. Following South Africa's economic growth in the first part of the 2000s (5.3% in 2005), the demand for Brazilian products has grown and, consequently, Brazilian exports increased by 32% from 2004 to 2005, reaching a total of $1.37 billion. This trend continued and, in 2008, exports reached $1.7 billion, 28% higher than in 2005. An analysis of the composition of these exports reveals that while only 12.7% are basic products and 4.8% semi-manufactured products, 82.4% are manufactured goods,[30] thus confirming Brazil's shift towards being an exporter of capital and technology. According to APEX, some of the most important sectors of the market are machinery, equipment, medical supplies, plastics, electronics, IT and food (especially meat). In addition, Brazil benefits from the dynamic production of South Africa's minerals: the country is considered the largest producer of platinum, chrome and gold; Brazil's imports of minerals and other goods from there totalled $772 million in 2008. In recent years, bilateral trade has diminished due to declining economic growth in both countries. In 2015, Brazil's exports to South Africa accounted for $1.35 billion, while imports totalled $644.6 million.

Economic relations between the two countries are also important in the context of IBSA, which contributed to the strengthening of trilateral trade relations between India, Brazil and South Africa, given that these were valued at a total of $10 billion in 2007. In this regard, the G-3 provides a great opportunity to explore the synergy among members by increasing investment and trade. The defence sector and science and technology have emerged in the area of cooperation between Brazil and South Africa. The former undemocratic regimes in Brazil and South Africa had developed efficient arms and aircraft industries as well as those of nuclear technology, which were seriously damaged after the adoption of neoliberalism in Brazil and the South African pact; as a result, there is now cooperation with a view to the resumption of these projects.

[30] Data compiled by the author from the World Bank and UNCTAD databases.

The multilateral dimension of African diplomacy

During the Cardoso government, Brazil did not fully exploit the emerging power status it had gained among developing countries but was seen just as an 'emerging market'; however this was not the case for Lula's diplomacy in relation to the multilateral diplomatic activities. This is evident in Brazil's efforts to create and develop the IBSA, ASA and, covering North Africa, the Summit of South American–Arab Countries (ASPA); these initiatives produced concrete actions in many areas and are important tools to strengthen South–South cooperation.

It is also important to acknowledge the potential of some of Brazil's agreements with regard to the African continent in future multilateral actions through, for example, the CPLP and ZOPACAS. The Palop countries have become a priority for the Foreign Ministry, particularly within the CPLP. These subjects will be addressed in the next chapter.

A new interaction between Brazil and Africa: The neo-Pentecostal churches in Africa

An important aspect of the recent Brazilian presence in Africa is the spread of neo-Pentecostal churches throughout the continent, especially in the Portuguese-speaking countries and South Africa. However, the character of these relations is mostly social, with no incentives from the Brazilian Government. We cannot consider it as a state policy or a foreign policy for Africa.

The fast-growing presence of Pentecostal churches in Africa has been an interesting phenomenon since the 1970s. Pentecostal churches first appeared in the United States around 1907, within the Protestant Church, and later became known as Assemblies of God.[31] The main characteristic of Pentecostalism is the experience with the 'Holy Spirit', but it is important to highlight that there are many strands of Pentecostalism. With the new social context in the 20th century and the uses of media, a reinterpretation gave space for the appearance of the neo-Pentecostal churches in the 1970s. It is important to bear in mind the differences between these two churches in the African continent. Pentecostalism spread the belief of 'Holy Spirit' against the 'Devil'; the neo-Pentecostals work more like business enterprises. Today, it is estimated that one quarter of the two billion Christians around the World are

[31] These Assemblies are different from the Brazilian Assembly of God.

Pentecostal or 'charismatic' (other churches that assimilated Pentecostal beliefs and practices into their existing Christian ways).[32]

The American Assemblies of God first started in Africa in Liberia and Angola. Today, the denomination has Churches in all countries of Sub-Saharan Africa. In South Africa, for example, in the apartheid period, the Pentecostal Church split in two – Apostolic Faith Mission (AFM), for white people, and Zion Christian Church, for black people. The AFM is one of the biggest in Africa nowadays. In Central Africa, for example, in what is now the Democratic Republic of the Congo, European missionaries came first and they established the Evangelical Mission of Congo. Later, the American Assemblies of God arrived, and they became very popular in the countries of the region.[33]

In Africa, Pentecostal churches have been covering activities that were the state's responsibility, such as building hospitals, universities and addressing HIV/AIDS. They also promise a prosperous spiritual and material life. According to Ampofo, the 'Men of God' are powerful.[34] They not only have cults but also TV and radio programmes, books, YouTube videos and many others ways to spread their thoughts. They have changed the religious, political and economic life of the continent. Concerning the African continent, it is not only foreign churches that come to Africa, but African churches also go abroad. From Nigeria, the neo-Pentecostal Redeemed Christian Church of God expanded to Kenya, South Africa, Cameroon, Benin, and further.[35] It is already present in 165 countries around the world. The Redeemed Church is a complex organism and has become a global institution. The Church has more than four hundred congregations in UK and five hundred in USA and, in addition to religious life, it also influences economic and political life.

Turning to the Brazilian-born neo-Pentecostal churches, one of the most important examples of the export of religion is the Brazilian Church

[32] Richard Vijgen, 'Pentecostalism: Massive Global Growth Under the Radar', Pulitzer Center, 9 March 2015, accessed 27 February 2018, https://pulitzercenter.org/reporting/pentecostalism-massive-global-growth-under-radar#slideshow-8.

[33] Pulitzer Center, 'Atlas of Pentecostalism', database, accessed 2 March 2018, www.atlasofpentecostalism.net.

[34] See Akosua Adomako Ampofo, 'Africa's fast-growing Pentecostal mega churches are entrenching old injustices against women', *QuartzAfrica*, 16 June 2017, accessed 27 February 2018, https://qz.com/1007819/pentecostal-churches-in-ghana-and-nigeria-are-entrenching-sexist-gender-roles-for-women.

[35] See Asonzeh Ukah, 'African Christianities: Features, Promises and Problems', Working Paper 79, Department of Anthropology and African Studies, Mainz: Johannes-Gutenberg-Universität, 2007, accessed 1 March 2018,www.ifeas.uni-mainz.de/Dateien/AP79.pdf.

established by Bishop Edir Macedo, Universal Church of the Kingdom of God (IURD). In contrast to many others, Universal has been present in both the religious and political life of peoples. In Mozambique, like Brazil, Universal Church publishes a newspaper, has a TV channel and has representatives in the congress and in government. It appeared after the civil war, a good time to attract followers, and they made the people believe that they would resolve all the country's problems. IURD follows the 'evangelisation mission' of neo-Pentecostal churches, and develops the belief that the more you give to the church the more you will receive in return. This promise to receive generated the name of 'market of faith'. They negotiate the receipt of blessing, finding a fertile ground in post-conflict countries.

In South Africa, the Universal Church arrived more than twenty years ago, and it has more than 382 temples around the country. Lusophone Africa was also fertile ground for IURD. In Angola since 1991, the Brazilian Evangelical Church has opened more than 230 temples and has 500,000 followers. In 2012, Universal Church and other neo-Pentecostal churches were closed for a period of time in the country after an incident in which thirteen people died at a 250,000-person worship service held at the Luanda Sports Citadel stadium.[36] The Universal Church was the first evangelical church to settle in Mozambique after the civil war. After some twenty-five years in the African country and with more than two hundred temples, many Mozambican politicians are linked to it. The IURD is currently present in thirty-nine countries; its strongest presence is in South Africa, followed by Angola, Côte d'Ivoire and Mozambique. Lastly, other neo-Pentecostal Brazilian churches on the African continent include the World Church of God's Power and the Renewed World Church; the New Jerusalem Pentecostal Evangelical Church is also present but is less influential.

Conclusions: Prestige, cooperation or business?

What does Brazil want to obtain through its relations with the African continent: to garner diplomatic prestige so as to get a permanent seat on the UN Security Council, to support the economic and social development in solidarity with Africa, or simply to do profitable business? Are these three dimensions mutually exclusive? It can be said that Brazil and Africa entered the world system simultaneously and this created strong

[36] See Anaxsuell Fernando Silva and Karen Susan Silva Pititinga Rosa, 'A Igreja Universal do Reino de Deus em Angola: faces da nova cartografia religiosa global', *Ciências Sociais Unisinos*, 53:2 (2017), 234–41.

historical and cultural identities, particularly in the case of the five Palop countries. Nevertheless, common language, culture and traditions are not enough to develop modern relations. Culturalist discourses essentially seek to legitimise government actions internally and externally. Brazil's African descendants know little about Africa, and the attempt to merge the problems of Africans with those of Afro-descendants makes more sense in historical rather than contemporary terms. Socioeconomic structures, not skin colour, are the central issue. Hence, it is essential to put naivety aside and recognise that Brazil and African countries are all market economies and their relations have an economic aspect.

Despite phases of varying intensity, Brazil's relations with the African continent have deepened since the early 1960s. It was Brazilian industrialisation and the African independences that created the new reality. Unlike the 19th century, there have been no complete interruptions and the economic axis has been paramount (along with technical cooperation) as it constitutes the sustainable basis on which nations build their relations. The political dimension gained strength at various times, such as during the Independent Foreign Policy period, in the second phase of the military regime and Sarney's government, and again under Lula. Diplomacy was an exploratory aspect in the first phase, while in the second phase it was very assertive due to adverse changes in the international arena, and then became multidimensional and ambitious in a third phase when the world stage permitted advances. The political credits accumulated during Lula's phase have not been completely spent under Dilma. When President Michel Temer assumed power with a neoliberal agenda in May 2016, Africa formally lost priority again.

Whereas world trade trebled from 2000 to 2010, the increase in trade between the BRIC countries and Africa was tenfold (from \$16 billion to \$157 billion). Moreover, Brazil–Africa trade grew fivefold from US\$ 4 billion to US\$ 20 billion in the same period. Thus, the policy of rapprochement with the African continent has proved fruitful, as the BRICS have streamlined the African economy. However, in the 21st century, Brazil has added multilateral coalitions, social cooperation and technology transfer through its now-traditional South–South cooperation with Africa. Therefore, there are political, economic and social dimensions at the international level, in keeping with Brazil's domestic actions and the insertion strategy to change the world order towards development and a multipolar order.

Recent administrations have clearly taken a comprehensive approach to South–South cooperation and tried to propose a more adequate and inclusive structure for the international system. It is not a question of demanding a new type of treatment by the more powerful partners, but rather of not demanding this from the less developed ones. The economic projection of the BRICS towards the African continent allowed an increase and diversification of investments and trade, even in sectors that were stagnant. The advanced capitalist countries of North America, Europe and Asia have had to meet the challenge with new projects and more advantageous conditions. This is consistent with the political and social agenda set out in Brazil since the beginning of Lula's government. Nor is it the former Third World strategy of the 1970s – a coalition against the North. The post-Cold War stage and globalisation have produced a new international environment in which Brazil needs strong partners to build a multipolar world order.

Brazil–Africa relations have become even more important in the current context of global financial crisis which has led to developing countries being threatened by falling commodity prices and declining foreign investments. It is therefore a critical time for partnerships with African countries, where there is a potential for both a closer relation and a risk of rupture of relations.

Since the 1970s and 1980s, the capital investments of the North Atlantic powers have sought developing regions for reproduction at higher profit rates (running away from stagnation, high wages and union struggles). The irony is that the formation of an industrialised semi-periphery, accumulating capital surpluses, has generated a new flow that now seeks the periphery, where there is a faster return on investments. Thus, Brazil–Africa cooperation is part of a historical movement that foreshadows a new economic cycle and a civilisational change, which will bring an end to five centuries of the North Atlantic grip on the southern part of the planet – the Anglo-American maritime empire over the large masses of land and population.

3

The Multilateral and Regional Dimensions of Current Brazil–Africa Relations

Paulo Fagundes Visentini

Introduction

The relations between Brazil and the African continent have always been marked by interests in particular countries, especially the former Portuguese colonies and South Africa. In addition, oil producers like Nigeria and Algeria were included. There has also always been informal diplomatic cooperation in forums where there were common interests, such as the UN and international financial institutions. However, since the 1980s more systematic initiatives have emerged, such as the Zona de Paz e Cooperação do Atlântico Sul (South Atlantic Peace and Cooperation Zone – ZOPACAS) and the Comunidade de Países de Língua Portuguesa (Community of Portuguese-speaking Countries – CPLP). But it was at the turn of the century that multilateral diplomacy asserted itself between Brazil and Africa, in addition to a more coordinated role in the World Trade Organisation (WTO) and in both the commercial and financial G-20s. The first to be highlighted at the regional level (besides the CPLP) is the formation of the IBSA Dialogue Forum (G-3), articulating Brazil, South Africa and India and, in another context, the Mercosur–SACU Agreement (Mercado Común del Sur – Southern Common Market – and Southern African Customs Union). However, the most daring and creative multilateral initiatives were the Cúpula América do Sul-Países Árabes (Summit of South American–Arab Countries – ASPA), which included several North African nations) and the Africa–South America (ASA) Summit, at which a new form of South–South articulation was developed between both Brazil and other countries in South America with the Arab countries and the African continent. Although the changes that have taken place at the global and regional levels since 2010 have hampered their progress, they were bold initiatives.

Multilateral diplomacy on the world stage

The multilateral interaction between Brazil and Africa takes place in various spheres and compositions. The UN, the WTO and the financial G-20 (also known as G-20 major economies) are global forums analysed herein. Other important forums with narrower scope, such as the ASA, the ASPA and the CPLP will also be analysed. Even though multilateral initiatives have not reached their full potential, they are mechanisms that bring groups of nations together to discuss general and specific matters and to promote common goals in global forums. Moreover, forums allow the different integration processes in the South Atlantic region to intersect, favouring trade between Mercosur, SADC and ECOWAS in particular.

The United Nations Organisation (UN)

The history of relations between Brazil and African countries in the United Nations has been marked by changes in the organisation's composition since its inception. Initially, only four African countries belonged to the UN, namely South Africa, Egypt, Liberia and Ethiopia; these were all formally independent at the time of its foundation. Like Brazil, they were granted the status of founding members following their accession to the Atlantic Charter. However, in the wake of the decolonisation process that swept much of Africa after the independence of Ghana in 1957 and the deepening of the Third World movement in the 1960s, new African states joined the organisation. When the Portuguese colonies gained their independence in 1975, there were fifty African members of the UN, making up 32.5% of all member states. During this period, the Brazilian position on issues of importance to Africa fluctuated and in the early years of the UN Brazil tended to be slow to act and also lacked political autonomy.

According to Pinheiro, Brazil's actions in support of the United States and the United Kingdom in conjunction with the Foreign Ministry's sympathetic stance on self-determination resulted in ambiguous discourse and practices regarding Africa.[1] Until the 1970s, the country's policy in the United Nations forums was generally to favour the positions defended by France and Portugal as antagonising these nations would have spoiled Brazil's economic development project. The Brazilian diplomatic representation supported colonialism in the United Nations Fourth Committee and aligned with the US position in its treatment

[1] Letícia Pinheiro, 'Brasil, Portugal e descolonização africana (1946–60)', *Contexto Internacional*, 4:9 (1989), 91–111.

of South Africa during the apartheid period, seeking not to isolate it completely.

Nevertheless, there were times when Brazil's actions diverged from the positions held by Western nations, especially under the Vargas Government (1951–54). During this period, it was generally believed that economic competition with the colonial areas was harmful to Brazil as it did not receive the external assistance offered to the African and Asian colonies. Thus, the support given for the participation of delegates from non-autonomous territories in the Information Committee was the first step towards closer relations with Africa. During Juscelino Kubitschek's administration (1956–61), the support to the Iberian dictatorships became a sort of 'foreign body' within the nationalist foreign policy project adopted by the Brazilian government with the launching of the Pan-American Operation in 1958, which had a clear anti-colonialist and pro-democracy content. However, the programme almost restricted Brazil's foreign policy to the Americas and, as a result, the independence of African countries that began during the time of President Kubitschek was handled only as a matter of protocol.

In 1960, the Year of Africa, the United Nations General Assembly defined what constituted 'non-self-governing territories' and declared the unconditional right of nations to independence through Resolution 1514 of its fifteenth session. The representations of Brazil, South Africa, Belgium, Spain, France and Portugal voted against Resolution 1542, which called on Portugal to adhere to Article 73 of the UN Charter and to provide information on their colonial territories; the US and the United Kingdom abstained. Despite the alignment of the Brazilian delegation with the US, some segments of society were already aware at the time that rapprochement with Africa was needed; Oswaldo Aranha, Álvaro Lins and José Honório Rodrigues[2] advocated this, among others. In that year, seventeen African nations became independent and joined the UN, and the Organisation established the guarantee of the right to unrestricted sovereignty as one of its aims. Brazil silently watched their emancipation. The foundations for a more effective rapprochement between Brazil and Africa were only laid with Quadros' and Goulart's Independent Foreign Policy, which encouraged decolonisation and helped the reconstruction process of the liberated nations.

[2] Representatives of Brazilian diplomacy. They defended pragmatic, progressive and realistic relations with Africa. See José Flávio S. Saraiva, *O Lugar da África: a dimensão atlântica da política externa Brasileira de 1946 a nossos dias* (Brasília: Ed. UnB, 1996), 43.

In 1961, when the liberation struggle began in Angola, the issue of the freedom of colonised peoples became a priority on the General Assembly and Security Council meeting agendas. For its part, Portugal took an intransigent position on its overseas territories and insisted that the United Nations had no jurisdiction to intervene; from 1962, it relied on the favourable vote or abstention of the United States in deliberations within the UN.[3] To the detriment of the Portuguese position, however, Brazil launched an African policy and took an effective stand on defending the self-determination of colonial peoples. The change in Brazil's attitude toward Africa reflected the shift in the dynamics of world trade and, in particular, an increase was seen in commercial activity between Brazil and the African continent. With the creation of UNCTAD in 1964, there was a widespread understanding among developing nations of the need to redefine some aspects of the international economy and to establish more favourable conditions for the least developed countries. Brazil, for instance, sought to leverage existing niche markets in order to allocate its growing industrial production, to project itself internationally and to serve as a link between the West and Africa. Moreover, Brazil was concerned about the privileged access granted to African countries, colonies or former colonies, within the European markets.

After a considerable setback in terms of closer ties between Brazil and the Third World countries during the first two Brazilian military governments, the collapse of the Salazar regime in the 1970s marked a turning point in relations between Brazil and Africa.[4] In 1973, Brazil began voting in favour of decolonisation. Thereafter, the country's actions at the UN aimed to support the independence movements and national reconstruction; indeed, Brazil was the first country to recognise the government of the Marxist-inspired MPLA in 1975, during Ernesto Geisel's administration. Figueiredo's administration deepened relations with Africa, and even the 'New Republic' of José Sarney (1985–90) maintained significant ties in the 1980s.

After the Cold War, there was a paradigmatic shift in the United Nations' focus, changing from a bipolar logic to a new vision of what constituted a threat to international peace and security. Thus, the new world order resulted in the United Nations remodelling its concept of

[3] See José Honório Rodrigues, *Brasil e África: outro horizonte*, 2nd ed. (Rio de Janeiro: Editora Civilização Brasileira, 1964).

[4] See Pio Penna Filho. *O Brasil e a África do Sul.* O arco atlântico da política externa brasileira (1918–2000) (Brasília: FUNAG/CESUL, 2008) and Henrique Altemani & Antônio Carlos Lessa. *Relações internacionais do Brasil: temas e agendas* (São Paulo: Saraiva, 2006), 159–93.

security to one in which the preservation of human security became vital; in itself, this notion might conflict with the historically established notion of state sovereignty. This change took place at the same time as the escalation of civil wars, internal conflicts and economic misfortunes that directly or indirectly threatened the security of the African people. The practical result of this new situation was the multiplication of peacekeeping operations, as well as the broadening of the contents of the UN Charter to counter intrastate conflicts, following the launch of the 'Agenda for Peace' of the then UN Secretary-General Boutros Boutros-Ghali (1997–2002). There have been sixty-seven missions since the creation of the UN, more than a third of which were in Africa. Except for the United Nations Operation in the Congo (UNOC, 1960–64) in response to the Congo crisis, all of the missions started in 1988 or later. Brazil's two last military administrations and the first civilian government were therefore marked by convergence between Brazil and Africa at the UN.

Brazil's stance was substantially modified in that period, for example refusing (under Collor de Mello) to comply with the UN request to provide troops to assist in the Namibian independence process in 1990. Four years later, however, during the Itamar Franco administration (1992–95), it actively participated in the supervision of elections in Mozambique. Overall, since 1948, Brazil has participated in thirty peacekeeping operations. Three of the five operations to which it sent troops targeted Africa: Suez (UNEF I), Angola (UNAVEM III) and Mozambique (UNOMOZ). In 1995, during the Fernando Henrique Cardoso (FHC) administration (1995–2002), the Peacekeeping Force sent to Angola during its civil war comprised 1,200 people.

Also in the FHC period, the cooperation agenda with Africa at the UN included the break of international pharmaceutical patents for HIV drugs. According to Lima,[5] fighting HIV/AIDS was one of the paradigms around which cooperation in the IBSA Dialogue Forum could be structured as regards the terms of the complementarity of the development, production and demand of drugs for the treatment of the disease. The epidemic was spreading dramatically in Sub-Saharan Africa as a whole, and South Africa in particular; by 2016, out of the 22.5 million people living with HIV/AIDS in Sub-Saharan Africa, 5.6 million were in South Africa.[6]

[5] See Maria Regina Soares de Lima, 'A política externa brasileira e os desafios da Cooperação Sul-Sul', *Revista Brasileira de Política Internacional*, 48:1 (2005), 24–59.

[6] Reuters, 'Factbox: Africa bears heavy AIDS burden, hope ahead', 4 March 2011, accessed 26 December 2018, www.reuters.com/article/us-aids-africa/factbox-africa-bears-heavy-aids-burden-hope-ahead-idUSTRE7232VJ20110304.

The Lula administration was a landmark for closer relations between Brazil and the African continent; levels of exchange reached unprecedented levels and the establishment of diplomatic ties intensified substantially. The areas in which cooperation was developed between Brazil and Africa under UN auspices include the fight against poverty and epidemics (mainly HIV/AIDS), food security and technology transfer among developing countries. The issue of eradicating hunger in particular garnered great efforts; the emergence of the trilateral IBSA Fund in 2004 – a South African initiative of South–South cooperation – can be attributed to an awareness of the need to encourage multilateral cooperation in the fight against hunger. India, Brazil and South Africa each contribute $1 million annually to the Fund, which became operational in 2006.

The end of East–West rivalry and Brazil's return to democracy after the military regime in 1985 broke Brazil's twenty-year absence from participating as a non-permanent member of the UN Security Council, and both factors revitalised the issue of reform of the UN's main body.[7] The current arrangement of the UN system is fiercely contested due to the legitimacy crisis which it has experienced since the US declaration of war on Iraq in violation of the UN Security Council's decision and in the face of claims from developed and developing countries. With the entry of Eritrea in 1993, African countries make up 27% of all UN members but, as former President Lula stated, none of the continent's current fifty-four countries is covered by the current formation of the Security Council.

In 2011, the inauguration of Lula's successor, Dilma Rousseff, coincided with the presence of all three IBSA countries as non-permanent members of the UN Security Council. Brazil has drawn the attention of the international community due to its active presence in the United Nations. In his inauguration speech, Foreign Minister Antônio Patriota indicated the new government would continue with the same policies when he reiterated the commitment to 'maintaining an active agenda with our partners in Africa – intensifying our cooperation and our dialogue with our brother continent'. It remains to be seen whether President Rousseff's departure in 2016 will result in significant changes in Brazil's foreign policy towards Africa.

World Trade Organisation (WTO), commercial G-20 and financial G-20

As globalisation deepens, economic and trade relations have become one of the influential lines in foreign policy; this drives the need to build an

[7] See Lima, 'A política externa brasileira', 24–59.

international economic agenda that answers the demands of developing economies. The new political geography that redefines international relations assigns a new role to the Southern countries and it constitutes one of the pillars for relations in the multilateral and financial arenas. Brazil's participation in the WTO is closely linked with the developmental bias of the Ministry of Foreign Affairs, which sets itself a mediating role between developed and developing nations in the organisation spectrum.

Brazil joined the WTO when it became operational in 1995. Cabo Verde's accession in 2008 brought the number of African nations in the organisation to forty-one together with the other 115 member states.[8] Among the various coalitions formed within the organisation, the commercial G-20 (also known as G-20 developing countries) must be highlighted. One of the main goals Brazil seeks to achieve through its participation in the WTO is the liberalisation of agricultural trade, a central topic of the agenda proposed in its Doha Development Round, which commenced in November 2001. The commercial G-20 came together in pursuit of this and other goals to counterbalance the protectionist decisions of the United States and the European Union – bastions of practices such as agricultural subsidies – against which the Cairns Group of nineteen agricultural exporting countries was not making definitive advances. The countries composing the commercial G-20 take individual positions on different issues but they converge in the view that the developed nations have plagued the competitiveness of others by making a selective liberalisation of sectors in their economies. The IBSA countries South Africa, Brazil and India are at the core of the G-20. The other African countries in the group are Egypt, Nigeria, Tanzania and Zimbabwe.

The common platform has substantially helped to minimise the commercial differences between countries and contribute to the achievement of related goals. Therefore, Brazil acquired the status of 'big winner' in the Cancun negotiation round (2003) when it spearheaded the formation of the G-21 or G+. Food security and the adjustment of imbalances in trade between central and peripheral countries are paramount issues for Africa. African countries, in turn, managed to benefit as they drew closer to Brazil and increased their mobilisation capacity in the WTO. In the Cairo Declaration (2005), African countries – which together form a separate bloc within the WTO – stated they had common interests with

[8] In Africa, Algeria, Comoros, Eritrea, Equatorial Guinea, Libya, Seychelles, South Sudan and Sudan are not full members of the WTO.

the G-20. However, the poorest countries of the African bloc resist some of the changes proposed by this coalition.

Cervo claimed that the Cancun Round represented the developing countries' first victory over the will of the Western countries.[9] The resolution of the Doha Round could benefit both large exporters of commodities, such as South Africa, and countries plagued by hunger. The cotton and sugar trade are the main issues in which African countries are more directly involved. The discussion on how to move forward is central in various international forums and, in terms of agriculture, the commercial G20 is crucial to maintaining dynamic negotiations.

Although formed in 1999, the financial G-20 (also known as G-20 major economies) gained notoriety only in 2008 with the onset of the international financial crisis. According to the rationale of the Brazilian government, the rise of the G-20 to the main international economic forum resulted not only from the crisis but also from the major developing countries' resilience to its worst effects. Such a situation would have enabled the heterogeneous group of developed and developing countries to seek joint solutions to combat the crisis. Currently, South Africa alone represents the African continent in the financial G-20.

In spite of the friction between Brazil and South Africa in 2012 due to the WTO dispute over anti-dumping measures in relation to Brazilian chicken exports, this did not generate a retreat in Brazil–Africa relations, nor did it represent a misalignment of the agendas within the G-20, for example. In 2013, a Brazilian became Director-General of the WTO. Roberto Azevêdo was elected with strong support from African countries, since his election represented a further step towards building a new global order. According to Antônio Patriota, this was an opportunity for emerging markets to show their leadership. In 2017, Azevêdo was re-elected to the post. Also in 2017, during the Hamburg Summit, consensus was reached on the establishment of a G-20 Partnership with Africa, in order to forge an inclusive environment of dialogue.

India–Brazil–South Africa Dialogue Forum (IBSA)

The IBSA, or G-3, was launched in 2003 and is a South African initiative of South–South cooperation. The Forum was established with the aim of improving coordination and cooperation among the three emerging countries at the trilateral and global levels, so that it could influence major negotiations such as the Doha Round in the WTO, UN reforms

[9] See Amado Cervo, 'Um balanço da reunião da OMC em Cancún', *Meridiano 47 Journal of Global Studies* 4:38–39 (2003), 1–32.

and the building of a New Economic Order and a multipolar world system.

At the Second IBSA Summit in South Africa in 2007, Brazilian diplomacy intensified trilateral cooperation and political articulation. The reform of the UN Security Council and the Doha Round were among the topics on the agenda. The alignment of the positions in the WTO rounds of negotiations is a priority for all three countries as they are part of the G-20 and together fight to open the markets of developed countries to the production of developing nations, as seen previously. Brazil, India and South Africa also set ambitious targets for the increase in trilateral trade. In June 2006, during the fourth meeting of the Trilateral Joint Commission in New Delhi, the Brazilian Foreign Minister, Celso Amorim, proposed a target of $15 billion by 2010. The three countries had already intended to reach $10 billion in trade by 2007. At the time, the Brazilian Minister also advocated increased efforts towards creating a free trade area between Mercosur, India and SACU, a group that includes South Africa, Botswana, Lesotho, Namibia and Swaziland. Accordingly, IBSA also appears as a relevant mechanism of rapprochement with South Africa, a major economic partner on the continent – as well as with other African nations.

Several working groups also take actions in health, science and technology, security, trade, transport and investment, and a diplomatic focus has been on the political potential of the group. During the Third IBSA Summit in New Delhi in October 2008, the leaders of the three countries reaffirmed their commitment to coordinate action in international politics in areas such as global governance, reform of the international financial system, energy, South–South cooperation, peace, security, regional integration and the fight against poverty.

The Brasília Declaration from the Fourth Summit of the IBSA Dialogue Forum in 2010 reiterated and deepened topics from the previous summit, and also added others such as 'the social dimensions of globalisation', 'Internet governance', 'the IBSA Fund', 'IBSA satellites' and regional issues such as Haiti (MINUSTAH support and donation of $2 million for the reconstruction of the country).[10] The situation in Chile, Iran and Afghanistan was also discussed, as well as regional integration issues like the New Partnership for Africa's Development (NEPAD) and the African Union.[11] At the 66th Session of the UN General Assembly

[10] India, Brazil and South Africa Dialogue Forum (IBSA), *Brasília Declaration*, Brasília, 2010.

[11] On the same day (15 June 2010), the Second BRIC Summit (Brazil, Russia, India and China), another multilateral dialogue forum, took place.

in September 2011, IBSA held a ministerial meeting to discuss issues concerning the UN configuration and its operations in various regions of the world.

The Fifth IBSA Summit (October 2011), which took place in Pretoria, South Africa, deliberated on various issues in the Declaration of Tshwane: reform of global governance, the economic and financial global crisis, the Millennium Development Goals, international trade, sustainable development, climate change, global food security, South–South cooperation, human rights, disarmament and non-proliferation, terrorism, transnational organised crime, intellectual property rights, Internet governance, energy, health, gender and regional issues. It is worth highlighting that the demand for a reform of the UN Security Council intended to expand both the permanent and the non-permanent members. These countries also urged the implementation of reforms on the International Monetary Fund, including those related to its electoral processes and the weight of the votes of developing countries.[12] Since 2008, the three countries have also held biennial joint naval exercises, called IBSAMAR, to strengthen maritime security cooperation. In 2014, the exercises were carried out on the South African coast. In 2016 the exercises conducted on the Indian coast were the most complex to date involving ships, airplanes and Special Forces of the three countries.[13]

The establishment of IBSA has played an important role in drawing the attention of the 'economic North' nations to the South's intention to make its voice heard on major global issues. To some extent, it influenced the G-8 to invite them to join its internal debates. The Forum is, therefore, performing the role of projecting its members onto the international stage, alerting the international community that these countries are willing and able to break the shell of their regional contexts and collaborate decisively for the progress of a multipolar order. However, in recent years the cooperation of the three countries within IBSA has, to some extent, been replaced by the BRICS group (Brazil, Russia, India, China and South Africa), which has gained more political weight. Consequently, there have been six annual BRICS summits between 2013 and 2018, while IBSA's tenth anniversary summit scheduled for May 2013 in New Delhi was cancelled and no other summit has been held since.

[12] India, Brazil and South Africa Dialogue Forum (IBSA), *Tshwane Declaration*, Pretoria, 2011.

[13] *The Economic Times*, 'IBSAMAR 2016: Navies of Brazil, India and South Africa to hold exercise off Goa coast', 23 February 2016, accessed 18 April 2018, https://goo.gl/E6cnkk.

Irrespective of the absence of summits since 2011, in October 2017 an official agreement was signed between India, Brazil and South Africa on the IBSA Fund for Poverty and Hunger Alleviation that became operational in 2006.[14] Until September 2017, the Fund had received $35 million in contributions and had implemented twenty-seven projects in twenty-one partner countries, in support of all seventeen Sustainable Development Goals.[15] This initiative has been a pioneer in terms of South–South cooperation. Meanwhile, the Sixth IBSA Summit was scheduled to take place in India in the first half of 2018 with the aim of reactivating the trilateral forum; however it was later rescheduled to 2019.

Community of Portuguese-Speaking Countries (CPLP)

Few countries have received the level of priority that Brazil's Foreign Ministry (also known as Itamaraty) has given to the CPLP, which brings together a population of nearly 250 million people in four of the five continents. Portugal, East Timor, Guinea-Bissau, Cabo Verde, São Tomé and Príncipe, Mozambique, Angola and Equatorial Guinea jointly seek to advance the areas of security, business, health and education through cooperation with Brazil. The Community originates from a Brazilian initiative – the foundation of the International Institute of the Portuguese Language (IILP) in 1989 – and, within the Community, the Palop (Officially Portuguese-speaking African) countries have been a priority for Itamaraty. Under Lula, this mechanism was commonly used to deepen relations with Africa, driven by its cultural and historical links with the five former Portuguese colonies; for example, in 2003 Brazil promoted consultations in order to identify possible measures to support Guinea-Bissau, which was going through a serious political and institutional crisis. In the same year, the Brazilian President made an official visit to São Tomé and Príncipe, Mozambique and Angola. At the time, investment possibilities in various areas of industry and commerce were discussed.

[14] MRE, 'Acordo entre o governo da República da Índia, o governo da República Federativa do Brasil e o governo da República da África do Sul sobre o Fundo IBAS para o alívio da pobreza e da fome', Nota 346, 17 October 2017, accessed 18 April 2018,,www.itamaraty.gov.br/pt-BR/notas-a-imprensa/17618-acordo-entre-o-governo-da-republica-da-india-o-governo-da-republica-federativa-do-brasil-e-o-governo-da-republica-da-africa-do-sul-sobre-o-fundo-ibas-para-o-alivio-da-pobreza-e-da-fome.

[15] UNOSSC, 'Launch of the 2017 IBSA Fund Overview of Project Portfolio Report and Exhibition', 11 September 2017, accessed 18 April 2018, www.unsouth-south.org/2017/09/11/launch-of-the-2017-ibsa-fund-overview-of-project-portfolio-report-and-exhibition.

Over the years, Brazil has developed strong bilateral cooperation programmes with the CPLP countries. Important actions include an agreement on the opening of technical education centres in East Timor and Angola and the provision of electronic voting machines for Guinea-Bissau's elections, which were delayed due to the 2012 military coup in the country. An agreement was also made with Mozambique to set up a factory of antiretroviral drugs. In 2010, the Brazilian government officially confirmed the creation of a Portuguese-speaking Countries University (UNILAB) in Brazil in order to unify the language and bring Brazilian, Palop and Timorese societies closer, as previously mentioned.

While presiding over the CPLP (2002–04), Brazil played a central role in the diplomatic initiatives that contributed to the return of democracy in São Tomé and Príncipe after the July 2003 coup. Cooperation with São Tomé's National Petroleum Agency was established to help the country develop its regulatory system and the bidding for the exploitation of its oil. Relations with Angola, a traditional partner in several areas, were expanded. With Mozambique, trade ties became closer and cooperation was established in the agricultural sector, among others. With all countries of the Community, cooperation programmes were implemented in the areas of agricultural development, the fight against AIDS and the fight against poverty. While visiting the CPLP headquarters in Lisbon, in 2008, President Lula stressed the Community's special responsibility to reverse the poverty in which some people live and the need to mobilise the international community in this struggle. During the Eleventh CPLP Summit in Brasília, in the second half of 2016, the two-year presidency was passed again to the Brazilian President, Michel Temer, who assumed the position under the motto 'CPLP and Agenda 2030 for sustainable development'.

Besides cultural and economic convergence, the members of the organisation are increasingly moving towards defence cooperation. In 2016 the CPLP revised its cooperation protocol in defence in order to ensure its compromise with peace and security. In 2017, the Seventeenth FELINO Exercises took place in September, in the Military Academy of Agulhas Negras (AMAN) in Resende, in Rio de Janeiro. It included military personnel from the nine CPLP member states. The FELINO series was created to regularise the execution of joint and combined military exercises, enabling the interoperability of the armed forces of the CPLP member states, as well as their training for use in humanitarian assistance and peace operations both within the CPLP and regional organisations; in either case, they are always under the authority of the United Nations.

Multilateral cooperation at the regional level

South Atlantic Peace and Cooperation Zone (ZOPACAS) and Southern Common Market and Southern African Customs Union (Mercosur–SACU)

The ZOPACAS had been established in 1986 during the Sarney administration, and after a considerable period of stagnation it resumed its activities in 2007 at the Ministerial Summit in Luanda (Angola).[16] The event resulted in the Action Plan of Luanda, which points to a number of areas in which cooperation can be intensified. The following step was the creation of working groups on economic cooperation, peace operations, environmental issues and the fight against transnational illicit activities. Between 2003 and 2010, cooperation agreements were signed in the field of defence with seven African countries: South Africa, Angola, Mozambique, Namibia, Equatorial Guinea, Nigeria and Senegal. Activities were carried out in the areas of military training, continental shelf mapping, science and technology, and trade. The creation of the Security Forces Training Centre in Guinea-Bissau ($3 million investment of the Brazilian government) and the military technical support to Angola and Namibia are examples of this military cooperation. In 2013, the Seventh Ministerial Meeting of ZOPACAS took place in Montevideo, Uruguay. It was attended by the defence ministers of the member states. The Brazilian Defence Minister Celso Amorim called attention to the need to reinvigorate ZOPACAS. The meeting endorsed the Montevideo Action Plan that gave special attention to cooperation in maritime safety. The restoration of ZOPACAS is important in itself, given the wide availability of mineral and natural resources in the South Atlantic that are crucial to the development of Brazil and African countries. With the discovery of new pre-salt oil fields off the Brazilian coast and the Gulf of Guinea, as well as the re-formation of the Fourth US Fleet and the growing strategic importance of the South Atlantic Ocean, ZOPACAS may prove to be a fundamental institutional forum for peace, sovereignty and development in this large geopolitical space.

Following the restructuring of SACU, the negotiations on the Framework Agreement were expanded to include other African countries.[17] In December 2008, the Preferential Trade Agreement (PTA) between Mercosur and SACU was signed, the aim of which was to eventually form a free trade area between the two blocs. The Mercosur–SACU PTA only came into force in October 2016, due to Mercosur demands for

[16] ZOPACAS will be further discussed in Chapter 5.

[17] South Africa, Botswana, Lesotho, Namibia and Swaziland are the members of SACU.

administrative and legal issues related to the agreement, and also due to intra-bloc issues. As previously mentioned, during the fourth meeting of the IBSA Trilateral Joint Commission in New Delhi in June 2006, the Brazilian Foreign Minister, Celso Amorim, supported increasing the efforts towards the creation of a free trade area comprising Mercosur, India and SACU. At the Ministerial Trilateral India–Mercosur–SACU Meeting, which took place in Geneva in November 2009, the participating ministers indicated the need for studies to be conducted with the aim of making a 'trilateral trade arrangement' at the same time as welcoming the preferential trade agreements of Mercosur–SACU and Mercosur–India.

Summit of South American–Arab Countries (ASPA)

In May 2005, the ASPA was formed as a bi-regional cooperation mechanism and a policy coordination forum; it resulted from a proposal made by President Lula in early 2003. This is an innovative initiative because it is a dialogue between the two regions, and not between a power and the region. The Summit was the cause of great discomfort in the US due to the establishment of direct links between the two regions and it represented a qualitative step forward in South–South cooperation. It comprises thirty-four countries – twenty-two Arab and twelve South American nations. South America is represented by Argentina, Bolivia, Brazil, Chile, Colombia, Ecuador, Guyana, Paraguay, Peru, Suriname, Uruguay and Venezuela. Arab countries comprise Algeria, Bahrain, Comoros, Djibouti, Egypt, Iraq, Jordan, Kuwait, Lebanon, Libya, Mauritania, Morocco, Oman, Palestine, Qatar, Saudi Arabia, Somalia, Sudan, Syria, Tunisia, United Arab Emirates and Yemen. The ASPA countries gather a population of 648 million people (260 million in the Arab region and 387 million in South America), and a nominal GDP of $4.87 trillion ($2 trillion in the Arab region and $2.87 trillion in South America).

The Brasília Declaration of May 2005 listed the goals of the signatory countries to articulate the regions and regional forums through eleven main approaches:

(1) Peace and security;
(2) Cultural cooperation;
(3) Economic cooperation;
(4) International trade;
(5) International financial system;
(6) Sustainable development;
(7) South–South cooperation;
(8) Science and technology;

(9) Information society;
(10) Action against hunger and poverty; and
(11) Development and social issues.

Reaffirming the principle of sovereignty and territorial integrity of states, the Declaration established ASPA's close bond with the UN Charter, especially with regard to the use of force in international relations.[18] Four Sectorial Committees were formed with the responsibility of executing the action plans initiated during the ministerial meetings.[19] Since 2005, eleven ministerial meetings have been held: two on the economy, two on culture, one on the environment, two on social affairs, one on water resources and combating desertification, and three meetings of Foreign Affairs Ministers. Brazil is the regional coordinator of ASPA in South America (until the consolidation of the General Secretariat of UNASUR – Unión de Naciones Suramericanas / Union of South American Nations), and the General Secretariat of the League of Arab States (LAS) is the coordinator of the Arab region. Business forums occur both during the summits and in trade missions organised by the member states, in which the Arab–Brazilian Chamber of Commerce is an active participant.

In the Second ASPA Summit of Heads of State and Government in March/April 2009 in Doha in Qatar, the international economic crisis was the main focus. Thus, there was even greater need for dialogue towards a new international financial system that was fairer, more equitable and without speculation, and in which the bloc would play an important role in the future global order. It can be said that ASPA made some progress on specific matters in a short time, and sought to address the great difficulties raised by the differences between countries, within the blocs and even in their own regions. A better apparatus is needed in UNASUR and the LAS, as well as the support of all members in the integration processes. Moreover, the priority given to economic and trade issues by the South American countries, as opposed to the Arab countries, which have higher expectations on political issues, is also an issue that needs to be addressed. It is worth noting that trade is one of the strongest gains; in fact, trade to Brazil reached $25.1 billion in 2011, most of the $27.4 billion traded between the two regions. The Federation of Arab–South American Chambers of Commerce was formed in

[18] Summit of South American–Arab Countries (ASPA), Brasília Declaration, Brasília, 2005.

[19] Economic cooperation; cultural and educational cooperation; scientific and technological cooperation; social and environmental cooperation.

Buenos Aires in April 2013 to stimulate trade between the regions and to foster closer relations.

The Third ASPA Summit of Heads of State and Government was scheduled for February 2011 but, due to the Arab Spring, it only took place in October 2012, in Lima, Peru. This was the first meeting between South American and Arab countries after the demonstrations of the Arab Spring and was attended by eleven leaders. The main topic was how to raise the cooperation potential (especially economic and commercial) affected by the political upheaval, and resume the level reached before the crisis. President Dilma Rousseff attended the Summit and stressed that South American and Arab economies could work together in the areas of energy, mining and tourism in order to expand trade and investment. Concerning politics, the President stated that Brazil supported the UN and LAS efforts to negotiate a solution to conflicts and it was willing to cooperate with the restructuring of nations that had gone through political and social changes. However, she stressed that only the Arab countries could find the solutions to their problems. In the Lima Declaration, the countries reaffirmed their commitment to further bi-regional relations and to consolidate ASPA through policy coordination. The cooperation agenda presented proposals on economic and financial

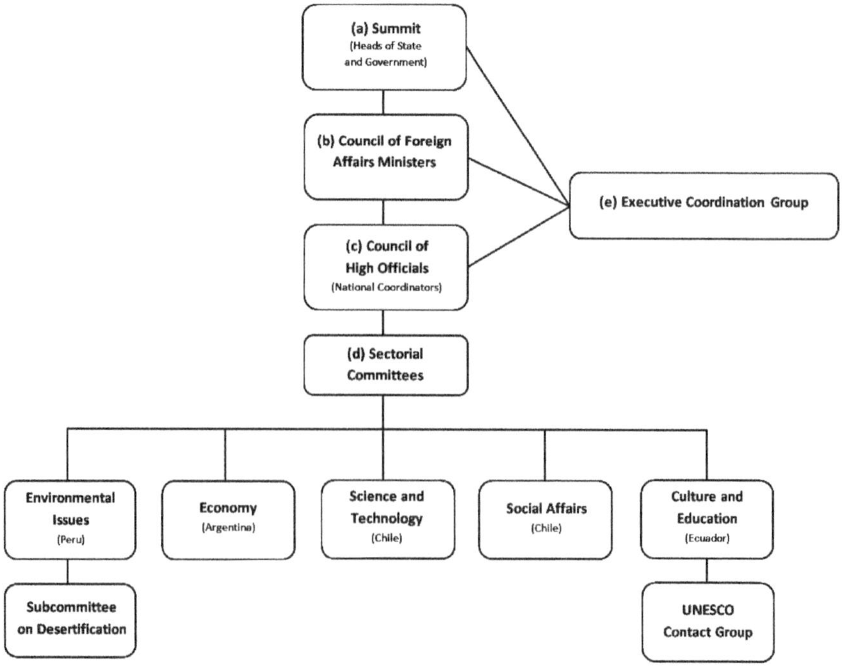

Figure 2 ASPA's coordination structure

matters; culture and education; the environment; social and development issues; and on science, technology and information. The Fourth ASPA Summit was held in November 2015 in Riyadh in Saudi Arabia. The summit approved the Riyadh Declaration to further promote political, economic, commercial, technological and environmental cooperation between Arab and South American countries. The Fifth Summit of Heads of State and Government of ASPA was scheduled to take place in Venezuela in 2018; by December 2018, this had not happened.

ASPA's coordination structure is executed according to the organisation chart in Figure 2, agreed at the Third Meeting of Foreign Affairs Ministers in Cairo in March 2009.

Africa–South America Summit (ASA)

As a result of closer relations between the Brazilian and Nigerian governments in 2005, ASA seeks regional cooperation and a coordinated international insertion of South America and Africa in global politics. The First Summit took place in November 2006 and led to the Abuja Declaration, in which the signatory countries recognised the need to deepen cooperation and press the developed countries to change the unequal economic order. In addition, an executive body was formed, the Africa–South America Cooperation Forum (ASACOF), to be coordinated by Brazil in South America, and Nigeria in Africa. According to the Declaration, ASA must act in the areas of multilateral cooperation; peace and security; democracy and human rights; trade and investment; development and infrastructure; energy and minerals; among others. ASA is a unique and strategic initiative because it combines two important regions of the Global South.

The Second ASA Summit was held in Venezuela (Isla Margarita) in September 2009. The resulting Nueva Esparta Declaration was built on the 2006 Declaration, reaffirming commitments and tracing the lines of action and inter-regional cooperation for the coming years. The topics discussed included the reform of the Security Council; the fight against drug trafficking; the strengthening dialogue and cooperation for the promotion of peace by the Peace and Security Council of the African Union, the Defense Council of UNASUR and the South Atlantic Peace and Cooperation Zone; and the formation of multilateral forums of cultural diversity.[20] It is also worth highlighting the fight against hunger and poverty, a goal that was reinforced by Dilma Rousseff's administration – through the Brazil Without Poverty Plan – and the election of the

[20] Africa–South America Summit (ASA), Nueva Esparta Declaration, Venezuela, 2009.

first Latin American to the position of Director-General of the United Nations Food and Agriculture Organisation (FAO) in 2011, the Brazilian José Graziano da Silva (re-elected in June 2015).

The Third ASA Summit was to be held in Libya but was postponed given the growing political instability in the country and the subsequent overthrowing of the Muammar Gaddafi government. The Fourth Meeting of the Council of Foreign Ministers of ASACOF in November 2011 recommended holding the Third Summit in Equatorial Guinea. The meeting was postponed a second time, at the request of the South American bloc. As intercontinental cooperation projects require more time to take shape, the Council of ASACOF proposed holding the summits every three years instead of two, interspersed with meetings at different levels to be determined by the parties. During the Rio+20 Conference on Sustainable Development in June 2012, the Nigerian President Goodluck Jonathan invited the Brazilian President to visit his country and called for the revitalisation of ASACOF as a platform for cooperation between the two continents.

The ASA Summit offers an historic opportunity for the two regions to shape a new paradigm of South–South cooperation, as was well illustrated at the Third Summit by the motto 'Strategies and mechanisms for strengthening South–South cooperation'; the Summit finally took place in Malabo, Equatorial Guinea, in February 2013. Thirty-six Heads of State and Government attended the 2013 meeting, and eleven South American and forty-eight African countries participated in working groups and meetings. President Dilma Rousseff attended the event because Brazil is the South American Regional Coordinator and seeks to increase the leverage of developing countries, through an alliance in multilateral forums in defence of common interests on the world political and economic stage. The Malabo Declaration was formulated during the meeting and addressed several important issues for cooperation between the two continents such as peace and security; political affairs, democracy, governance and human rights; cooperation in multilateral forums; investment, trade, industry and tourism; science and technology; and institutional management. Although the Fourth ASA Summit, which had originally been planned to be held in Quito, Ecuador, in 2016, was later postponed until May 2017, the meeting has not taken place yet.

Conclusions

The main objective of this chapter was to present Brazil and Africa relations beyond the supposed historical ties and the solidarity between

Brazilians and Africans. It can be affirmed that the intensification of political, economic, cultural and security relations that has taken place since the 2000s was intended to promote and strengthen South–South cooperation. In this sense, the different multilateral forums were an area of paramount importance. The development of so many initiatives with diverse themes and scopes was made possible by the favourable international environment – an emerging multipolar world order – and governments that perceived the time was right to actively defend their interests in the international arena; this was done either through traditional organisations, drawing the attention of Northern countries to the demands of the South, or through the creation of new initiatives that emerged as both an alternative and a space to create agendas and policies designed to meet the demands of peripheral countries.

4

Brazil's Development and Financial Cooperation with African Countries

Gerhard Seibert

Introduction

Since President Lula came to power in 2003, Brazil has increasingly used development cooperation as a foreign policy tool to strengthen political and economic relations with African countries as part of the country's global power aspirations, notably that of deepening ties with the entire Global South. This diversification of external partners sought to increase autonomy and reduce dependency on the United States and other industrialised countries. While the objectives of the Lula government were similar to those of presidents Jânio Quadros and João Goulart (1961–64) and Ernesto Geisel (1974–79), the domestic and international political and economic contexts were significantly different. On one hand, rhetorically Lula maintained the former discourse of cultural affinities, including assertions of Brazil's African-ness and of Brazil as the second-largest black nation after Nigeria; on the other hand, he replaced the supposed existence of a racial democracy by stressing that Brazil had a moral and historic debt with Africa due to the contribution of more than four million African slaves to the construction of Brazilian society and culture.

Development cooperation projects were expected to further Brazil's national prestige and visibility in the target countries and strengthen bilateral relations in the political and economic areas. According to White, development cooperation was one of three broad categories of Brazil's Africa strategy under Lula, together with political diplomacy and trade and investment.[1] Brazil used development cooperation with the Global South in general and Africa in particular as a tool to increase the country's soft power in international relations. Joseph Nye perceived the concept of soft power as the capacity of strong states to exercise

[1] Lyal White, 'Understanding Brazil's New Drive for Africa', *South African Journal of International Affairs*, 17:2 (2010), 228.

influence over other countries through the attractiveness of their culture, values and institutions, without military or diplomatic coercion. From a complementary perspective, Stolte assesses Brazil's increased engagement in development cooperation as part of the country's ambitious quest for Great Power status, including a permanent seat on the UN Security Council, an explicit goal of the Lula presidency.[2]

The votes of the then fifty-three African countries were considered crucial to the country's quest to become a permanent member of the UN Security Council, as well as the election of Brazilian diplomats as head of international organisations. In addition to political objectives, development cooperation was also expected to foster Brazilian companies' access to African markets. The importance of African countries grew after South American neighbours refused to recognise Brazil as regional leader and to back the country's ambitions for a permanent seat on the Security Council.[3] With regard to political objectives, the diplomatic efforts paid off when the votes of African countries resulted in the election of the Brazilian diplomats José Graziano da Silva and Roberto Azevêdo as directors-general of the UN Food and Agriculture Organization (FAO) in 2011 (re-elected in 2015) and the World Trade Organization (WTO) in 2013 (re-elected in 2017) respectively. The leading positions in two international organisations were expected to advance the country's international visibility, prestige, status, and influence. Initially, Brazil's macroeconomic stability and economic growth enabled the expansion of international cooperation on all levels. However, in recent years the country's economic and financial crisis that began under the Dilma government has raised doubts about the sustainability of the scope of Brazil's development cooperation. This chapter examines and analyses the concepts, dimensions, practices and trends of Brazil's development cooperation in the agriculture, health and education sectors; it also addresses the areas of military and financial cooperation, which have generally received less attention but are equally important to the country's ambitious engagement in African countries.

[2] Christina Stolte, *Brazil's Africa Strategy: Role conception and the drive for international status* (New York: Palgrave Macmillan, 2015), 36.

[3] Adriana Erthal Abdenur, 'Organisation and Politics in South-South Cooperation: Brazil's technical cooperation in Africa', *Global Society*, 29:3 (2015); Stolte, *Brazil's Africa* Strategy, 145.

The scale and regional impact of Brazil's development cooperation in Africa

Unlike other providers of international development assistance, Brazil has not published regular annual reports and statistics and, in contrast to other non-Development Assistance Committee (DAC) countries and multilateral organisations, it does not report official development assistance (ODA) data to the Organisation for Economic Cooperation and Development (OECD). Brazil applies neither the criteria for ODA nor the standards of aid effectiveness of the DAC of the OECD. However, in 2010, 2013 and 2016, the *Instituto de Pesquisa Econômica Aplicada* (IPEA – Institute of Applied Economic Research) did publish the first three reports on Brazil's engagement in bi- and multilateral development cooperation in the period from 2005 to 2009, the year 2010 and the period from 2011 to 2013, respectively. From 2005 to 2009, Brazil's annual development cooperation almost doubled from R$384.2 million ($158.1 million) to R$724 million ($362.2 million) and it totalled R$2.9 billion ($1.43 billion) over the five-year period. Of this amount, 76.1% represented contributions for international organisations and regional development banks, while 5.4% was spent on humanitarian aid, 9.8% on foreign student scholarships and 9.7% on technical cooperation.[4] A considerable share of the country's contributions to UN organisations remains within its own borders, since they also finance projects executed in Brazil. During the five-year period, 7.3% of the R$155.3 million in humanitarian aid went to Africa, and predominantly to Guinea-Bissau which received about half of this proportion. The geographic distribution of other cooperation expenditures is not clearly specified in the report.[5]

In 2010, Brazil granted development assistance of R$1.6 billion ($923 million), a marked increase of 91.2% over the previous year.[6] Contributions to international organisations and peace missions represented 69.7% of the total, while humanitarian aid, scholarships and scientific cooperation and technical cooperation accounted for 17.5%, 6.4% and 6.3% respectively. Of the full amount, R$965 million (66.3%) was spent

[4] IPEA, *Cooperação Brasileira para o Desenvolvimento Internacional: 2005–2009* (Brasília, 2010).

[5] Abdenur, 'Organisation and Politics in South-South Cooperation'.

[6] The OECD estimates that Brazil's development cooperation in 2010 was only $500 million, according to the DAC criteria of ODA that do not include peace missions. See OECD 'Brazil's Development Cooperation', n.d., accessed 26 December 2016, www.oecd.org/dac/dac-global-relations/brazil-development-co-operation.htm.

on multilateral cooperation and R$491 million (33.7%) on bilateral development assistance. To put this into the international perspective, in 2010 Brazil's international development assistance of $597 million (without contributions to multilateral organisations) was between that of Portugal ($431.8 million) and South Korea ($900.6 million), but well below that of the United Kingdom ($8 billion) and France ($9.15 billion), countries with a comparable GDP.[7]

African countries received R$64.7 million (22.6%) of Brazil's bilateral cooperation with regions, which totalled R$286.5 million. Cabo Verde had 24.4% of this, Guinea-Bissau 21.2%, Mozambique 13.3%, São Tomé and Príncipe 10.4% and Angola 7.2%; the remaining 23.5% was shared among another forty-three African countries that benefited from development cooperation with almost a hundred Brazilian entities in that year. As for the R$101.7 million in technical cooperation financed by forty-four institutions of the Brazilian federal administration, 53.3% was allocated to Latin America and the Caribbean, 39.5% to Africa and 7% to Asia. São Tomé and Príncipe, Mozambique, Cabo Verde and Guinea-Bissau were the main beneficiaries of Brazilian technical cooperation in Africa. In 2010, Brazil's educational cooperation totalled R$63 million, 97% of which went to scholarships for foreign students. About R$31 million of this financed 1,643 scholarships for undergraduate students (*Programa de Estudantes-Convênio de Graduação* – PEC-G) at forty-seven Brazilian universities; 1,211 (73.7%) of these students were from the five Palop countries and 118 (7.2%) from other African countries. A further R$14.6 million financed scholarships for 440 postgraduate students (*Programa de Estudantes-Convênio de Pós-Graduação*, 20% of whom were from the Palop (officially Portuguese-speaking African) countries and 1% from other African countries. In 2010, Brazil's humanitarian aid totalled R$284.2, about R$130 million of which was granted to Haiti's reconstruction after the devastating earthquake. Bilateral humanitarian aid represented 43.2% of the total amount and benefited seventeen African countries.[8]

In late 2016, IPEA published its third report on Brazil's international development cooperation for the period from 2011 to 2013. The country's development cooperation in the three-year period covers the activities of ninety-three different government institutions in 159 countries with total expenditures of R$2.8 billion ($1.5 billion), 56% of

[7] Carlos R.S. Milani, *ABC 30 Anos. História e Desafios Futuros* (Brasília: Agência Brasileira de Cooperação, 2017), 81.

[8] IPEA, *Cooperação Brasileira para o Desenvolvimento Internacional 2010* (Brasília, 2013).

which was with international organisations. On an annual basis, Brazil disbursed R$985.3 million ($588.4 million) in 2011, R$1,004.4 million in 2012 ($513.8 million), and R$857.3 million ($396.8 million) in 2013, thus considerably less than the peak in 2010. The downward trend is even more marked in dollars due to the increasing devaluation of the Brazilian currency over the three-year period. Five per cent each of the total R$2.8 billion was spent on educational cooperation and UN peacekeeping missions, 13% each on technical and scientific cooperation and humanitarian aid, 1% on the protection and support of refugees, while the remaining 7% went to technical cooperation. The annual expenditure for technical cooperation declined from R$76.4 million ($45.6 million) in 2011 to R$68.8 million ($31.8 million) in 2013. The Agência Brasileira de Cooperação (ABC – Brazilian Development Agency) disbursed 71.6% of the total R$211.6 million expenditure for technical cooperation from 2011–2013 and spent R$40.3 million of this on the management of technical cooperation projects. Mozambique and São Tomé and Príncipe headed the list of beneficiary countries of the R$106.6 million in bilateral Brazilian technical cooperation for the three-year period, receiving R$19.7 million and R$7.7 million respectively. In terms of regional distribution Africa received R$62.8 million (46.4%) of the R$135.3 million for technical cooperation.

Over the three-year period, Brazil spent R$382.8 million on humanitarian cooperation, R$288.1 million of which went to food aid distributed through the World Food Programme (WFP). Somalia (17.4% of the total) and Ethiopia (7.5%) were among the top five food recipients. Altogether, another twenty-three African countries benefited from Brazilian food aid, particularly rice, beans and maize.[9] In addition, six African countries received medical drug donations, including Benin, Burkina Faso, Cabo Verde, Côte d'Ivoire, Democratic Republic of the Congo (DRC), and São Tomé and Príncipe. Between 2011 and 2013, the Brazilian government spent R$19.9 million on support for refugees within its borders. From 2010 to 2015, the number of foreigners seeking refuge in Brazil rose drastically from 966 to 28,670, before falling significantly by 64% to 10,308 in 2016. At the end of 2013, Brazil was hosting 5,256 recognised refugees from seventy-nine different countries, 1,062 of whom were from Angola (20.4%), 617 from the DRC (11.9%), and 258 from

[9] Algeria, Burkina Faso, Burundi, Cabo Verde, Cameroon, Central African Republic, Chad, DRC, Gambia, Guinea-Bissau, Kenya, Madagascar, Mali, Mauretania, Mozambique, Niger, Republic of Congo, São Tomé and Príncipe, Senegal, Sudan, Swaziland, Uganda and Zimbabwe.

Liberia (5%).[10] By April 2016, the number went up to 8,863, including 1,420 from Angola and 968 from the DRC.[11] This figure had risen again by December that year to 9,552 refugees of eighty-two nationalities. As far as African countries are concerned, most of the newly recognised refugees in 2016 came from the DRC (189), followed by Angola (26), Guinea-Conakry (19), Cameroon (17), Nigeria (16), Ghana (14) and Togo (12).[12] Finally, over the three-year period, Brazil contributed to sixteen UN peace missions, including in the DRC (Monusco), Darfur (Unamid), Côte d'Ivoire (Unoci), Sudan (Unmis), Somalia (Unsoa), Central African Republic (Minurcat) and Western Sahara (Minurso). These operations received R$130 million in funding.[13] The aim of Brazil's sizeable contributions to peacekeeping operations in Africa and beyond was to compensate for its lack of participation in the principal international security activities.[14]

Technical cooperation: Concepts and projects

Brazil's development cooperation has focused on technical cooperation because, unlike other bilateral donors, legally it can only provide financial resources in the form of loans to finance large infrastructure projects executed by Brazilian companies abroad. Under Brazilian legislation, other forms of financial aid can only be conceded to other countries under very restricted circumstances. However, whereas the OECD considers bilateral loans to developing countries and multilateral agencies with a grant element of at least 25% to be official development assistance, Brazil only considers grants to other countries and international organisations part of its international development cooperation.[15] In the period of 2005 to 2013, Brazil disbursed a total of $295 million for international technical cooperation. This amount represented only 7% of Brazil's total expenditure on international development cooperation for that period. From 2005 to 2010, the annual expenditure on technical

[10] IPEA, *Cooperação Brasileira para o Desenvolvimento Internacional 2011–2013* (Brasília, 2016).

[11] UNHCR–ACNUR, 'Dados sobre refúgio no Brasil', 2018, accessed 30 December 2016, www.acnur.org/portugues/recursos/estatisticas/dados-sobre-refugio-no-brasil.

[12] Ibid.

[13] IPEA, *Cooperação Brasileira 2011–2013.*

[14] Stolte, *Brazil's Africa Strategy*, 47.

[15] IPEA, *Cooperação Brasileira 2005–2009.*

cooperation increased sharply from $11.4 million to 57.8 million, before declining steadily to $31.8 million in 2013.[16]

The country's technical cooperation is coordinated by the ABC, which reports directly to Itamaraty, the Foreign Ministry, as is the case with development agencies in most countries. The agency was established in 1987 with the institutional and organisational assistance of the UNDP to manage international assistance received by Brazil from industrialised countries; however, in the early 2000s it also became a provider of technical cooperation, predominantly for Latin America, the Caribbean and Africa.[17] Between 1987 and 2015, Brazil received bilateral technical cooperation of $6.01 billion, an annual average of about $207.4 million. Germany ($2.55 billion), France ($1.39 billion) and Japan ($1.05 billion) were the three main providers of the technical cooperation received in this period.[18] Currently, the ABC is organised in nine departments; two of these deal with assistance received, five with assistance provided abroad and another two with administration, planning and public relations.[19] As already pointed out, the provision of technical cooperation has become an important instrument of Brazil's foreign policy, and particularly during the Lula presidency.[20] It is not by coincidence that Brazil's main partners of technical cooperation in Africa have all supported its claim for a permanent seat on the UN Security Council. South–South cooperation is seen as an important means of promoting foreign relations, projecting Brazil internationally and contributing to a better insertion in the global context.[21] Nevertheless, in recent years the country has still received more than it has spent on international cooperation. According to the OECD, in 2015 Brazil received official

[16] IPEA, *Cooperação Brasileira 2011–2013*, 15.

[17] From 1950, a number of different agencies created within the Foreign Ministry managed and coordinated the development assistance provided by several Western donor countries. In the 1970s, Brazil began providing some technical cooperation to African countries, but the projects were executed by individual ministries and government agencies without any coordination by the Foreign Ministry.

[18] Milani, *ABC 30 Anos*, 94.

[19] Ibid., 61.

[20] Carlos Alfonso Iglesias Puente, *A cooperação técnica horizontal brasileira como instrumento da política externa: a evolução da cooperação técnica com países em desenvolvimento – CTPD – no período 1995–2005* (Brasília: Fundação Alexandre Gusmão, 2010), 232.

[21] Ibid., 262–3.

development assistance of $998.7 million, considerably more than the development assistance it disbursed annually between 2011 and 2013.[22]

Although Latin America and the Caribbean and Africa received roughly an equal share of the ABC budget from 2002 to 2007, Africa received about 10% more between 2008 and 2012 and then significantly more than Latin America and the Caribbean in the two following years. The projects coordinated, implemented and monitored by the ABC are carried out by 335 different public, private and non-government entities and focus on sectors such as tropical agriculture, health, education, vocational training, energy, biofuels, public administration and social protection.[23] These organisations had often been recipients of international development cooperation in the initial stage of their existence.[24] Generally, ABC is in charge of the operationalisation costs of the projects, including air fares and daily allowances for national consultants, technicians and instructors, but the various national partner organisations usually pay for the salaries of their staff while abroad.[25] The ABC has estimated that the participating Brazilian institutions and organisations account for 80% of the project expenditure by providing human resources, infrastructure and equipment.[26] Consequently, the budget data provided by the ABC do not cover the total expenditure on Brazil's technical cooperation with developing countries, but only represents a small share of these costs. Despite the efforts to centralise the management of international development assistance to bring it more in line with foreign policy priorities, individual ministries and other state agencies have continued to conduct technical cooperation projects abroad autonomously. In addition, as technical cooperation is provided by many different entities with their own decision-making systems, it does not seem to be an instrument of one single policy, but rather of a multiplicity of interests.[27]

[22] OECD–DAC, 'Recipient Countries', 2018, accessed 8 December 2017, https://public.tableau.com/views/OECDDACAidataglancebyrecipient_new/Recipients?:embed=y&:display_count=yes&:showTabs=y&:toolbar=no?&:showVizHome=no; IPEA, *Cooperação Brasileira 2011–2013*.

[23] ABC, '335 Entidades Brasileiras Parceiras', 2012, accessed 27 December 2016, www.abc.gov.br/Gestao/EntidadesParceiras.

[24] Puente, *A cooperação técnica*, 125.

[25] Iara Costa Leite et al., *Brazil's Engagement in International Development Cooperation: The state of the debate*. Evidence Report no. 59 (Brighton: Institute of Development Studies, 2014), 40.

[26] Puente, *A cooperação técnica*, 126.

[27] Costa Leite et al., *Brazil's Engagement*, 8.

Brazil emphasises that it is different from traditional providers of development assistance in that it shares with Africa a history of colonial domination and has its own experience of poverty and underdevelopment. In general, projects of technical cooperation are based on experiences with similar programmes, which have already been successfully implemented in Brazil in the recent past. In fact, Brazil's social policies have significantly reduced poverty and hunger, but the country has certainly not yet overcome these problems. From 2001 to 2012, Brazil reduced poverty from 24.3% to 8.4% and the income of the poorest 20% of the population increased three times as much as that of the wealthiest 20%.[28] In addition, the execution of the projects is based on practices applied by multilateral organisations such as the United Nations Development Programme (UNDP).[29] Brazil's official discourse emphasises that Africa's problems are very similar to its own. Brazil claims that its geographic proximity with Africa means that the soils and climate of its tropical regions are similar to those of the African continent; this is considered a comparative advantage in development cooperation, especially with regard to tropical agriculture and medicine. In addition, Brazil draws attention to the advantage of the implantation of its projects and programmes in partner countries by civil servants who have gained experience in executing similar initiatives at home. Brazil expects the partner countries to participate with a share of their own resources in the projects, a rule that has frequently caused problems when they failed to meet their obligations.[30] In addition, Hirst points out that many partner countries have a lack of adequately trained administrative personnel, thus hindering the necessary continuation to consolidate the initiated projects.[31]

Nevertheless, White believes that thanks to Brazil's nuanced approach to Africa 'there is a greater sense of mutual partnership and reciprocity in the relationship, which is not always the case with other established and emerging powers in Africa'.[32] In 2015, when Brazil's development cooperation with Africa was already declining, Lula's Foreign Minister, Celso Amorim, proudly quoted a Kenyan university professor who

[28] Felipe Leal Ribeiro de Albuquerque, 'Cooperation on Food Security with Africa as an Instrument of Brazil's Foreign Policy (2003–2010)', *Brazilian Journal of International Relations*, 4:3 (2015), 565.

[29] Puente, *A cooperação técnica*, 114.

[30] Ibid., 152.

[31] Mónica Hirst, *Aspectos Conceituais e Práticos da Atuação do Brasil em Cooperação Sul-Sul: os Casos de Haiti, Bolívia e Guiné-Bissau*. Texto para Discussão (Brasília: Instituto de Pesquisa Econômica Aplicada, 2012), 14.

[32] White, 'Understanding Brazil's New Drive', 239.

claimed that there was a Brazilian solution for every African problem.[33] Brazil defines its development assistance as South–South cooperation, a concept of technical cooperation between developing countries first established in the Buenos Aires Action Plan of 1978.[34] It perceives South–South cooperation as a horizontal relationship between equal partners in search of mutual benefits, guided by international solidarity, non-interference in the internal affairs of partner countries and without any imposition of political or economic conditionality. These principles correspond to those of Brazil's foreign policy, which are also based on the country's Southern identity.[35]

Despite the official discourse of horizontal relations with partner countries, Brazil's cooperation is not free of either asymmetries or self-interest, but driven by various political and social interests.[36] In practice, asymmetries between Brazil and African partner countries are inevitable as the technology and human resources in the latter are less developed.[37] Besides, the projects generally involve the provision of human resources, technology and equipment from Brazil. A number of authors have questioned the country's denial of any commercial or economic interests related to its development cooperation. White, for example, is of the opinion that 'Brazil's engagement with Africa has entailed a three-pronged pursuit of political diplomacy, strategic commercial interests and development cooperation'. He argues that the seamless link between business interests and development cooperation makes Brazil's approach to business and development in Africa unique when compared with both new players like China and India and traditional ones like the United States and Europe.[38] Stolte, however, affirms that economic and business interests were not the main drivers of Brazil's development cooperation with Africa, but were primarily a means of achieving its foreign policy objectives by increasing its international prestige and credibility

[33] Celso Amorim, 'Um Balanço das Relações Brasil–África', *Diálogos Africanos*, 1(2015), 26.

[34] Puente, *A cooperação técnica*, 78.

[35] Costa Leite et al., *Brazil's Engagement*, 17.

[36] Adriana Erthal Abdenur and João Marcos Rampini, 'A Cooperação Brasileira para o Desenvolvimento com Angola e Moçambique: Uma Visão Comparada', in *Política Externa Brasileira, Cooperação Sul – Sul e Negociações Internacionais*, edited by Haroldo Ramazini Júnior and Luís Fernando Ayerbe (São Paulo: Editora Cultura Acadêmica, Fundação Friedrich Ebert, Instituto de Estudos Econômicos e Internacionais – IEEI–UNESP, 2015), 89.

[37] Puente, *A Cooperação Técnica*, 73.

[38] Lyal White, 'Emerging Powers in Africa: Is Brazil any different?' *South African Journal of International Affairs*, 20:1 (2013), 118.

and winning new international partners for its foreign policy initiatives globally.[39]

The principle of non-interference means that Brazil maintains cooperation relations with any country, irrespective of considerations of 'good government' or whether its political regime is democratic or dictatorial. As a result of such pragmatism, 'in its bilateral relations Brazil has often proven reluctant to directly condemn or single out human rights violators, expanding cooperation as well as commercial relations with theses regimes.'[40] Similarly, White states that Brazil's poor regard for inclusive democracy in some of the countries with Brazilian investments 'contradicts Brazilian ambitions as an emerging power and a moral leader of the South'.[41] Officially, Brazil's cooperation is not only presented as selfless, but also as demand-driven and responding exclusively to requests from individual partner countries. However, Stolte affirms that Brazil has, in fact, actively presented itself as a development model for African countries; Lula himself repeatedly stressed his country's development successes arguing that the application of Brazil's development strategy would help bring poverty in the continent to an end.[42]

Even though Brazil claims that its development cooperation is based on different principles of equitable relations unlike traditional donor countries, it has executed a few large projects in Africa triangulated with those countries, in particular with Japan, Canada, the USA, Germany, France, Italy, Norway and the United Kingdom. Trilateral cooperation projects permit Brazil to share know-how and experiences, as well as costs, which is advantageous given its comparatively limited financial resources. In addition, trilateral cooperation with traditional development assistance providers has furthered Brazil's role as an emerging power in development cooperation.[43] There are also some trilateral cooperation projects with international organisations such as UNDP, UNICEF, FAO, WFP and the International Labour Organization (ILO). From 2009 to 2015, the share of budgeted trilateral technical cooperation with international organisations executed by the ABC increased from 1.9% to 73.8%.[44]

[39] Stolte, *Brazil's Africa Strategy*, 137.

[40] Adriana Erthal Abdenur and Danilo Marcondes de Souza Neto, 'Brazil's Development Cooperation with Africa: What role for democracy and human rights', *SUR – Revista Internacional de Direitos Humanos*, 19 (2013), 27.

[41] White, 'Emerging Powers in Africa', 121.

[42] Stolte, *Brazil's Africa Strategy*, 111.

[43] Ibid., 76.

[44] Milani, *ABC 30 Anos*, 227.

Brazilian technical cooperation is made up mainly of small projects with a duration of two years, renewable for another two; however, Brazil also began executing so-called structuring projects with a larger scope and duration in 2008. Unlike the small projects, structuring projects are expected to produce a systematic impact and remain sustainable over the long run. The ABC has executed twelve structuring projects in Africa: including five in Mozambique and three in São Tomé and Príncipe. Until 2014, the total ABC expenditure for the twelve projects was $26.9 million.[45] The ABC claims to have carried out technical cooperation projects in forty-two African countries.[46] This considerable geographical dispersion combined with the prevalence of small short-term projects has inevitably limited the impact of Brazil's development cooperation on the partner countries.[47]

However, due to the common language, shared colonial history and supposed cultural affinities, about half of the ABC's technical cooperation in Africa has been allocated in the five Portuguese-speaking countries: Angola, Cabo Verde, Guinea-Bissau, Mozambique and São Tomé and Príncipe.[48] The common language affords Brazilian technical cooperation in these countries advantages that they do not have in Anglophone and Francophone countries. While Brazil's official discourse stresses the shared colonial history with these countries, it downplays the country's support for Portuguese colonialism during most of the Cold War period.[49] As already pointed out in Chapter 1, Brazil's technical cooperation with the former Portuguese colonies began after they had gained independence in 1975, initially predominantly human capacity building actions carried out in Brazil. The country signed bilateral cooperation agreements with Cabo Verde in 1977, Guinea-Bissau in 1978, Angola in 1980, Mozambique in 1981, and São Tomé and Príncipe in 1984.[50]

[45] ABC, 'Projetos Estruturantes', n.d., accessed 24 December 2016, www.abc.gov.br/Gestao/ProjetosEstruturantes.

[46] ABC, 'Países Parceiros da Cooperação Sul-Sul Brasileira', n.d., accessed 24 December 2016, www.abc.gov.br/Gestao/PaisesParceiros.

[47] Puente, *A Cooperação Técnica*, 242.

[48] In 1995, Namibia became the first non-Portuguese-speaking African country to benefit from Brazil's technical cooperation (Puente, *A Cooperação Técnica*, 181).

[49] Generally the affirmation of a shared colonial history disregards the differences in Portuguese colonialism in Brazil from the 16th century to the early 19th century from that in Africa from the late 19th century until the last quarter of the 20th century.

[50] Kamilla Raquel Rizzi, 'Relações Brasil – PALOP: 40 anos de cooperação para o desenvolvimento no Atlântico Sul (1974/75–2015)', *Revista Brasileira de Estudos Africanos*, 1:1 (2016), 151.

Portugal, the former colonial power, also concentrated its development assistance in this same group of countries. Inevitably, the two countries are competitors in development cooperation rather than partners in the Palop. The concentration of Brazil's technical cooperation in the Palop demonstrates that, in fact, it is not guided exclusively by its commercial and economic interests. Although this might be true in the case of Angola and Mozambique, where Brazilian companies have made considerable investments and bilateral trade is significant, it does not apply to the three small Palop countries. Brazilian trade and investments are largely insignificant in these countries, notably in Guinea-Bissau and São Tomé and Príncipe. However, cooperation projects in the three small countries serve as showcases for Brazil's development cooperation for third countries, and thus indirectly contribute to Brazil's foreign policy goals. In addition, Brazil has geopolitical interests and security concerns in the South Atlantic where these countries that are all members of ZOPACAS are located. Moreover, the Brazilian presence in these countries draws attention to its claim for a leading role within the CPLP vis-à-vis Portugal, which has similar political aspirations of leadership within the small nine-country community formed in 1996.

Until 2010, the last year of the Lula presidency, the ABC's technical cooperation with Africa increased significantly in terms of both the value and number of projects. Brazil has prioritised Africa as the focus of technical cooperation over its own Latin American region.[51] Between 1995 and 2005, the ABC projects in Africa represented \$6.6 million, equivalent to 52% of the agency's total budget of \$12.7 million during this period.[52] From 2005 to 2015, 49.7% of the ABC's total expenditure for technical cooperation went to Africa, whereas Latin America and the Caribbean accounted for 31.9%. From 2000 to 2010, the agency's annual budget for projects in Africa rose from \$808,000 to \$19,845,000, and the number of projects expanded accordingly from 4 to 253. As already noted, these amounts do not include the financial contributions of other Brazilian entities to these projects. During the Dilma Rousseff government (2011–16), there was a sharp decline in the ABC budget for Africa and the number of projects, due to different political priorities and Brazil's economic crisis. Indeed, due in part to the depreciation of the Brazilian currency, the ABC's annual budget for Africa dropped from \$13.7 million (50.6% of the total budget) to \$5.1 million (71.4%) between 2011 and 2014 and the number of projects fell from 233 (29.8% of the total) to 161 (41.8%) in the same period.

[51] Stolte, *Brazil's Africa Strategy*, 107.
[52] Puente, *A Cooperação Técnica*, 158.

From 2010 to 2014, the average costs per project in Africa went down by almost 60% from $78,438 to $31,488.[53] In the triennium from 2015 to 2017, the ABC executed a total budget of $59.5 million for projects in twenty-four African countries, including military training and Brazil's contribution to trilateral projects; this represents an annual average of about $19.8 million. The main recipient countries were Guinea-Bissau ($10.1 million), Mozambique ($9.8 million) and São Tomé and Príncipe ($6.0 million). In terms of projects during the three-year period, by far the largest share of the budget ($26.5 million) went to the three regional cotton development projects in West Africa (Cotton-4 + Togo), Malawi and Mozambique, and Tanzania, Kenya and Burundi, followed by the vocational training centres in São Tomé ($3.2 million) and in Guinea-Bissau ($3.1 million).[54]

Main national partners and sectors of technical cooperation

During the five-year period from 2010 to 2014, agriculture accounted for 33.4% of the agency's technical cooperation with African countries. The *Empresa Brasileira de Pesquisa Agropecuária* (EMBRAPA – Brazilian Agricultural Research Corporation) is ABC's most relevant partner in this sector. EMBRAPA was established in 1973 and is attached to the ministry of agriculture; it is headquartered in Brasília and has delegations all over the country and a total staff of 9,859 people, 2,224 of whom are researchers. In 2006, EMBRAPA opened a regional office for Africa in Accra, Ghana and it has been involved in several larger agricultural development projects in various African countries. EMBRAPA began the Cotton-4 project based in Bamako, Mali, in 2008 to conduct research on the genetic improvement of cotton to increase crop quality and productivity in the cotton-producing countries of Mali, Burkina Faso, Chad and Benin. Togo joined the project at the start of the second phase in 2014. The aim of the second phase is to make the production chain of cotton in the five countries more competitive, adapt competitive technologies in small properties and strengthen the local partners' institutional capacities to develop adequate technical solutions for the cotton sector. Based on the experiences gained in West Africa, EMBRAPA initiated two other regional cotton projects in 2015: the Shire Zambezi Cotton Project with Malawi and Mozambique and the Victoria Cotton

[53] ABC, 'Execução Financeira 2000–2014', 2010, accessed 24 December 2016, www.abc.gov.br/Content/ABC/imagens/africa_financeiro.png.

[54] Execução Orçamentária da ABC de 2015 a 2017, received 27 March 2018 through the Electronic System of the Citizen Information Service (e-SIC).

Project with Tanzania, Kenya and Burundi. The projects are politically associated with Brazil's position in favour of the abolition of cotton subsidies provided by the United States and other Western countries, since they reduce global cotton prices and negatively affect Brazil's cotton sector and the development possibilities of African cotton-producing countries.[55] Until 2016, the ABC financed the project with a total of $2.9 million. Part of these funds stem from the *Instituto Brasileiro de Algodão* (IBA – Brazilian Cotton Institute); this institute was established in 2010 to receive payments from the US Commodity Credit Corporation as a partial solution for the cotton litigation between the two governments within the WTO due to the controversial subsidies paid by the US government to its cotton producers.[56]

Mozambique has hosted three larger projects in which EMBRAPA has been involved. From 2010 to 2014, the corporation participated in a trilateral technical support project with the US Agency for International Development (USAID) and Mozambique to strengthen and restructure the research and innovation capacity of the Agricultural Research Institute of Mozambique (IIAM). The goal of the project was to improve IIAM's research management, development and technology transfer to help Mozambique to achieve self-sufficiency in food production. From 2011 to 2015, it also participated in another trilateral food security project with USAID and Mozambique. The project, entitled 'Technical Support to Mozambique's Nutrition and Food Security Programmes', was executed as part of the US Government's Global Hunger and Food Security Initiative (GHFSI) with the aim of making Mozambique self-sufficient in vegetable production. The project included the introduction of Brazilian vegetable plants in Mozambique, the evaluation of irrigation systems and the systematisation of the experimental area for organic vegetable production research in IIAM's experimental agricultural station Umbelúzi in Boane, Maputo province. More than seventy different vegetable species were tested and the adaptability of many of these could be approved. In addition, the project provided human capacity building courses for local researchers, agronomists, extension workers and farmers.[57]

In 2011, in conjunction with the Japan International Cooperation Agency (JICA) and the Mozambican government, EMBRAPA launched a third trilateral agricultural development programme, the *Programa de Cooperaçao Tripartida para o Desenvolvimento da Agricultura da*

[55] Albuquerque, 'Cooperation on Food Security', 572.
[56] Milani, *ABC 30 Anos*, 120.
[57] 'Projetos Estruturantes', EMBRAPA.

Savana Tropical em Moçambique (Trilateral Agriculture Development Cooperation Programme in Mozambique's Tropical Savannah), better known as ProSAVANA, in the Nacala Corridor in northern Mozambique. The project seeks to increase agricultural productivity and production in this region. It is based on Brazil's own experience in large-scale agricultural transformation of large swaths of south-central Brazil (the arid Cerrado region) into export-oriented monoculture agriculture, to the detriment of small farmers and the Amerindian population. The project was implemented with Japanese assistance in the 1970s. The large project in Mozambique covers an area of about 14 million ha in nineteen districts in Nampula, Niassa and Zambezia provinces, with 4.5 million inhabitants. It has become Brazil's most controversial development project in Africa and has repeatedly triggered protests by local farmer communities and civil society organisations, with the support of Brazilian partner organisations. They have accused the project of primarily addressing the interests of foreign agro-business at the expense of the needs of small local famers.

These suspicions were reinforced when an agricultural risk capital investment fund for the Nacala Corridor was simultaneously launched in Brasília and Maputo in 2012. Registered in Luxembourg, the Nacala Fund was expected to attract private investments of $500 million to develop 300 ha in the cultivation of rice, maize, soya and cotton in the first phase of the project.[58] In 2013, small farmers asked for the immediate suspension of the project, arguing that private investments in large-scale cultivation of export crops would result in the loss of their lands. Even though the local government rejected the concerns of the local farmer communities as unfounded, nine Mozambican civil society organisations initiated a campaign in mid-2014 aimed at terminating the project on the grounds that it would benefit only the interests of agro-business and put the existence of thousands of small famers at risk. Again, the people in charge of ProSAVANA considered the allegations groundless. At the public presentation of ProSAVANA's master plan, in May 2015, local famers again accused the project of being incompatible with the reality of the peasant communities. The national project coordinator dismissed this and affirmed that, on the contrary, the goal of the project was to improve peasant life. Finally, in early 2016, the government sought to improve the dialogue with the rural communities by allowing them to

[58] Elga Lessa de Almeida, 'Entre o Discurso Solidário e a Ação Pragmática da Cooperação Brasileira em Moçambique: os casos dos projetos de implantação da fábrica de medicamentos antirretrovirais e o ProSavana', *Caderno CRH, Salvador*, 29:76 (2016), 63.

participate more in the project implementation.[59] Nevertheless, in October 2017 local farmer organisations again rejected the implementation of the project arguing that it would benefit large-scale monocultures and export-oriented agribusiness, while small farmers would lose their lands. The Mozambican project coordinator appeased the protesting farmers by reassuring them their lands would not be taken away.[60] As a result of falling commodity prices and the consecutive protests, the Nacala Fund has not become operational and was finally closed in 2014. Nevertheless, the fierce protests have seriously questioned claims that Brazilian cooperation is, by definition, not associated to commercial interests.[61] At the same time, the results and the future of the project have become increasingly uncertain.

EMBRAPA has also executed many other projects in several other African countries. From 2010 to 2012, the corporation carried out a rice-cultivation project worth $2.4 million in Senegal. In 2010, EMBRAPA established the Agricultural Innovation Marketplace, a partnership to enhance agricultural innovation and development in Brazil, Latin America, the Caribbean and Africa. In Africa, the project, which involves a number of international donors, is currently conducting agricultural research projects in Benin, Burkina Faso, Cameroon, Ethiopia, Ghana, Kenya, Nigeria, Mali, Mozambique, Tanzania, Togo and Uganda. In 2014, EMBRAPA launched another trilateral project with Angola's Ministry of Agriculture and the FAO with the objective of strengthening the capacities of public agricultural research institutions, and in this way, furthering food security and national agricultural development in that country.[62] In addition, EMBRAPA has regularly held capacity building courses in Brazil for researchers, technicians and farmers from the various African project countries. Despite the extensive engagement abroad, an advisor of EMBRAPA confessed that although the corporation had been engaged in international development cooperation more frequently since 2008, they had not been given the previous experience, training or awareness-raising they required. He affirmed that there was no internal capacity building in the technical cooperation sector even by 2017. In

[59] Gerhard Seibert, 'Brazil's Engagement with Africa', in *Africa South of the Sahara 2017*, 46th edition. (London: Routledge, 2016), 48.

[60] Alfredo Júnior, 'Camponeses querem travar o ProSavana', *Voz da América*, 24 October 2017, accessed 23 December 2018, www.voaportugues.com/a/camponeses-querem-travar-prosavana/4084596.html.

[61] Almeida, 'Entre o Discurso Solidário', 65.

[62] 'Projetos Estruturantes', EMBRAPA.

fact, the advisor stated that EMBRAPA did not have the organisational and technical capacities to operate outside Brazil.[63]

In the period from 2010 to 2014, the health sector represented 15.5% of the ABC projects in Africa. The *Fundação Oswaldo Cruz* (Fiocruz) is the agency's main partner in the health sector. It was founded in 1890 and is headquartered in Rio de Janeiro. The foundation has gained an international reputation in the development of scientific research and technologies in the public health sector and the successful control of yellow-fever and Chagas disease.[64] Reformed in the 1970s, the foundation is associated with the Brazilian Health Ministry and employs more than 7,500 people; it set up an international cooperation division, the Centre for International Relations in Health (CRIS), in 2009. Fiocruz cooperates with other public health institutions worldwide. In 2008, the foundation opened a regional office for Africa in Mozambique's capital Maputo to highlight its South–South vocation. Maputo's neighbouring city of Matola is home of an antiretroviral (ARV) generic drugs manufacturing factory, one of Fiocruz's major projects in Africa with an investment of $21 million. Mozambique was expected to contribute $5.4 million to this amount. The factory for the production of ARV generic drugs for the treatment of HIV/SIDA and several other drugs, initially promised by President Lula during his first visit to Mozambique in 2003, was part of a bilateral cooperation agreement signed in 2008 with the Health Ministry and the *Sociedade Moçambicana de Medicamentos* (SMM – Mozambican Medical Drugs Society), the operator of the factory. Subsequently, Fiocruz provided Mozambican technicians with human capacity building courses, in Brazil and elsewhere. When Lula visited Maputo in November 2010 during his last visit to Africa as head of state, he called the project a revolution in the fight against HIV/AIDS in Africa.[65] However, the factory only started operations in mid-2012 due to consecutive delays mainly caused by financial constraints as a result of Mozambique's failure to provide its agreed counterpart contribution. The Mozambican government acquired a former private serum plant in Matola, but then stated it lacked the funds for the

[63] Milani, *ABC 30 Anos*, 65.

[64] Janiffer Zarpelon, *Cooperação para o desenvolvimento do Brasil na área da saúde com os PALOP*, Oficina do CES no. 414 (Coimbra: Centro de Estudos Sociais, 2014), 8.

[65] Adriana Abdenur and Danilo Marcondes, 'Brazilian South-South cooperation in public health: Dilemmas of the ARV factory initiative', in *Mozambique and Brazil. Forging New Partnerships or Developing Dependency?* edited by Chris Alden, Sérgio Chichava, and Ana Cristina Alves (Johannesburg: Jacana Media, 2017), 184.

building's necessary renovation works. The problems were overcome after the Brazilian mining company, Vale, granted the Mozambican government $4.5 million to make the project feasible.[66] Initially, the plant equipped with machinery purchased in Brazil only packaged, stored and distributed ARV drugs that had been manufactured in Brazil. It was only in August 2013 that the plant started to produce its own ARV and other drugs. By 2015, the factory, which has forty-five employees, claimed to have reached the stage of producing 19 million pharmaceutical units of four essential drugs entirely in Mozambique.[67] However, during the year 2017, the factory did not produce any drugs at all due to internal problems. Instead, it was decided to replace the production of ARV by that of analgesics (paracetamol) and six other essential drugs in 2018, since the ARV (nevirapina), which production technology foundation Fiocruz had transferred to Maputo, had become obsolete for the treatment of HIV. Brazil's Ministry of Health financed this change of production with R$5 million.[68]

The project was based on Brazil's domestic approach to HIV/AIDS prevention and treatment with generic drugs. Brazil's public health system (SUS) has provided HIV/AIDS patients with free access to ARV generics since 1996.[69] The plant also represents and disseminates Brazil's official policy abroad that developing countries must have the right to produce generic drugs in cases of epidemics, as in the case of HIV/AIDS in Southern Africa, a region severely affected by HIV/AIDS prevalence. This position against pharmaceutical patents to reduce drug costs of public health programmes in the fight against endemic diseases has been defended by the Brazilian government and several developing countries against the interests of large multinational pharmaceutical companies backed by industrialised countries.[70] In addition, Fiocruz has run several institutional and human capacity building programmes for the public

[66] Almeida, 'Entre o Discurso Solidário', 57.

[67] Fundação Osvaldo Cruz, 'Relatório de Atividades Internacionais 2014–2015', Centro de Relações Internacionais em Saúde (Rio de Janeiro 2016), accessed 27 December 2016, https://portal.fiocruz.br/sites/portal.fiocruz.br/files/documentos/fiocruz_relatorio_de_atividades_internacionais_2014–2015.pdf.

[68] Amanda Rossi, 'Em vez de remédio contra Aids, fábrica financiada pelo Brasil em Moçambique produzirá analgésico', UOL Notícias, 6 December 2017, https://noticias.uol.com.br/saude/ultimas-noticias/bbc/2017/12/06/em-vez-de-remedio-contra-aids-fabrica-financiada-pelo-brasil-em-mocambique-produzira-analgesico.htm?cmpid=copiaecola.

[69] Abdenur and Marcondes, 'Brazilian South-South cooperation', 180.

[70] Adriana Erthal Abdenur, 'Organisation and Politics in South-South Cooperation: Brazil's Technical Cooperation in Africa', *Global Society*, 29:3 (2015), 335.

health sectors in Angola, Cabo Verde, Guinea-Bissau, Mozambique, and São Tomé and Príncipe. Projects in the health sector have not been restricted to Fiocruz. Another larger health project, jointly executed by ABC, the Health Ministry, the Federal University of Minas Gerais (UFMG) and the Fundação Hemominas, is the Blood and Sickle Cell Treatment Centre at the Komfo Anokye Teaching Hospital in Kumasi, Ghana, financed with a Brazilian government grant of $13.7 million. The Centre's foundation stone was laid in 2010 in the presence of a Brazilian delegation headed by the ambassador in Accra, Luis Fernando Serra. The Centre was to include a blood transfusion centre and an out-patient clinic for sickle cell and other blood diseases.[71] However, it seems the construction was not completed because the Ghana National Petroleum Corporation donated $4.5 million in 2016 to the same project after it had been paralysed for some years due to a lack of funds.[72] Besides the Palop countries, Brazil has signed public health cooperation agreements with the following countries in Africa: Benin, Botswana, Burkina Faso, Burundi, Cameroon, Republic of Congo, Ethiopia, Gabon, Ghana, Libya, Namibia, Nigeria, Kenya, and Zambia.[73] However, there are no data available to confirm whether these agreements have actually been implemented.

Education accounted for 23% of ABC's technical cooperation in the period from 2010–2014. The *Serviço Nacional de Aprendizagem Industrial* (SENAI – National Service for Industrial Training) is in charge of technical cooperation in the area of vocational training; it was founded in 1942 and is entirely financed by compulsory contributions of the private sector. In Brazil, SENAI employs 22,595 people and provides vocational training courses in twenty-eight areas of professional specialisation. It is the only national partner organisation whose technicians are paid by the ABC.[74] Between 1999 and 2014, SENAI inaugurated vocational training centres in the capitals of Angola, Cabo Verde, Guinea-Bissau, and São Tomé and Príncipe. The construction of another vocational centre in Maputo was one of the ABC's twelve large-scale projects for the

[71] *Ghanaian Chronicle*, '$13.66m Blood & Sickle Cell Centre for KATH', *Modern Ghana*, 29 November 2010, accessed 23 December 2018, www.modernghana.com/news/306308/1/1366m-blood-amp-sickle-cell-centre-for-kath.html.

[72] *Citifmonline*, 'GNPC donates $4.5m for construction of sickle cell centre', 9 March 2016, accessed 23 December 2018, http://citifmonline.com/2016/03/09/gnpc-donates-4-5m-for-construction-of-sickle-cell-centre.

[73] Ministério da Saúde, 'Acordos Internacionais', n.d., accessed 28 December 2016, http://portalsaude.saude.gov.br/index.php/o-ministerio/principal/leia-mais-o-ministerio/279-aisa-raiz/aisa/24941-acordos-internacionais.

[74] Milani, *ABC 30 Anos*, 63.

period of 2010 to 2014, but did not come to fruition due to the agency's financial constraints. Between 2000 and 2008, the vocational centre at Cazenga in Luanda trained almost 19,000 participants. The management of the centre was transferred to the Angolan authorities in 2005. Currently, it receives about 1,200 students annually; they are trained by thirty teachers, most of whom did their own vocational training in Brazil.[75] In addition to the construction of these centres, SENAI has also provided human capacity building services for the Brazilian companies Odebrecht in Angola, Vale in Mozambique and Petrobras in Tanzania.

Brazil has also provided technical cooperation in the field of higher education. With Brazil's assistance, Cabo Verde inaugurated its first public university in 2006. In 2011, four Brazilian universities and two local universities began setting up the Open University of Mozambique, a project budgeted at $30 million over a nine-year period. Drawing on Brazil's experience of distance learning since 2005, the institution offers a course in public administration and three courses for the training of primary and secondary teachers (biology, mathematics and pedagogy). Although the project was expected to train 5,500 primary and secondary school teachers and 1,500 public servants by 2014, only 590 students were enrolled in March 2014 and 15% of the students had abandoned their studies between 2011 and 2014. Of the ten university campuses originally planned in the country's provincial capitals, only three have actually been constructed: in Maputo, Beira and Lichinga. From the start, the three campuses were affected by a lack of space for teachers and students, poor Internet access, insufficient didactic material, and the absence of adequately equipped libraries. Some of the selected students resided far from the campuses in remote places without Internet access, which made their participation impossible.[76] In 2016 Brazil ceased to fund the project due to budget constraints. At the time, only about 680 students had actually completed their courses at the Open University.[77]

The *Universidade da Integração Internacional da Lusofonia Afro-Brasileira* (UNILAB – University of International Integration of Afro-Brazilian Lusophony) is another cooperation project in higher education that is related to Africa but based in Brazil; it was created as a public

[75] ABC, 'Centro de Formação Brasil-Angola', n.d., accessed 27 December 2016, www.abc.gov.br/Projetos/CooperacaoSulSul/CentroFormacaoAngola.

[76] Oreste Preti, 'A Universidade Aberta do Brasil em Moçambique: a experiência de um programa de cooperação internacional no continente africano', *Pesquisa de Debate em Educação*, 3:1 (2013).

[77] Aires Zarina Bonifácio Mombassa and Eucidio Pimenta Arruda, 'História da Educação a Distância em Moçambique: perspectivas atuais e as contribuições do Brasil', *Práxis Educativa*, 13:3 (2018), 12.

federal university in 2010. The Lula government expected the university to admit 5,000 students, half from Brazil and the other half from the five Portuguese-speaking African countries and East Timor. UNILAB's mission of educational cooperation with Africa was highlighted by inaugurating the main campus in the small town of Redenção in the Northeastern federal state of Ceará on 25 May 2011; this is Africa Day and commemorates the foundation in 1963 of the Organisation of African Unity (renamed African Union in 2002). The choice of Redenção was also emblematic as it was Brazil's first municipality to abolish slavery when the 116 slaves in the locality were granted freedom in 1883, five years ahead of the country's general abolition in 1888. In 2014, UNILAB opened an external campus in São Francisco do Conde in Bahia, one of the three federal states with the highest percentage of Afro-Brazilians in the population. In October 2017, 6,803 students were enrolled at UNILAB, including 102 postgraduate students and 2,706 students of distance learning. However, the university achieved far from its proclaimed objective of parity in the enrolment of students from abroad. At the time, only 1,031 (25.8%) of the 3,995 undergraduates came from the six so-called partner countries.[78] In fact, there was a downward trend in the proportion of foreigners; 610 (30%) of the 2,056 students were foreigners in August 2014, and 888 (26.1%) of the 3,398 undergraduates in November 2016.[79]

In addition, the number of students from the individual countries was very unequal, although they had been offered the same enrolment numbers, irrespective of each country's population size. While 622 (60.3%) of the foreign students came from small Guinea-Bissau, only 151 (14.6%) and 32 (3.1%) were from the much larger countries of Angola and Mozambique respectively.[80] One possible reason for this great disparity is that university education in Guinea-Bissau is almost non-existent, while Angola and Mozambique have several public and private universities throughout the countries. UNILAB also has a long way to go in terms of quality of education, scientific research and other indicators. Five years after it was set up, the university occupied the

[78] UNILAB, 'Unilab em números', n.d., accessed 9 December 2017, www.unilab.edu.br/unilab-em-numeros.

[79] Ibid.; Susanne Ress, 'Racialization through "Time" in Brazil's Cooperation in Higher Education: An ethnographic case study of UNILAB' in *International Perspectives on Race (and Racism): Historical and contemporary considerations in education and society*, edited by Diane Brook Napier (Hauppauge, NY: Nova Science Publishers, 2015), 6.

[80] 'Unilab em números' UNILAB.

174th position in the 2016 ranking of a total of 195 Brazilian universities.[81] Ress, who recently conducted ethnographic research in Redençao, argues that the UNILAB version of a supposedly shared history of slavery with Africa reduced complex and diverse histories of colonialism and slavery that exist on both sides of the Atlantic to Brazil's own history of slavery, confining Africans and Africa mainly to the past and almost rendered contemporary Africa invisible.[82] The selection procedure of applicants to UNILAB from the partner countries is conducted by the local Brazilian embassies. UNILAB tries to attract students to study in a small, newly established university in a remote place by providing them all with a monthly grant of R$530 ($161) during their undergraduate studies, which is not common practice in other Brazilian universities. However, in July 2017, UNILAB's dean announced the end of the grants for future foreign students, alleging budgetary constraints. The decision was tantamount to refusing to admit foreign students in the future as they would not be able to afford studying at UNILAB without the modest financial support. Following ten days of fierce protests within and outside the institution, the dean was obliged to revoke his decision.

Generally, Brazilian universities provide places for foreign undergraduate students as part of the above-mentioned PEC-G created in 1965. Unlike the students who apply for admission at UNILAB, since 2015 applicants to PEC-G from the Palop countries and East Timor (where Portuguese is also the official language), have been obliged to present the official Brazilian Certification of Portuguese Language Proficiency CELPE-Bras (*Certificado de Proficiência em Língua Portuguesa para Estrangeiros*).[83] Between 2000 and 2017, PEC-G provided 7,373 scholarships for undergraduate courses at Brazilian universities for applicants from nineteen different African countries. However, almost two thirds of these students came from two countries, namely Cabo Verde (41.5%) and Guinea-Bissau (18.4%), followed by Angola (10.0%) and the Democratic Republic of the Congo (6.6%).[84] For scholarships financed by the postgraduate programme PEC-PG, 567 applicants were selected from fourteen African countries between 2000 and 2016. The vast majority of the beneficiaries came from Mozambique (279) and Cabo Verde

[81] *Folha de São Paulo*, 'Ranking Universitário Folha 2016', 2017, accessed 23 December 2018, http://ruf.folha.uol.com.br/2016.

[82] Ress, 'Racialization through "Time"'.

[83] This rule was revoked in 2018.

[84] MRE, 'Exchange Program for Undergraduate Students', n.d., accessed 23 December 2018, www.dce.mre.gov.br/EN/PEC/PECG/php.

(132), followed by Angola (62) and Guinea-Bissau (39).[85] The number of scholarships is comparable to that of Portugal, which granted 5,774 university scholarships to students from the Palop countries between 1999 and 2009.[86] In terms of the total African student population, Brazil lags far behind countries such as France, China, United States, United Kingdom, South Africa, Saudi Arabia, Canada and Germany.[87] In 2016, only 15,803 (0.2%) of the 8,052,254 undergraduate students at Brazil's 2,407 higher education institutions were foreigners; 4,251 (28%) of these were Africans. The African students came from Angola (1,928), Guinea-Bissau (1,017), Cabo Verde (561), South Africa (185), Benin (154), Mozambique (147), São Tomé and Príncipe (139) and the Republic of Congo (120).[88] In 2013, Brazil's Ministry of Education announced it would provide $2.7 million through its foundation *Coordenação de Aperfeiçoamento de Pessoal de Nível Superior* (CAPES – Coordination for the Improvement of Higher Education Personnel) to forty-five projects to enhance higher education in the five Palop countries and East Timor, which would be carried out by twenty different Brazilian universities. As part of the programme, Mozambique received twenty-two projects, followed by Cabo Verde (10), Angola (9), Guinea-Bissau (2), São Tomé (1) and East Timor (1).[89]

In addition to bilateral development cooperation coordinated by the ABC, Brazil has been engaged in trilateral cooperation within the India–Brazil–South Africa (IBSA) Dialogue Forum. The IBSA Forum was established in 2003 by India, Brazil and South Africa with the goal of strengthening political, strategic and economic cooperation between the three emerging powers, as well as to seek their greater involvement in issues of global governance. On the political level, IBSA held five annual summits of the three heads of state between 2005 and 2011, but the

[85] MRE, 'Programa de Estudantes-Convênio Pós-Graduação', n.d., accessed 15 June 2018, www.dce.mre.gov.br/PEC/PG/historico_Africa_3.png.

[86] Ana Benárd da Costa, 'Cooperação portuguesa com os PALOP ao nível superior: Impactos e Desafios', in *Formação Superior e Desenvolvimento. Estudantes Universitários Africanos em Portugal*, edited by Ana Benárd da Costa and Margarida Lima de Faria (Coimbra: Almedina, 2013), 25.

[87] Jane Marshall, 'Mobility of African Students – Europe losing ground', *University World News*, 17 November 2016, accessed 23 December 2018, www.universityworldnews.com/article.php?story=20161117045045147.

[88] INEP, *Censo da Educação Superior 2016. Divulgação* (Brasília: Ministério de Educação, 2017), 32.

[89] Fábio Takahashi, 'Brasil financiará melhoria de ensino superior na África', *Folha de São Paulo*, 6 June 2013, accessed 23 December 2018, www1.folha.uol.com.br/educacao/2013/06/1290566-brasil-financiara-melhoria-de-ensino-superior-na-africa.shtml.

trilateral forum has been largely eclipsed by the BRICS group that was formally established in 2009. Nevertheless, IBSA has operated a Facility for Poverty and Hunger Alleviation (IBSA Fund) since 2006 with a modest annual contribution of $1 million per member. The IBSA Fund, which is managed by the Special Unit for South–South Cooperation at UNDP, has undertaken small projects in Burundi, Cabo Verde, Comoros, Guinea-Bissau, Sierra Leone and Sudan; Cambodia, East Timor, Laos and Vietnam; Fiji; Guyana, Haiti and Saint Lucia; and Palestine. By the end of 2017, it had disbursed a total of $32 million. The projects have been conducted in the areas of food security, energy, health, education, capacity building and rural development with the aim of contributing to the fulfilment of the Millennium Development Goals. The IBSA Fund claims that the projects are replicable and scalable and that they can be disseminated to other interested developing countries as examples of best practices to fight poverty and hunger.[90] Nevertheless, Brazil has carried out far more trilateral technical cooperation projects in Africa with Western countries and Japan than as part of the IBSA Fund.[91]

Military and financial cooperation in Africa

Military cooperation is an area of bilateral cooperation that has received comparatively little publicity from the Brazilian authorities despite its significant expansion in recent years. Only 1% of ABC projects were in military cooperation during the Lula presidency, but this rose to 16% during the Dilma presidency. Celso Amorim was the Defence Minister during Dilma's first term from 2011to 2014; he had contributed considerably to making Africa a priority in Brazil's global foreign policy when serving as Lula's Foreign Minister.[92] Despite its overall success, in recent years Brazil's military cooperation has also suffered a few setbacks due to technical and financial constraints; this has raised doubts about the sustainability of the country's engagement in defence cooperation. The discovery of huge pre-salt oil reserves in Brazil's territorial waters by Petrobras in 2008 increased the country's security concerns in the South Atlantic, which is already of crucial importance for Brazil's economy.

[90] IBSA Fund, '2017 On-going Projects Reports', 2018, accessed 23 December 2018, http://tcdc2.undp.org/IBSA/projects/projects2017.htm.

[91] Adriana Erthal Abdenur and Danilo Marcondes de Souza Neto, 'O Brasil e a cooperação em defesa: a construção de uma identidade regional no Atlântico Sul', *Revista Brasileira de Política Internacional*, 57: 1 (2014), 4.

[92] Guilherme Ziebell de Oliveira, 'Política Africana do Brasil: Mudança entre Lula e Dilma?' *Conjuntura Austral*, 6:29 (2015), 41.

More than 90% of Brazilian oil is produced on offshore platforms and about 95% of the country's international trade is transported on the Atlantic.[93] Consecutive Brazilian defence guidelines, such as the National Defence Policy (2005, updated 2012), National Defence Strategy (2008, updated 2012), and National Defence White Book (2012), stressed the relevance of West and Southern African countries as potential partners in security cooperation in the South Atlantic.[94] As part of its maritime defence strategy in the region, Brazil has invested in the increase of its naval capacity, including the expansion of operations to the other side of the South Atlantic, and the planned establishment of an integrated surveillance system to monitor its vast exclusive economic zone. At the same time, Brazil has increased military cooperation with several African countries, particularly with Nigeria, Namibia, South Africa and the five Palop countries. In 1994, Brazil signed a defence cooperation agreement with Namibia and since then has become the main supplier and training partner of the country's Navy. Between 2003 and 2013, Brazil's Naval Academy trained a total of 1,315 naval officials from Namibia. However, this engagement with Namibia's Navy has not translated into new business opportunities for Brazil's defence industry, since Namibia signed an agreement with a Chinese company in 2011 for alternative supply of military hardware. In 2012, the Chinese-built warship *Elephant* arrived in Walvis Bay. The ship was also expected to serve as a logistical support vessel, including local cadet training. Namibia's sailors had previously gone to Brazil's Naval Academy for training.[95]

Since 1994, Brazil has signed other military cooperation agreements with Cabo Verde, South Africa, Guinea-Bissau, Mozambique, Nigeria, Senegal, Angola, and Equatorial Guinea.[96] In recent years, Brazil has trained navy personnel from South Africa, Angola, Guinea-Bissau, Mozambique, Nigeria, and Senegal. Brazil maintains naval advisory missions in Walvis Bay, Namibia (since 1994), Cabo Verde (2013) and São Tomé and Príncipe (2015). In the latter country, the Brazilian Navy trained 120 soldiers between 2014 and 2017 to establish a marine corps of the local Coast Guard. In addition, Brazilian and South African arms

[93] Abdenur and Neto, 'O Brasil e a cooperação em defesa', 9.

[94] Pedro Seabra, 'Brazil as a Security Actor in Africa: Reckoning and challenges ahead' *GIGA Focus Latin America*, 7 (2016), 2.

[95] Abdenur, Adriana Erthal Abdenur, 'China in Africa, Viewed from Brazil', *The Journal of Asian Studies*, 74:2 (2015), 262; Seabra, 'Brazil as a Security Actor', 4.

[96] Ivair Santos, 'A influência militar e das industrias brasileiras de armamento na África', *Portalafro*, 14 June 2015, accessed 23 December 2018, www.portalafro.com.br/a-influencia-militar-e-da-industria-de-armas-brasilieras-na-africa.

producers have cooperated since 2007 in the production of short-range air-to-air A-Darter missiles, which entered production in 2015.[97] In 2014, Brazil and Angola signed an agreement on the construction of seven patrol boats for the latter's Navy. At an estimated cost of $170 million, the first four vessels were to be built in Brazil and the other three in Angola. However, in 2016 the deal was revoked because the Brazilian shipyards lacked the logistical capacity to keep the agreed deadline for the delivery of the vessels.[98] Nevertheless, on the whole, public and private Brazilian arms dealers have successfully increased their sales to African countries, as had already happened in the 1980s. To capitalise on government incentives to promote Brazil's defence industry, several construction companies including Norberto Odebrecht and Andrade Gutierrez have established defence branches to participate in the growth of arms production.[99] Since 2012, Brazil's aircraft manufacturer, Embraer, has been selling its Super Tucano A-29 military training and light combat aircraft to Angola, Burkina Faso, Ghana, Mali, Mauretania, Nigeria and Senegal.[100] In 2016, Brazil went back on its 2009 promise to donate Tucano training aircraft of its Air Force to Mozambique due to cutbacks in the military budget in the financial crisis.[101] From 2000 to 2013, Brazil supplied small arms and ammunition worth more than $70 million to twenty-eight African countries. The main clients were Algeria, Botswana, South Africa, Kenya, and Angola.[102] The sales contributed to Brazil's position as second-largest small arms exporter in the Western Hemisphere.[103] In 2013, Brazil was one of the first countries that signed the UN Arms Trade Treaty (ATT) aimed at regulating the

[97] Ministério de Defesa, 'Brasil e África do Sul fortalecem cooperação na área de defesa', 21 March 2014, accessed 30 December 2016, www.defesa.gov.br/index.php/noticias/8406-parceria-brasil-e-africa-do-sul-fortalecem-cooperacao-na-area-de-defesa.

[98] Seabra, 'Brazil as a Security Actor', 4.

[99] Abdenur, 'China in Africa', 263.

[100] *Defense Industry Daily*, 'Super Tucano Counter-Insurgency Plane Makes Inroads in Africa', 12 April 2017, accessed 23 December 2018, www.defenseindustrydaily.com/super-tucano-counter-insurgency-plane-makes-inroads-into-africa-07348.

[101] Seabra, 'Brazil as a Security Actor', 4.

[102] Nathan Thompson and Robert Muggah, 'The Blue Amazon: Brazil asserts its influence across the Atlantic', *Foreign Affairs*, 11 June 2015, accessed 23 December 2018, www.foreignaffairs.com/articles/africa/2015-06-11/blue-amazon.

[103] Abdenur and Neto, 'Brazil's Development Cooperation', 23.

international trade of conventional arms, but had still not ratified it in August 2017.[104]

As already noted, Brazil does not include its financial cooperation with developing countries in the official statistics of its international development cooperation. However, credits provided by several Brazilian financial institutions have been an important instrument to expand the country's investments and exports in African countries. The bulk of investment projects executed in African countries have been financed by the *Banco Nacional de Desenvolvimento* (BNDES – Brazilian Development Bank), which is responsible to the Ministry of Development, Industry and Foreign Trade. In late 2013, BNDES opened a regional Africa office in Johannesburg, South Africa, to increase its engagement on the continent. Until 2007, BNDES had conceded loans totalling $742 million to finance twenty-nine infrastructure projects in African countries. From 2007 to 2015, the institution approved additional loans for Brazilian investments in Africa worth $4.15 billion. The bulk of this amount was provided to finance infrastructure projects in Angola (84%), with the remainder going to Mozambique (10.7%) and Ghana (5.2%). The large construction companies of Norberto Odebrecht, Camargo Corrêa, OAS, Construtora Queiroz Galvão and Construtora Andrade Gutierrez have been the major beneficiaries of these loans. Since 2014, these construction companies and the oil company, Petrobras, have been the principal targets of the operation *Lava Jato* (Car Wash) by the country's Federal Police, which is investigating a series of corruption cases that have also involved many prominent politicians from all the main political parties, including former President Lula, who has repeatedly denied any wrongdoing. Several politicians and company managers have already been detained, tried and sentenced to prison terms in what has become by far Brazil's major corruption scandal ever. The criminal investigations have also included several loan arrangements that benefited these companies in Africa. In October 2016 BNDES announced it was suspending the disbursement of $4.7 billion for twenty-five loans conceded to the five construction companies for investment projects abroad that were under investigation as part as the *Lava Jato* operation. The measure affected projects in nine Latin American and African countries, including four projects in Angola, one in Ghana and one in Mozambique.[105] In

104 UN Office for Disarmaments Affairs, 'The Arms Trade Treaty', n.d., accessed 5 January 2018, www.un.org/disarmament/convarms/att.

105 Danielle Nogueira, 'BNDES suspende US$4,7 bi de desembolso a obras no exterior', *O Globo*, 11 October 2016, accessed 23 December 2018, http://oglobo.globo.com/economia/bndes-suspende-us-47-bi-de-desembolso-obras-no-exterior-20274312.

March 2017, after an in-depth inquiry, BNDES resumed the payment of a loan for a road construction project by Andrade Gutierrez in Ghana. The project started in 2013; it represented a total investment of $202 million, 70% of which was financed by BNDES.[106] BNDES has also opened credit lines for twelve African banks totalling between $300 million and $400 million to finance Brazilian exports to the continent. In these financial operations, the African banks assume the risk of the local importers.[107]

The main institution financing exports is the *Câmara de Comércio Exterior* (CAMEX – Chamber of External Trade), which is also associated with the Ministry of Development, Industry and Foreign Trade. CAMEX has conceded loans worth $640 million for export promotion as part of the food security programme *Mais Alimentos Internacional* (More Food International), which was initiated in 2010 under the name *Mais Alimentos África* (More Food for Africa). The project, which was renamed in 2012 when Cuba was included, is based on the *Programa Mais Alimentos* (More Food Programme) executed in Brazil since 2008 with the aim of increasing food production by modernising family-run farms. The goal of the African programme, which is coordinated by the Ministry of Agrarian Development, is to help small farmer families boost food production and create employment in rural areas in the five participating African countries Ghana, Kenya, Mozambique, Senegal and Zimbabwe. In 2011, CAMEX disbursed credits of $240 million and a further $400 million in 2012. As part of the programme, Ghana, Mozambique and Zimbabwe benefited from credits worth $95.5 million, $97.6 million ad $98.6 million respectively, with a fifteen-year term and 2% annual interest; this was for the acquisition of tractors, agricultural machinery and other inputs from Brazil, where more than a hundred companies participate in the export promotion initiative.

The *Programa de Financiamento às Exportações* (PROEX – Export Financing Programme) is the main export promotion instrument operated by CAMEX. It has existed since 1991 and is managed by the state-owned *Banco do Brasil*. PROEX either finances the Brazilian exporter

[106] BNDES, 'BNDES retoma desembolsos para mais dois contratos de exportação de serviços de engenharia' 16 March 2017, accessed 23 December 2018, www.bndes.gov.br/wps/portal/site/home/imprensa/noticias/conteudo/bndes-retoma-desembolsos-para-mais-dois-contratos-de-exportacao-de-servicos-de-engenharia.

[107] Francisco Góes, 'Acordo entre BNDES e banco africano eleva potencial de exportações para o continente', *Valor Econômico*, 4 December 2015, accessed 23 December 2018, www.valor.com.br/brasil/4342050/acordo-entre-bndes-e-banco-africano-eleva-potencial-de-exportacoes-para-o-continente.

or the foreign importer. The programme's export financing for Africa decreased from $266 million in 2005 (54% of the total) to only $20.2 million in 2010 (4%). PROEX offers two modalities for export promotion: PROEX financing for Brazilian companies with an annual turnover up to R$600 million with terms of financing that vary between sixty days and ten years and a maximum of 85% of export value above two years; and PROEX equalisation for companies of any size with financing terms of between sixty days and fifteen years with up to 100% of export value. From 2010 to 2016, Angola ($62.8 million) was by far the main African beneficiary of PROEX financing export credits, followed by Mozambique ($44.7 million), Zimbabwe ($33.4 million), Ghana ($32.5 million), Senegal ($28.5 million), South Africa ($22.1 million), and Morocco ($8.6 million). In the same period, Angola was also the African country with by far the biggest share of PROEX equalisation export credits ($158.8 million), followed by Ghana ($38.8 million), South Africa ($17.9 million), Mozambique ($17 million), Algeria ($13.6 million), Ethiopia ($8.7 million), and Egypt ($4.9 million).[108]

In addition, Brazil has renegotiated or pardoned bilateral debts with African countries to give these countries access to new credits, since the BNDES rules do not permit the concession of loans to countries indebted to Brazil. Consequently, the debt relief was also expected to benefit Brazilian trade and investments in the continent. During the Lula government, bilateral debts with African countries worth almost $1 billion were rescheduled or pardoned, at the time almost 75% of their total outstanding debts with Brazil. In 2013, President Dilma rescheduled another $900 million with twelve African countries. However, neither export promotion by PROEX credits nor debt forgiveness to permit African countries to contract new loans have been able to halt the marked decline in Brazil's foreign trade with Africa in recent years. From 2000 to 2011, Brazil's trade with African countries increased six fold, from $4.2 billion to $27.6 billion. With annual growth rates of 16%, Brazil achieved the second-highest rise in trade with Africa, after China.[109] Despite such impressive growth rates, Brazil's trade with the entire African continent of fifty-four countries was worth about the same as that with Germany, but far from the levels of Brazilian trade

[108] Ministério da Indústria, Comércio Exterior e Serviços, 'Programa de Financiamento às Exportações – Proex', n.d. accessed 11 December 2017, www.camex.gov.br/financiamento-e-garantia-as-exportacoes/programa-de-financiamento-as-exportacoes-proex.

[109] Stolte, *Brazil's Africa Strategy*, 99.

with Argentina, the United States or China.[110] In 2013, Brazil's external trade with Africa reached a record $28.5 billion but it then fell steadily from $26.8 billion in 2014 to $17 billion in 2015 and to $12.4 billion in 2016. At the same time, Africa's share of Brazil's foreign trade also decreased from 5.7% in 2013 to 3.9% in 2016. The Brazilian economy started to recover in 2016 and, as a result, trade with Africa increased by 20% in 2017 to $14.9 billion, equivalent to 4% of the country's foreign trade. Until 2016, the downward trend in the trade relations with Angola, traditionally one of Brazil's five most important trading partners in the continent, was particularly dramatic. From 2013 Brazilian exports to Angola fell from $1,271 million to $540 million in 2016, while imports from Angola declined in the same period from $727 million to just $72 million. However, in 2017, exports to Angola recovered to $670 million and imports increased to $266 million.[111]

Conclusions

In the mid-2000s, Brazil emerged as a rising power in international development cooperation. The Lula government used international cooperation as a foreign policy tool in its quest to be recognised as a major global player in a multipolar world. Africa played a particular role in this strategy, since the neighbouring continent comprises fifty-four countries. Brazilian diplomacy has claimed comparative advantages in bilateral relations with Africa due to similar geographic and climatic conditions and a shared history resulting from the Atlantic slave trade and the consequent 50% share of the Brazilian population of at least partial African descent. Brazil's development cooperation is conceived as South–South cooperation based on a horizontal relationship between equal partners providing mutual benefits. The country claims that, as a developing nation with its own experience of underdevelopment, it is in a better position than traditional donor countries to provide adequate projects of technical cooperation that enhance the socioeconomic development of the African partner countries. The ABC has coordinated and monitored the bulk of Brazil's technical cooperation projects. Until 2011, the ABC budget in general and for Africa in particular increased considerably both in terms of value and the number of projects. However, due

[110] Ibid., 135.

[111] Ministério da Indústria, Comércio Exterior e Serviços, 'Balança comercial brasileira: Países e Blocos', accessed 15 April 2018, www.mdic.gov.br/index.php/comercio-exterior/estatisticas-de-comercio-exterior/balanca-comercial-brasileira-mensal-2.

to Brazil's economic crisis, there has since been a steady decline in the budget and the number of projects, which raises doubts about the sustainability of the scope of Brazil's development cooperation. In addition, the problems encountered during the implementation of several projects in Africa, as well as the fierce political contestation in the case of ProSAVANA in Mozambique, have raised questions about the superiority of Brazil's technical cooperation and the claimed absence of commercial interests associated to bilateral development cooperation. Despite a few innovative approaches, Brazilian development cooperation as a whole is possibly more similar to the practices of other industrialised countries in the field than official political rhetoric suggests. The expansion of Brazil's weaponry exports in Africa and the ongoing criminal investigation into the concession of government loans for the construction of large infrastructure projects by Brazilian companies in African countries put the ethics of the country's relations with Africa in question. Irrespective of considerations about the supposed superiority of Brazilian technical cooperation in qualitative terms, it must be considered a success as a foreign policy strategy, since it made an undeniable contribution to raising the country's visibility and prestige in its desire to play a major role in global politics in the 2000s.

5

The South Atlantic in the Framework of Brazil–Africa Relations

Analúcia Danilevicz Pereira

Introduction

The South Atlantic is an extremely important axis for Brazil largely due to relations with the African continent. In a superficial analysis made by some critics, the Brazilian strategy is defined as paradoxical in that it appears to be fostering diplomacy with the poorest countries that have little influence in the global geopolitical context and even less significance in the Brazilian balance of trade. However, it is necessary to evaluate some political and economic trends linked to the ever-enlarging globalisation process. Mention must be made of the fact that Brazil is not only a traditional (and now competitive) exporter of primary products, services and manufactured goods but also of capital and technology. Africa is one of the most suitable targets for Brazilian investments because it is one of the last natural borders still receptive to expanding business in sectors like oil, gas and mining; moreover, the continent also emerges as an important space for political and diplomatic exchanges. On the other hand, there are global disputes over access in the region to the increasingly scarce raw materials required by the traditional powers that have intensified their aggressive and interventionist actions.

Thus, from the Brazilian perspective, the South Atlantic provides a solid connection with Africa (especially South Africa) and Asia through the Indian Ocean. In addition to the south of the African continent becoming a logistical base, it has emerged that the South Atlantic (and also the Indian Ocean) is full of energy resources with gas and oil reserves in the pre-salt layer. There have been new discoveries on both Atlantic coasts and in considerable parts of the Indian Ocean. As a result, not only must sovereignty over the territorial waters be clearly defined and the necessary security for navigation in the Ocean maintained, but any militarisation initiative by extra-regional powers in these maritime spaces must be blocked.

The increasing economic importance of the South Atlantic is accompanied by growing international pressure on the region. It is important to note the expanding military presence of the United Kingdom (with the support of the United States) due to the dispute with Argentina over the Malvinas/Falklands Islands. Therefore, the countries on both coasts are guaranteed economic rights but they must also assume duties and responsibilities on political, environmental and public safety issues to ensure effective control and maintenance of state sovereignty. Moreover, regional countries need to demonstrate maritime power, both in terms of defence and also so that they can work together to tackle the great challenges and processes that are part of the South Atlantic strategic context. It is also urgent to control the maritime routes and illegal activities in the Ocean as well as the exploration of natural resources in international waters.[1]

The historical importance of the South Atlantic to Brazil–Africa relations

The strategic importance of the South Atlantic can be analysed from many perspectives. However, geopolitics must be taken into consideration when evaluating forces that drive the formulations of foreign policy and its impact on international relations. Relations between Brazil and the African continent are old and deep, and the links are stronger than with Portugal. It is not only about the 'Africanisation' of Brazil due to the arrival of the first slaves and the foundation of a socioeconomic structure that lasted throughout colonial and imperial Brazil, but also the establishment of a strategic axis of political and economic-commercial relations that gained its own dynamics in the 17th century by gradually reducing Portugal's capacity to interfere.

With the advent of the *Pax Britannica*, the South Atlantic, Brazil and Africa acquired a new meaning in the global strategy of the hegemonic power of the 19th century, and this caused the potential of the Brazil–Africa axis to stagnate. However, it is difficult to explain why it took so long for Brazil to rebuild an African policy. In the early 20th century, some Brazilian authorities expressed interest in Africa, not as a supplier of labour as in previous centuries, but as a place to trade.[2] The trade was

[1] See Daniel Flemes and Alcides Costa Vaz, *Regional Security Contexts as Constraints for a Common Agenda: Security policies of India, Brazil and South Africa*, GIGA Working Paper no.160 (Hamburg: GIGA German Institute of Global and Area Studies, 2011).

[2] After the 1930 Revolution in Brazil, Afrânio de Melo Franco, Foreign Minister, sought to give impetus to a new trade policy, that led to the trade agreements of

not constant or on a large scale, and European domination undoubtedly controlled or inhibited relations until decolonisation in Africa. Nevertheless, foreign policy was guided by the United States–Western Europe axis and, as a result, it took some time for Brazil to see the African continent as an area for cooperation. Not only did it close its doors to internationalisation, but also to the possibility of overcoming its economic agro-export model.

During the Second World War, there was fresh interest in Africa and notably northern Africa. At the time, the Foreign Minister Osvaldo Aranha decided to send a diplomatic agent to the region as its strategic importance in the war was increasing. Vasco Leitão da Cunha was chosen for the position and was to study the possibility of establishing a consulate in Algiers. Missions were sent to determine the possibility of military cooperation with the Allies before sending the Brazilian Expeditionary Force in 1942.[3]

In the decade following the war, between 1945 and 1955, Brazil's non-participation in Africa's evolution led to discontinuity in relations again. Brazil limited itself to formal and small manifestations in favour of the first African emancipations, announcing its support for 'reconciliation' between the new States and their former colonial powers. Despite the rhetoric in support of a 'union of all people in the work of international reconciliation', the South American continental policy and maintaining the link with Western Europe was Brazil's main concern.[4]

It is curious to note that even when Brazil was isolated as a result of the strength of American capitalism and European impairment (when Europe saw Africa as its last opportunity to be reborn as a power pole), Brazil rejected the possibility of expanding trade with the Soviet Union, Eastern European countries and China that, together, comprised about one billion potential clients.

This can be observed in the government policy of Juscelino Kubitschek (1956–61). His government was focused on the Pan-American Operation or on the idea of the valuation of Latin America, and it showed no great enthusiasm for the explosion of African independence; there were ten independent countries in 1958 and seventeen new countries achieved their freedom in 1960. The Brazilian reaction was limited to

1931 and 1932 with the United Kingdom; this extended reciprocal treatment to the colonies, protectorates and territories under the British mandate that was no less favourable than that accorded to any other country. See footnote 3.

[3] José Honório Rodrigues, *Brasil e África: outro horizonte* (Rio de Janeiro: Editora Civilização Brasileira, 1964), 225.

[4] João Fernandes Café Filho apud Rodrigues, *Brasil e África*, 227.

formal recognition of their independence. Despite the Brazilian government's commitment to American policy, the neglect of the African processes proved a mistake that soon brought harmful consequences. In fact, Brazil took some time to identify itself as a 'historical and strategic partner' for the new African nations, which reveals the lack of a vision of the future international system. According to Rodrigues,

> The lack of attention to Africa, whose West salient is a few hours flight from our Northeast coast, and the importance of the South Atlantic, which is the base of our plans for economic cooperation and strategic defence, impose new directions for our foreign policy. Neither the lesson of the Great War [...] nor our links with Africa taught us that probably our manifest destiny, which emerged from the past, collides in the present and will advance in the future, is to have broad intercontinental policies to improve our protection and security and to develop our foreign trade.[5]

The Independent Foreign Policy, from 1961 to 1964, brought a more consistent approach but was followed by a period of distancing during the first two military governments (1964–69). Relations between Brazil and Africa, especially with Lusophone countries, improved greatly in the Médici government and until the end of Sarney's government (1969–90), with strong cooperation in several areas. However, relations cooled again during the neoliberal governments of Fernando Collor de Mello (1990–92) and Fernando Henrique Cardoso (1995–2002) at a time of globalisation. It was at the turn of the century, especially from the beginning of the Lula government (2003–10), that the African continent finally became a priority for Brazil.

Besides being a trade route and an important geo-economic space, the South Atlantic is also a development pole. In this context, it is worth recalling that Brazil's projection towards Africa and Asia was followed by that of China and India towards South America and Africa. The South Atlantic therefore emerges as a platform for the creation of strategic partnerships between the countries lying on its coast and between these countries and the Asian States, and proves to be decisive to the development of South–South Cooperation policies. Within the dynamics of such politics, it is in the African continent that coalitions in the South converge.

Brazil and the South Atlantic

Taking into account the vast territory under Brazilian jurisdiction, the country needs to have the ability to project political power, especially in

[5] Rodrigues, *Brasil e África*, 218. Translated by the author.

what concerns the sea. Brazil has a privileged position – the Caribbean and North Atlantic lie to the north; Antarctica to the south; and, the West African coast to the east (1,500 nautical miles away).[6] The east and south-east coast are favourable for locating ports and are the most productive areas in the country; most navigation goes via this route. It should also be noted that Brazil has a coastline of more than 7,500 km (4,660 miles) in length (four times longer than that of Angola), and 320 km (200 miles) of territorial sea with a sea bed of 4.4 million square km (1.7 million square miles) and rich underwater natural resources. It is therefore no surprise that there is great national interest in preserving the territorial integrity and natural resources, given the area's economic and political potential.

The South Atlantic is of particular importance to Brazil, especially due to the recent (and increasing) interest of countries like the United Kingdom, United States, Germany, France, Russia, China and Japan. The proximity to Antarctica (its privileged position between three oceans is seen as vital to Brazilian navigation) and its climatic effects over the territory must be taken into account when formulating Brazil's policy for the region. As most of Brazil's foreign trade is via the ocean, and considering the strong fishing activities and oil exploration in the South American continental shelf, the Brazilian Navy had to develop its navigation capacities in deep waters. Fostering security in the region must be seen as one of the main objectives of national security.

Consequently, Brazil opened a debate on the delimitation of the territorial sea. The United Nations Convention on the Law of the Sea (UNCLOS) of 1982 came as a result of this discussion that dated back to 1970. Thus, Brazil's intention to set 200 nautical miles was defended in the final report of UNCLOS. Article 76 of UNCLOS defines the demarcation process of the Outer Limits of the Continental Shelf beyond 200 nautical miles. According to the Convention, after its ratification each country would have a ten-year period to submit an application for the extension of this limit, based on the scientific mapping of the continental shelf. The Brazilian mapping had already been started in 1987 and was delivered in 2004; the operation cost $40 million, half of which was financed by Petrobras. In the United Nations report, Brazil claimed the inclusion of the Amazon cone, the Brazilian North chain, the Victoria and Trinity chain, the São Paulo plateau and the south continental shelf. The United Nations allowed the full inclusion of the São Paulo plateau

[6] A nautical mile is a unit of measure of length or distance equivalent to 1.151 land miles.

and 75% of the other claimed areas. However, Brazil is still pursuing the area initially claimed.

The enlargement of Brazilian rights to maritime territory is accompanied by greater obligations in the South Atlantic. After the ratification of the International Convention for the Safety of Life at Sea and the International Convention on Maritime Search and Rescue, Brazil had to set up a monitoring system of vessels located in the maritime area, and became responsible for search and rescue vessels and shipwrecked people. As a result, the country increased its maritime area of monitoring and surveillance from 4.5 million square km (1.73 million square miles) of its continental shelf to almost 14 million square km (5.4 million square miles).

In addition to legal responsibilities, Brazil seeks to consolidate its position in the South Atlantic using non-traditional programmes to project power. The development of public policies fostering fisheries, coastal navigation, scientific research and tourist activities constitute this 'subjective' element of consolidating Brazil's involvement. In this sense, and considering also the proximity to Africa, Brazil's engagement is understood as contributing to the improved control of the area. By relying on good relations with countries on the other coast, Brazil distances itself from Washington and is better able to defend its national interests while facing France and the United Kingdom – countries that already have territorial possessions in the South Atlantic. Moreover, it is interesting to note that cooperation and the use of law are traditional in Brazilian foreign policy – they converge with the political context of multilateralism and are linked with Brazil's historical and cultural ties with the African continent.

During his first speech as President, Lula stressed the importance of strengthening these historical ties with the African continent and emphasised his determination to help develop Africa's great potential. The speech marked the return of Brazilian foreign policy towards the other side of the Atlantic, which since then has become a declared priority for the government of Brazil. During Lula's eight years in government, he headed twelve official missions in Africa accompanied by entourages of business executives as an expression of the real interest in expanding Brazilian business interests in the region. The missions also assisted in the rapprochement between the Mercosur countries and the Africans. Celso Amorim, Minister of Foreign Affairs of the Lula government, made sixty-seven visits to Africa, going to thirty-four different countries. Amorim and Samuel Pinheiro Guimarães – general secretary of the Ministry of Foreign Affairs – gave priority to the African continent in the training of diplomats, and restructured the Department of African Affairs and the Middle East; he formed a Department for African Affairs, with three divisions and its own budget. Moreover, seventeen new embassies were opened. Less than one year after the start of her first mandate (2011–14), President Dilma Rousseff indicated the continuity of the African policy when she attended the IBSA Dialogue Forum meeting in South Africa, and with subsequent visits to Angola and Mozambique.

Africa's importance to Brazilian policy can also be demonstrated in numbers. According to the World Bank Report, in 2009, 50% of Brazilian international development projects financed by the Agência Brasileira de Cooperação (Brazilian Development Agency – ABC) were allocated to the African continent.[7] In 2011, the figure rose to almost 60% and totalled more than $22 million. The technical cooperation projects are also of great relevance to Brazilian foreign policy, where Africa represented 46.4% of all technical cooperation undertaken by ABC between 2011 and 2013, that is R$62.8 million (around $18 million). The Palop countries, mainly Mozambique, are among Brazil's main partners in Africa.[8] However, technical cooperation has subsequently declined significantly. Even if critics question the validity of getting involved with poorer countries with limited participation in the Brazilian balance of trade, Africa appears as an excellent destination for Brazilian exports and investments as well as serving as a trade route to the Indian Ocean. Moreover, as the report of the World Bank/IPEA points out, Brazilian knowledge of medicine and tropical agriculture constitutes a unique opportunity for African countries to import effective solutions for development in these two areas. In addition, there is African interest in the Brazilian social assistance projects. Social inequality is similar on both sides of the Atlantic, and the outstanding success of social programmes such as *Fome Zero* (Zero Hunger), has led to the implementation of adaptations of these social assistance systems in Angola, Kenya and Senegal, among others, since 2003. Even though it is still early to make an assessment of the results obtained, the initiatives demonstrate Brazil's intended long-term involvement in Africa.

Similar interests between the two sides, the search for common solutions to common issues, the importance of safeguarding peace in order to strengthen regional development and integration, and increasing trade with the Southern African nations comprise the major premises of Brazil's African policy. Despite the great international recognition

[7] The World Bank and IPEA, *Bridging the Atlantic: Brazil and Sub-Saharan Africa South-South partnering for growth* (Brasília: IPEA, 2011).

[8] Carlos R.S. Milani. *ABC 30 anos História e Desafios Futuros* (Brasília: Agência Brasileira de Cooperação, 2017), 76.

of the importance of Brazil's development cooperation with Africa, the Brazilian government has gradually reduced the amount disbursed since 2013.[9] It is necessary to analyse geo-economic and geo-strategic dimensions in order to evaluate the renewed importance of the South Atlantic in the 21st century.

The geo-economic dimension: Cooperation and development

It should be noted that the South Atlantic comprises four large archipelagos and islands of different importance and size, as well as different nationalities, with an extensive coastal region that covers part of the American, African and Antarctic continents. The African coast extends from Senegal to the Cape, with more than 7,800 km (4,847 miles), of which 1,200 km (745 miles) are the Angolan and Namibian Deserts. There are twenty-one countries on this coast, including the island nations of Cabo Verde and São Tomé and Príncipe. The few natural ports include Freetown, in Sierra Leone; Boma, in the Republic of Congo; Libreville, in Gabon; Douala, in Cameroon; Luanda, in Angola; Walvis Bay, in Namibia; and Cape Town, in South Africa.

The eastern South American coast starts at the Orange Cape in North-eastern Brazil and extends to the Tierra del Fuego Cape. It is 10,800 km (6,710 miles) long, of which 5,970 km (3,710 miles) belong to Brazil, 330 km (205 miles) to Uruguay and 4,500 km (2,795 miles) to Argentina. The maritime area of the British islands in the South Atlantic must be added to this. The South American coast has many natural ports, such as Recife, Salvador, Rio de Janeiro, Paranaguá, Santos, Porto Alegre and Rio Grande. The Antarctic coast extends from the Antarctic Peninsula to the Maud Land (or Queen Maud Land), opposite Cape Town. This is one of most difficult coastal regions in the world to access, particularly the Weddell Sea. Due to the geo-strategic separation of the southern region of the Atlantic Ocean and Antarctica into two different subsystems, 60° S latitude was defined as the limit of the South Atlantic region. As such, the Ocean can be accessed in three ways – through the North Atlantic, the South Pacific and the Indian Ocean. This interconnectivity is one of the principal reasons for the call for security cooperation and the maintenance of the South Atlantic area as a pacific zone and a development space.

However, in light of the renewed strategic importance of the South Atlantic and Brazil–Africa relations, it is essential to go further and

[9] Milani, *ABC 30 Anos*, 76–77.

consider the economic alliances as fundamental to the development of both margins of the ocean, as well as the importance of Antarctica. Hence there is a need to improve Brazil's protection and defence facilities and to strengthen bonds of cooperation and friendship.

Fishing is a key activity for the coastal communities and is in urgent need of vigilance and control. The ineffective combat of predatory fishing by foreign ships with high technology that disrespect environmental law results in economic and social damage that must be tackled. However, one of the most relevant factors to consider in relation to security in the region is merchant shipping, since about 95% of Brazilian exports and imports pass through the South Atlantic. According to the Brazilian Navy, the Brazilian and possibly the African Continental Shelf have huge resources of polymetallic nodules (found in abundance in the Peruvian Basin) containing metals of great economic value, as well as monazitic sand with significant uranium concentration.

In addition to Brazil's new pre-salt reserves, there are also reserves on the Argentinean Continental Shelf as well as considerable offshore reserves of petroleum in the Gulf of Guinea, mainly in Nigeria, Angola, Gabon and Equatorial Guinea. On the Western Coast of Africa, Namibia also possesses vast deposits of gas, and South Africa has deposits of coal.

With the discovery and exploration of the pre-salt layer, the region gained even more economic importance, which makes the need to regulate oil exploration, and also the other aforementioned resources, a crucial measure for countries on both margins. The geo-economic relevance of the Ocean is also strengthened by the fact that it borders Antarctica, which is considered a new frontier for exploration. This area will undoubtedly be subject to greater international pressure in the near future.

The geo-strategic dimension: The urgent consolidation of a peace and cooperation zone

Brazil has developed policies for the exchange of military techniques with African countries and India, creating a complex securitisation network that interconnects the three continents. Given the increasing geo-economic importance of the South Atlantic, the military exchanges between the two margins assume a relevant role in the relations between the three countries.[10] It is worth highlighting the biennial joint exercises of the Indian, Brazilian, and South African navies, IBSAMAR, that have

[10] See Flemes and Vaz, 'Regional Security Contexts'.

regularly taken place since 2008. This important repeated multilateral event has gone almost unnoticed by the local population of the countries involved. India and Brazil have strong navies totalling more than 50,000 ships, much more significant in terms of numbers than that of South Africa, and can therefore play the coordination role in the future. On the other hand, South Africa has a long coastal area (it is a bi-oceanic country) and a limited naval capacity to monitor and protect it, thus creating an opportunity for all three navies to act in these areas. Moreover, the Cape of Good Hope is used increasingly as a trade route. (It is worth recalling that the action of Somali pirates made the Suez route very dangerous.)

The trilateral relations between India, Brazil and South Africa (IBSA) are very well consolidated, and in conjunction with regional neighbours inclined to multilateralism, this can constitute a new distribution of power and – according to Kornegay – represents the 'geopolitical and geo-economic reunification of Gondwana' (the former mega-continent that united South America, Africa, India and Australia).[11] From the trilateral perspective, the geo-strategic logic of IBSA is clear – the objective is to create a maritime liaison between the South Atlantic and the Indian Ocean. What each country seeks through this depends on their individual and joint political will to form the geopolitical and strategic terms of the 21st century.[12] The last IBSAMAR took place off the West Coast of India in February 2016 with the participation of five vessels, as well as helicopters and aircraft from India.

In spite of some limitations in terms of regional security – especially in the case of India and South Africa – relations between the IBSA members seem to strengthen the regional objectives of its parties. Furthermore, the three countries occupy a relevant international position; the acronym may not only fortify this position but also be a way of promoting a new political orientation. IBSA emerges at a new crossroads in world history in which there is a leadership vacuum in terms of global political legitimacy and geopolitics marked increasingly by energy and resources competition. This aspect is also related to the threat of environmental deterioration on a global scale. Therefore, IBSA could assume a role that promotes a new orientation for the geopolitics of energy in favour of a new responsibility (ethical and pro-conservation) as the cornerstone of global governance.

[11] Francis Kornegay, *South Africa, the Indian Ocean and the IBSA-BRICS Equation: Reflections on geopolitical and strategic dimension*, ORF Occasional Paper (New Delhi, 2011), 12.

[12] Ibid., 1.

As mentioned earlier, the South Atlantic is of particular importance to Brazil, especially due to the recent (and increasing) interest of states like the United Kingdom, United States, Germany, France, Russia, China and Japan. Historically, the proposal of a South Atlantic security organisation went back on the agenda in 1977 at the initiative of the Commander of the Uruguayan Navy. The organisation that would be known as the South Atlantic Treaty Organisation (SATO) would follow the North Atlantic Treaty Organisation (NATO) model. The Brazilian government rejected the Uruguayan proposal, advocating that SATO would lead to an arms race in the region and that the Southern countries would not have the required capacity to face a possible 'Soviet threat' without North American support. The Brazilian rejection brought South Africa and Argentina closer, an alliance that would soon be dismantled due to the dispute over the Malvinas/Falkland Islands in 1982. South Africa started to encourage a rapprochement with Bolivia, Paraguay and Chile in order to implement the SATO proposal. Chile drew closer to South Africa through a huge irrigation project in conjunction with the United Kingdom. However, the idea of setting up the organisation was gradually put aside because it could not have functioned according to the initial plan.

Nevertheless, Brazil felt the need to guarantee the region's security and therefore had to revise the original idea of SATO. The question was then how to implement the mechanism and its composition. In the late 1980s, Brazil proposed the Zona de Paz e Cooperação do Atlântico Sul (South Atlantic Peace and Cooperation Zone –ZOPACAS) as a counterpart to SATO. Due to its regional importance, Brazil obtained the support of the countries bordering the South Atlantic Ocean. However, South Africa and Namibia were not included in the proposal because South Africa's apartheid regime was isolated and Namibia was still ruled by the South Africans. The change of position came after the 50th United Nations General Assembly in 1986, when the Resolution A/RES/41/11 defined the South Atlantic as a peace and cooperation zone.[13] The second and third articles of the Resolution called on the regional countries to unite in order to maintain peace by the demilitarisation of the area, the non-introduction of mass destruction weapons and non-nuclearisation. It is interesting to note that when voting took place, the Resolution received 124 votes in favour, eight abstentions (all from Western countries) and one vote against – from the United States. The idea of South Atlantic

[13] See Moses Bangani Khanyile, 'South Africa's Security Relations with the Mercosur Countries' (PhD dissertation, Pretoria: University of Pretoria, Faculty of Humanities, 2005).

demilitarisation and denuclearisation was not supported by the developed countries, considering that they have clear interests in the region's natural resources.

The fifth article of the Resolution was of great relevance to South Africa as it established the end of the apartheid regime and the self-determination and autonomy of Namibia. Moreover, it determined the end not only of all aggressions between the regional states but also that of any kind of support for colonialism and racism and their consequences. Therefore, the Resolution covered four of the region's problematic issues: environment, socioeconomic development, peace and security, and the emancipation of South Africa and its neighbours.

The first ZOPACAS meeting took place in Rio de Janeiro in 1988, the second in Abuja, Nigeria in 1990, and the third in Brasília in 1994. However, the fourth meeting in South Africa in 1996 is considered unique for many reasons. Under the 'Bridging the South Atlantic' theme, the gathering emphasised the region's importance for both coasts. ZOPACAS activities were supported by many organisations such as the International Maritime Organisation (IMO). Since 1994, Brazil has been South Africa's biggest partner in South America, and one of the biggest in the Southern Hemisphere. In 1995, about 50% of the South African exports went to Brazil, and South Africa had a foreign trade surplus with Brazil. In that year, Otto Maia became the first career diplomat to be appointed ambassador to South Africa.

Nelson Mandela's visit to Brazil in 1998 when he signed the Memorandum of Understanding Concerning Consultations on Issues of Common Interest was another landmark in Brazil–African relations. Further agreements on technical cooperation, double taxation, promotion and security of investments followed. Mandela's successor, Thabo Mbeki, visited Brazil in 2000 when he also met Mercosur leaders. Before the constitution of IBSA and the later realisation of IBSAMAR joint military exercises, South Africa and Brazil had already been part of three exercises under North American influence – the ATLASUR (a biannual naval event that took place for the first time in 1993 involving Brazil, Uruguay, Argentina and South Africa), UNITAS (naval exercises that involved the aforementioned countries plus Chile, Colombia, Ecuador, Paraguay, Peru, Venezuela and the United States) and the TRANSOCEANIC.[14] Unlike the others, the last is a transport control exercise that does not involve ships. In addition to the exercises sponsored by

[14] See Moses Bangani Khanyile, 'South Africa's Post-1994 Military Relations with the Mercosur Countries: Prospects and challenges', *Strategic Review for Southern Africa*, 26:2 (2004).

the US, bilateral initiatives also took place such as the Brazilian Task Group with South Africa and Brazil; an exercise with Uruguay, Brazil and Argentina; and another with South Africa and Chile.

Lula's arrival coincided with the end of the Mbeki government when Brazil and South Africa increased their diplomatic and military interaction in the IBSA framework. Steeped in a positive perception of South–South Cooperation as a means of achieving greater political autonomy and international prominence, the politics of both countries converged and relations were intensified and improved through BRICS (Brazil, Russia, India, China and South Africa) and IBSA. The two international mechanisms have different objectives but are equally important for the foreign policy of the two countries. While BRICS gives more importance to the reform of global governance and the financial system, IBSA aims to contribute to the construction of a new international architecture and also seeks to deepen mutual knowledge in specific areas, such as public administration and governance, tributary and customs administration, agriculture, human settlements, science and technology, commerce and investments, culture, defence, social development, education, energy, environment and climate changes, health, information society, transportation, and tourism, among others.

Through the IBSA Fund and the action of work groups, the three countries are improving their know-how and technical cooperation in the above areas. It is also important to stress the work of IBSA Ocean which is a research group in the Antarctic continent. At its second meeting, four main areas of action and a master plan were defined, namely:

- Variability and Climate Changes (the construction of a joint database and the IBSA Earth System Model are planned);
- Impact of Climate Changes on Ecosystems, Carbon Fluxes and Biogeochemistry (including ecosystems offshore and on the coastline);
- Impact of Global Changes on Living Beings, on Biodiversity and on Management planning (including the harmful algal blooms and fishing);
- Regional Ocean Observing Systems.

Although lacking military involvement, this is very relevant to the understanding of the security space that the three countries are developing.

Political and strategic coordination and cooperation for development: The cases of the South Atlantic Peace and Cooperation Zone and the Gulf of Guinea Commission

The creation of ZOPACAS in 1986 and the Gulf of Guinea Commission (GGC) in 2001 represent initiatives was linked to the developing countries' perception of changes in the distribution of world power. The current international system is constituted by multiple centres of power, which allow strategic areas to emerge due to the role played by their economic growth potential due to their energy resources, among other things.

Even though created at different times, the motivations and objectives of these organisations have now converged. Their member countries share the perception that the South Atlantic is an area of stability in the region where political, economic and military ties can be developed. The South Atlantic is therefore perceived as a space of furthering cooperation for development, security and greater international projection. Preserving this area from tensions and conflicts is extremely important to the global balance, given the large amount of minerals and energy resources in the region that are essential for the development of all nations.

The region is again part of the calculations of extra-regional strategic powers largely due to the South Atlantic's particularities as a route of passage and trade, as a means of access and flow of energy products, and the strengthening of state capacity of the region's countries. Thus, ZOPACAS and GGC have gained more prominence in the regional order, seeking to increasingly develop greater cooperation on strategic issues. Therefore, the point of convergence between the two organisations is clearly the need to develop political and strategic coordination mechanisms in order to ensure sovereignty and the maintenance of dialogue between the states involved.

The South Atlantic Peace and Cooperation Zone (ZOPACAS)

As observed above, ZOPACAS was formed as a result of the pressure placed on Brazil to take a position in light of the South Atlantic situation due to changes in the dynamics of the Cold War (Washington–Moscow rapprochement).[15] However, US rhetoric was still about the continuing

[15] The creation of ZOPACAS was inspired by the Akinyemi Doctrine, launched ten years earlier. This doctrine was an initiative of a group of strategists and political thinkers from Nigeria that raised for the first time the idea of political cooperation between Nigeria, Angola and Brazil, around the South Atlantic, in quite different terms from those defended in the SATO initiative. This Nigerian initiative postulated a non-alignment of the South Atlantic countries based on

bipolar dispute. Therefore, as part of the Western bloc, Brazil was expected take into account the US accusations about the Soviet Union's plan to get close to the South Atlantic area, considered to be part of Western dominance (Africa was under European control and the whole American continent under US control). However, despite some internal differences, Brazil avoided positioning itself in such a way because it did not perceive the Soviet Union as a threat and also doubted the veracity of the US claims.[16]

On the other hand, some surrounding countries raised objections to Brazil's failure to take a position as they believed Brazil was about to support SATO – which aimed to militarise the Ocean, behaving as a NATO 'complement' to impede the Soviet projection in the South Atlantic area.[17]

In this framework, and by defending the non-militarisation of the South Atlantic, Brazil proposed creating an autonomous mechanism without the interference of extra-regional powers, and which would allow discussion between the regional countries on security issues and cooperation opportunities. The inclusion of 'cooperation' within the ZOPACAS group showed the growing importance Brazil was giving to the countries on the other side of the Atlantic in the international context of the oil shock and economic protectionism of the world's leading economies. It is important to remember that Brazil started to abandon the ideological barriers of its foreign policy from the mid-1970s and boosted its relations with the African continent, especially with the former Portuguese colonies.

Finally, Brazil sought not only to establish a cooperation policy with the new independent African countries, but also to revise its relations with Portugal and South Africa, positioning itself in favour of the end of the apartheid regime and the independence of Namibia. In this context, Brazil's association with SATO would trigger an undesirable reaction from African countries that considered this pact as a likely source of regional insecurity, and a threat to the independent nations' stability and

---

the main intention of keeping the ocean free of bipolar tensions. See Marcelo A. de M. Jardim, 'A Zona de Paz e Cooperação do Atlântico Sul' (dissertation, Brasília: Instituto Rio Branco, 1991).

16 Andrew Hurrell, 'The Politics of South Atlantic Security: A survey of proposals for a South Atlantic Treaty Organization', *International Affairs*, 59:2 (1983), 179–93.

17 Francis Kornegay 'South Africa, the South Atlantic and the IBSA-BRICS Equation: The transatlantic space in transition', *Austral: Brazilian Journal of Strategy and International Relations*, 2:3 (2013), 92, translated by the author.

to world peace.[18] The Brazilian Foreign Ministry therefore decided not to sacrifice the recent efforts to foster political relations with Africa and to stress the use of the South Atlantic based on inter-regional relations distinguished by its horizontal nature (South–South).

The ZOPACAS group is currently formed by the three countries of the east coast of South America with coastline in the South Atlantic (Brazil, Argentina and Uruguay), and twenty-one countries of the west coast of Africa (given that South Africa and Namibia were not initially part of the forum).[19] The First Ministerial Meeting of ZOPACAS in 1988 was attended by representatives of all initial twenty-two member countries. At this meeting, the aim was to exchange preliminary information on the points of convergence between them, emphasising the interrelationship of peace, security and development issues. In addition, there was strong rhetoric against any kind of intervention from foreign powers, citing the situations in the Malvinas and in Southern Africa, such as the Angolan civil war, the apartheid regime and the Namibia occupation. The final document of the meeting expressed the determination to study mechanisms to strengthen and increase cooperation ties between the countries involved, including the exchange of technological and scientific knowledge and considering issues about the environment and the South Atlantic resources. On this occasion, mention was also made of the importance of UNCLOS as an essential pillar in the process of strengthening cooperation and promoting studies on the subject.[20]

During the 1990s, ZOCOPAS weakened, reflecting the international situation marked by the end of the Cold War and the globalisation process. This framework led to the loss of the geo-strategic importance of the South Atlantic, as well as the political and diplomatic retreat by the neoliberal governments in power. As a result, the consolidation of ZOPACAS was not only affected by international and regional political changes, but also by the economic circumstances of the South American and African continents. The difficulty of allocating resources in order to achieve the ZOPACAS aims and the lack of institutionalisation of the forum came together with a change in priorities (realignment to North

[18] Joy Ogwu, 'Nigeria and Brazil: A model for the emerging South-South relations?' in *South-South Relations in a Changing World Order* edited by Jeker Arlsson (Uppsala: Scandinavian Institute of African Studies, 1982), 102–27.

[19] Angola, Benin, Cabo Verde, Cameroon, Côte d'Ivoire, Democratic Republic of the Congo, Equatorial Guinea, Gabon, Gambia, Ghana, Guinea, Guinea-Bissau, Liberia, Namibia (joined 1990), Nigeria, Republic of Congo, São Tomé and Príncipe, Senegal, Sierra Leone, South Africa (1994) and Togo.

[20] United Nations General Assembly, *Resolution A/43/512 (1988) Annex – Zone of Peace and Cooperation of the South Atlantic* (New York: 1988).

powers), causing inertia and neglect of the organisation and its strategic objectives.

In this scenario, the forum was almost abandoned but was saved by a Brazilian initiative to revitalise it and refocus, given the imminent end of the Cold War. As such, the Third Ministerial Meeting of ZOPACAS was held in 1994; this was the first to be attended by South Africa under the chairmanship of the African National Congress (ANC). This meeting was central to the definition of a cooperative agenda as it adopted the Declaration of Commercial Cooperation in the South Atlantic. Furthermore, ZOPACAS gained more status by also adopting the Declaration of Denuclearisation of the South Atlantic and the Declaration of Maritime Environment.[21] However, the following meetings took place without any great advance and still under the impact of the economic marginalisation of South American and African countries during the 1990s. In African countries, the economic crises worsened due to problems intrinsic to the creation of States. In Brazil, the neoliberal government policies resulted in a change of priorities related to international affairs. A Fourth Ministerial Meeting of ZOPACAS took place in Walvis Bay, South Africa, in 1996 and a fifth meeting in Buenos Aires, Argentina, in 1998.

Significant changes in the world scenario took place between the meetings in Buenos Aires (1998) and Luanda (in 2007), speeding up the trend towards the multipolarisation of the international system. The 2000s were marked by the abandoning of the neoliberal route in Latin American and African countries. It is worth mentioning that China's rapid rise was one of the main drivers of change in Africa and especially in Angola – the country that initiated the revitalisation of ZOPACAS in 2007. Thus, African countries received major investments and financing from the 'Washington Consensus' and the 'Beijing Consensus' that accelerated their economic and social growth. For instance, this new situation meant a major change in Angola, a country just coming out of a civil war; it raised the possibility of shared leadership in Southern Africa with South Africa. It should be noted that, while Nigeria and South Africa seemed to be more focused on coping with their internal problems, Angola projected itself regionally and internationally with relative autonomy. This projection was supported mainly by its oil sector, in which China has invested significantly.

On the other side of the South Atlantic, Brazil was also making important changes in its foreign policy, and multilateralism again became a priority mechanism of regional and international performance. This can

[21] United Nations. General Assembly, *Resolution A/49/467 (1994) Annex IV – Zone of Peace and Cooperation of the South Atlantic* (New York, 1994).

be observed in the deepening of the regional integration project and the launch of the Unión de Naciones Suramericanas (Union of South American Nations – UNASUR) in 2004, the entry into IBSA and BRICS, and also Africa's placement as the central axis of Brazil's foreign relations. Along with the country's economic stability and growth, a new vulnerability emerged, raising the question of the delay in the modernisation of the armed forces, and the country's weaknesses in the defence of its sovereignty. In this context, President Lula da Silva supported the continuation of the efforts to consolidate the ZOPACAS, and included its revitalisation in the Brazilian White Paper on National Defence. In the framework of ZOPACAS, Brazil helped with military training in several coastal countries and provided technical assistance for the mapping of the continental shelves.

The Luanda meeting in 2007 was therefore an attempt to revitalise the forum. The presence of representatives from twenty-four member states demonstrated that they were all interested in resuming the cooperation project in the South Atlantic. As a result of the meeting, the Luanda Action Plan defined an agenda for the three key issues: disarmament and non-proliferation; cooperation for development; and economic issues. In accordance with the objectives, working groups were formed for the discussion of problems such as economic cooperation for the eradication of poverty, combating transnational crimes, peace, stability and security, scientific research, environmental issues and the implementation of joint projects in these fields.[22]

However, 2007 was also marked by the start of the global financial crisis. The crisis demonstrated the fragility of the financial system sponsored by the United States and Europe, thus providing opportunities for the emerging countries. Accordingly, although the ZOPACAS revitalisation process started advancing due to the countries' increased participation, the Zone subsequently slowed its activity as concerns about economic stability developed among the member countries. However, at the Montevideo meeting in 2013, the Brazilian Defence Minister Celso Amorim called attention to the need to reinvigorate the forum, suggesting the inclusion at ZOPACAS of seminars on defence issues in the Action Plan. He also highlighted the importance of expanding defence cooperation, saying: 'In today's world, it is very difficult to say exactly where, how and what external interventions will take place in any conflicts that may arise'.[23]

[22] Kornegay, 'South Africa, the South Atlantic', 94.

[23] *Defesanet*, 'ZOPACAS – Amorim propõe ações para fortalecer cooperação em Defesa', 16 January 2013, www.defesanet.com.br/geopolitica/noticia/9322/

There was also discussion on that occasion about the need for the African Union to join forces with ECOWAS (the Economic Community of West African States) and the CPLP (the Comunidade de Países de Língua Portuguesa – Community of Portuguese-speaking Countries) in response to difficult situations in the Democratic Republic of the Congo (DRC) and Guinea-Bissau. Moreover, the Montevideo meeting was marked by the definition of four major areas for cooperation: mapping and exploitation of the seabed; environmental cooperation (oceanography, fisheries and others); security (defence, maritime safety and combating transnational crimes); and transport (ports, maritime and air transport).

Although the multilateral forum has been weakening for years, Brazil and Africa have made persistent attempts to firmly consolidate ZOPACAS. Such a framework is strengthened mainly due to the fact that the extra-regional threats have changed in the South Atlantic area; this is not only related to the potential expansion of natural gas and oil production on both sides of the Ocean (that can be considered part of the 'oil route'), but also to the strengthening of state capacity of some countries in the region. So over the coming years, the awareness of the benefits provided by the prospect of cooperation between the two South Atlantic margins will be extremely important to maintain ZOPACAS as an initiative of key significance to the nations' future.

The Gulf of Guinea Commission (GGC)

The Gulf of Guinea Commission, formed in November 1999, united the region's countries around the idea that it was necessary to develop a mechanism for cooperation and political coordination for conflict resolution, as well as the regulation and harmonisation of natural resource exploitation. The formation of this organisation was due mainly to Nigerian President Olusegun Obasanjo (1999–2007), who had brought back the autonomist discourse and the continental projection aim.[24]

In July 2001, the constituent treaty of GGC was signed in Libreville, Gabon, by eight of the region's countries: Angola, Cameroon, DRC, Equatorial Guinea, Gabon, Nigeria, Republic of Congo, and São Tomé and Príncipe. It is important to bear in mind that African oil production is concentrated in the Gulf of Guinea (70%), in other words, the

---

ZOPACAS---Amorim-propoe-acoes-para-fortalecer-cooperacao-em-Defesa, accessed 17 December 2018. Translated by the author.

[24] See Barcelona Centre for International Affairs (CIDOB), CIDOB International Yearbook 2008. *Country Profile: Nigeria and its regional context* (Barcelona, 2008).

Commission brings together the largest oil producers in Sub-Saharan Africa. In fact, Nigeria and Angola stand out not only for their production levels, but also because they are longstanding members of the Organisation of Petroleum Exporting Countries (OPEC), while Gabon, Equatorial Guinea and the Republic of Congo joined the organisation recently.[25]

At a meeting of the member countries in 2006, Carlos Gomes of São Tomé and Príncipe was nominated to the Executive Secretariat with a three-year mandate. It was decided that the headquarters would be in Luanda, with the Angolan government then in charge of the budget for its operation for one year. In the 2006 declaration, the Commission underlined its central role in resolving and dealing with regional conflicts (caused by the lack of delimitation of maritime boundaries, the economic and commercial exploitation of natural resources located within the territorial limits, and other issues), and cooperation for development and security was considered a central concern. Furthermore, in accordance with the principles of the African Union, the Commission strengthened the non-aggression pacts and mutual assistance.[26]

In 2007, the Commission officially began its operations and maritime threats to the Gulf countries were therefore dealt with together. The second meeting took place in Luanda in November 2008 and served to integrate GGC into the regional dynamics. It should be noted that, even though the leadership of GGC was originally Nigerian, Angola's increasing role led to closer ties between the two countries. According to Kornegay, the two countries operate in a complementary form inside the Commission: Angola plays an important role in the Regional Centre for Maritime Security in Central Africa (known by the French acronym CRESMAC) – due to its leadership in the Economic Community of Central African Countries (ECCAS) – while Nigeria leads the creation of a naval force for the region, prepared with regard to the defence and security of the Gulf of Guinea oil industry.[27]

[25] Abel Esterhuyse, 'A Iraquização da África. Africom: a perspectiva sul-africana', *Air & Space Power Journal Edição em Português*, 21:1 (2010), 78. Gabon was a member of OPEC from 1975–95 and rejoined the organisation in 2016. Equatorial Guinea and the Republic of Congo joined OPEC in 2017 and 2018 respectively.

[26] Abel T. García, La política exterior de Estados Unidos hacia el Golfo de Guinea durante la administración de W. Bush (Buenos Aires: CLACSO, 2011), 432; Eugênio Costa Almeida and Luís Manuel B. Bernardino, 'A Comissão do Golfo da Guiné e a Zona de Paz e Cooperação do Atlântico Sul. Organizações Interzonais para a persecução da Segurança Marítima na Bacia Meridional Atlântica', *Revista Militar* 2532 (2013), 43–61.

[27] Kornegay, 'South Africa, the South Atlantic', 96.

The growing diplomatic activities of Angola were evident at the Luanda Conference on Peace and Security in the Gulf of Guinea in 2012, which was organised by the Angolan government and GGC. The Luanda Declaration expressed the countries' major concerns on security; the focus was on internal vulnerabilities linked to underdevelopment, arbitrary borders, the porosity of those borders and the conflicts caused by disputed territories, piracy, illegal trade and illegal immigration issues.[28] According to the Declaration, environmental threats and illegal fishing are also problems that GGC seeks to combat autonomously.

Besides the consensus on the need for the Gulf of Guinea region to remain peaceful, there was discussion on creating common policies to combat the possible threats to security. Furthermore, the Luanda Declaration states the intention of the countries in the region to work closely with other regional organisations on implementing a long-term strategy in order to achieve the security and development objectives regarding the use of the sea and territories. Thus involves cooperation with the African Union, the United Nations, the South Atlantic Peace and Cooperation Zone, the Economic Community of Central African Countries, and the Economic Community of West African Countries.

Similarly, the Conference held in Yaoundé in June 2013 called on regional organisations to work together on Gulf security. As such, the Third Meeting of the Heads of State and Government of the Guinea Gulf Commission held in Malabo, Equatorial Guinea, in August 2013 was attended by representatives of ECOWAS and ECCAS. During the meeting, new positions were created and people appointed to them.[29] At the 2013 meeting, Miguel Trovoada, former President of São Tomé and Príncipe (1991–2001) and Executive Secretary of GGC from 2009–14, stated that the Gulf of Guinea Commission had moved on to a new phase as it had managed to fulfil two objectives in five years without presidential meetings: (1) consolidation as an autonomous sub-regional institution of Africa allowing it to gain international visibility and establish important dialogues with other regional organisations; and (2) the consolidation of its own strategy to combat threats in the maritime area of the Gulf of Guinea.[30]

[28] IRI, Luanda Final Declaration of the VIth Meeting of Member States of the Zone of Peace and Cooperation of the South Atlantic, 18–19 June 2007.

[29] Namely: Nigeria, Executive Secretary; Angola, Assistant Executive Secretary for Political Affairs; Cameroon, Assistant Executive Secretary for Natural Resources; Gabon, Financial Director; Equatorial Guinea, Managing Director and President. In addition, Ghana and Liberia were also represented at the meeting.

[30] See more at: *Dnotícias*, 'Comissão do Golfo da Guiné propõe órgão para questões de defesa e segurança', 10 August 2013, www.dnoticias.pt/

In August 2013 and in line with the proposal made by the then Angolan President, José Eduardo dos Santos (1979–2017), the VIII Council of Ministers of the Gulf of Guinea Commission advocated the creation of a security and defence committee, under the authority of the Executive Committee, due to increased maritime insecurity in the area. Furthermore, it stressed that the main objectives of the institution are defence, peace and security; combating piracy and other unlawful acts at sea; marine environment protection; maritime communications; the prevention, management and resolution of conflicts; the cooperation and harmonisation of policies on exploitation of marine resources; and the delimitation of the Exclusive Economic Zones (EEZ).[31] It should be noted that Angola plays a very important role in the South Atlantic organisations as it works hard to make GGC the main decision-making mechanism on the security and defence of the Gulf of Guinea region. This position constitutes a strategic aspect that can connect the agendas of African and South American organisations. In addition, GGC itself already provides a suitable platform for the strategic convergence of pan-African agendas.[32] The collaboration between regional organisations not only ensures they join forces in political cooperation, but also strengthens the discourse of autonomy and the development of a common strategy for the Gulf of Guinea and for the South Atlantic.

The Gulf of Guinea Commission has resized its activities through a process of broadening and deepening since 2007 – a decisive year for the African Atlantic coast due to the discovery of new energy resources. Since then the organisation has dealt more specifically with security and defence affairs on the coast so that the states in the region develop a common strategy focusing on possible threats to security. In this context, Angola, São Tomé and Príncipe, Nigeria and Equatorial Guinea have been the Commission's most important actors.

The South Atlantic Peace and Cooperation Zone and the Gulf of Guinea Commission: The increasing relevance of the South Atlantic

The two regional organisations, ZOPACAS and GGC, have converging interests and perceptions. Above all, they define the South Atlantic as a multilateral cooperation area for the provision of security and, consequently, foster conditions for the development of the region's countries.

---

hemeroteca/400603-comissao-do-golfo-da-guine-propoe-orgao-para-questoes-de-defesa-e-seguranca-FODN400603, accessed: 11 December 2018.

[31] Ibid.

[32] Kornegay, 'South Africa, the South Atlantic', 96.

The South Atlantic area receives worldwide attention not only due to its commercial routes and as a source of energy products, but also because it contains many mineral resources of great economic relevance. Thus, it is an area of fundamental geo-economic and geo-strategic importance. Although of great importance since the colonial era, the region has gained more visibility with the discovery and exploitation of offshore oil reserves and the geopolitical turn to the South. This draws the attention of extra-regional powers already present in the region due to their military control of several islands in the South Atlantic passage.

The region's importance and strategic significance in the production and exploration of hydrocarbons must be seen in a much broader context which is dominated by the interests both of traditional powers and today's major world consumers, such as India and China.[33] Indeed, studies indicate that the Persian Gulf's position as a major supplier of oil may gradually be transferred to the Gulf of Guinea. The Gulf of Guinea occupies a key geo-strategic position; in addition to being a large oil region with over 15% of world production, it connects the other African sub-regions; for example, the construction of the important 'Chad–Cameroon' pipeline and its possible extension will link Niger, the Central African Republic, Sudan and Libya – an area with more than 250 million inhabitants.[34] Moreover, oil from the Gulf of Guinea stands out for its quality, the fact that most of its reserves are located offshore and therefore less vulnerable to crises and conflicts, and the ease of transportation to international markets.

In these matters, the geo-strategic importance of the South Atlantic region should be seen in a broader context as global powers are striving to ensure control of the main oil and natural gas regions. This raises extremely important issues for coastal countries, such as the militarisation of this space and consequently new challenges for regional countries in their cooperation projects. These are of relevance to both GGC and ZOPACAS, and foster cooperation mechanisms between the two organisations. Undoubtedly, the South Atlantic has become one of the most thriving areas in the early 21st century because of its production and exploitation of hydrocarbons, and its importance for international maritime transport. Hence, an analysis should be made of how the extra-regional powers have responded to the autonomous movements of the South Atlantic countries and how concerns have converged in the South Atlantic region.

[33] See Eduardo Beny, *A nova geopolítica do petróleo: do Golfo Pérsico ao Golfo da Guiné* (Lisbon: Novo Imbondeiro, 2007).

[34] García, *La política exterior*, 394.

The Euro-American response

The revitalisation of the geopolitical and geo-strategic importance of the South Atlantic in international relations was recognised by the developed countries that were major players in Africa and they have responded to these autonomous movements by reinforcing their military presence or by stimulating triangular cooperation.[35] The United States announced it would be setting up the United States Africa Command (AFRICOM) when the Gulf of Guinea Commission resumed its activities in March 2007, and a meeting took place on the revitalisation of ZOPACAS in June that year. Since then, the US command for Africa has dissociated itself from the EUCOM (European Command) and the CENTCOM (US Central Command), claiming that this would give its armed forces a more effective and integrated approach. When the formation of AFRICOM was announced, the US Defence Secretary, Robert M. Gates, defined the function of the command as the 'cooperation supervisor for security, partnerships capacity building, defence support to non-military missions and, if directed, military operations within the continent'.[36]

An analysis of the setting up of AFRICOM reveals the strategic importance the continent acquired for US foreign policy in the second term of President George W. Bush (2004–09), notably in terms of security after the 9/11 attacks.[37] The US military presence in the Gulf region increased dramatically; no activity was recorded in 2004 but in 2006 the US Navy made continuous incursions in the region.[38] Mention should also be made of the US concern about China's growing involvement in Africa through increased trade and cooperation in the defence area. African countries favoured developing relations with China, which has undoubtedly emerged as an alternative to US influence.

Veiled behind the War on Terrorism strategy, the United States revealed its interest in the oil reserves in Africa when it set up AFRICOM, in order to reduce its dependence on the Middle East at a time when underlying tensions in the region endangered US access to energy resources. The Gulf of Guinea where, as noted, 70% of Africa's oil

[35] See Mônica Hirst, 'Países de renda média e a cooperação Sul-Sul: entre o conceitual e o político', in *Brasil, Índia e África do Sul: desafios e oportunidades para novas parcerias* edited by Maria Regina Soares de Lima and Mônica Hirst (São Paulo: Paz e Terra, 2009).

[36] Esterhuyse, 'A Iraquização da África', 75; Ian Taylor, *The International Relations of Sub-Saharan Africa* (London: The Continuum International Publishing Group, 2010), 28.

[37] Taylor, *The International Relations*, 24.

[38] García, *La política exterior*, 420.

production is concentrated, was already supplying 20% of US demand in 2007.[39]

From the start, the action of AFRICOM did not have the direct support of any African leader, except that of Mali.[40] As a result, it was decided to have AFRICOM headquarters in Stuttgart, Germany instead of Africa, as originally planned. In addition, its operations are supported by a base on Ascension Island in the South Atlantic and another in Djibouti in a strategic region of East Africa.[41] This therefore not only represents an undesirable presence of an extra-regional power in Africa but also a possible threat in the South Atlantic region.

In 2009, the United States also initiated the Regional Maritime Awareness Centre in the Gulf of Guinea, and plans to extend it to Cabo Verde in order to control and identify vessels transiting the region. Under the auspices of this initiative, the US positioned a surveillance radar in São Tomé and Príncipe in 2009. Thus, the US has full control of vessels that travel through Central Africa, particularly on the Nigerian and Angolan coasts where most of the Gulf's oil is produced,[42]

Through the sale of arms and military training, the US seeks to retain key regimes in power in Africa, especially among oil exporters. President Jimmy Carter's Persian Gulf policy of taking strategic positions in the South Atlantic and signing bilateral agreements with certain countries has therefore been resumed with the aim of reducing the financial and political costs of direct intervention,[43] In 2008, the US also relaunched the Fourth Fleet in the South Atlantic, where it had served between 1943 and 1950 – thus militarising the space again. This was officially with the aim of safeguarding the region from illicit trafficking and terrorism. According to Arraes, in practice the US quickly intervened whenever there was any instability contrary to their interests in the South Atlantic.[44] The reactivation of the Fourth Fleet was also intended to show emerging powers, like China, that the search for natural resources could be through military manoeuvres and use of force. But, in addition to demonstrating to China that it could take military action in the region,

[39] Esterhuyse, 'A Iraquização da África', 77–78.

[40] See Jeremy Keenan, *The Dark Sahara: America's War on Terror in Africa* (London: Pluto Press, 2009).

[41] Ian Taylor, *The International Relations*, 29.

[42] See Almeida and Bernardino, 'A Comissão do Golfo da Guiné'.

[43] Daniel Volman and Jeremy Keenan, 'The origins of AFRICOM: The Obama administration, the Sahara-Sahel and US militarization of Africa', *Concerned Africa Scholars Bulletin*, 85 (2010), 84–90.

[44] Virgílio Arraes, 'Estados Unidos: um possível significado para a Quarta Frota', *Meridiano*, 47: 97 (2008), 25.

the US showed South Atlantic countries (such as Brazil, Angola and Nigeria) its intention to monitor the South Atlantic with the clear objective of ensuring the regular supply of oil from African countries and, in the future, from the Brazilian pre-salt fields, in an effort to diversify energy sources.

It is interesting to note that US actions in South America go through the US Southern Command (SOUTHCOM), in which the Fourth Fleet is integrated. Thus, the US has bases in Colombia and Peru; a training centre in Fuerte Aguayo, Chile; and a 'humanitarian aid' centre in El Chaco, Argentina. It should be stressed that the province of El Chaco is located above the Guarani Aquifer, the largest cross-border potable water source in the world and second-largest underground water source, and it is also located near the Triple Frontier (that between Brazil, Argentina and Paraguay). In addition, Washington has a partnership with Bogotá, embodied in its Plan Colombia.[45] Therefore, the South Atlantic region is increasingly the focus of US strategic interests, especially in relation to natural resources. The US role in the region and its strategic demands operate against the principles of regional organisations such as ZOPACAS and GGC, which pursue a demilitarised South Atlantic area, and without the presence of extra-regional forces. In this framework, instability is an important variable that can soon take the form of conflict as it is also important to consider the historical European interests in the region.

While the US has a prominent position in the South Atlantic, European powers are traditional actors in Africa and they maintain their presence in the region in many ways through joint ventures with US policies. France is clearly trying to recover lost influence in Africa, but the UK and Portugal are also historical and maritime powers who regard the South Atlantic area as vital to their global power – so their action should not be overlooked. France first tried to maintain its hegemony in more politically fragile countries that were rich in natural resources in an effort to ensure the neo-colonial scheme which Verschave characterised as Françafrique; but on the other hand, as France cannot afford full hegemony, it strives to achieve its objectives in African countries through multilateral military efforts (particularly in the partnership with the UK and the US).[46] With the launch of the new 1996 defence policy,

[45] See Indira Olivo and Ernesto Navarro, 'EUA instalam novas bases militares na América do Sul, *Brasil de Fato* (30 May 2012); Arraes, 'Estados Unidos', 26.

[46] See François-Xavier Verschave, *De la françafrique à la mafiafrique* (Bruxelas: Éditions Tribord, 2004).

France tried to retain and strengthen its position in oil-producing countries like Cameroon, Gabon and the Republic of Congo.[47]

While France tried to implement its foreign policy more decisively, the United Kingdom implemented the Mayall policy (1986) of damage limitation. As noted by Clapham, regardless of the party in power, the common understanding in Whitehall seems to be that maintaining strong ties with Africa is more harmful than profitable.[48] Therefore, the United Kingdom intervenes only indirectly in the region, maintaining the 1997 policy of the Blair government. Since then, the United Kingdom has preferred to support actions by non-governmental organisations (NGOs), international organisations, companies, etc., as opposed to direct action on the continent.[49]

Whereas the British news talks about immigration and social and development issues, the British government specialises in arms sales to Africa, namely to South Africa, Algeria, Angola, Eritrea, Ethiopia, Kenya, Namibia, Sierra Leone, Somalia, Sudan, Uganda, Zambia and Zimbabwe. This is one of the priorities of the British Department for International Development.[50] In 2012, the British government demonstrated its intention to consolidate its place in the South Atlantic by sending a modern military Royal Navy ship, the destroyer HMS Dauntless, to the Malvinas/Falklands for the thirtieth anniversary of the end of the war to take the islands back from the Argentinians. In the South Atlantic, it is worth remembering that Whitehall also gave the Ascension Islands to AFRICOM and to NATO.

Interestingly, British domains permeate the South Atlantic; this ensures the expansion of the defence powers of the country's national territory, as well as their vital lines of maritime communication. The

[47] See Samuel S. Ndutumu, *Géopolitique Maritime du Golfe de Guinée au XXIe Siècle* (Paris: L'Harmattan, 2012); Shaun Gregory, *French Defense Policy into the Twenty-First Century* (Houndmills: Macmillan Press; New York: St. Martin's Press, 2000); Guy Martin, *Africa in World Politics: A pan-African perspective* (Asmara: Africa World Press, 2002).

[48] Christopher Clapham, Africa and the International System: The politics of state survival (Cambridge: Cambridge University Press, 1996), 88.

[49] Taylor, *The International Relations*, 48–49; see also Charles Ukeje and Wullson Mvomo Ela, *African Approaches to Maritime Security – The Gulf of Guinea* (Abuja: Friedrich-Ebert-Stiftung, 2013).

[50] Taylor, *The International Relations*, 39; see also Paul Williams, 'Britain and Africa after the Cold War: Beyond damage limitation?' in *Africa in International Politics: External involvement on the continent* edited by Paul Williams and Ian Taylor (London: Routledge, 2004).

Atlantic islands represent considerable strategic value, since they form the so-called 'geo-strategic triangles'.[51]

Only one of the triangles is not formed exclusively by territories under British control; this is the one closest to South America and is composed of Brazilian domains (Fernando de Noronha, Trinidad) and the Malvinas/Falklands – occupied by the British, but with sovereignty challenged by Argentina. The other two triangles are British: one, consisting of Ascension, St. Helena and Tristan da Cunha, is the support base in the Cape Route; and the other is composed of Gough, South Shetland, Georgia and South Sandwich. It should be noted that two large military bases equipped for air operations are located in Ascension and the Malvinas/Falkland Islands, which has the largest base in the South Atlantic.[52]

There is also a Portuguese geo-strategic triangle in the South Atlantic formed by the islands of the Azores, the archipelago of Madeira and Portugal, which contributes significantly to enhancing Portugal's functional power.[53] In addition, it has four former colonies in the Ocean that are home to a large number of Portuguese people, as well as the Portuguese community in South Africa. As a result, Portugal seeks to place itself as a country that binds Europe with the thriving Atlantic market – in a broad sense, without differing between North or South.[54]

The global financial crisis had a dramatic effect on the Portuguese economy, and as a result it intensified its policy of positioning Portugal as a pivot in the Europe–Africa relationship. In 2007, the same year as the Angolan initiative to revitalise ZOPACAS, Portugal was presiding over the Council of the European Union and the EU–Brazil and EU–Africa summits were launched as well as a strategic partnership with Cabo Verde. In addition to these summits, the 'Angola–European Union Joint Way Forward' agreement was signed in 2012. Portugal was clearly attempting to draw closer to its former colonies under the aegis of the European Union despite resistance from some African countries.[55]

[51] Therezinha de Castro, *Geopolítica: princípios, meios e fins* (Rio de Janeiro: Bibliex, 1999), 22.

[52] Ibid., 19.

[53] Luís Carlos Falcão Escorrega, 'Da Importância Geopolítica e Geoestratégica dos Açores no Actual Contexto Estratégico', *Revista Militar*, 2497/2498 (2010), 203.

[54] Martin, *Africa in World Politics*, 50; see also José Manuel D. Barroso, 'Um Portugal Atlântico ou um Portugal Europeu?' Speech 13/773, Algarve Business Forum, 5 October 2013.

[55] See Eli A Penha. *Relações Brasil-África e a Geopolítica do Atlântico Sul* (Salvador: EDUFBA, 2011).

It is also important to remember that Portugal belongs to NATO and therefore condones the organisation's strategies for the South Atlantic and the extension of its action area beyond the North Atlantic. A strategy defined at the NATO meeting in Lisbon in 2010 determined that intervention was possible in the South Atlantic as they believe the alliance is affected by issues beyond its borders in the north. The Atlantic Basin Initiative (ABI) emerged at this time; it would eliminate the separation between the North Atlantic and South Atlantic, with NATO taking responsibility for safeguarding.[56]

In October 2010, Brazil's Minister of Defence, Nelson Jobim, was invited to a round table on the ABI held in the Transatlantic Relations Centre at Johns Hopkins University in Washington, DC. The Minister highlighted the structural problems in this project, emphasising the fact that the circumstances of the North and South Atlantic are different. Minister Jobim also stressed several negative aspects of the ABI, such as the fact that it could open up a space for NATO's intervention in the South Atlantic region under various pretexts.[57]

These measures, which reflect the enhancement of the geopolitical importance of this region, do not represent actual benefits to coastal countries, and they interfere directly in their interests, especially in the context of ZOPACAS and GGC. The possibility of further European and US presence, and thus the militarisation of the South Atlantic, creates new challenges for countries in the region as it is a priority area and also essential for the development and safety of these nations.

Conclusions

It is important to underscore that, from Brazil's perspective, Africa is not simply a connection to Asia. The South Atlantic has witnessed discoveries of a myriad of natural resources, such as the Brazilian pre-salt or the new oil deposits in the Gulf of Guinea and on the Angolan coast – where Brazil is already investing and cooperating with the supply of technical resources for exploration. As a result, there is an urgent need to assure sovereignty over the territorial waters, maintain security in the oceans for navigation and block any militarisation initiative in these spaces by extra-regional powers. The need of the United States to control safer and cheaper oil deposits than those of Venezuela and the Middle East should also be considered as well as its close military relations with

[56] Marco Aurélio de Andrade Lima, *A iniciativa da Bacia do Atlântico: um risco para o Brasil?* (Rio de Janeiro: Escola Superior de Guerra, 2011), 29–32.
[57] Ibid., 32.

South Africa – from where it could enter the African continent and then the South Atlantic.

Despite criticisms, the countries in the region must develop military capacities whilst also emphasising ZOPACAS; this is particularly important due to the attempts to militarise the region, for instance, the Malvinas situation (UK), the re-creation of the Fourth Fleet (United States) and AFRICOM, and the US presence in South America through bases installed in the Colombian territory and elsewhere.

Brazil has understood the great potential of turning the South Atlantic into a security and energy supplier community, and seeks leadership in this project through its assertive policy of international projection. South Africa is located in a key position between the Indian and Atlantic Oceans and has a strong economy; it is therefore almost inevitably included when seeking engagement with the African continent.[58] It is interesting to note that the resolution of the African regional conflicts (for example, Angola and South Africa) boosted an 'African Turn of the Tide' and allowed Brazil to act in the rapprochement with and between these countries. The expansion of this relationship broadens the options inside SADC, which may lead to a joint maritime security plan that will bring the region closer to Brazil and, thus, strengthen IBSA. While the South Atlantic does not have an institutionalised organisation, as is the case of IOR-ARC (Indian Ocean Rim Association for Regional Cooperation), the international relations of the region should lead to a new transatlantic maritime security architecture.[59] The creation of the South American Defence Council, led by Brazil, is a step in this direction.

When addressing the resumption of the strategic importance of South Atlantic and Brazil–Africa relations, consideration must also be given to economic alliances as a key component for the development of both sides of the Ocean, as well as the significance of Antarctica, which is the only territory in the world without a defined sovereignty. Hence there is a need to improve the conditions for protection and defence and to deepen the cooperation ties and the good relations between those states.

In order to fully defend the sovereignty of its seas, Brazil needs to be in a consistent institutional architecture along with the coastal countries of Africa. In this regard, ZOPACAS plays an essential role for security. Only an institution with established objectives and ethics can provide a place for discussion, exchange of information and technical needs. Thus, the revitalisation process that ZOPACAS has seen in recent years – headed by Brazil and Angola – is of the utmost importance.

[58] Kornegay, *South Africa, the Indian Ocean*, 6.
[59] Ibid., 16.

However, ZOPACAS is still experiencing many difficulties. Many of its early challenges – such as South Africa's occupation of Namibia and the development of nuclear weapons by the apartheid regime – have been resolved. On the other hand, new and growing challenges make it necessary for ZOPACAS to become more consistently institutionalised and for its member states to work harder so it may be consolidated as a respected regional political actor.

Historically, the least developed nations have pursued integration and cooperation by working together to find a solution to their problems and to increase development. This can be seen in the pan-Africanism of the late 19th century and in today's integration mechanisms like the African Union (AU) and others. In the case of the Gulf of Guinea region, until 2001 the countries were scattered across different regional organisations: while some belonged to ECOWAS,[60] others were part of SADC[61] or ECCAS.[62]

It is clear that, since the turn of the century, the African continent has taken positive steps towards a new international insertion. Political processes have advanced and there is a clear intention to contain armed conflicts (in the awareness that many of these are related to foreign interests from extra-regional powers). Also, we have witnessed economic growth associated with satisfactory macroeconomic performance and an increase in self-confidence of the elites evidenced by new forms of political, economic and social relations. This African scenario can be identified as a new renaissance in the continent; its status in the world has risen and there is an optimistic environment.

However, Brazilian and African states' foreign policies have perceived the great potential of transforming the South Atlantic into a community of security and energy supply, as an alternative to the Euro–US system in the North Atlantic. Despite criticisms, regional countries must develop military capabilities whilst also emphasising the importance of ZOPACAS, especially given the militarisation attempts in the region noted above. These initiatives also include the proposal to create an Atlantic community that brings the North and the South of the Atlantic Ocean together in a geopolitical unit.

[60] Côte d'Ivoire, Togo, Benin, Nigeria and Ghana.
[61] Angola and DRC.
[62] Angola, Cameroon, Chad, DRC, Gabon, Equatorial Guinea, Republic of Congo, and São Tomé and Príncipe.

6

Africa in Brazil: Slavery, Integration, Exclusion

Antonia Aparecida Quintão

Introduction: The heritage of slavery for Afro-descendants

In discussing recent affirmative action policies with underlying racial elements in Brazil it is necessary for us to take a retrospective view that contextualises the trajectory of black men and women: the conquest, the struggles and the protagonism of the Negro descendant movements are inherent in the discussions and actions addressing the denouncement of racism and the formulation of inclusive politics.

The past and present of the Afro-Brazilian population and their descendants remain deeply related and need to be evaluated to enable future thinking. The Afro-descendants of the entire Americas went through a specific historic experience, namely, slavery; they were and continue to be marked by this fate. This historic past in conjunction with current racial prejudice still represents a severe obstacle for Afro-descendants. The official historiography in Brazil has long transmitted the deprecating idea of the passive and submissive Negro, who accepted enslavement without any reaction, because the institution of slavery had already been familiar in the African homeland.

This image of passivity and submission was contradicted by the sphere of permanent tensions that marked Brazil during almost four centuries of slavery: the conflicts that involved the black brotherhoods (slaves and freedmen), who venerated black saints such as Saint Elesban, Saint Iphigenia, Saint Benedict and, the most popular among them, Our Lady of the Rosary of Black Men.

Among slaves, there were also frequent suicides, murders of masters, uprisings and escapes; maroon communities (*quilombos*) were also formed that constituted eloquent manifestations of active resistance and can be interpreted as a strategies of disruption as they were not simple hideaways, but attempts of liberation and the construction of a new model of society inspired by African communities.[1]

[1] Kabengele Munanga, ed., *Estratégias e políticas de combate à discriminação racial* (São Paulo: Edusp, 1996). For more information on the maroon communities, see footnote 32.

As the historian Joel Rufino dos Santos writes: 'It is about making the Brazilian Negroes visible by this recovered past [...] Although this may seem a task of less importance, it is a first and indispensable step to promote them to the condition of Brazilian citizens.'[2]

The transition from slave labour to free labour

The second half of the 19th century was marked by a period of profound changes in the Brazilian economy. Prado Júnior's characterisation of the economic evolution during this period stresses the following developments: the progress of agricultural production, the nascent industries, the multiplication of commercial houses and banks, the accumulation of capital, demographic growth, the increase in international trade, the construction of railways (and to a lesser degree motorways), the establishment of the telegraph network, the strength of foreign loans and the progressive occupation of the national territory.[3] Coffee was the Empire's main cash crop and fundamentally needed two favourable inputs: an abundance of both land and labour. The latter was provided by the slave trade, which eventually was prohibited due to pressure from the British in 1850. The price of slaves began to increase, favouring their transfer from Brazil's economically decadent regions, particularly from the north-east to the south-eastern coffee-growing regions.

Another solution to satisfy the growing demand for labour was the adoption of free labour, with the first attempts at this dating back to 1850. The planter contracted workers in Europe; they agreed to sell him their labour, and the national government financed their journey. However, the transition to free labour was a slow process. 'Even on the eve of the abolition of slavery, slave labour was very widespread in São Paulo, Rio de Janeiro and Minas Gerais. Incidentally, these were the provinces most opposed to the abolition of slavery.'[4]

According to Prado Júnior, Brazil's international position on the question of slavery had become difficult since 1865, since liberation had already taken place in the United States; Brazil, together with Cuba, remained the only countries of the Western Hemisphere to permit slavery.[5] However, there were no uniform positions on this question. On the one hand, the northern regions had few reasons to defend slavery, even though many of these provinces had sold many slaves through the

[2] Joel Rufino dos Santos. *O que é racismo* (São Paulo: Brasiliense, 1983), 54.
[3] Caio Prado Júnior, *História Econômica do Brasil* (São Paulo: Brasiliense, 2006).
[4] Jacob Gorender, *O escravismo colonial*, 3rd ed. (São Paulo: Ática, 1980), 562.
[5] Prado Júnior, *História Econômica*.

internal slave trade. On the other hand, the coffee-producing areas of the south-east were the stronghold of the pro-slavery reaction. Yet, even within them, differences existed with regard to the degree of the commitment to the institution of slavery. For example, although captivity still had deep roots in the Paraíba Valley, the agriculture of west São Paulo had privileged conditions to adopt wage labour due to its better financial circumstances.

The 1870s were marked by increased tensions in slave labour relations. Discipline was tightened in the organisation of slave labour in that the master class feared for the survival of the institution. Thus they sought to get maximum productivity from slaves by using coercion and corporal punishment. This was widely reported by the paper *A Redenção*[6] ('The Redemption'), in the section 'scenes of slavery': 'The state of the corpse was horrible: buttocks flocked, broken head, one eye perforated, three ribs fractured. The forensic experts declared that the death was caused by the injuries. However, the master reported that he had died of colic.'[7]

The emancipatory laws

Emancipatory laws were enacted consecutively as a result of external and internal pressures beginning in 1871 and finally ending slavery in 1888.

The Law of Free Birth (*Lei do Ventre Livre*)

This law of 28 September 1871, also known as the Rio Branco Law, established that, thereafter, the children of slaves born in the Empire were considered 'free'. The master would leave the child with the mother until the age of eight when he could either deliver him/her to the government in exchange for compensation or keep the child until the age of

[6] The paper *A Redenção* was founded in January 1887 in the city of São Paulo. Created and published two times a week by the lawyer Antônio Bento, an advocate of the republic and the abolition of slavery, the periodical was defined as 'abolitionist, commercial and news journal'. *A Redenção* emerged as another instrument of the social and political struggle. In that period, many abolitionists worked as journalists or started writing to defend the cause of the captives. They promoted escapes of slaves and supported them to hide and live far away from the authorities. *A Redenção* contested slavers' ideas, tried to convince society about the need for change, and denounced farmers, judges, delegates and politicians, as well as other papers considered enemies of the cause. It ceased publication after the abolition of slavery in May 1888.

[7] *A Redenção*, vol. 1, January 1887, p.1.

twenty-one, using his/her services in exchange for the cost of his/her upkeep. This law stands out for the recognition of the property right through the compensation of the 'harmed' master. Alternatively the master could choose to keep the free child until the age of twenty-one and this was, in fact, frequently what they decided to do. Few children were handed over to the state: 118 out of the 400 children registered until 1885.

The Sexagenarian Law

This law, also known as Saraiva-Cotegipe, was adopted on 28 September 1885 to grant freedom to slaves over the age of sixty. However, as compensation, they had to work without payment for another five years. Even when this law was promulgated, it triggered a reaction since few slaves succeeded in reaching this age and these were mostly sick, disabled, or unfit for work. In other words, they were costly for owners and it was therefore advantageous to grant them freedom as the masters no longer had any obligation to them.

The Golden Law (*Lei Áurea*)

This famous law was approved on 13 May 1888 and marked by its extremely laconic character:

1) Slavery in Brazil is declared extinct.
2) Conflicting provisions are revoked.

There was no concern to ensure the survival of the liberated slaves. No action was taken to guarantee them lands, as abolitionists such as Joaquim Nabuco demanded insistently. No compensation rights were considered for the former slaves and their descendants; thus, they were abandoned to their own fate. According to the sociologist Florestan Fernandes (1920–95), the masters were freed from any responsibility for the maintenance and security of the freemen:

> As no collective impulse was expressed that led the whites to discern the necessity, the legitimacy and the urgency of social measures to protect the Negro (as person and as group) in this transition phase, to live in the city presupposed that he was condemned to an ambiguous and marginal existence.[8]

The difficult transition from slave to free labourer was aggravated by the prejudice against blacks, which assumed even more complex

[8] Florestan Fernandes, *A integração do negro na sociedade de classes*, vol. 1, 3rd ed. (São Paulo: Ática, 1978), 28.

configurations in order to consolidate the hierarchy of the social groups. Considered '*peças*' (pieces), 'barter object', 'thing', 'monetary exchange', 'merchandise belonging to the masters' they carried the marks of slavery on their bodies and the stereotypes imposed by whites that emphasised a vision of blacks as lazy, indolent, stupid, incapable, idle, soulless individuals, who by nature were servile and accustomed to submission.

The Afro-descendants, now freed, frequently were not hired even when labour was required. In addition, a decree of the newly established Brazilian Republic, dated 28 June 1890, determined that Africans and Asians could only be admitted to Brazil's ports with the authorisation of the National Congress. The same legislation was reaffirmed by the then President Getúlio Vargas, who decreed on 18 September 1943:

> Art. 1 – Every foreigner can enter Brazil when the requirements established by this law are met.
> Art. 2 – The admission of the immigrants will take into account the necessity to preserve and develop, in the ethnic composition of the population, the most appropriate characteristics of their European descent, as well as the defence of the national worker.

During over three centuries of slavery, Brazil received about five million slaves from diverse regions of Africa, which leads us to think of African cultural pluralism within Brazilian territory. However, soon after the formal abolition of slavery, the debate on the question of miscegenation was stimulated by concerns about the identity of Brazilian society. Analysed with scepticism by American and European travellers, feared by the elites, the racial question slowly seemed to become a central topic that shed light on Brazil's destinies.

Brazilian racial identity

The question of the constitution of a Brazilian 'racial identity' was first strengthened by the racial interpretations of theorists from outside the country. The 'race' factor was then understood as a type of vital influence in the civilising potential of a nation and racial theories published in Europe and particularly in France caused a great impact in Brazil. Brazil was portrayed in these reports as the first great example of 'the degeneration of a tropical country' of mixed races. At the time, social Darwinist authors were much quoted in Brazil due to their theories of black inferiority, the degeneration of 'mulattoes', and tropical decadency.

According to these intellectuals, the 'promiscuity' that occurred in colonial times had produced degenerated and unstable individuals, who were thus incapable of accompanying the progressive development.

Many Brazilian intellectuals believed in this claim and used the thoughts of European social Darwinism in their own theories. A good example is that of Raimundo Nina Rodrigues (1862–1906), considered the founder of scientific anthropology in Brazil. He believed that the inferiority of the Negro race could be established beyond any scientific doubt and claimed that it was impossible that the intelligence of 'representatives of inferior races' could achieve 'the high level reached by the superior races'.[9] This approach considered studies and essays that focused on the black race and even the question of miscegenation. Nina Rodrigues himself believed in a Brazil radically divided between a white south and a mestizo and degenerated north. Although interpretations of national authors varied, their fear for Brazil's racial future was predominant. Many argued that a white future was the only way to rescue Brazil from degeneration.

The theory of whitening

It was a 'thesis' that sought to outline new solutions for the 'discredited' national racial panorama, which caused great apprehension within Brazil's elites and intellectuals.

This new thesis, at the time called the 'theory of whitening' of the races, was grounded on deterministic racial theories developed in Europe. Ambiguity was the main particularity of this theory, since miscegenation was conceived both as an evil that should be eradicated and as a solution for Brazil's racial question. Using principles of eugenics, some authors suggested the possibility of the depuration of black and mixed-race characteristics after a few generations. This position was endorsed by 'national science'.

João Baptista Lacerda (1846–1915) was a physician and specialist in 'physical anthropology' who represented Brazil in the First Universal Races Congress in London in 1911; like most anthropologists of the time, he was very familiar with the scientific methods and techniques developed in Europe, as well as with the deterministic racial theories. According to Lacerda, there was no reason for concern since the black race would tend to disappear in about a century due to the abolition of slavery and the dispersion of the former slaves. A similar analysis was elaborated in the 1920s by Francisco José de Oliveira Viana (1883–1951); he believed progressive aryanisation would take place in Brazil

[9] Rodrigues, Raimundo Nina, *As Raças Humanas e a Responsabilidade Penal no Brasil* (Salvador: Livraria Progresso, 1957), 28.

not only due to white immigration, but also because of racial mixing and the mortality of black and mixed-race people.

Contrary to current interpretations that the 'ideology of whitening' had appeared in Brazil at the end of the 19th century, the anthropologist Andreas Hofbauer, argues that the 'ideas of whitening' were already present in the foundations of Brazil's colonial society. For Hofbauer, the idea of whitening went through several reformulations over the centuries and was adjusted to the values of each era, since it is linked primarily to the specific characteristics of power relations in Brazil.[10]

From 1930, Brazilian anthropologists, including Arthur Ramos (1903–1949), sought inspiration and resources in cultural anthropology widely practiced in scientific centres abroad (principally in the United States, with the culture-centred school of Franz Boas). From a cultural vision, it developed images about the 'Negro question' and criticised or brought several solutions from 'biologist' concepts that predominated until the 1930s. The concept of culture was added to the concept of race. This broke up the pessimistic consensus that hung-over Brazil's 'ethnic reality' and opened more optimistic perspectives for the nation's future.

Blacks ceased to be an exclusively pathologic and negative presence and figured as a factor that contributed positively to Brazilian culture and to the constitution of Brazilian nationality. This optimism characterised the work of Gilberto Freyre (1900–87), a former student of Boas and one of the best-known Brazilian intellectuals abroad. He consecrated the representation of a soft and 'democratic' racial situation in colonial Brasil, with images of masters and docile and passive slaves; this characterisation became even more marked when the author contrasted it with the North American situation. With his analysis that included the influence of evolutionism, which strictly hierarchised the human races, Gilberto Freyre strengthened the ideal of whitening in his work and vividly showed how the white elite acquired cultural traits through reciprocal contact with Africans and to a lesser extent, with Amerindians.

After a period of relative 'neglect', the racial question returned in the 1950s to the centre of interest of Brazilian intellectuals following research on race relations sponsored by UNESCO. This time, based on the study of social scientists including Florestan Fernandes, Roger Bastide (1898–1974) and Oracy Nogueira (1917–96), the Afro-Brazilians are analysed and understood as a group that faces several obstacles for their participation in Brazilian society, and as a result they distanced

[10] Andreas Hofbauer, 'Uma história de branqueamento ou o negro em questão' (PhD dissertation, São Paulo: Universidade de São Paulo, 1999), 375.

themselves from the model of 'racial democracy' that Brazil intended to present.

It is important to stress that the aim of the UNESCO project was to understand and make a scientific analysis of societies, in which race relations supposedly were less tense. The purpose was not to debate the formation of the 'Brazilian national character', but to analyse the situation of the descendants of slaves. The project included the city of Salvador da Bahia, and the south-east region was represented by the cities of São Paulo and Rio de Janeiro. Thales de Azevedo (1904–95) conducted the research in Bahia, Luíz de Aguiar Costa Pinto (1920–2002) in the city of Rio de Janeiro and Florestan Fernandes and Roger Bastide in the city of São Paulo.

As result of this research project, three major paradigmatic disruptions were observed:

a) The use of the category 'race' as a category of analysis, which points to the existence of racial prejudice in Brazil despite the ideal of racial democracy;
b) The use of the word 'identify' by researcher Thales de Azevedo, which means the beginning of the perception of the racial question from the category 'identity';
c) The birth of the idea of a 'myth' associated to racial democracy; this idea was defended by the São Paulo Sociology School (*Escola de Sociologia Paulista*) whose leading spokesman was Florestan Fernandes.

The reality of Brazil's Afro-descendant population

According to the 2010 population census, Brazil was estimated to have 191 million inhabitants, 91 million of whom classified themselves as whites (47.7%), 15 million as blacks (*pretos*) (7.6%), 82 million as mixed-race (*pardos*) (43.1%), 2 million as Asians (*amarelos*) (1.1%) and 817,000 as Amerindians (*indígenas*) (0.4%).[11] Compared with the population census in 2000, we see a sharp increase in persons who classified themselves as blacks and mixed-race, perhaps reflecting the implementation of affirmative action policies in the country. The 2010 census thus indicates that over half of the Brazilian population (51.7%) are 'Negro' (black and mixed-race).

[11] According to the official Brazilian demographic classification Negroes (*negros*) are subdivided into blacks (*pretos*) and mixed-race (*pardos*). In the English translation, Afro-descendants, Afro-Brazilians or blacks refer to both groups.

The report *Retrato das Desigualdades de Gênero e Raça* published in 2011 by the Instituto de Pesquisa Econômica Aplicada (IPEA – Institute of Applied Economic Research), pinpoint some important and significant indicators. [12] With regard to schooling, 16.6% of Brazilian women had higher education vis-à-vis 12.2% of men; however, the schooling rate of white women is higher than that of Afro-descendant women, corresponding to 23.8% and 9.9% respectively.

As far as the labour market is concerned, the participation rate of persons over the age of sixteen is 58.9% for women and 81.6% for men; the unemployment rates range from 12% for Afro-descendant women to the lowest of white men (5%). The formal sector participation is the highest among white men (43% with regular employment registration, including social security number), while Afro-descendant women have the lowest rate (23% with regular employment registration).

In relation to distribution by sector of activity, Afro-Brazilian women are concentrated in the social services sector (34% of the female workforce), and in services related to education, health, social and domestic services. Differences of gender and race mark the insertion of women in the job market: there are fewer women than men, they occupy differentiated spaces and exercise the most precarious functions. With regard to the data on income and poverty, the above-mentioned document indicates that although the average income has increased, inequalities have persisted. The incomes of black women continue to be at the bottom of the social hierarchy, corresponding to 30.5% of incomes of white men, who are at the top with the highest incomes. In 2009, black men and women corresponded to 72% of the 10% of Brazil's poorest population. Irrespective of sex, colour or race, the most outstanding inequalities in relation to income concentration are found in the Northeast and Midwest regions.

Although income indicators have revealed a slight decline in the gap between the incomes of whites and Afro-Brazilians, largely due to public policies (education, job market, family allowance (*bolsa família*), etc.), changes in social mobility are still slow; in addition a culture remains active, which is a collective imaginary of racism and male chauvinism that needs to be deconstructed so that in fact a culture of equality of gender and race and of true racial democracy settles in Brazil. When the poverty indicators are disaggregated by gender, race and/or ethnicity, it is possible to see that poverty in Brazil does in fact have a sex and a colour: black women living in poverty are among the poorest of the

[12] Instituto de Pesquisa Econômica Aplicada – IPEA, *Retrato das desigualdades de gênero e raça* (Brasília: 2011).

poor. Thus, it is relevant to examine the role of affirmative policies in the struggle against this serious impediment to the right of citizenship.

Organisations of black women

The contemporary black women's movement emerged in the context of the feminist and anti-racist struggle of the 1970s, which sought to embody the so-called 'specific questions' affecting Afro-Brazilian women. In the late 1980s, they established their organisation with its own physiognomy and national character; its aim was to intensify the debates and actions to combat racial and gender oppression. To this day, the mobilisation and organisation of Afro-descendant women groups is increasing, both from centres within the black or feminist movements, and autonomously by groups formed only by Afro-descendant women with their own agendas. Between 1984 and 1994, fifty feminist organisations that focused on the racial question appeared in sixteen federal states including Paraná, Santa Catarina and Rio Grande do Sul, where 83% of the population is white.

Different concepts prevail within the black women's movement with regard to its constitution; however, at the first national seminar of Afro-descendant women (1993), the participants elaborated a more unified conceptualisation:

> The movement has been constituted from the crossing of questions of gender, race and social class. It should be autonomous, independent, and composed of women from different social and political movements (for example, from Afro-descendant, trade unionist, popular or partisan movements). It should primarily be articulated with the Afro-Descendant and feminist movements, in that these incorporate and support the struggle of Afro-Descendant women maintaining its particularity'.[13]

From 1985, the first collectives of Afro-descendant women emerged, and meetings were organised on a federal state level. Two meetings (in 1988 and 1991) and two seminars (in 1993 and 1995) were held on a national level. At these events, the perspectives of Afro-descendant women were defined; they constructed a collective space of intervention, evaluation and reflection on their struggle and made it possible to exchange experiences, challenge positions and deepen the debates on the movement's organisational direction. Simultaneously, relations with

[13] Matilde Ribeiro, 'Antigas personagens, novas cenas: mulheres negras e participação política' in *Mulher e Política. Gênero e feminismo no Partido dos Trabalhadores* edited by Ângela Borba, Nalu Faria and Tatau Godinho (São Paulo: Fundação Perseu Abramo, 1998), 199.

the Afro-descendant and feminist movement were developed; however, they were unable to tackle their inner diversity. Afro-descendant women were very critical about the black and feminist movements and their leadership: frequently equality between women is assumed when talking about 'women' and the ethnic and social differences and ensuing conditions are rarely taken into account; and when talking about the 'Afro-descendants', differences between men and women are not always considered.

The feminist meetings, thematic networks, debates and seminars were the formal channel of dialogue between Afro-Brazilian and white women. The Afro-Brazilian women had an outstanding participation in the feminist movement after 1985. The Ninth National Feminist Meeting in 1987 was a milestone as the Afro-descendant women exercised strong pressure with regard to the absence of their specific questions and also decided to organise the First National Meeting of Black Women. They subsequently participated in the Tenth and Eleventh National Feminist Meetings (1989 and 1991).

It should be noted that actions to change inequality should be taken by movements in different spheres to guarantee dialogue and pressure state institutions to implement democratic public policies that impact the daily life of the population, particularly that of women, Afro-descendants and Afro-descendant women; they should aim, for example, for guarantees of entry and permanence in the job market and the educational system, and for guarantees of anti-racist legal arrangements, both the already existing (the law that makes racism non-bailable and imprescriptible) and the creation of new ones; actions aimed at equal rights based on group membership (gender, race), as well as programmes combatting poverty and social exclusion.

A milestone in racial equality

The 1951 Afonso Arinos Law

As the last country in the world to end slavery and the first with a self-proclaimed 'racial democracy'[14], Brazil exposed itself to international public humiliation in 1951 when the African American dancer, Katherine Dunham, hired for a show in São Paulo, was barred from a luxury hotel in the city on the grounds of race. Immediately after this extremely embarrassing affair for Brazilian diplomacy, the National Congress

[14] Gevanilda Santos, *Relações raciais e desigualdades no Brasil* (São Paulo: Selo Negro, 2009), 119.

approved a law submitted by the federal deputy Afonso Arinos (1905–90) that determined punishment for those who discriminated against persons because of their race. Excerpts of this law are as follows:

> Art. 1 – It is a misdemeanour punishable under this law for a commercial or educational establishment of any kind to refuse to host, serve, attend or receive a client, buyer or student on the grounds of race or colour.
> Art. 6 – [...] prevent the access of anybody to any public service position or to the service in any unit of the armed forces on the grounds of race or colour.

The Afonso Arinos Law was positive in that it recognised the existence of racism in Brazil. If there is a law against racism, it means it exists and cannot be denied. On the other hand, the law did not in fact make racism a crime; it was a mere misdemeanour that could be punished with a small fine. Nevertheless, such actions, in addition to beginning to meet the collective interests of the Afro-descendant community, were important because they raised society's awareness of the racial discrimination suffered by almost half of the Brazilian population.

Africa and the Afro-descendant movement in the 20th century

Brazil–Africa relations and African topics were not considered in the black movement's dialogue with the political parties. References to Africa and government programmes were only included in the period of the Brazil's democratic opening in the 1980s due to the Workers' Party (PT).[15] Already from 1945, a social Afro-descendant movement was developing, which is demonstrated by the formation of the Experimental Theatre of the Black (*Teatro Experimental do Negro*), founded in Rio de Janeiro in 1944. The Afro-Brazilian population's constant struggles to organise and gain recognition for their key role in the construction of Brazil have deeply marked the political history of the entire Brazilian nation.

The 1970s marked the rebirth of the struggle against racial discrimination alongside the fight for democratic liberties. Strictly speaking, it would be more appropriate to call the initiatives and institutions that multiplied in Brazil after the 1970s 'black movements' (*movimentos negros*) rather than a black movement due to their diversity and frequent splits and divergences; however, there is no doubt that their common

[15] Irene Vida Gala, 'The External Politics of Lula's Government to Africa. The external Politics as an instrument of affirmative action...Though not only' (dissertation, Brasília: Instituto Rio Branco, 2007).

objective was to combat racism and struggle to improve the living conditions of the Afro-Brazilian population.

In this context, the rediscovery of Africa had an important function in the activists' process of instrumentalisation, because it expanded the awareness of their own origin and opened up the possibility for action. The designation 'black movement' gained visibility after July 1978 when the United Black Movement Against Racial Discrimination (MNUCDR – *Movimento Negro Unificado Contra a Discriminação Racial*) was founded in São Paulo following strong protests against the death of a black youngster from São Paulo after being violently assaulted by the police and accused of stealing fruit in a local market.

Historically, the MNUCDR constituted an example for the African Diaspora in South America by organising the first major protest in modern Brazil against racism and channelling the support of Afro-Brazilian religious leaders (*Candomblé* and *Umbanda*), the Catholic Church, the Brazilian Bar Association (OAB), the Brazilian Press Association (ABI), the Movement for Amnesty for political prisoners of the military dictatorship (1964–85) and many other civil society sectors that engaged in this struggle. During the 1980s, MNU centres opened in all Brazilian states, several Afro-descendant entities were formed and cultural, political and academic meetings became national events. Also in the 1980s, there were more international cooperation programmes for complaints of acts of racism and the provision of more efficient legal support; these included the obligation to comply with the Caó Act (anti-discrimination law of 1989). SOS-Racism, an international anti-racist organisation with national branches, founded in France in 1984, spread to several states and led to new experiments of managing these defence organisations in the public sphere with the support of lawyers, academics and social workers, among others.

In the 1990s, the black movement clearly grew as a social movement, and non-governmental organisations sprang up to lead the anti-racist battle in the area of culture, the development of research, and the provision of institutional support for victims of racism and police violence, religious practices and women. The 21st century began with the World Conference against Racism, Racial Discrimination, Xenophobia and Related Intolerance in Durban in 2001, which resulted in affirmative action policies for the Afro-Brazilian population.

Affirmative action policies

Affirmative action policies can be defined as a set of measures in the public and private spheres that create special and temporary conditions which allow social groups suffering from discrimination to achieve emancipation, autonomy and equal opportunities. They are temporary actions because they must serve as a lever that fills the gap until the specific established goals are achieved. They can also be conceived as reparatory, compensatory and/or preventive actions that seek to correct a situation of discrimination and inequality by means of the social, economic, political and/or cultural appreciation of these groups. They allow the beneficiaries to compete equally in the educational area and in the labour market and simultaneously correct the inequalities in the access to opportunities. These actions are typically designed for groups defined by race, colour, religion or sex.

It is worth mentioning that the goal of these public policies is to systematically combat discrimination and reduce the inequality that affects some groups more severely because of race and gender, as is the case of black women. They also seek to integrate different existing social groups through the recognition and respect for their cultural diversity. This idea tries to confer a positive identity to groups that are stereotyped and stigmatised and assumes that the living together of different people helps prevent future prejudiced visions and discriminatory practices.

The first record of an attempt at affirmative action in Brazil stems from 1968 when staff of the Ministry of Labour and the Supreme Court of Labour were in favour of establishing a law that would oblige private enterprises to employ a minimum number of Afro-Brazilian employees, 20%, 15% or 10% according to demand and the type of activity, as a way of addressing racial discrimination in the labour market. However, this law was never drawn up during the military dictatorship (1964–85).

In the 1980s, the black parliamentarian Abdias do Nascimento (1914–2011) drafted a bill proposing 'compensatory action' for Afro-descendants. The proposals included the incorporation of a positive image of the Afro-Brazilian family in education; introducing the history of African civilisations and Africans into schooling in Brazil; reserving 20% of vacancies in the civil service for Afro-descendant women and men; scholarships for black students; and incentives for the elimination of racial discrimination in private enterprises. This bill, however, was not approved by the National Congress.

In 1988, the centenary of the abolition of slavery (*Lei Áurea*), the Palmares Cultural Foundation attached to the Ministry of Culture was set up to support the social mobility of the Afro-Brazilian population. In the same year, Brazil's New Constitution was adopted; this brought social improvements like the protection of women in the labour market as part of social rights, and a quota of jobs in the public service for disabled people. This set of initiatives within the public service shows that there was some recognition of the problem of racial, ethnic and gender discrimination, and of restrictions for the disabled. The 1988 Federal Constitution states:

> Art. 5 – All are equal under the law, without any distinction whatsoever, guaranteeing Brazilians and foreign residents in the country the inviolability of the right of life, liberty, security and properties, under the following terms: [...]
> XLI – The law will punish any offending discrimination of the fundamental rights and liberties;
> XLII – The practice of racism constitutes a non-bailable and irrevocable crime subject to imprisonment, under the law.

In 2002, Itamaraty, the Foreign Ministry, launched a scholarship programme aimed at helping Afro-descendant candidates to participate in public selection processes for diplomatic careers by enabling them to acquire reading materials and learn foreign languages. This measure allows all candidates to compete under equal conditions by giving access to the specific knowledge that is evaluated in the selection exams. Theoretically it leads to greater representation and participation of the Afro-descendant population in the Foreign Ministry and the Brazil's diplomatic corps which, even today, is almost exclusively composed of representatives of the white population.

It is argued that affirmative actions help combat racial inequality and strive to compensate the Afro-Brazilian population for the discrimination suffered or for disadvantages due to lower levels of education, income and housing.

> Therefore, in the first instance, this set of compensatory actions focuses on the attempt to correct the disadvantageous situation historically imposed on the blacks and, in the last instance, it is directed to promoting a democratic society that cannot be achieved without equality.

It is not just to make blacks and whites equal so that they can undertake fair competition. Despite considering the existence of a void between the capacity of competition between the two groups, it is understood that the socioeconomic differences between both are generated not only by competitive ability, but also by unequal selective patterns, based on racist criteria that, among others, explain how blacks with university degrees have earned a lower salary than whites with second-tier diplomas for the same functions.[16]

[16] Ronald Walters, 'O princípio da ação afirmativa e o progresso racial nos Estados Unidos', *Estudos Afro-Asiáticos*, 28 (1995), 131.

In addition to the anti-discriminatory practice, the set of affirmative actions not only corrects and compensates past and present discrimination, but will also prevent new cases of discrimination by defining punishments for transgressors, creating multiple oversight mechanisms and building social promotion agencies for discriminated groups; in other words it is about creating an equal society where everyone has the chance to be successful depending on their efforts and abilities.

The persistent challenge of educational inclusivity

The exclusion of Afro-descendant students from public universities remains a continuing problem. Both qualitative and quantitative research and academic studies conducted by respected research institutions such as the *Instituto Brasileiro de Geografia e Estatística* (IBGE – Brazilian Institute of Geography and Statistics) and IPEA, leave no doubt about the severe exclusion of the Afro-descendant population in Brazilian society.

The systematic comparison of racial status and the socioeconomic indicators of income, schooling, social class and family situation since 1929 allows us to conclude that:

> In Brazil, the racial condition constitutes a factor of privilege for whites, and exclusion and disadvantage for non-whites. Some statistics frighten those who are socially concerned and committed to the search for equality and equity in human societies.[17]
>
> a) Out of the total of Brazilian university students, 97% is white, while 2% is Afro-descendant.
> b) Among 22 million Brazilians, who live below the poverty line, 70% is Afro-descendant.
> c) Out of 53 million Brazilians who live in poverty, 63% is Afro-descendant.[18]

In 2014, the same author demonstrates again the prevalences of persistent inequality among the black population. According to the *Pesquisa Nacional por Amostra de Domicílios* (PNAD – National Household Sample Survey), the average schooling of black men is 6.9 years and of black women is 7.4 years, while that of white men is 8.7 years and white women is 8.9 years.

[17] Ricardo Henriques, *Desigualdade Racial no Brasil: evolução das condições de vida na década de 90*. Texto para Discussão, n. 807 (Brasília: IPEA, 2001).
[18] Ibid.

Numerous public schools in the country have difficulty in accommodating all students' specificities and needs. Schools are often unable to cope with the consequences of the socioeconomic inequalities, particularly in the most vulnerable communities.[19]

In 2016, inequality of unemployment was shown to be higher among blacks (7.5%) and mixed-race (6.8%) than among whites (5.1%). Child labour is higher among mixed-race (7.6%) and blacks (6.5%) than among whites (5.4%).

Social inequalities are reinforced in education. The illiteracy rate is 11.2% among blacks; 11.1% among mixed-race people; and 5% among whites. Until the age of fourteen, there is little variation in the school attendance rates of white and black populations as the access to school is similar. However, the difference increases from the age of fifteen. While 70.7% of white adolescents are in high school, the rate drops to 55.5% among blacks and 55.3% among those of mixed-race. The gap increases again in the third year of high school, at the end of basic education: 38% of whites, 21% of mixed-race, and 20.3% of blacks have adequate education in Portuguese, while 15.1% of whites, 5.8% of mixed-race and 4.3% of blacks have adequate schooling in mathematics.[20]

The question that arises concerns how long the Afro-Brazilian population will have to wait for equal access to and permanence in higher education, or a tuition-free public university of good quality. In a country, where the resistance to confront and combat prejudices and racial discrimination is great, poor white students and poor black students are not equal, for the first are discriminated once: by the socioeconomic condition; and the latter twice: by the socioeconomic condition and by racial inequality. Thus, the so-called universal policies defended by several segments of Brazilian society are unlikely to bring the substantial changes that the Afro-Brazilian population have long awaited. As Munanga stated as far back as 2003:

> In the search for appropriate tools and instruments to speed up the process of change in this unjust situation suffered by the black population, quotas are proposed as the best solution. The argument that the quota system will allow unqualified students to enter university does not hold because the competitiveness of entrance exams will continue to be respected. The

[19] Ricardo Henriques, 'O custo do racismo', 21 November 2014, accessed 19 January 2018, www.geledes.org.br/o-custo-racismo-por-ricardo-henriques.

[20] Mariana Tokarnia, 'Educação reforça desigualdades entre brancos e negros, diz estudo', acessed 19 January 2018, http://agenciabrasil.ebc.com.br/educacao/noticia/2016-11/educacao-reforca-desigualdades-entre-brancos-e-negros-diz-estudo.

> only difference lies in the fact that aspiring candidates who identify themselves in their registration as black or Afro-descendants benefit from the quota. Their exams are corrected and classified separately; those who pass will take up the vacancies foreseen according to the established quota. In this way, the merits are respected and the excellence in this specific universe is guaranteed.[21]

The exclusion of Afro-descendant lecturers in Brazilian public universities is also a significant problem. The lack of systematic data on the racial composition of lecturers and researchers in universities deserves a deep reflection. How can researchers theorise about race relations in Brazilian society if they are unaware of the race relations of which they are part and that they help to reproduce? An example of a racial census, a result of surveys made by Afro-descendant lecturers in their respective universities in the early 2000s presented the following results:[22]

a) University of Brasília (UnB) – 1,500 professors, fifteen of whom are Afro-descendants;
b) São Carlos Federal University (UFSCar) – 670 professors, three of whom are Afro-descendants;
c) Rio Grande do Sul Federal University (UFRGS) – 1,300 professors, three of whom are Afro-descendants;
d) Goiás Federal University (UFG) – 1,170 professors, fifteen are Afro-descendants;
e) Minas Gerais Federal University (UFMG) – 2,700 professors, fifteen are Afro-descendants;
f) Pará Federal University (UFPA) – 2,200 professors, eighteen are Afro-descendants;
g) Pontifical Catholic University of Minas Gerais (PUC-MG) – 1,700 professors, seventeen are Afro-descendants;
h) Rio de Janeiro State University (UERJ) – 2,300 professors, five are Afro-descendants;
i) Campinas State University (Unicamp) – 1,761 professors, five are Afro-descendants;

[21] Kabengele Munanga, 'Uma abordagem conceitual das noções de raça, racismo, identidade e etnia',paper presented at the 3º Seminário Nacional Relações Raciais e Educação, PENESB, Universidade Federal Fluminense, Rio de Janeiro, 5 November (São Paulo: Attar Editorial, 2003).

[22] These data are from a pioneer research included in the book *Inclusão Étnica e Racial no Brasil: a questão das cotas no ensino superior* (Attar Editora, 2005). The author is José Jorge de Carvalho, Ph.D. in Anthropology, professor at the University of Brasília (UnB) and researcher of the CNPq (National Council for Scientific and Technological Development). The researcher analyses the racial quotas, reservation of university vacancies for blacks and Amerindian people, and the ethnic and racial formation of both the student and professorial bodies.

j) University of São Paulo (USP) – 4,705 professors, twenty are Afro-descendants;
k) Rio de Janeiro Federal University (UFRJ) – 3,200 professors, including twenty Afro-descendants.

With regard to USP, certainly the country's most important university, it is worth noting that only three of the 504 professors in the Faculty of Philosophy, Arts and Human Sciences (FFLCH) are black and one of these is African.

In the case of UFRJ, information provided by university staff belonging to the Education Workers Union (SINTUFRJ) indicates that the Health Science Centre (CCS), which is the university's biggest academic unit with about eight hundred professors, employs only three Afro-descendants. As for UERJ, the situation is even worse in that at least half of the Afro-descendant professors are in two academic units stigmatised as less prestigious: The Department of Physical Education and the Teacher Training Centre.

The selection processes for professors, in which candidates are almost exclusively white, cannot be seen as the simple result of the selection committee's rational decisions based on entirely impersonal patterns:

> The selections are actually the result of a complex equation that involves variables such as the academic policy (external and internal pressures in favour of certain candidates), networks of relations within the academic community (research topics, theoretical affiliations, areas of activity) besides, of course, the merit and academic trajectory of each one (published articles and books, research experience), the relevance of which varies according to the profile of the desired candidate (senior or junior researcher, etc.). Ultimately the selection procedures for professors are not only governed by impartiality. Given these shocking data, the Ministry of Education should investigate the selection processes held and seek to find out whether the public vacancies are allocated within some criteria of social interest (including racial plurality) and, if, for example, it is not the time for a faculty that has five hundred white professors and three Afro-descendants to start racially integrating its faculty staff, independent of the specific capacity of the selection committees to evaluate the candidates according to allegedly universalist criteria of scientific merit.[23]

Despite all the data unequivocally exhibiting the racial inequality in Brazil, many social scientists at public universities reject proposals of affirmative actions on the grounds that scientifically races do not exist

[23] José Jorge de Carvalho, *Inclusão Ética e Racial no Ensino Superior* (Brasília: Universidade de Brasília, 2003), 167.

and they displace the problem to biology; in fact, what is at stake is racialization, constructed as a social representation that generates chronic and systematic inequalities.

In 2016, an institutional campaign of the Federal University of Juiz de Fora (UFJF), which questioned the small number of black teachers in higher education, gained followers in Brazil in the social media. Organised by the Department of Affirmative Actions, banners with the question 'how many black teachers do you have?' and the hashtag #nãoécoincidência (it is not a coincidence) were placed all over the city campus in the Zona da Mata in Minas Gerais. Many responders answered the question on the Internet, thus presenting a retrospective of their school life.

A survey also conducted by the Department of Affirmative Actions of the UFJF revealed that only twenty out of the institution's approximately one thousand teachers were black. To carry out the study, each department was asked to identify the teachers who recognised themselves as black or were recognised as such.[24]

Subsequently, research published in 2017 noted that in USP, one of the largest universities in Brazil, only 1.8% of active teachers were black. In a university that has pioneered discussions on racial inequality since its formation, the researcher Viviane Angélica faced difficulties in starting her research due to the lack of a racial census of teachers, mainly due to the low number of blacks in teaching. 'I came across the question: if USP is the university that has the most jobs on the racial issue in the country, then why do they not have black teachers? Who made this debate?' she explains.

The low number of black teachers in the university is also due to the hiring process. The researcher says that the process of entry is random, there are no process steps that evaluate racial inequalities, and the hiring process conducted only takes into account the level of candidate excellence. Angélica shows that there are families of teachers at the university, with 'solemn surnames', which indicates that the process of entry also functions as a form of inheritance.[25]

[24] Márcia Maria Cruz, 'Número de professores negros em universidades públicas gera debate', accessed 19 January 2018, www.em.com.br/app/noticia/gerais/2016/02/03/interna_gerais,731244/numero-de-professores-negros-em-universidades-publicas-gera-debate.shtml.

[25] Leandra Rajczuk Martins, 'Perfil racial dos docentes da USP analisa baixo índice de professores negros', accessed 19 January 2018, https://paineira.usp.br/aun/index.php/2017/03/23/perfil-racial-dos-docentes-da-usp-analisa-baixo-indice-de-professores-negros.

The Afro-descendant black women and the media

Another area where existing racist prejudices and stereotypes are continuously reproduced and diffused is the Brazilian media, in particular television. Being a white man in a male chauvinist, racist and exclusionary society means receiving daily benefits and advantages. There are many privileges: small, medium and large that help increase these advantages and the concentration of resources that Brazilian racism bestows in everyday life, and therefore whites benefit on a daily basis from social, economic or cultural capital that has been distributed unequally according to racial criteria: waiting less time to be attended in public and private spaces, facility in obtaining a letter of recommendation, access to an important and prestigious contact in the academic world, a psychological reinforcement of one's personal image or the ease of obtaining a new source of income. Being white in Brazil means taking advantage of Afro-Brazilians on a daily basis, and to be an Afro-Brazilian women means to suffer even greater disadvantage. White men and black women are located on the two opposite extremes of the socioeconomic continuum in Brazil. Even if races do not exist in the biological sense of the term, the social representation of the difference is racialised phenotypically; suffice to look at the Brazilian television, from soap operas to advertising.

> The constant supply of images that strengthens the identification with the hegemonic model, and the prohibition of icons that would allow the construction of other projects of identification mean that, currently, the media are the most efficient among the most capable means for the edification of discourses about the differences. They repeat in daily life, hour after hour, the idea that the other is the unequal, the negative, the inferior, with a character that still one does not know if it is human, or almost human, or non-human.[26]

Brazil is a multicultural society, but race relations are marked by deep violence, subordination and segregation, and are guided in the representation of the Afro-descendant population as incapable, inferior and accustomed to submission; these situations are camouflaged by the myth of racial democracy that continues to prevent an understanding of the extent and the magnitude of racism, segregation and exclusion of Afro-descendant men and women in the country. The symbolic exclusion, the non-representation and distortions of the image of the Afro-descendant

[26] Ivair Augusto Alves dos Santos, 'O movimento negro e o estado (1983–1987): o caso do Conselho de Participação e Desenvolvimento da Comunidade Negra no Governo de São Paulo' (M.A. dissertation, Campinas: Universidade Estadual de Campinas, 2005).

woman in the media are painful, cruel and prejudicial forms of violence that could be dealt with in the context of human rights. Article XIX of the Universal Human Rights Declaration states: 'Everyone has the right to freedom of opinion and expression; this right includes freedom to hold opinions without interference and to seek, receive and impart information and ideas through any media and regardless of frontiers.'

This means that Afro-descendants should have access to all means of communication and public opinion. However, to guarantee the respect of fundamental rights to access to media, ethical codes must be elaborated that respect the norms of pluralism and human rights. Throughout history, the black woman has been the major victim of the deep racial inequality in Brazilian society. Research conducted reveals a dramatic picture and its drama is not only in the pessimist socioeconomic conditions, but also in the daily negation of the condition of being a black woman through racism and sexism that permeates all areas of life. To the Afro-descendant woman, who possesses the physical 'attributes' accepted by the hegemonic aesthetic standard, the role of 'mulatto woman' is reserved. The authorised stereotyped image is that of sensuality and seduction. And she is offered a 'labour market' that alienates her and submits her to the exposure of her body for the delight of tourists and for the reinforcement of the so-called Brazilian 'racial democracy'.

Sex tourism and the traffic of women and children currently cause almost one million victims. Afro-descendant youth and adolescents are frequently victims of this violence that has increased alarmingly, and the denunciations of torture, beatings and even homicides are on the rise. Brazilian television prohibits Afro-descendant women the right to have their own aesthetics, their history, their culture, their desires and feelings. From the imaginary perspective, the country opted for an artificial standard of European inspiration, expressed in the massive presence of white and blonde women. When insertion occurs, the prevailing image of the black woman is mostly that of an opportunistic, stupid, seductive and permissive servant. These stereotypes cause a sensation of impotence against images that present this social segment as inferior beings, lacking human qualities. In this way, exploitation, exclusion, violence, humiliation, contempt, rape, trafficking, slavery and even death are justified.

Racism in the media is not only measured by Afro-descendants having greater or less visibility, but also by the proposed typologies of being black. The representations of ethnic conflicts either deny that racism exists at all, or individualise racial aspects by suggesting that conflicts can be solved at the individual level, thus rendering unfeasible solutions that demand social intermediations rather than particular ones. The black movements are demanding that the media act with social responsibility, so that they no longer reproduce stereotypes and strengthen prejudices. Television is a vital part in the everyday life of millions of Brazilians. It is necessary to reflect about the impact that a message of racist content produces in a population that has struggled for centuries against stigmatisation and exclusion.

The great challenge is to combat discriminatory practices motivated by Brazilian racism because the media is the mirror of society and vice-versa. It is urgent to draw up educational proposals aimed at changing the hegemonic aesthetic code and demanding the equitable participation of segments of society historically discriminated against. In fact, Brazilian society needs to be plural in its representations and must demand that the media is committed not to create and diffuse stereotyped images that reinforce racist feelings and practices.

The state's role in the promotion of racial equality and affirmative action policies

President Lula: Strategic change in the policy of racial equality

President Luís Inácio 'Lula' da Silva (2003–10) allowed an important change to take place by promoting a meaningful racial equality policy. This new phase was inaugurated with the setting up of the Secretaria Nacional de Políticas de Promoção da Igualdade Racial (SEPPIR – the National Secretariat for Policies to Promote Racial Equality) on 21 March 2003 – a long-claimed demand of the black movement. The President appointed Matilde Ribeiro (2003–08), a black intellectual, activist and researcher, as SEPPIR's first secretary, with the status of minister. The main task of SEPPIR was to implement a national policy promoting racial equality through policy coordination between other ministries, federal state governments and municipalities, as well as civil society. The sectors that have received most attention from SEPPIR are labour, health, education and the maroon communities.

The setting up of SEPPIR represented a breakthrough in the Brazilian state's treatment of racism and racial inequalities. In addition, it opened a communication channel with organised civil society, in particular the black movement that for decades had highlighted the severe consequences of these inequalities for the country's development. Not by coincidence, it was founded on the same date chosen by the United Nations as the International Day for the Elimination of Racial Discrimination – a reference to the Sharpeville Massacre of 21 March 1960 in Johannesburg, South Africa, which had a significant role in the international mobilisation to end apartheid.

The role of SEPPIR is to develop policies that promote equality and protect the rights of individuals and racial and ethnic groups, notably Afro-Brazilians affected by racial discrimination and other forms of intolerance. It articulates with public entities and other institutions and is also active in monitoring the execution of cooperation programmes with public and private national and international organisations tackling racial equality issues.

On 9 January 2003, shortly after his inauguration, President Lula passed the Law 10.639 that made it mandatory to include Afro-Brazilian and African history and culture in the official school curriculum. African history, the struggle of Afro-Brazilians, the culture and role of Afro-Brazilians in the formation of Brazil's society therefore became part of the curriculum. This law identifies the school as a fundamental space to combat racism and racial discrimination. However, fifteen years after the implementation of this law, its real result remains problematic due to the lack of knowledge and appropriate didactic material, and inadequately trained teachers.

Also in 2003, the National Policy for the Promotion of Racial Equality (PNPIR) was also adopted under decree 4886. This aimed to reduce racial inequalities through the defence of rights, affirmative actions and the articulation of the gender and race dimensions. In February 2004, the Minister of Education, Tarso Genro (2004–05), established a new secretariat: The Secretariat of Further Education, Literacy and Diversity (SECAD) to combat the many dimensions of educational inequalities in Brazil. This sought to develop and implement educational inclusion policies by considering the particularities of Brazilian inequalities and ensuring the respect and appreciation of the multiple contours of the country's ethnic-racial, cultural, gender, social, environmental and regional diversity.

Mention must also be made of another law passed in 2004, namely Bill 3627, which reserves study places in Federal Institutions of Higher Education (IFES) for students from public high schools, with specific quotas for Afro-descendants and Amerindians. The University for All Programme (ProUni) established by the Lula government in 2005 reserved scholarships in private higher education institutions that account for more than 80% of Brazil's higher education sector for students from public schools and students with scholarships from private schools; 30% of these scholarships were reserved for Afro-descendants and Amerindians. Although non-profit institutions had granted their own scholarships until 2004, they defined the number of scholarships available, the reduction in fees, the courses, etc. ProUni introduced federal tax exemptions in exchange for these universities offering integral or partial quotas in graduate courses.

Candidates for ProUni scholarships are pre-selected on the basis of marks obtained in the National High School Exam (ENEM) and they must then provide evidence of family income, which cannot exceed three times the national minimum wage if the scholarship is to be considered; candidates must also have concluded high school education in a public school or in a private school with a full scholarship of the institution. Over the years, the programme has proved to be an important public policy instrument for access to and democratisation of higher education. In 2005, more than 100,000 study places were filled by students from low-income groups, including about 30,000 Afro-descendants.

Decree 6872 of 4 June 2009 adopted the National Plan of the Promotion of Racial Equality (PLANAPIR). Based on the definitions of the First Conference of the Promotion of Racial Equality (I CONAPIR) held in Brasília in July 2005, this plan defined a set of actions related to the following: labour and economic development, education, health, cultural diversity, human rights and public security, so-called traditional peoples and communities, foreign policy, social development and food security, and infrastructure and youth.

Law 12.288 of 20 July 2010 established the Statute of Racial Equality, which defines the main areas known by public institutions to overcome racial inequalities: health, education, culture, sports and recreation; freedom of conscience and faith; access to land and housing; and labour and media. It also created institutional intervention mechanisms such as the Permanent Ombudsmen in Defence of Racial Equality, within SEPPIR.

Science without Borders (CsF) is an academic programme set up on 26 July 2011 which seeks to promote the consolidation, expansion and internationalisation of science and technology, innovation and Brazilian competitiveness through international exchange and mobility. The initiative was a result of the joint efforts of the Ministries of Science, Technology and Innovation (MCTI) and of Education (MEC) by means of their respective development institutions – CNPq[27] and CAPES – and MEC's secretariats of Higher Education and of Technological Education. The aim of the four-year project was to promote international exchange by providing 101,000 scholarships for graduate and postgraduate students to do internship abroad; this would give them the opportunity to have contact with competitive educational systems in the fields of technology and innovation. In addition, it sought to attract foreign researchers

[27] *Conselho Nacional de Desenvolvimento Científico e Tecnológico* (National Council for Scientific and Technological Development).

who wanted to settle in Brazil or establish partnerships with Brazilian researchers in the programme's priority areas and to create opportunities for researchers working in enterprises to receive special training abroad.

Afro-descendants account for 25.2% of the vacancies offered by the programme since ethnicity was included in the Science without Borders' registration form in 2013. Overall, 69,000 beneficiaries of the programme answered the question about colour. That is, one in four of these exchange students was black.[28]

In 2017 the Ministry of Education announced the end of fellowships for undergraduate students in Science without Borders. The programme continues to work only for postgraduate students (postgraduate, master's, doctorate and postdoctoral).

The official claim is that the programme did not yield results and the financial resources of about R$ 3.2 billion could be used for other more urgent priorities, such as buying school meals for students in basic education.[29]

In 2012, Law 12.711, popularly known as the 'quota law', was adopted by President Dilma Rousseff on 29 August. It reserves study places for students from public schools, Afro-descendants and Amerindians, and fixes at a minimum of 50% the access of those categories to federal universities and the federal institutions of technical education at high school level.

An analysis of the results of these initiatives shows that, in the first year, ProUni[30] – the University for All Programme – achieved almost the same results as the quota policies during three years to improve social inclusion of poor and black students in higher education: 112,275 attended in the first year of ProUni vis-à-vis 150,000 students included in university quotas in the three years of the quota law. And in the last year of available data, the University for All Programme granted 306,726 scholarships, of which 70% were full and 30% partial scholarships.

From 2003 to 2014, more than 1.2 million scholarships for lecture hall students were granted and more than 223,000 scholarships for

[28] Governo do Brasil, 'Ciência sem Fronteiras já beneficiou 17,5 mil negros com bolsas de estudo no exterior', 29 November 2015, accessed 19 January 2018, www.brasil.gov.br/educacao/2015/11/ciencia-sem-fronteiras-ja-beneficiou-17-5-mil-negros-com-bolsas-de-estudos-no-exterior.

[29] Ibid.

[30] ProUni University For All Programme provisional measure 213/September 2004/ Draft Law no. 3,582/2004/ Law 11,096/January 2005 Programme for providing full or partial scholarships for the low-income population. Some of the scholarships should be for black, mixed-race and Amerindian students, in proportion to the numbers of these ethnic groups in the population of each federal state.

students of Distance Education (EAD). Most scholarships were granted for night classes: 74% compared with 19% in the morning shift, 4% in the afternoon and 3% in the evening. There were more women than men (53% women and 47% men) among the beneficiaries. In terms of colour, 45.8% of the scholarship holders were white, 50.8% were black and mixed-race, 1.8% were of Asian descent and 0.1% remained unclassified. Amerindians were not included in the percentages but in absolute numbers represented 1,887 fellows.[31]

President Dilma's government and the maroon communities (*quilombos*)[32]

Brazil's 1988 Constitution guarantees the existing maroon communities the right to communal land titles. In 2014, President Dilma Rousseff's first term came to an end without any change in the slow pace of maroon land titling, just as with her predecessors Luís Inácio 'Lula' da Silva and Fernando Henrique Cardoso. Until 13 November that year, President Dilma' administration had titled only nine lands, all partially. More than 1,400 persons were waiting for the process to be completed by the National Institute of Colonisation and Agrarian Reform (INCRA).[33]

> Currently, 140 maroon estates, where 229 communities live, are titled, but some only partially. The regularised areas are home to 12,428 families; this represents 5.8% of the 214,000 families estimated by SEPPIR as the maroon population in Brazil. The federal states with the most titled maroon lands are Pará

[31] Márcia Lima and Paulo Ramos, Educação e políticas de promoção da igualdade racial no Brasil de 2003 a 2014. Análise 31 (São Paulo: Friedrich-Ebert-Stiftung Brasil, 2017), 19–20.

[32] Under Decree 4887 of 2003, maroon communities (*comunidades quilombolas*) are ethnic-racial groups, according to criteria of self-classification, with their own historical trajectory, provided with specific territorial relations and with Afro-descendant ancestry related to resistance against historical oppression. The property rights of these communities have been established since the Federal Constitution of 1988. A survey of the Cultural Foundation Palmares (FCP) mapped out 3,524 maroon communities in Brazil. Other sources, however, estimate there are about 5,000 communities. In 2007 the Quilombola Social Agenda (ASQ) was established to coordinate the actions within the Federal Government through the Brazil Quilombola Programme (PBQ). '*Quilombo*' refers historically to hideouts of runaway slaves.

[33] INCRA – *Instituto Nacional de Colonização e Reforma Agrária* is a federal authority of the Brazilian Public Administration. The institute was created by decree 1.110 of 9 July 1970 with the priority mission to carry out the agrarian reform, maintain the national register of rural properties and manage the public lands of the state. It is implemented in the entire country by means of thirty regional superintendents.

> (fifty-four estates) and Maranhão (fifty-two), largely as a result of the action of the two state governments. The Pará Lands Institute (Iterpa) titled forty-six estates, and in Maranhão all were regularised by the Maranhão Institute of Colonisation and Lands (Iterma). The first titling of a maroon estate occurred in 1995 during the government of Fernando Henrique Cardoso, seven years after the Federal Constitution had assured the maroons the property of their lands. During President Lula's two terms, eight estates were titled and another four were partially regularised, benefiting 1,059 families. In his government the first decree of expropriation of maroon lands was issued nationally and, until the end of his two terms, forty-three decrees were issued benefiting the maroon communities. By 13 November 2014, President Dilma had partially regularised nine maroon estates, where 1,192 families live. The total number of regularised estates represents a very modest area of 2,497,164 hectares. This acreage corresponds to only 8.5% of the total area to be titled.[34]
>
> In 2015 ten maroon land titles were recognised. Partial titles were delivered by INCRA to the lands of the maroons Jatobá (Patu – Rio Grande do Norte), Serra da Guia (Poço Redondo – Sergipe), Kalunga (Cavalcante, Monte Alegre and Teresinha de Goiás – Goiás), Lagoa dos Campinhos (Amparo de São Francisco and Telha – Sergipe), and Conceição das Crioulas (Salgueiro – Pernambuco). A total of 7,328 hectares benefited 797 families.
>
> With the 2015 decree, this number increased to 164 the regularised maroon lands, where 253 communities live. According to INCRA, 1,500 cases remained without titles, 87.5% of which had no identification reports, which are necessary for the procedure.

In 2016 there was only one single recognised maroon land title regularised. After President Dilma was ousted in May of that year, Antônio Oliveira Santos took over the position of General Coordination of Regularisation of Maroon Territories within INCRA. The 2017 budget was cut by 50% compared to the 2016 budget.[35] Just as in the year before, only one maroon land title was regularised in 2017.

Under Dilma Rousseff, Law 12.990 of 9 June 2014 that introduced a quota system for public sector employment was an important achievement of the black movement, representing a significant advance in the struggle for racial equality:

[34] Comissão Pró-Índio de São Paulo, 'Terras Quilombolas – governo Dilma titula apenas nove terras, todas parcialmente', 21 December 2015, accessed 19 January 2018, http://comissaoproindio.blogspot.com.br/2014/11/terras-quilombolas-governo-dilma-titula.html.

[35] 'Terras quilombolas em 2015: apenas 10 terras tituladas', ibid.

> Art. 1 – 20 % of vacancies offered in public job selections for permanent positions and public employment within the federal civil service, municipalities, public foundations, public enterprises and parastatals controlled by the state are reserved for Afro-descendants under this law.
> Art. 2 – Applications for the vacancies reserved for Afro-descendant candidates (*candidatos negros*) may be made by individuals who, on registration, declare themselves to be black (*pretos*) or mixed-race (*pardos*), according to the criteria of colour or race used by the Brazilian Institute of Geography and Statistics (IBGE).
> § 1. In the event of a false representation, the candidate will be eliminated from the selection process and, if already appointed, this will be subject to cancellation of employment in the public service after an administrative procedure, in which the candidate is assured of the right to challenge and full defence, regardless of other applicable penalties.
> Art. 3 – Afro-descendant candidates compete concomitantly for the reserved vacancies, and the vacancies determined for full competition, according to their classification in the job selection.
> Art. 6 – This law shall enter into force on the date of its publication and will be valid for a period of ten years.

Deprived of the hegemonic levers used by the white sectors to dispose, define, finance and control research, Afro-descendants confront the challenge of freely constructing their theses without subordination to dominant models. It is important to note that the Afro-descendant question does exist within Brazilian society and not outside it, and is never isolated from the national question. There is no analysis that can be done with possible political efficiency than that which views the Afro-descendant within Brazilian society. The attempts to improve the situation of the Afro-descendant population should take the particularities of the different regions and the various configurations of the national landscape into consideration.

In December 2013 the UN General Assembly proclaimed 2015 to 2024 as the International Decade for People of African Descent (Resolution 68/237); this highlights the need to strengthen national, regional and international cooperation to ensure Afro-descendants enjoy full economic, social, cultural, civil and political rights, and are able to participate fully and equally in all areas of society.[36]

[36] UNESCO – United Nations Educational, Scientific and Cultural Organization, 'International Decade for People of African Descent (2015–2024)', 2015, accessed 7 December 2018, https://en.unesco.org/decade-people-african-descent/objectives.

The General Assembly states that 'recognition, justice and development' are the focus of the International Decade for People of African Descent. Its main objectives are:

- To promote the respect, protection and fulfilment of all human rights and fundamental liberties of Afro-descendants, as acknowledged by the Universal Declaration of Human Rights;
- To promote greater knowledge and respect for the diversified heritage, culture and contribution of people of African descent to the development of societies;
- To adopt and strengthen national, regional and international legal frameworks according to the Durban Declaration and Programme of Action[37] and the International Convention on the Elimination of all forms of Racial Discrimination, and to ensure its full implementation.[38]

The implementation of the Action Programme of the International Decade for People of African Descent, approved by the General Assembly, is to take place at various levels. At a national level, the States must take concrete and practical actions through the adoption and effective implementation nationally and internationally of legal frameworks, policies and programmes to combat racism, racial discrimination, xenophobia and correlative intolerance faced by Afro-descendants, bearing in mind the particular situation of women, young girls and boys.

At regional and international levels, the international community and the international and regional organisations are called to raise awareness about and disseminate the Durban Declaration and Action Programme and the International Convention on the Elimination of all Forms of Racial Discrimination, to help the States in the full and effective implementation of the commitments made in the scope of the Durban Declaration and Action Programme, collect statistical data, incorporate human rights in the development programmes, and honour and preserve the historic memory of Afro-descendant persons, among others. The International Decade for People of African Descent was officially launched in Brazil on 22 July 2015, during the opening of the Afro-Latino-American and Caribbean women's festival. The event took place in Brasília and was attended by Jorge Chediek, the Envoy of the

[37] United Nations, 'The Durban Declaration and Programme of Action', Durban Review Conference, Geneva, 20–24 April 2009, accessed 7 December 2018, www.un.org/en/durbanreview2009/ddpa.shtml.

[38] OHCHR – United Nations Office of the High Commissioner Human Rights, 'International Convention on the Elimination of All Forms of Racial Discrimination', 1969, accessed 7 December 2018, www.ohchr.org/EN/ProfessionalInterest/Pages/CERD.aspx.

UN Secretary-General for South-South Cooperation, among representatives of other authorities.

Chediek emphasised Brazil's importance on the world stage as the second-largest country with a black population, after Nigeria. He also highlighted that 'the UN does not accept or tolerate racism' and presented the organisation's three objectives for the Decade for People of African Descent: 'to strengthen the adoption of national, regional and international repercussion measures so that the Afro-descendants enjoy full economic, social, cultural and political rights; to promote greater knowledge about the diversity of Afro-descendant race and cultures; to approve and strengthen legal milestones on a national, regional and international level to eliminate all forms of racial discrimination.'[39] According to the then Minister of Women, Racial Equality and Human Rights, Nilma Limo Gomes (October 2015–May 2016), 'the Decade is an opportunity for countries to ponder and submit measures to overcome racism, aiming at promoting inclusion and social equality'.

The Temer government (2016–18) and the reduction in resources for policies promoting racial equality

The neoliberal government of Michel Temer has not dedicated the same attention to the Afro-descendant population as the governments of Lula da Silva and Dilma Rousseff. The Temer government executed only R$ 1.4 million of the R$22 million authorised by the National Congress as budget for racial promotion policies in 2017, equivalent to only 6% of the available resources.

The proposed budget for the promotion of racial equality policies in 2018 was just R$ 16 million, corresponding to a reduction of 34% compared with 2017. To contextualise, in contrast, from January to June 2017, the Temer administration spent R$ 100 million on official advertising to defend the reform of Brazil's Social Security (*Reforma Previdenciária*) advocated by his government. Besides removing resources from the area, the Temer government also stopped allocating resources to 'support the sustainable development of the maroon communities, Amerindian people and traditional communities.' In the analysis of Carmela Zigoni, political adviser of the Institute of Socioeconomic Studies (INESC), the reductions in the Temer government's proposed budget for

[39] ONUBR – Nações Unidas no Brasil, 'ONU e governo brasileiro iniciam planejamento da Década Internacional de Afrodescendentes', 3 March 2015, https://nacoesunidas.org/onu-e-governo-brasileiro-iniciam-planejamento-da-decada-internacional-de-afrodescendentes.

policies promoting racial equality reveals the deeply rooted mechanisms of institutional racism in Brazilian society.

Conclusions

The Golden Law, which officially abolished slavery in Brazil, was signed on 13 May 1888, completing 130 years in 2018. However, organisations of the black movement see no reason to celebrate and, since the early 1980s, this has been considered as a national day of struggle against racism. The objective has been to show that the legal abolition of slavery did not guarantee real conditions of social inclusion for the black population.

On the contrary, with the end of slavery, the ruling classes did not contribute to the inclusion of the ex-slaves as free workers, nor did they seek to create conditions for them to have a proper participation in society. Access to land, a key resource for ensuring the survival of their families, was not ensured for blacks, who were also excluded from the labour market, which was reserved for white workers, especially European immigrants.

Hence, the black population has sought to overcome the disastrous consequences of the abolitionist model imposed by the elites. In this context, the African continent has become an important reference for black movement organisations, primarily because it offers and expands the awareness about Afro-descendant origins and contributes decisively to the construction of the black identity of the militant.

The greatest challenge now is to think about the political conjuncture in contemporary Brazil allied to the struggles of the black movements and to understand the relationship between structural racism and the current economic model. In this process, affirmative actions play fundamental roles in overcoming entrenched inequalities in society. Their scope must be broadened because they are compensatory measures; they refer to the past to demand compensation for the damages caused. This seems contradictory, because affirmative actions look to the future by imposing a reflection on the inequalities of opportunities, and demanding a redistribution of resources because advantages have been and continue to be granted to one group to the detriment of another. Finally, affirmative actions set new standards and create new models that can serve as a reference and example for the new generations.

As far as higher education is concerned, there has been a breakthrough in the fight against Brazilian racism since the first universities instituted the quota system for blacks in the early 2000s. Currently, blacks and mixed-race people account for 27% of enrolments in higher education compared with just 8% before the introduction of quotas.[40]

This increase in schooling, however, has not yet had a great effect on employment. Research conducted by the Ethos Institute presents extremely worrying data: in 2016, blacks and mixed-race people accounted for only 34% of the employees in the country's top 500 companies.[41]Another study, conducted in 2016 by the SEADE Foundation[42] in partnership with Dieese[43] for the metropolitan region of the city of São Paulo, revealed that even with higher education, blacks and mixed-race people received only 65% of the salary obtained by whites in the same conditions.[44]

In his first documented act as interim President, Michel Temer presented his ministerial reform, reducing the number of ministries from thirty-two to twenty-three. The Ministry of Racial Equality, Women and Human Rights was among the those dissolved.[45] After taking office in May 2016, Temer cut public spending in strategic areas such as health and education. This inevitably aggravated the situation of socioeconomic segments already living in a situation of great vulnerability. There was, therefore, a racial factor within the execution of cuts to public policies that cannot be ignored. To think of a true transformation project for Brazilian society, such as a new economic proposal articulated with the fight against racial inequalities, the historical agenda of the black movement demands the inclusion of factors of gender and race.

[40] Luisa Bustamante and Maria Clara Vieira, 'Vergonha Brasileira', *Veja* 50:47 (2017), 81.

[41] Instituto Ethos, *Perfil Social, Racial e de Gênero de 500 maiores empresas do Brasil e as suas ações afirmativas* (São Paulo, 2016), www3.ethos.org.br/wp-content/uploads/2016/05/Perfil_Social_Tacial_Genero_500empresas.pdf.

[42] The State System of Data Analysis Foundation, known as the SEADE Foundation, is an agency of the Secretariat of Planning and Regional Development of the State Government of São Paulo. It is a national reference center for the production and dissemination of socioeconomic and demographic analyses and statistics.

[43] The Inter-Union Department of Statistics and Socioeconomic Studies (DIEESE). It was founded in 1955, with the objective of developing research to support the demands of trade unions, federations and national confederations of workers.

[44] SEADE, 'Instrução maior eleva fosso salarial entre branco e negro', 15 November 2017, accessed 19 January 2018, www.seade.gov.br/instrucao-maior-eleva-fosso-salarial-entre-branco-e-negro.

[45] Zero Hora, 'Temer (PMDB) elimina ministério que defendia mulheres, negros e LGBT', *Enio Verri*, 13 May 2016, accessed 19 January 2018, http://enioverri.com.br/temer-pmdb-elimina-ministerio-que-defendia-mulheres-negros-e-lgbt.

7

Brazil–Africa Relations After Lula: Continuity Without Priority

Gerhard Seibert & Paulo Fagundes Visentini

Introduction

A former trade union leader, Luís Inácio 'Lula' da Silva was the first politician from the left-wing Worker's Party (PT) to assume the Brazilian presidency. During Lula's two terms, foreign policy was an extremely important instrument to boost the country's development and international standing, just as it had been in the 20th century after the 1930s, albeit with varying paradigms. In addition to the national component, the foreign policy aimed to foster the development of its neighbouring countries on the other side of the Atlantic, from which the ancestors of a large proportion of Brazil's population had originated. Brazilian diplomacy therefore paid special attention to Africa by strengthening ties with several countries and developing an 'active, affirmative and purposeful' diplomacy. Brazil based its insertion in the African continent primarily on South–South (or horizontal) cooperation and the promotion of trade and investments. With this perspective, Lula intended to deepen and diversify ties with African countries by creating various initiatives to foster trade, investment, technical and cultural cooperation and also cooperation in security and defence. Therefore the delegations of Lula's frequent visits to African countries always included representatives of large Brazilian companies. The development projects presented to African countries were in the form of missions, seminars, small and large projects involving infrastructure and capacity building, mostly coordinated by the Brazilian Development Agency (ABC) and carried out by Brazilian technical institutions such as the Oswaldo Cruz Foundation (Fiocruz), the Brazilian Agricultural Research Corporation (EMBRAPA), the National Service for Industrial Training (SENAI), and dozens of other smaller organisations. The inauguration/reopening of seventeen embassies in African countries under the Lula administration also illustrates Brazil's foreign policy offensive in the continent.

In addition to bilateral relations with specific countries, Brazil–Africa relations were also strengthened within multilateral forums, such as the

UN and the WTO. It is important to highlight the favourable global political context during the 2000s in which the Lula government was projected internationally, when countries in the Global South were able to challenge the hegemony of the traditional powers and play a more active role in the international system. Demands of institutional reforms of the UN system leading to greater and more adequate representativeness of emerging powers were accompanied by the creation of new multilateral initiatives such as the India–Brazil–South Africa Dialogue Forum (IBSA), the Brazil, Russia, India, China and South Africa (BRICS) grouping, and other summits for South–South dialogues and cooperation; these were presented as viable alternatives to traditional international political structures that had remained largely unchanged since the end of the Second World War. However, the question that arose was whether these advances were already consolidated and sustainable over time.

As already indicated in the previous chapters, Brazilian policy on Africa has retracted in all sectors since the end of the Lula administration. Although officially still prominent on the Brazilian foreign policy agenda, in fact, Africa was no longer a priority. One reason for this decline was the economic recession facing Brazil in the early 2010s. The recession, together with the fall in commodity prices generated budget constraints, which in turn affected Brazil's foreign policy initiatives and its international projection. Significantly, in 2012, the ABC budget for technical cooperation programmes and projects with Africa – an important political instrument for the promotion of Brazil's bilateral relations – fell by 25%, and, consequently, many projects were discontinued.[1] In addition, Brazil's economic and financial problems triggered a retreat in its economic and commercial relations, strategic partnerships and also with regard to the provision of humanitarian aid. Although Presidents Dilma Rousseff and Michel Temer never made Africa a foreign policy priority, they sought to some extent maintain Brazil's international insertion project established in the previous decade under Lula. However, Brazil was eventually forced to take a more restrained stance towards its foreign engagements not only because of financial constraints, but also due to a more adverse external political environment and a severe domestic political crisis; the latter was marked by the controversial impeachment of Dilma Rousseff, who was definitively removed from office in August 2016, and the ongoing criminal investigation *Lava Jato* (literally 'Car

[1] Patrícia Campos de Mello, 'Brasil recua e reduz projetos de cooperação e doações para a África' *Folha de São Paulo*, 22 March 2015, accessed 8 December 2018, www1.folha.uol.com.br/mundo/2015/03/1606466-brasil-recua-e-reduz-projetos-de-cooperacao-e-doacoes-para-a-africa.shtml.

Wash') launched in 2014 by the Federal Police into massive corruption schemes involving large companies and the country's political class that has already resulted in the trial and sentencing of more than a hundred businesspeople and politicians, including Lula.

The Dilma Rousseff administration (2011–16)

During her almost five and a half years in office, Dilma's administration sought to sustain the active and ambitious diplomacy of her predecessor. At first sight, Dilma's election symbolised the continuity of Brazil's international insertion project, but in fact it was more a case of 'continuity without priority'. Her Foreign Ministers, Antônio Patriota (2011–13), Luiz Alberto Figueiredo (2013–14) and Mauro Vieira (2014–16), were all career diplomats and they formally reaffirmed their intention to maintain the pattern of relations with the African continent. However, as domestic politics became more complex and challenging, foreign policy steadily shifted away from the president. In addition, Dilma Rousseff did not consider international affairs a personal priority. This is demonstrated by the reduction in the number of official trips abroad she made as President, notably to the African continent. Whereas Lula had made visits to twenty-three different African countries in eight years, Rousseff visited only six in five and a half years. She made her first trip to Africa in October 2011, visiting South Africa (attending the Fifth IBSA Summit), Angola and Mozambique. During her second visit to Africa, in February 2013, she attended the Third Africa–South America (ASA) Summit in Malabo, Equatorial Guinea; before returning to Brazil, she also went to Abuja for talks with the Nigerian President. In March 2013, she visited South Africa to attend the Fifth BRICS Summit of Heads of State and Government. Two months later, she participated in the Fiftieth Anniversary Summit of the African Union in Addis Ababa, Ethiopia, as a special guest. In December that year, Dilma returned to South Africa, this time for the funeral of Nelson Mandela, accompanied by her four predecessors Luís Inácio Lula da Silva, Fernando Henrique Cardoso, Fernando Collor de Mello and José Sarney. This was her last visit to an African country.

Dilma's position broke with her predecessors' more active presidential diplomacy. As already pointed out, this withdrawal from the international stage was not only from the presidency but also included a budget cut for international cooperation projects and a reduction in the diplomatic staff. It is important to recall that, from 2013, along with questions about Brazil's internal politics, some of the Brazilian middle class started to oppose the country's South–South cooperation, claiming that it was too ideologically oriented without generating adequate benefits for the country's national interests. According to Cervo and Lessa, the Rousseff administration represented a decline in Brazilian foreign policy efforts. However, they also note that, in addition to the weaknesses of her government, the internal and external political and economic contexts were very different from when Lula was in power.[2] Marcondes and Mawdsley draw attention to another important aspect of Rousseff's foreign policy, namely that just a few months after she took office she made it clear she was interested in a result-orientated diplomacy, with more concrete achievements and less political 'symbolism'.[3] Such a stance may be perceived as an attempt by the President to contain the animosities of a national elite that pressed for more concrete foreign policy results.

The resulting decline in Brazil's development cooperation was quite significant; however, in relation to the Americas and the Caribbean, Africa remained in a relatively privileged position and suffered proportionally fewer cutbacks. Despite budget cuts, the African continent was the main recipient of South–South technical cooperation projects financed by Brazil between 2011 and 2014, with between 50.6% (2011) and 71.4% (2014) of the reduced annual budgets.[4] The focus was mainly on cooperation projects building infrastructure and empowering the institutional capacities of African countries. It is important to note that parallel to the difficulties and dilemmas in Brazilian politics (and which had a direct impact on its international projection and therefore on its partnerships in development cooperation), the African continent was in a sort of 'Age of Choices', that is, there were alternative providers of development cooperation and business opportunities. In this context, other external actors were able to neutralise the effects of the Brazilian withdrawal, with an emphasis on India and China.

The Michel Temer administration (2016–18)

Following the May 2016 start of President Dilma Rousseff's controversial impeachment process due to accusations of fiscal irresponsibility, then-Vice-President Michel Temer took over as Brazil's interim President

[2] Amado Luiz Cervo and Antônio Carlos Lessa, 'O declínio: inserção internacional do Brasil (2011–2014)', *Revista Brasileira de Política Internacional* 57:2 (2014), 133–51.

[3] Danilo Marcondes and Emma Mawdsley, 'South–South in Retreat? The transitions from Lula to Rousseff to Temer and Brazilian development cooperation', *International Affairs* 93:3 (2017), 681–99.

[4] ABC, 'Execução Financeira', 2010, accessed 10 May 2018, www.abc.gov.br/Content/ABC/imagens/africa_financeiro.png.

until the end of the term of office in December 2018. The internal situation remained turbulent: there were questions about the legitimacy of the newly established government and of its institutions, deepening political polarisation within society, civil-military tensions, unpopular economic austerity measures, social instability, and the ongoing *Lava Jato* investigations. All these factors ended up weighing negatively on Brazil's international insertion, including its relations with African countries.

In the wake of promoting changes and disruptions with the previous government, in May 2016, José Serra of the PSDB (Brazilian Social Democracy Party, the party of former President Fernando Henrique Cardoso), a politician and not a career diplomat, was appointed Foreign Minister. In his first public declaration, Serra criticised the mistakes and exaggerations of the previous Lula and Dilma administrations, especially with regard to South–South cooperation, which he considered too ideologically oriented.[5] He emphasised that Brazilian foreign policy would now prioritise the signing of trade agreements and attracting foreign investments to Brazil. Despite Serra's rhetoric against South–South cooperation, he stated that Brazil would remain 'open' to developing countries with an internal market capable of absorbing Brazilian products, including African countries. José Serra resigned for health reasons in February 2017 and was replaced by Aloysio Nunes – also a political affiliate of the PSDB. Nunes drew attention to the importance of Brazil's continuity within BRICS and IBSA. To some extent, he wanted to go back to the positions of previous governments, albeit minimally. Two months after his appointment, Nunes made a trip to Namibia, Botswana, Malawi, Mozambique and South Africa in search of business and investment opportunities for Brazilian companies. His mission was officially announced as a concrete sign of the priority Brazil placed on its relations with Africa. In October that year, he made another trip to Africa, visiting Ghana, Nigeria, Côte d'Ivoire and Benin to strengthen political, economic and cultural ties with these countries, and South Africa, where he participated in the Eighth Meeting of the Trilateral Ministerial Commission of IBSA held in Durban. At the time, his ministry declared that relations with Africa constituted a permanent priority of the Brazilian government. In February 2018, he made a short visit to Luanda where he announced the concession of new Brazilian loans of $2 billion to finance investments and imports from Brazil.

[5] Adriana Erthal Abdenur, 'Brazil-Africa Relations: From boom to bust?' in *Africa and the World. Bilateral and Multilateral International Diplomacy* edited by Dawn Nagar and Charles Mutasa (London: Palgrave Macmillan, 2018).

Undeniably, the new Brazilian foreign policy under Temer began to respond to the interests of the conservative segments of society, both politically (distancing themselves from what they considered an ideologically minded foreign policy) and economically (prioritising economic relations with the advanced economies and with the countries considered to be of greater economic potential within the developing world). Thus, under Temer, Brazilian foreign policy became orientated predominantly by the North–South axis, and the previous autonomist project and diversification of foreign relations have been stopped or put on hold. While many of the multilateral initiatives (such as the BRICS) were maintained, the government demonstrated its preference for strengthening bilateral relations with countries considered politically and economically relevant to the detriment of multilateral forums. Therefore, even if the main multilateral initiatives developed and strengthened under Lula were formally maintained (IBSA, BRICS, the South Atlantic Peace and Cooperation Zone – ZOPACAS, the Summit of South American–Arab Countries – ASPA, ASA, and the Community of Portuguese-speaking Countries – CPLP), the effect of the lack of sustainability resulted in negative consequences for Brazil's involvement and image abroad.

The relations between Brazil and Africa were predominantly determined by the economic-commercial aspect. Apart from the officially Portuguese-speaking African (Palop) countries, Nigeria, South Africa and Senegal were among the few countries that maintained strong ties with Brazil. Despite initial statements by Foreign Minister Serra in May 2016 about the possibility of closing some African embassies established under the Lula presidency, Brazilian diplomats in the African continent said that Brazil would maintain its commitment. In fact, contrary to what happened in the 1990s, the Temer administration did not close any of Brazil's thirty-eight diplomatic representations in Africa. In addition to President Temer's different foreign policy approach, new challenges began to weigh on Brazil–Africa relations, notably: (i) the main Brazilian public and private companies (the 'national champions')[6] operating in the African continent faced an unfavourable political-economic scenario of intense difficulties (the result of anti-corruption operations) in both Brazil and Africa; and (ii) new budget cuts, which again had direct effects on cooperation projects in several countries.

[6] Such as Petrobras, Norberto Odebrecht, Camargo Corrêa and Vale, among others present in Africa since the 1970s.

Declining trade and investments

As outlined in Chapter 2, during the first decade of the 2000s Brazil's economic relations were marked by the intensification of Brazilian investments in the African continent, especially in energy, mining and construction. These investments came primarily from large Brazilian companies that were in an internationalisation process supported mainly by public financing in the form of credits from the Brazilian Development Bank (BNDES). Between 2007 and 2015, BNDES financed Brazilian investments in Africa with loans of $4.2 billion. In December 2013, the bank opened a regional Africa office in Johannesburg to further boost Brazilian investments in the continent. The large construction companies were the main beneficiaries of the funds, and the total amount was divided between just three countries: Angola (84% of the loans), Mozambique (10.7%) and Ghana (5.2%). In October 2016, BNDES announced the suspension of the disbursement of $4.7 billion for twenty-five loans conceded to the construction companies Norberto Odebrecht, OAS, Queiroz Galvão, Camargo Côrrea and Andrade Gutierrez for foreign projects, on the grounds that they were under investigation in the *Lava Jato* operation for suspicion of corruption. The measure affected nineteen projects in six Latin American countries and four projects financed with $809 million in Angola (all by Odebrecht) and one each in Ghana and Mozambique (both by Andrade Gutierrez), financed with $202 million and $320 million respectively. Following investigations, the bank resumed the payment of three loans in March 2017, including one for a road construction project by Andrade Gutierrez in Ghana. As a result of the *Lava Jato* investigations, BNDES loans to finance Brazilian projects in Africa in 2016 accounted for only 1% of the annual average disbursed in the eight previous years: $6 million vs. $446 million.[7]

According to the Brazilian Ministry for Industry, Foreign Trade and Services (MDIC), the trade flows between Brazil and Africa in the first year of Dilma's government continued to grow, reaching $27.7 billion in 2011. This was followed by a slight decline in 2012 to $26.5 billion. In 2013, Brazil's trade with Africa peaked at $28.5 billion. Thereafter and in line with the general downward trend in its foreign trade, figures then dropped steadily to $26.8 billion in 2014, $17 billion in 2015 and only $12.4 billion in 2016; this was due not only to Brazil's domestic economic crisis, but also to the economic decline in African oil-producing

[7] Amanda Rossi, 'O aeroporto fantasma feito pela Odebrecht em Moçambique, que o BNDES financiou e tomou calote', *BBC Brasil*, 27 November 2017, accessed 7 December 2018, www.bbc.com/portuguese/brasil-42074053.

countries. In 2017 Brazil's trade with Africa increased to $14.9 billion, accompanying the beginning of a modest recovery in its overall economy.[8] The figures demonstrate that the positive results until 2013 were due to the combination of two factors: commodity and capital exports. It is important to emphasise that the *Lava Jato* anti-corruption investigation, initiated in 2014, affected the Brazilian transnational companies operating in African countries in particular. In turn, the consequent disinvestments by these large companies also contributed to the retraction in relations with African countries in other sectors.

Between 2003 and 2011, Brazil was the eleventh-largest foreign investor in Africa with an annual average of 2.8% of total foreign investments in terms of value. The Brazilian investments were concentrated in the energy, mining and construction sectors. During this period, Angola, Mozambique, South Africa, Libya, Egypt, Guinea-Conakry and Namibia were the main destinations for Brazilian investments.[9] From 2007 to 2011, Brazilian investments in Africa increased by 10.7%, less than investments in Africa made by other emerging economies; for example, Turkey increased its investments in the continent by 49.5% in the same period.[10] In recent years, several Brazilian companies in Africa have disinvested as a result of Brazil's economic crisis and the *Lava Jato* investigations in fraud and corruption schemes. Responding to demands by local enterprises to counteract this trend, Brazil signed Agreements for Cooperation and Facilitation of Investments (ACFI) with Angola, Mozambique and Malawi in 2015 to promote investments in these countries. In Malawi, the mining company Vale was Brazil's sole investor that accounted for 26% of the country's total foreign direct investment. This investment was related to the construction of the 912 km Nacala Corridor railway (567 miles) that links the Moatize coal mine with the port of Nacala in Tete province in Mozambique and crosses 237 km (147 miles)of Malawian territory. In 2007, Vale signed an exploration concession for the Moatize coal mine. The coal extraction at the

[8] 'Balança Comercial Brasileira: Países e Blocos', Ministério da Indústria, Comércio Exterior e Serviços, accessed 8 May 2018, www.mdic.gov.br/index.php/comercio-exterior/estatisticas-de-comercio-exterior/balanca-comercial-brasileira-mensal-2.

[9] Pedro da Motta Veiga and Sandra Polónia Rios, *Os investimentos brasileiros na África: características, tendências e agenda de política*. Texto CINDES 39 (Rio de Janeiro; Centro de Estudos de Integração e Desenvolvimento – CINDES, 2014), 16,17, 21.

[10] Paula Adamo Idoeta, 'Ainda como investidor pequeno, Brasil está na corrida para fincar pé na África', *BBC Brasil*, 9 May 2012, www.bbc.com/portuguese/noticias/2012/05/120504_brasil_africa_fdi_pai.

Moatize mine started in 2011. In March 2017, the Japanese company Mitsui took over 15% of Vale's 95% in the Moatize mine for $255 million and paid $513 million for half of Vale's 70% stake in the Nacala Logistic Corridor. In doing so, Vale sought to mitigate possible risks and to reduce capital investments. The Nacala Logistic Corridor, Vale's biggest foreign investment ever of $4.4 billion, was inaugurated in May 2017 in the presence of Mozambican President Filipe Nyusi and Brazil's Foreign Minister Aloysio Nunes. From 2016 to 2017, coal production in Moatize increased from 5.6 million tons to 11.2 million tons.

Vale's investment in a copper mine in neighbouring Zambia, already mentioned in Chapter 2, was less successful. In 2017, the joint venture (50% each) of Vale and the South African-based African Rainbow Minerals (ARM), established in 2009, sold its 80% stake in the Lubambe Copper Mine in Chililabombwe in the Copper Belt for $97.1 million to the Australian private equity firm EMR Capital Group. Vale and ARM had spent more than $400 million building the mine, but decided to exit the project due to financial losses.[11] Already in 2014, Vale was hit by a major setback in Africa when the government of Guinea-Conakry revoked a concession for half of the Simandou iron ore mine held by its joint venture with the Israeli company Beny Steinmetz Group Resources (BSGR); supposedly, the latter had obtained the exploration concession in 2008 by paying bribes to the previous government. The group always fiercely denied any wrongdoing and alleged it was the victim of a conspiracy. In 2010, Vale had agreed to pay $2.5 billion for 51% stake in BSGR's concession; however, the Israeli company had only invested $160 million for developing the mine but it had not paid anything for the exploration license. When the two companies lost the concession, Vale had actually paid only a first instalment of $500 million to BSGR. In March 2015, Vale formally transferred its 51% interest in the joint venture back to BSGR but demanded compensation from BSGR for the lost investments. Consequently, Vale sought international arbitration against BSGR in an attempt to recover the failed investment in the Simandou iron ore mine.[12]

[11] Hemanth Kumar, 'EMR Capital Buys 80% Interest in Zambia's Lubambe Copper Mine', *Mining Technology*, 15 August 2017, www.mining-technology.com/news/newsemr-capital-buys-80-interest-in-zambias-lubambe-copper-mine-5901451.

[12] Jon Yeomans, 'Inside Simandou: The mining project that has cursed all who come near it', The Telegraph, 5 June 2017, accessed 7 December 2018, www.telegraph.co.uk/business/2017/06/05/inside-simandou-mining-project-has-cursed-come-near.

The state-owned oil company, Petrobras, had been another major investor in Africa. The company has been severely hit by the corruption schemes investigated since 2014. The Federal Police estimated that altogether nearly $3 billion was diverted from the company's accounts by fraudulent practices. From the late 1970s, the company's operational centre in Africa was in Angola, but it was also engaged in the oil sectors of Benin, Equatorial Guinea, Gabon, Libya, Namibia, Nigeria, Senegal and Tanzania after the company's African investments expanded during the Lula administration. In 2011, the acquisition of an oil block in Benin by Petrobas for $34.5 million involved the payments of bribes of $10 million. One of the beneficiaries of the kickbacks was Eduardo Cunha of the Brazilian Democratic Movement (MDB), former president of the Chamber of Deputies, the lower house of Brazil's National Congress, and protagonist of Dilma's impeachment process. He was detained from October 2016, and in November 2017 was sentenced to fourteen and a half years imprisonment for corruption and money laundering.[13] In 2013, Petrobras established a joint venture for oil and gas production in Africa by selling 50% of its subsidiary Petrobras Oil & Gas for $1.5 billion to the Brazilian investment bank BTG Pactual (40%) and the London-based Helios Investment Partners (10%), engaged in private investments in Africa. As already mentioned, by 2016, Petrobras Oil & Gas was only producing oil in Angola and Nigeria, and was conducting oil exploration activities in Gabon and Tanzania. Subsequently, Petrobras sold its interests in three of these countries. As part of its disinvestment plan in Africa, in November 2017 Petrobras announced the beginning of the sale of the joint venture that still owned the concessions of two oil fields in Nigeria.

Brazil's bus manufacturer Marcopolo exports buses to several African countries. The company's sales in Africa represent about 5% of its global annual production. Besides factories in China, India, Australia, Argentina, Columbia and Mexico, the company has production plants in Johannesburg, South Africa, and in Suez, Egypt. The production at the Marcopolo plant in Johannesburg, established in 2000, increased from 258 units in 2013 to 334 units in 2015, but then fell to 298 units in 2016. In 2017, production rose again by 18.8% to 354 units. The company in Suez, GB Polo Bus Manufacturing Company, is a joint venture with the local manufacturer GB Auto SAE, established in 2008. At the time, Marcopolo expected the plant to produce 1,500 units in 2009 and

[13] *CartaCapital*, 'Lava Jato: 41ª fase foca em operações da Petrobras na África', 25 May 2017, accessed 7 December 2018, www.cartacapital.com.br/politica/lava-jato-41a-fase-foca-em-operacoes-da-petrobras-na-africa.

up to 5,000 units annually from the fifth year. During the turmoil of the Arab Spring, production was temporarily suspended in 2011 and subsequently reached a total of just 2,175 units by mid-2013. From 2014 to 2015 the number of units produced in the Suez plant more than doubled from 776 to 1,190 units before falling again to 693 in 2016. In June 2017, Marcopolo reduced its participation in the joint venture from 49% to 20% because efforts to improve the performance of the factory had failed due to exchange rate, political and market problems.[14]

The engineering and construction company Norberto Odebrecht has been one of Brazil's major investors in Africa. As indicated in Chapter 2, the company has focused its economic activities in Angola, where it has been involved since 1984 when it was engaged in the construction of the Capanda hydroelectric dam. Although it is the country's largest private sector employer, the number of Angolan employees decreased from 11,787 to 9,601 from 2015 to 2016. In 2016, Odebrecht employed a total of 10,284 people (12.9% of its total workforce of 79,616) in Africa as a whole.[15] In addition to engineering and construction, Odebrecht's activities in Angola also include participation in a sugar cane plantation for the production of sugar and ethanol, a large shopping mall in Luanda and the supermarket chain *NossoSuper* with thirty-one shops. In August 2017, Odebrecht sold its 16.4% stake in the Catoca diamond mine in Lunda Sul province. Currently, Odebrecht is also engaged in construction works in Ghana and Mozambique. In the past, the company had projects in Botswana, Djibouti, Libya, Gabon, Equatorial Guinea, Guinea-Conakry, Liberia, the Republic of Congo and South Africa. In 2009, Odebrecht's projects in African countries generated $2,420 million of income, corresponding to some 10% of the company's overall revenues in that year.

Corrupt business practices have meant the company has been severely affected by the investigations of the *Lava Jato* operation. Marcelo Odebrecht, the company's former president, was detained in June 2015 and subsequently tried and sentenced to nineteen years and four months of imprisonment for corruption. Among others, the company admitted paying bribes estimated at $900,000 between 2011 and 2014 to Mozambican government officials to obtain the order for the construction of the Nacala International Airport; initially this was budgeted for $90 million

[14] *Marcopolo*, 'Resultados do Exercício em 2017', 21 February 2018, accessed 19 May 2018, http://ri.marcopolo.com.br/ptb/3366/Relatrio%20da%20Administrao%202017.pdf.

[15] Odebrecht, '2017 Odebrecht uma grande transformação', n.d., accessed 20 May 2018, www.odebrecht.com/sites/default/files/relatorio_anual_2017.pdf.

but ultimately cost $216.5 million.[16] Co-financed with a $125 million loan by BNDES, Mozambique's first new airport since independence in 1975 was inaugurated in late 2014. The BNDES loan for the airport had been made possible by Brazil's cancellation of Mozambique's previous bilateral debts of $315 million in 2004. In 2015, the modern airport, the second largest in Mozambique after Maputo, was awarded the International Property Awards prize for best architectural design for public buildings in Africa. Despite a capacity of 500,000 passengers per year, Nacala airport receives less than 20,000, while the expected international flights never arrived; moreover, the airport receives only two domestic commercial flights operated weekly by *Linhas Aéreas de Moçambique* (LAM) from Maputo and two private flights operated by Vale. In comparison, Nampula airport, 190 km (118 miles) from Nacala, operates fifty-seven flights a week. As the Nacala airport functions with less than 4% of its capacity, its operational costs are twice the receipts.[17] Its unsustainable external debt led to Mozambique's failure to repay the instalments of the BNDES loan in November 2016 and, as a result, the bank activated the export credit insurance to recover the overdue instalments of $7.5 million in June 2017. This was the first default experienced by the BNDES in operations contracted by foreign governments. Subsequently, direct negotiations took place between the governments of Brazil and Mozambique on the repayment of the $125 million BNDES credit for the Nacala airport.[18]

The construction and engineering company Camargo Corrêa was also affected in Brazil by the *Lava Jato* investigations due to the payments of kickbacks; its African activities focused on Angola where it has built roads, power lines, schools, and hospitals. From 2007 to 2012, the BNDES conceded the company loans of $213.1 million for its projects in Angola. In Mozambique, the company was contracted by Vale for construction works in the Moatize coal mine and the port of Nacala. In addition, Camargo Corrêa heads a consortium contracted by the Mozambican government in 2008 for the construction of the 1,500 MW Mphanda-Nkuwa hydroelectric dam on the Zambezi, 60 km (37 miles) downstream of the existing Cahora Bassa Dam. In 2010, the Mozambican

[16] 'Corrupção: Os tentáculos da Odebrecht em Angola e Moçambique', *Deutsche Welle*, 25 April 2017, www.dw.com/pt-002/corrupção-os-tentáculos-da-odebrecht-em-angola-e-moçambique/a-38569474.

[17] Rossi, 'O aeroporto fantasma'.

[18] *BNDES*, 'Nota à imprensa: BNDES aciona seguro de crédito para operações com Moçambique', 24 June 2017, accessed 7 December 2018, www.bndes.gov.br/wps/portal/site/home/imprensa/noticias/conteudo/bndes-aciona-seguro-de-credito-para-operacoes-com-mocambique.

government authorised the construction of the Mphanda-Nkuwa dam. The dam, budgeted at $2 billion, has been controversial due to the need to relocate local inhabitants and the expected negative environmental impact. After taking over the Portuguese cement company Cimpor in 2012, Camargo Corrêa established the subsidiary InterCement, which owns cement factories in Angola, Cabo Verde, Egypt, Mozambique and South Africa. The company is market leader in the sector in Cabo Verde and Mozambique.[19]

Andrade Gutierrez, another Brazilian construction and engineering company, has operated in more than forty countries since 1948. In Africa, it was responsible for the construction of infrastructure projects in Algeria, Angola, Cameroon, the Democratic Republic of the Congo (DRC), Equatorial Guinea, Ghana, Guinea-Conakry, Libya, Mali, Mauretania, Mozambique and the Republic of Congo. The company's construction projects in Africa have been carried out by its Portuguese subsidiary Zagope, acquired in 1988. Headquartered in Portugal, Zagope has access to European development funds for the financing of projects in Africa. In 2015, Zagope was renamed Andrade Gutierrez Europa, África, Ásia (AG EAA). In March 2017, the BNDES resumed the disbursement of the $202 million loan for the company's road construction project in Ghana initiated in 2013, following suspension in 2016 due to the *Lava Jato* corruption investigation. However, a $320 million loan remained suspended and hence construction works, initiated in 2014, were interrupted for the Moamba Major hydroelectric dam on the Incomáti River in Maputo province in Mozambique, which would also have provided the region's population with drinking water.[20]

Since its involvement in the *Lava Jato* scandal, the construction company Queiroz Galvão has lost almost two thirds of its revenues, dismissed more than half of its personnel and several former executives have been sentenced to prison terms. In 2005, the company began to expand its activities to Africa; its International Construction branch has been engaged in Angola, Ethiopia, Gabon, Ghana, Equatorial Guinea, Libya, Mozambique, Namibia, Kenya, Senegal and Tanzania. In 2018, Queiroz Galvão was only active in road and airport construction in

[19] Camargo Corrêa, 'Group's Business', accessed 20 May 2018, www.camargocorrea.com.br/en/Group.html.

[20] *Macauhub*, 'Governo de Moçambique negoceia reinício das obras da barragem de Moamba-Major', 8 February 2018, accessed 7 December 2018, https://macauhub.com.mo/pt/2018/02/08/pt-governo-de-mocambique-negoceia-reinicio-das-obras-da-barragem-de-moamba-major.

Ghana and in real estate development, an urban requalification project and urban cleaning services in Luanda, Angola.[21]

The construction company OAS, founded in 1976, started its expansion to Africa in 2009. In 2012, Vale signed two contracts worth $242 million with OAS for construction works in the Nacala harbour and the Nacala Logistics Corridor railway. In 2013, the company's revenues in Africa represented 35% of its income abroad. At the time, OAS employed 6,000 people in Africa, 300 of whom Brazilians.[22] In 2015, five OAS executives were sentenced to prison terms of between four and sixteen years for their involvement in bribery schemes in Brazil. Subsequently, the company dismissed more than 15,000 employees and requested court protection from creditors before presenting a proposal to restructure debts of almost $2.5 billion. Although it has also been severely affected by the *Lava Jato* operation, OAS has maintained representations in Angola, Côte d'Ivoire, Equatorial Guinea, Guinea-Conakry, Mozambique and Namibia.

International cooperation

Until 2010, Brazil stepped up its international cooperation efforts for the development of Southern countries. While this took shape in various forms, technical cooperation was the most important instrument; however, it has been affected by consecutive budget cuts since Rousseff's government. Nevertheless, the ABC, part of the Foreign Ministry and responsible for coordinating and monitoring Brazil's technical cooperation, has remained one of the main agents of bi- and multilateral development projects. Despite the financial constraints, a few large cooperation projects were initiated or completed. In 2014, the ABC inaugurated the second phase of the experimental cotton station in Sotuba, Mali, to provide technical support to the West African cotton-producing countries Mali, Chad, Benin and Burkina Faso as part of the Cotton-4 project.[23] At the same time, Togo joined the regional cotton

[21] Queiroz Galvão, 'Construção Internacional', 14 July 2016, accessed 20 May 2018, www.grupoqueirozgalvao.com.br/en/construcao-internacional.

[22] Roberto Rockmann, 'Infraestrutura e serviços estimulam negócios na África', *Valor Econômico*, 25 October 2013, accessed 23 December 2018, www.valor.com.br/brasil/3316182/infraestrutura-e-servicos-estimulam-negocios-na-africa.

[23] The first phase of the project, 'Support for the Development of the Cotton Sector of the C-4 Countries (Benin, Burkina Faso, Chad and Mali)', or Cotton-4, was launched in 2008 and was extended until December 2013. It aimed to contribute to increasing the competitiveness of the cotton production chain in the C-4 countries.

project, which was implemented by EMBRAPA. Encouraged by the experience of the Cotton 4 + Togo project, in 2015 EMBRAPA initiated two similar regional cotton projects in Malawi and Mozambique, and Tanzania, Kenya and Burundi. Finally in 2013, after consecutive delays, an antiretroviral drugs manufacturing factory, established by Fiocruz in partnership with the *Sociedade Moçambicana de Medicamentos* (SMM) in Maputo, started local drugs production. However, as noted, in 2017 it was decided to replace the production of antiretroviral (ARV) drugs by that of analgesics and six other essential drugs, since the ARVs introduced from Brazil had become out-dated for the treatment of HIV. In 2014, SENAI inaugurated a vocational training centre in São Tomé, the fourth in Portuguese-speaking African countries. However, a fifth vocational training centre in Maputo did not pass the planning phase due to financial problems. The large Trilateral Agriculture Development Cooperation Programme in Mozambique's Tropical Savannah (ProSAVANA), in Mozambique's Nacala Corridor, launched by EMBRAPA together with the Japanese Cooperation Agency in 2011, has repeatedly met fierce opposition from local small farmers, who have accused the organisations in charge of the project of primarily serving foreign agribusiness interests. During the first term of the Dilma presidency, the ABC reduced its technical cooperation both in financial terms and with regard to the number of projects. The ABC's budget executed in African countries dropped from $13.7 million in 2011 to only $5.1 million in 2014, considerably less than the agency's $19.8 million budget for Africa reported for 2010, the last year of the Lula presidency. The number of projects in Africa fell from 253 in 2010 to 223 in 2011 and to just 138 in 2013, but then increased to 161 in 2014 despite a lower budget in that year. In fact, the ABC's average project expenditure in Africa declined from $60,639 in 2013 to $31,488 in 2014.[24] Inevitably, Brazil's overall development cooperation suffered a similar decline affected by a downward trend during the Rousseff presidency. As already shown in Chapter 4, the country's total annual cooperation expenditure dropped from $923 million in 2010 to $396.8 million in 2013.

Nevertheless, ongoing high-level political and diplomatic contacts between Brazil and Africa resulted in the opening of negotiations and even the signature of several new agreements in various areas such as technical cooperation and defence. Driven by Brazil's geo-strategic interests in the South Atlantic region, the latter was one of the areas of

[24] Agência Brasileira de Cooperação, 'África – Execução Financeira 2000–2014', 2010, accessed 8 May 2018, www.abc.gov.br/Content/ABC/imagens/africa_financeiro.png.

bilateral cooperation relations that least felt the retraction. Agreements on defence were signed with Angola, Nigeria, Senegal, South Africa, Namibia, Equatorial Guinea and Mozambique. In October 2013, the First Session of the Brazil–Nigeria Mechanism of Strategic Dialogue also took place. In the same year, Celso Amorim, now Defence Minister, travelled to Cabo Verde to discuss the strengthening of security conditions in the South Atlantic, and to inaugurate Brazil's permanent naval mission in Praia in support of the modernisation of Cabo Verde's Coast Guard. In 2014, Brazil's Navy established another naval mission centre in São Tomé to boost the maritime security cooperation with the archipelago in the oil-rich Gulf of Guinea. In September that year, two major developments in the area of defence cooperation marked Brazil–Africa relations: (i) the agreement to sell seven 500-ton Brazilian patrol vessels produced by the state-owned company *Empresa Gerencial de Projetos Navais* (EMGEPRON) to the Angolan Navy; and (ii) the announcement of joint defence studies and military technological research by Brazil and South Africa, in order to win new markets and become strong enough to compete with more developed countries in the defence industry sector. However, in 2016, the Angolan Navy cancelled the order for the construction of the seven patrol boats on the grounds that the Brazilian shipyard lacked the logistical capacity to deliver them in time.

Brazil's role in peace processes and in political and humanitarian crisis in Africa has also been important. In recent years, Brazil has participated in UN Peacekeeping Missions in Western Sahara (MINURSO), Central African Republic (MINUSCA), DRC (MONUSCO), Sudan (UNISFA) and South Sudan (UNMISS). The Brazilian presidency of the UN Peacebuilding Commission Guinea-Bissau Configuration (PBC-GB) has been presented as another example of Brazil's engagement in conflict-stricken regions; it was established in December 2007 to promote peace and political stability in this small country marked by continuous political instability. In May 2018, the Brazilian diplomat, José Viegas Filho, was appointed Special Representative of the UN Secretary-General in Guinea-Bissau, becoming the ninth foreign diplomat in this position since 1999.[25] Despite the ambitions and efforts of Brazil and other regional and international mediators, such as the UN and ECOWAS, the long lasting political crisis in Guinea-Bissau has largely remained unresolved; however, there has not been another military coup since 2012.

[25] UNIOGBIS, 'Secretary-General appoints José Viegas Filho from Brazil as Special Representative for Guinea-Bissau', 7 May 2018, accessed 13 May 2018, https://uniogbis.unmissions.org/en/secretary-general-appoints-josé-viegas-filho-brazil-special-representative-guinea-bissau.

Still on the issue of humanitarian cooperation, in 2014, Brazil provided food and medical aid worth $9.6 million through the UN to combat the Ebola epidemic in the three West African countries of Guinea-Conakry, Liberia and Sierra Leone. This modest amount represented the bulk of Brazil's total humanitarian aid of only $11.9 million disbursed in Africa in that year. This total was more than the $6.9 million the country spent on humanitarian aid in Africa in 2013, but considerably less than the total amount of $65.2 million made available in 2012.[26]

Multilateral dimensions of Brazil–Africa relations

In the multilateral sphere, Brazilian diplomacy clearly got less engaged although formerly policies remained for almost all the different initiatives set up during the Lula administration. In addition to the lack of political support and cuts in the cooperation budget on the domestic front, there was a retraction of the regional political leaderships worldwide due to internal problems and a more adverse international environment in the aftermath of the 2008 international financial crisis (falling prices of oil, raw materials and other commodities, important for Brazil and for the African countries). Officially the foreign policy strategies and objectives were maintained during the Rousseff government, but real efforts were significantly less than under Lula. Nevertheless, initially relations with Africa suffered relatively little in the sphere of South–South cooperation.

The inauguration of Dilma Rousseff in 2011 coincided with the presence of all three IBSA countries as non-permanent members of the UN Security Council. Brazil had drawn the international community's attention through its active presence in the United Nations, a role undertaken to emphasise its ambitions of a permanent seat in a reformed UN Security Council. In his inauguration speech, Foreign Minister Antonio Patriota indicated that the new government would continue with the same policies when he reiterated the commitment to 'maintaining an active agenda with our partners in Africa – intensifying our cooperation and our dialogue with our brother continent'. However, despite this announcement, already before President Dilma's contested departure in 2016, in fact Brazil's foreign policy for Africa suffered a significantly different approach.

Nevertheless, in the first years of Dilma's presidency, Brazil's diplomacy benefited from its more active Africa policy and had two successful candidatures in international organisations. In 2011, Brazil's candidate

[26] Campos de Mello, 'Brasil recua e reduz projetos'.

José Graziano da Silva was elected Director-General of the FAO thanks to the votes of African countries. In June 2015, he was re-elected for a second four-year term with 177 out of the 182 votes of member countries. In May 2013, the Brazilian diplomat, Roberto Azevêdo, was elected as Director-General of the WTO with strong support from African countries. He received ninety-three votes from the 159 member countries that participated in the ballot. As Brazil had always struggled against the protectionist trade policies of Western countries, his election was presented as a further step towards building a new global order. Azevêdo had been head of Brazil's delegation in the WTO and had campaigned against the policy of agricultural subsidies in Western countries. According to then-Foreign Minister Antonio Patriota, Azevêdo's election was an opportunity for emerging powers to show their leadership capacities. In February 2017, Azevêdo was re-elected unopposed to the post. As one of the world's largest exporters of agricultural commodities, Brazil has a particular political interest in the leadership of the two organisations.

On the multilateral level Brazil continued to consider the nine-member CPLP as a space to strengthen South–South relations and promote the Portuguese language internationally. At the community's Tenth Summit of Heads of State and Government, in Díli, East Timor, in 2014, Equatorial Guinea was admitted as the ninth member country, with Brazilian support. The country's admission had been controversial due to its regime's notorious record of human rights violations; moreover, Portuguese was introduced as the country's third official language – after Spanish and French (since 1998) – in the former Spanish colony by presidential decree in 2010 to fulfil the CPLP's formal admission requirements. At the Eleventh CPLP Summit held in Brasília in November 2016, Brazil assumed the organisation's rotating two-year presidency. Besides diplomatic, cultural and economic cooperation, the members of the organisation have increasingly moved towards defence cooperation. In 2016, the CPLP revised its cooperation protocol in defence to guarantee its commitment to peace and security. In September 2017, Brazil hosted the seventeenth annual FELINO Exercises in the Military Academy of Agulhas Negras (AMAN) in Resende, in Rio de Janeiro. Military personnel from all nine CPLP member states participated in the exercise; they had previously taken place in Brazil in 2002 and 2006. The FELINO series was created in 2000 to regularise the execution of joint and combined military exercises, fomenting the interoperability of the armed forces of the CPLP member states, as well as their training for use in humanitarian assistance and peacekeeping operations both within the CPLP and regional organisations; in either case, they always would operate under the authority of the United Nations.[27]

In 2013, the Seventh Ministerial Meeting of ZOPACAS took place in Montevideo, Uruguay, attended for the first time by the defence ministers of the twenty-four member states. The Brazilian Defence Minister, Celso Amorim, called attention to the need to reinvigorate ZOPACAS, which had been inactive after the Cold War and was only reactivated at its Sixth Ministerial Meeting in Luanda in 2007 after a ten-year interruption. The meeting endorsed the Montevideo Action Plan that focused in particular on cooperation in maritime safety. The restoration of ZOPACAS was considered important in itself, given the huge mineral and natural resources in the South Atlantic that are crucial to the development of both Brazil and African countries in the region. ZOPACAS was expected to become a fundamental institutional forum for peace, sovereignty and development in this large geopolitical space following the discovery of new oil fields off the Brazilian coast (pre-salt) and the Gulf of Guinea, as well as the re-formation of the Fourth US Fleet and the growing strategic importance of the South Atlantic Ocean. It was evident that, even at a time of retraction in its external performance, the security of Brazil's strategic environment remained important in the foreign policy agenda. In Montevideo, the ZOPACAS member countries agreed to meet annually during the UN General Assembly to assess the organisation's achievements. In addition, a contact group made up of Argentina, Brazil, Uruguay, Angola, Cabo Verde, Nigeria and South Africa was created to monitor the implementation of the decisions taken. In October 2013, Brazil hosted the I Seminar on Maritime Surveillance and ZOPACAS in Salvador to debate security and surveillance of maritime traffic, search and rescue operations at sea. In November 2015, also in Salvador, the Brazilian Defence Ministry organised a three-day seminar for representatives from ZOPACAS member states on international peace missions. In June 2016, Brazil hosted a seminar in Rio de Janeiro on South Atlantic maritime security, focusing on the ZOPACAS member countries, in cooperation with the International Maritime Organisation (IMO).[28] However, ZOPACAS has not held any other ministerial meeting since 2013, which suggests that Brazil's attempts to fully reactivate the regional organisation have been unsuccessful.

[27] CPLP, 'Segurança e Defesa', n.d., accessed 13 May 2018, www.cplp.org/id-4271.aspx.

[28] MRE, 'Zona da Paz e Cooperação do Atlântico do Sul', 2011, accessed 12 May 2018, www.itamaraty.gov.br/pt-BR/politica-externa/paz-e-seguranca-internacionais/151-zona-de-paz-e-cooperacao-do-atlantico-sul.

Although many issues associated with Brazil's relations with India and South Africa have shifted to the BRICS meetings in recent years, the trilateral IBSA Dialogue Forum set up in 2003 has not been completely inactive. During Dilma Rousseff's government, the Fifth IBSA Summit of the three heads of state took place in Pretoria, South Africa in October 2011; they deliberated on various issues in the Declaration of Tshwane: reform of global governance, economic and financial global crisis, the Millennium Development Goals, international trade, sustainable development, climate change, global food security, South–South cooperation, human rights, disarmament and non-proliferation, terrorism, transnational organised crime, intellectual property rights, Internet governance, energy, health, gender, and regional issues. They also repeated the demand for a reform of the UN Security Council, aimed at increasing the number of both permanent and non-permanent members. The three countries also urged the implementation of reforms in the International Monetary Fund, including reforms of electoral processes and the weight of votes of developing countries. However, the Sixth IBSA Summit scheduled for 2013 in New Delhi to celebrate the tenth anniversary of the trilateral organisation did not take place. Although India announced in late 2016 that it would hold the postponed summit in 2017, this did not happen either. Nevertheless, the three countries have continued working together in the areas of defence and development cooperation. Since 2008, they have held biennial joint naval exercises called India–Brazil–South Africa Maritime (IBSAMAR) to strengthen maritime security cooperation. In 2014, the exercises were carried out off the South African coast. In February 2016, exercises conducted off the Indian coast were the most complex to date, involving ships, airplanes and Special Forces of the three countries. In October 2018 the Sixth IBSAMAR exercises were held in South African waters. The India, Brazil and South Africa Facility for Poverty and Hunger Alleviation (IBSA Fund), operational since 2006 and managed by UNDP, has implemented development projects in thirteen Southern countries to advance the fight against poverty and hunger. The three countries have financed the Fund with a modest annual contribution of $1 million each. Africa received 28.9% of the funds, Latin America and the Caribbean 25.7%, Arab countries 23.7% and Asia 21%.[29] As already suggested, the cooperation of the three countries within IBSA has, to some extent, been replaced in recent years by the BRICS group, which has gained more political weight.

[29] UNDP, 'Finances', IBSA Fund, n.d., accessed 12 May 2018, http://tcdc2.undp.org/IBSA/finance/finances.htm.

At the Third ASA Summit in 2013, the euphoria from the time of its creation in 2006 had dissipated. Little progress had been made with the defined objectives and the focus was mainly on organisational issues of the structure and formation of a permanent council. Thirty-six Heads of State and Government attended the 2013 meeting, and eleven South American and forty-eight African countries participated in working groups and meetings. President Dilma Rousseff attended the event because Brazil was the South American Regional Coordinator and sought to increase the leverage of developing countries through an alliance in multilateral forums in defence of common interests on the world political and economic stages. It was through this forum that the timid Brazilian post-Lula action sought to assist African partners with programmes to combat poverty and AIDS. In 2015, the seminar 'Rethinking ASA' reviewed its work in the ten years since its creation and made a commitment to intensify diplomatic relations among the countries participating in the Summit. However, as the internal problems plaguing several countries at the time demanded urgent attention, the effective actions of this South–South forum continue to be few and far between. It is, therefore, not surprising that the scheduled Fourth ASA Summit in Quito, Ecuador in 2016, was later postponed to May 2017 and has still had not taken place by the time of writing.

Following the restructuring of the Southern African Customs Union (SACU), a market of about 65 million consumers in South Africa, Lesotho, Namibia, Botswana and Swaziland, the negotiations on the Framework Agreement were expanded to include other African countries. The negotiations to create the Preferential Trade Agreement (PTA) between the Mercado Común del Sur (Southern Common Market – Mercosur) and SACU started in December 2000, while the agreement signed in 2008 only came into force in October 2016 due to Mercosur's demands related to administrative and legal issues of the agreement, and intra-bloc issues. In 2015, Brazilian exports to SACU accounted for $1.36 billion, with a positive trade balance of some $720 million in favour of Brazil.[30]

The ASPA remained one of the main bi-regional initiatives. In the period from 2013 to 2014, trade between the two regions was very significant ($33 billion). In addition, cultural cooperation gained prominence under the coordination of the Arab, African and South American

[30] MRE, 'Entrada em vigor do Acordo de Preferências Comerciais MERCOLUL-SACU', 4 April 2016, accessed 12 May 2018, www.itamaraty.gov.br/pt-BR/notas-a-imprensa/13717-entrada-em-vigor-do-acordo-de-preferencias-comerciais-mercosul-sacu.

Library and Research Center (Bibli-ASPA) in São Paulo. At the Third ASPA Summit of Heads of State in 2012, after the Arab Spring, President Dilma Rousseff drew attention to the potentials for cooperation in the areas of energy, mining and tourism in order to expand trade and investment between South American and Arab countries. In the meetings that followed, the desire to deepen cooperation among the countries of the summit was reinterpreted, but no new projects and initiatives were proposed. The Fourth ASPA Summit was held in November 2015 in Riyadh in Saudi Arabia. The summit approved the Riyadh Declaration to further promote political, economic, commercial, technological and environmental cooperation between Arab and South American countries. The Fifth Summit of Heads of State and Government of ASPA was scheduled to take place in Venezuela in 2018, a country that has for some years faced a very serious political-economic crisis. However, the summit was not held in 2018 without any justification by the organisation.

Conclusions

Since Lula's departure from the presidency, there has begun a perceptible decline in Brazilian engagements in the African continent, because they were unsustainable in adverse political and socioeconomic contexts. His successor, Dilma Rousseff, officially sought to continue the project of Brazilian international insertion and the priority attributed to Africa; however, the challenges of the deteriorating domestic socioeconomic situation as well as an increasingly adverse external environment made the attempts somewhat half-hearted. In fact, Dilma never attributed the priority and visibility to Brazil's relations with Africa as her predecessor had done, whereas her overall foreign policy approach was much more utilitarian and commercially oriented. During her presidency, the budget for technical cooperation projects in African countries was reduced considerably. However, until 2013, Brazil's external trade with Africa continued to increase. As far as Michel Temer is concerned, the results of his two and a half-year government are yet to be analysed more thoroughly. However, the declared shift from the South–South axis to the North–South seems to remove Brazil (albeit tentatively) from the position of uncontested candidate for regional power. Concomitantly, former claims of a permanent seat for Brazil at the UN Security Council largely disappeared from the foreign policy agenda. In turn, this made Brazil's respective diplomatic offensive in African countries outmoded. After Temer assumed the presidency, there was evidence of a further decline in the relations with the African continent on all levels, and of

Brazil's South–South cooperation in general. This does not necessarily mean that Brazil will further withdraw from Africa, but probably it will try to maintain and consolidate existing political relations, cooperation, investments and trade with the continent whenever possible and advantageous for Brazil's political and commercial interests, irrespective of the ideological position of its respective government. As the last sixty years have shown, the difference in foreign policy approach lies more in the scope, intensity and priority attributed to Brazil's relations with African countries, rather than in an extensive withdrawal from the neighbouring continent.

Conclusions

Paulo Fagundes Visentini

Only time will tell whether all the processes and developments described in the preceding chapters simply represent political discourse (prestige diplomacy), economic interest ('soft imperialism') or an association between two peripheries of the world system in the pursuit of socio-economic development (South–South Cooperation). Fundamentally, the three aspects complement each other because diplomacy and effective support for social development can only result from economic cooperation. Brazilian domestic contradictions interact with those of African nations. It is an ongoing process involving many actors, various goals and a complex regional and global environment. However, despite all Brazil's efforts, there has been a lack of coordination within the government and between the government, society and business, as well as an absence of strategic vision in the private sector. Similarly, although more financial resources have been invested, they are still insufficient for the proposed policy, and corporate sectors react strongly to the allocation of more resources for Brazil–Africa relations.

It is however undeniable that the relationship between Brazil and the African continent has deep historical roots, as both sides of the South Atlantic were inserted into the world system within the Portuguese Maritime Empire. What would eventually become Brazil was Europeanised and Africanised simultaneously, and it was the contribution of enslaved Africans that enabled colonisation. They knew the tropical environment, which was often fatal to Europeans. The slave trade lasted approximately three and a half centuries and in Portuguese America miscegenation was more frequent than in Anglo-Saxon and French America.

The contacts between the two South Atlantic shores (of people and goods) continued for nearly half a century after Brazil's independence in 1822, being interrupted only by the anti-slavery patrols of the British Navy and the European occupation of the African continent. The economic structure that gave rise to these transatlantic relations ceased to exist. As each side evolved separately, despite cultural and environmental similarities, mutual ignorance deepened. European and North American studies on Brazil and Africa were the only references to a scarce number of readers on the reality of 'the other side'. Brazil and Africa began to see each other through a mirror, distorted by the gaze of third parties (i.e. colonial powers).

In the 20th century, until the 1960s, Brazil maintained trade in Africa only with Apartheid South Africa, and supported Salazar's Portugal in maintaining its African empire only for 'sentimental' reasons, without any economic or diplomatic benefit. It was largely an internal issue of the Brazilian conservatives. The industrialisation of Brazil in the 1950s and the African decolonisation in 1960s would change the situation. The Independent Foreign Policy (PEI) of the Quadros and Goulart administrations emphasised the importance of South–South relations, particularly with the socialist countries. But the growing political cleavage within Brazilian society was aggravated by an unexpected political event parallel to the African independences: the Cuban Revolution. Worse even, Cuba had a very assertive African policy and Brazilian initiatives were inevitably affected, with criticism from both national and Washington conservatives.

The implantation of the military regime in Brazil by a coup in 1964 produced an ideological reaction that slowed the rapprochement with Africa in the second half of the 1960s. It was only with the 'Economic Miracle' of the 1970s that Brazil resumed contacts, strengthened by the 'Responsible Pragmatism' of the Geisel administration. Until the second half of the 1980s, economic and technical cooperation, and cultural relations, were as strong as during the Lula administration decades later. Moreover, the regime made daring diplomatic moves to make up for lost time, recognising the MPLA Marxist government in Angola and strongly criticising Apartheid South Africa, in addition to becoming a significant exporter of arms to African and Middle Eastern nations.

It was Brazil's debt crisis, the opening up of the political system (which complicated the process of diplomatic decision-making), and the implementation of neoliberalism that produced another downturn of relations with Africa. At the same time, Africa faced the problems created by the IMF's economic adjustment policies and the effects of the end of the Cold War, since African states ceased to be courted by the superpowers. There was no complete interruption of relations, but rather a more selective focus on the major trading partners from Africa. The North–South axis was now predominant in Brazilian foreign policy. Multilateral initiatives such as ZOPACAS and CPLP, as well as participation in UN Peacekeeping Operations in Africa, continued, as well as the discrete, but effective performance of the large Brazilian public and private companies on the continent.

With the changes occurring in the international economic framework in 1999, Brazil, implementing a neoliberal strategy under the second Cardoso government, resumed a more active diplomacy in Africa, as well as domestic policies of social and political inclusion for Brazilians of African descent. The Lula da Silva government (a centre-left coalition), which came to power in 2003, gave a strong impetus and a new sense of direction to these actions. In addition to the domestic social agenda that accompanied South–South cooperation, traditional economic interests and prestige diplomacy, President Lula da Silva initiated a bold multilateral diplomacy and began to promote Brazilian investments on the continent.

In addition to qualitatively deepening cooperation and the formulation of joint strategies with African states in international economic organisations such as the IMF, World Bank and the WTO, Lula da Silva's administrations created alternative multilateral forums for cooperation. Besides the creation of the trilateral IBSA Dialogue Forum, two important multilateral forums were set up, the South America–Africa Summit (ASA) and the Summit of South American–Arab Countries (ASPA), which launched an innovative, high profile diplomacy. These initiatives enjoyed a certain acceptance on the African continent that, since the turn of the century, had been experiencing economic growth and a significant political prominence, largely due to the growing presence of emerging powers such as China and India, among others.

The creation of the African Union and the start of the New Partnership for Africa's Development (NEPAD) in 2001, as well as other initiatives in the security field, were instruments that, at the same time, propelled the continent after 'two lost decades' towards socioeconomic and political renewal. It is important to emphasise that also the cultural and academic connections had a great impact, especially from the Brazilian end. For the first time, dialogue and direct reciprocal knowledge exchanges with African countries were established. Students, professors, researchers and technicians crossed the South Atlantic in both directions, in large numbers, starting a significant portfolio of projects, some of which are still ongoing.

The new international projection of Brazil and the results obtained, however, were not positively absorbed by the powers that traditionally considered Africa as their area of influence, as well as the United States, which began to have strategic interest in the African continent. Towards the end of the Lula administration, the sub-prime and the Euro crises, with a profound impact on the world economy, undermined the scenario that supported the 'active, affirmative and purposeful' diplomacy of Foreign Minister Celso Amorim. During the first year of Dilma

Rousseff's rule, there was the Arab Spring, which hit parts of (North) Africa politically and economically. The emergence of the BRICS (Brazil, Russia, India, China and South Africa) absorbed and took to a higher level the most expressive part of the foreign policy agenda that Brazil developed with Africa, while obscuring also the projection of IBSA. The IBSA Dialogue Forum provided an international stage for India Brazil and South America, which had no permanent seat in the UN Security Council, unlike the other two BRICS members.

In this sense, the tension between transoceanic cooperation focused on the North Atlantic (due to the history of capitalism) and another centred on the South Atlantic (based on South American integration in association with Africa, and South–South cooperation) is a fundamental contradiction. Brazil–Africa relations are therefore crucial. The integration of the North Atlantic is now complete, and many analysts have focused on the role of the Pacific Ocean. But few realise the importance of the emerging ocean spaces of the South Atlantic and the Indian Ocean, a route connecting Brazil (and the West) to Asia. Most of the oil of South America, Africa and South Asia is found in these two oceans. Thus, it is vital to defend the sovereignty over these natural resources and the demilitarisation and security of these strategic sea routes. This clearly explains the geopolitical logic behind the IBSA strategy and even that of Brazil–Africa relations.

Obviously, Brazil's strengthening of ties with African states serves to promote the country's international image as a global player (prestige diplomacy). Nevertheless, it is important to both sides of the South Atlantic because bilateral relations and the common multilateral actions are central to enhancing the international role of African countries and hence contribute to the emergence of a multipolar order. Another benefit for Africa is to master old challenges by balancing the cooperation opportunities with Europe and the US on the one hand, and take advantage of the new opportunities with the Chinese, Brazilian and Indian presence on the other hand. This is a prerequisite for Africa's social and economic development.

Lula's African policy was made possible not only by the increase in commodity prices in the 2000s, but because the agenda of the War on Terror attracted US attention to the Middle East and Central Asia and left more political space for Africans and Latin Americans. Consequently, the economic crisis and the effects of the Arab Spring eroded initiatives such as ASA and ASPA. Likewise, terrorism, which was already present in Saharan Africa, was intensified, attracting the attention of the US and France to the continent.

To complete the set of difficulties, President Dilma Rousseff did not give priority to Africa or foreign policy, which she neglected under the slogan of 'continuity without priority'. In addition to the domestic economic crisis, she faced an increasingly better articulated conservative opposition, a hostile media and criticism of the North Atlantic powers. When she considered her re-election, the pressure and the street protests increased exponentially, culminating in her dismissal in May 2016. Thereupon Vice-President Michel Temer assumed government and appointed politicians of the opposition PSDB (Cardoso's Party) to command diplomacy. If there still remains some foreign policy strategy in place, it has been characterised by a posture of opposition to the more politicised actions taken during the Lula administrations.

Most likely Brazil's current withdrawal from Africa, as in the 1960s and 1990s will eventually be reversed, but there is a new element to be considered. During consecutive governments, among the most effective tools of the relationship were Brazil's internationalised large companies, public and private, in construction, mining, energy and services, which were seriously hit by the anti-corruption *Lava Jato* operation. As a result, they have been partly excluded from a number of countries and, coincidentally, have been replaced by European, North American, Chinese and Indian companies. All of this will jeopardise both Brazil and many African states.

The future of Brazilian foreign policy is uncertain, but it should be clarified here that the Africa policy developed by Brazil, along with the unequivocal national interests, included a strategy to leverage the development of African nations. The general strengthening of the geopolitical South is a relevant step for any change in the international order towards multipolarity and multilateral management via the UN. It would be naïve to believe that Brazil only wanted to 'please Africans' in order to win votes to join the UN Security Council as a permanent member, for the simple reason that such support in the General Assembly would have a very limited effect (besides the fact that Africans are not naïve). What Brazilian diplomacy aspired to contribute, as Foreign Minister Celso Amorim explained on several occasions, was: (1) the expansion of the Security Council with representatives from developing nations (including Brazil, of course); (2) broadening the power of the General Assembly as a way of unblocking the veto mechanism in the UN Security Council and giving voice to the smaller nations; and (3) to make the Economic and Social Council (ECOSOC) the driving force of the UN in its task of promoting economic and social development, rather than a predominantly security based agenda.

African governments must, in turn, overcome their dependence on external assistance that began during the Cold War and intensified in the 'lost decade'; it is time to seek further development and integration processes under the challenge of globalisation. There is an urgent need to put aside certain aspects of colonial heritage, notably the fragmentation of countries observed especially in the configuration of small and unviable nations. At the same time, it is necessary to deepen cooperation ties within the Global South, which reverses the tendency towards marginalising the continent.

Brazil is far more than a commercial partner for the African continent; it is one that can reduce some internal obstacles (political, economic and social). On the other hand, Africa's economic, political and cultural situation can also be useful for Brazil. As a developing nation, there is always a sort of 'First World temptation' for Brazilian elites, which regard the country as 'white, Western and Christian'. The old Brazilian elite still shows strong traits of colonisation, always admiring the Northern nations and neglecting the South and even their own country. A society that receives African students should also send students and tourists to Africa, as this would contribute to the development of Brazil's identity.

In this context, the relationship between Brazil and Africa, as part of South–South cooperation, has formed an indispensable tool. The expansion of relations between Brazil and Africa was so rapid and diverse that it is difficult to obtain information on its impact, since it has been disseminated through many governmental, scientific, business and social organisations. But further analysis is required, owing to the inevitable politicisation and polarisation of the topic over the last two decades. If these relations were of less importance, there would not have been a broad alliance of internal opponents, from conservatives to ultra-left, to liberals, each launching their own critique. For some critics, too much was done, without return; for others it was too little; and for some, it was wrong and harmful to Africans. Thus, the compliments (and expectations) were huge as well as the criticisms. If, on the one hand, it is true that Brazil's third approach to post-colonial Africa is currently in decline, it must be recognised that, on the other, each approach was qualitatively more intense than the previous one. More than attracted by racial rhetoric, many African leaders have regarded Brazilian public policies as important, effective examples and tools to fight poverty in their own countries. The election of the right-wing candidate Jair Bolsonaro in October 2018 and two weeks later the appointment of Ernesto Araújo to the Ministry of Foreign Affairs signal the adoption of a foreign policy similar to Donald Trump's world perspective. In fact, the President-elect of Brazil is explicit in his admiration for the American President.

A retired army captain and member of the National Parliament for nearly thirty years, he is a self-styled right-winger and conservative. Thus, these characteristics seem to signal a foreign policy of strong ideological bias, with the purpose of reversing the diplomatic profile inaugurated by Lula da Silva. As for the place of Africa in Brazil's foreign policy, which began to retreat with Dilma and even more with Temer, the new government indicates an even greater deepening of this process – especially because the aforementioned Foreign Minister, although being a career diplomat, has forged an unusually militant campaign in support of Bolsonaro.

However, this can be misleading: the radical discourse of the campaign covered up the absence of a coherent project, the unpreparedness of the President and the general fragmentation of his political support base. Three distinct groups can be identified as forming his support base: (1) the ideological, made up of Pentecostal Church leaders and politicians close to the President, particularly his son Eduardo Bolsonaro and member of Parliament Onyx Lorenzoni (manager of the new government); (2) the military, strongly represented by General Antônio Mourão (the new Vice-President) and General Augusto Heleno Pereira, who have a more realistic approach; and (3) the ultra-neoliberal economic team, composed of elements of lesser relevance, such as the 'super minister' of the economy, Paulo Guedes.

Most likely there will be an unstable government and erratic behaviour, with difficulty posed in articulating its heterogeneous and fluid base of support. For example, the situation created with the abrupt end of Cuban cooperation in the More Doctors Programme (*Programa Mais Médicos*) that provides health services for remote regions and poor urban neighbourhoods drew intense criticism from the mayors of the affected municipalities. After Bolsonaro's statement that the Brazilian Embassy in Israel was to be transferred to Jerusalem, Egypt cancelled the trip of a Brazilian commercial mission to the country, whereupon the national agribusiness and the Chamber of Commerce with the Arab States alerted the government to the harmful consequences for Brazil's significant food exports to Arab countries. But the statement made by the future Economy Minister Paulo Guedes about Mercosur as being irrelevant to Brazil was answered hours later by the Brazilian National Confederation of Industry, which stated that Mercosur *was* relevant to Brazilian exports and important in preventing the overwhelming entry of Chinese products into the region (while also implying that he should be better informed). Along the same lines, the Ministry of Foreign Affairs is hardly likely to abandon its diplomatic investment in Africa; since it is of interest to the military due to the peacekeeping missions in which Brazil participates, it helps to counterbalance the growing Chinese presence on the continent and, finally, it serves the economic interests of Brazilian exporters. As in other phases of diplomatic history, the initial neglect should give way to pragmatism.

Brazil–Africa Relations: A Chronology[1]

Colonial and Imperial period

1538 The first African slaves arrive in Brazil.

1630 Dutch occupation of Northeast Brazil (Pernambuco, Sergipe and Maranhão).

In West Africa, the Dutch West India Company occupies the fort Elmina in present-day Ghana (1637) and Luanda and São Tomé (1641).

1648 With the help of Brazilians, the Dutch are expelled from Luanda, which brings Brazil closer to Angola. Subsequently, the Dutch return São Tomé to the Portuguese (January 1649).

1654 End of Dutch occupation of Northeast of Brazil.

1681 The number of black slaves brought from Angola to Brazil reaches one million.

1694 The discovery of the first gold deposits in Minas Gerais increases use of slave labour for its exploitation.

1695 The Maroon community (*quilombo*) of Palmares is destroyed and its leader, Zumbi, is killed; it reached its height between 1624 and 1654, when it housed about thirty-five thousand inhabitants.

1796 Fathers Cipriano Pires Sardinha and Vicente Ferreira Pires are sent by the Portuguese government on a diplomatic mission to Dahomey (present-day Benin), the place of origin of most of the slaves brought to Salvador in this period.

1811 Death record on a slave ship voyage: the 'São José Indiano' crew loses 121 of the 667 slaves on board.

[1] Information collected and adapted from: Itamaraty; Eugênio Vargas Garcia, *Cronologia das Relações Internacionais do Brasil* (Rio de Janeiro: Contraponto, 2000); Paulo Fagundes Visentini, *A Política Externa do Regime Militar Brasileiro* (Porto Alegre: Editora UFRGS, 2011); and Paulo Fagundes Visentini, *Relações Internacionais do Brasil: de Vargas à Lula* (São Paulo: Fundação Perseu Abramo, 2008).

1815 The British Representative at the Vienna Congress proposes condemnation of the slave trade. Portugal agrees to the abolition of slaves on the African coasts north of the Equator in a treaty with the United Kingdom.

1817 The United Kingdom and Portugal agree on the mutual right to visit and search ships suspected of illegal trade in slaves and set up joint judgement committees in Rio de Janeiro and Freetown, Sierra Leone.

1822 Independence of Brazil and establishment of the First Empire. Angola stands with Portugal.

Movement in Luanda and Benguela wants union between Brazil and Angola, the main provider of slave labour for the Brazilian economy.

The Obá Osemwede of Benin and the Ologum Ajan of Lagos are the first to recognise the independence of Brazil.

1826 In a convention on the Slave Trade with the United Kingdom, Brazil assumes the Portuguese commitments of 1817 and agrees to stop the slave trade in 1833.

1827 Portugal refuses accreditation of Brazilian consul in Luanda

1831 The Feijo Law against the slave trade is approved. Due to its non-application, it is known as the law 'for the English to see'.

1835 Malês Revolt, rebellion of Muslim slaves in Salvador. Two hundred Africans accused of involvement in the revolt are deported to West Africa.

1836 Coffee becomes Brazil's main export product.

1845 Brazil informs the United Kingdom of the end of the conventions on the slave trade signed in 1817 and 1826.

The British Parliament sanctions the Aberdeen Act, allowing slave ships to be captured and tried by the Admiralty High Court.

1850 Eusébio de Queiroz Law abolishes slave trade in Brazil. The law is effectively enforced and Portuguese traffickers are expelled from the country.

Hermenegildo Niteroi appointed consul general in Liberia, Brazil's first diplomat in an independent African country.

1866 Decree provides for freedom to the so-called 'slaves of the nation' who serve in the Brazilian Army.

1871 Approval of the Law of Free Womb, which frees slaves' newborn children.

1884 Ceará declares the abolition of slavery in that province.

1885 Promulgation of the Saraiva-Cotegipe Law, which frees sexagenarian slaves and seeks to placate the intense abolitionist campaign.

1888 The 'Lei Áurea', signed by the princess regent D. Isabel, decrees the abolition of slavery. Throughout the period of slavery about four million slaves were brought to Brazil.

1889 Proclamation of the Republic.

First Republic and Vargas Era (1889–1945)

1911 Honorary consulate in Senegal becomes a career consulate.

1920 General consulate is opened in Mozambique.

1922 The Lloyd Brazilian Shipping Company establishes a direct merchant line with Africa.

1926 First consul assumes position at the consulate of Cape Town.

1933 The book *Casa-Grande & Senzala* (*The Masters and the Slaves*) by Gilberto Freyre is published in Brazil.

1936 South African Union sends first special mission to South America to analyse trade prospects and diplomatic missions on the subcontinent.

1938 A commissariat of trade responsible for the regions of West and Northern Africa is established.

1939 First direct trade agreement between Brazil and South African Union.

1943 South Africa opens a consulate in Rio de Janeiro.

National Developmental Phase (1945–64)

1948 Formal diplomatic relations are established with South Africa.

1951 Representation with Ethiopian Empire, based in Cairo, is established.

1953 The Treaty of Friendship and Consultation is signed with Portugal, which limits the Brazilian diplomatic position on the Portuguese colonies in Africa.

1955 Diplomat Bezerra de Menezes participates as observer in Bandung Conference

1956 Brazil is one of the first countries to recognise the independence of Tunisia, opening a consulate in Tunis the following year.

1957 Diplomat Sérgio Corrêa do Lago writes a memorandum which recommends sending a mission to African and Asian countries to gather information on a possible reorientation of Brazilian diplomacy.

Jun. Portuguese President Francisco Craveiro Lopes visits Brazil under protests. At the end of the trip, the two countries issue a joint communiqué reaffirming support to Portugal.

Dec. Oswaldo Aranha writes a strongly critical letter to the Brazilian President, denouncing the Brazilian position towards Africa and advising a reorientation of foreign policy in favour of the independence of African countries.

1959 Sep. Portuguese exile George Agostinho da Silva establishes Centre for Afro-Oriental Studies (CEAO) at Federal University of Bahia (UFBA).

1960 Diplomatic relations are established with Ghana.

Jan. Brazil recognises French Cameroon's independence.

Aug. Brazil recognises Congo-Léopoldville's independence.

Oct. Brazil recognises Mali's independence.

Dec. Ethiopian Emperor, Haile Selassie, visits Brazil. During this visit, there is a coup attempt in Addis Ababa.

1961 Jan. A former colonial official, Henrique Galvão, hijacks the Portuguese ship 'Santa Maria' on the South American coast with the aim of inciting a rebellion in Angola. Galvão is given political asylum in Brazil by President Jânio Quadros.

Mar. Jânio Quadros advocates an 'Independent Foreign Policy' and appoints Raymundo Sousa Dantas, a black journalist, as ambassador to Ghana (who remains in Accra until 1963). The writer Rubem Braga is appointed ambassador in Morocco, and the painter Cícero Dias is appointed to the newly opened Brazilian Embassy in Tunisia.

The Working Group for Africa is formed by Foreign Ministry (Itamaraty).

Mission headed by Foreign Minister Afonso Arinos is sent to Senegal to participate in the commemorations of the first year of independence. He visits Cameroon and Sierra Leone on their independence day, as well as Côte d'Ivoire, Ghana, Guinea and Nigeria.

Apr. Government establishes the Brazilian Institute of Afro-Asian Studies (IBEAA) based in Rio de Janeiro (dissolved by military regime in 1964).

		Embassies in Dahomey, Nigeria and Senegal are established under Jânio Quadros Administration.
	Jul.	First fifteen African students with higher education scholarships arrive in Brazil from Cabo Verde, Cameroon, Ghana, Guinea-Bissau, Nigeria and Senegal.
	Sep.	Foreign Minister Afonso Arinos attends the First Conference of Non-Aligned Countries in Belgrade.
1962	Jan.	Brazil, Cameroon, Côte d'Ivoire, Ghana, and Nigeria found Alliance of Cocoa Producing Countries (COPAL)
		Diplomatic relations are established with Togo and Mali.
		Embassy opens in Algeria.
		South American and African producers sign first International Coffee Agreement
1963		Senegal establishes embassy in Rio de Janeiro, which is transferred to Brasília in 1970.
	Sep.	Foreign Minister Araújo Castro makes the 'Three-D's Speech' (Disarmament, Decolonisation and Development) at the UN General Assembly.

Military Regime (1964–85)

1964		Léopold Senghor, President of Senegal, visits Brazil, and commercial and cultural agreements are signed.
1965		Trade mission sent to West Africa visits Cameroon, Côte d'Ivoire, Ghana, Liberia, Nigeria and Senegal.
1966	Aug.	Foreign Minister Juracy Magalhães affirms: 'Everything that is good for Portugal is received with great pleasure by Brazil'.
	Sep.	Second trade mission to Africa, visiting Côte d'Ivoire, Ghana, South Africa, Angola and Mozambique.
1967		Despite protests by African countries, Brazilian Navy vessel visits Angola.
		Deputy General Secretary for Africa and the Middle East is established in Itamaraty; African Affairs are no longer integrated in Eastern European Division.
		Agreements with Portugal, which allows the intensification of commercial ties with the Portuguese colonies, are ratified.
1968		Formation of the Afro-Brazilian Chamber of Commerce (AfroChamber) in São Paulo by the black deputy and businessman Adalberto Camargo, who also becomes its first president.

	Jul.	Diplomatic relations are established with Congo-Léopoldville (later Zaire and now the Democratic Republic of the Congo – DR Congo).
	Oct.	Diplomatic relations are established with Sudan.
1969		Despite UN protests, Brazil allows South African Airways stopover in Rio de Janeiro.
1970		Diplomatic relations are established with Zambia.
1972		In the Year of the Luso-Brazilian Community; Brazil signs new treaties with Portugal that allow the former to expand its operations in Portuguese colonies.
	Apr.	Brazilian Embassy is inaugurated in Kinshasa, Zaire.
	Oct.	Foreign Minister Mário Gibson Barboza visits Dahomey, Cameroon, Côte d'Ivoire, Ghana, Liberia, Nigeria, Senegal, Togo and Zaire, and signs agreements for technical and cultural cooperation.
1973		Gibson Barboza visits Egypt and Kenya, where he signs technical and cultural cooperation agreements.
		Candido Mendes de Almeida sets up the Centre for Afro-Asian Studies (CEAA) at University Candido Mendes in Rio de Janeiro.
	Sep.	First trade mission organised by AfroChamber visits Dahomey, Cameroon, Côte d'Ivoire, Ghana, Liberia, Nigeria, Senegal, Togo and Zaire.
	Nov.	Brazil abstains in voting on UN resolution on the recognition of Guinea-Bissau's unilateral declaration of independence.
	Dec.	Brazil refrains from voting on a resolution in favour of the end of the right granted to Portugal to represent its colonies in the United Nations.
1974		Brazil–Nigeria Joint Declaration, signed in Brazil, condemns apartheid and defends a peaceful solution of the question of Portuguese colonies.
		Zaire's embassy in Brasília is inaugurated.
		Establishment of diplomatic relations with Equatorial Guinea.
		Brazil opens embassy in Tripoli, Libya.
	Apr.	The Carnation Revolution in Portugal overthrows the dictatorship of Marcello Caetano. Brazil is the first state to recognise the left-wing Military Junta.
	Jul.	Brazil recognises the independence of Guinea-Bissau.

	Aug.	Diplomatic representations are opened in Gabon, Mauritius, Sierra Leone, Zaire, Kenya and Ghana.
	Dec.	Ambassador Ítalo Zappa, head of the Department of Africa, Asia and Oceania of Itamaraty, meets Agostinho Neto (MPLA) and Samora Machel (Frelimo) on African soil. Machel criticises Brazil's complicity with Portuguese colonialism.
		Brazil establishes diplomatic relations with Guinea-Bissau.
1975	Feb.	At a meeting in Dakar, Brazil condemns the new US Foreign Trade Law along with other countries producing raw materials.
		Frelimo rejects Brazilian proposal to establish a special diplomatic representation in Lourenço Marques (now Maputo).
		Diplomat Ovídio de Andrade Melo inaugurates Brazil's special representation in Luanda after the Angolan liberation movements MPLA, UNITA and FNLA agree to the proposal.
	Jun.	Brazil is not invited to Mozambique's independence celebrations.
	Jul.	Brazil recognises independence of Cabo Verde and São Tomé and Príncipe.
	Nov.	On the exact day of Angolan independence (11 Nov.), Brazil is the first state to recognise the MPLA government.
		Brazil votes in favour of a resolution banning the sale of strategic raw materials to South Africa.
1976		Embassies are opened in Angola, Upper Volta (now Burkina Faso), Lesotho and Mozambique.
1978		The Brazilian Ambassador in Monrovia is accredited in Côte d'Ivoire.
		Brazilian Embassy is inaugurated in Lomé, Togo, and the Togolese Embassy is established in Brasília.
1979		Cooperation agreements come into effect with Nigeria.
	Mar.	Brazilian embassy is opened in Dar es Salaam, Tanzania.
	May	Agreements signed between Petrobras and Angolan state oil company Sonangol.
	Aug.	Visit of the President of Zambia, Kenneth Kaunda.
1980		Diplomatic relations are established with Burundi and the Republic of Congo (Brazzaville).
	Apr.	Diplomatic relations are established with Zimbabwe.

Jun. The Minister of Foreign Affairs, Ramiro Saraiva Guerreiro, visits Angola, Mozambique, Tanzania, Zambia and Zimbabwe.

Sep. Speech by Saraiva Guerreiro at the UN General Assembly shows concern about Third World development.

Nov. Brazil sends delegation to the Second Southern Africa Development Coordination Conference in Maputo.

1981 President of Mali, Moussa Traoré, visits Brasília and signs cooperation agreements establishing a Joint Commission between the countries.

Jan. Brazil establishes diplomatic relations with Rwanda.

Feb. Brazil condemns threat of South African attack on Mozambique.

Mar. In a message to the National Congress, President Figueiredo highlights the importance of political equality between Latin America and Africa.

Jun. Bilateral cooperation agreements are signed with Algeria, and a joint commission is set up.

Sep. Brazil–Mozambique General Cooperation Agreement is signed.

1982 Embassies are established in Lusaka, Zambia and Yaoundé, Cameroon.

Jul. Cooperation agreements signed with the Republic of Congo during the visit of President Denis Sassou Nguesso.

Aug. Itamaraty promotes four seminars on Brazilian technology on African soil.

1983 Brazil–Morocco Trade Agreement is signed.

Mar. Brazil sends observer to the Seventh Summit of Non-Aligned Countries.

Foreign Minister Saraiva Guerreiro visits Côte d'Ivoire, Gabon and Guinea-Bissau.

Apr. Four Libyan airplanes, allegedly transporting medical supplies but loaded with armaments, supposedly intended for the Sandinista National Liberation Front, are seized on their way to Colombia. After two months of negotiations, Brazil decides to return the Libyan cargoes with all the weapons and does not lose the contracts previously signed with the African country.

Aug. Executive Secretary of the United Nations Economic Commission for Africa, Adebayo Adedeji, visits Brazil to discuss its participation in African development.

Nov. President Figueiredo visits Algeria, Cabo Verde, Guinea-Bissau, Nigeria and Senegal. First visit of a Brazilian president to Africa.

1984 Cameroonian embassy established in Brasília.

Mar. Petrobras signs commercial agreement with NNPC, the Nigerian state oil company.

Apr. President Figueiredo visits Morocco, while Brazil receives a delegation from the League of Arab Countries.

Aug. Trade agreement is concluded with Gabon.

Foreign Minister Saraiva Guerreiro visits Zaire and Republic of Congo.

The New Republic Period (1985–90)

1985 Cabo Verde's President, Aristides Pereira, visits Brazil. Pereira visits again in 1987 and 1990.

Jun. Brazil advocates Namibia's independence.

Brazil condemns South Africa's entry into Botswana during attacks on the armed wing of the African National Congress (ANC) in Gaborone.

Jul. Brazil condemns the South African apartheid regime.

Agreement is reached on the setting up of the Brazil–Ghana Joint Commission.

Aug. Despite criticism from the South African ambassador, Brazil decides to prohibit, by decree, cultural, artistic and sporting exchanges with South Africa.

Sep. In the UN Security Council, Brazil declares the invasion of Angolan territory by South African troops to be illegal.

Diplomatic relations are established with Botswana.

1986 Mar. Brazilian missionaries are abducted in Angola.

Itamaraty calls for the postponement of a Libyan military visit to sign contracts for future arms purchases.

May President Sarney visits Cabo Verde and signs trade agreements.

Brazil condemns South African attacks on Botswana, Zimbabwe and Zambia.

Jun. Brazil sells military trucks to Angola.

	Jul.	Brazil supports sanctions against South Africa.
	Aug.	Brazilian embassy is inaugurated in Zimbabwe.
		President Sarney sends message of support for SWAPO and condemns apartheid.
	Oct.	UN General Assembly approves draft Brazilian resolution establishing the South Atlantic Peace and Cooperation Zone (ZOPACAS).
		President of Algeria, Chadli Bendjedid, visits Brazil.
	Nov.	Foreign Minister Abreu Sodré visits Angola, Cameroon, Nigeria and Zimbabwe with a focus on supporting ZOPACAS. Brazil–Cameroon Joint Commission established
1987		Diplomatic relations are established with Somalia.
	Feb.	President of Zaire, Mobutu Sese Seko, visits Brazil.
	Mar.	President of SWAPO, Sam Nujoma, visits Brazil.
	May	Desmond Tutu, South African Archbishop, visits Brazil.
		Brazil condemns South African attack on Maputo.
	Jun.	During a visit to Cairo, Abreu Sodré expresses concern to the Egyptian government about the situation in Southern Africa and South–South relations.
1988	Jan.	Memorandum from the US State Department condemns Brazil's sale of arms to Libya.
	Apr.	Mozambican President Joaquim Chissano visits Brazil.
	Jun.	President-in-Office, Ulysses Guimarães approves request for political asylum by Abule Magari, a South African guerrilla.
	Jul.	Brazil condemns execution of the 'Sharpeville Six' in South Africa.
		First Meeting of the South Atlantic Countries, in Rio de Janeiro.
	Dec.	Brazilian General Péricles Gomes takes over the leadership of the international force to verify the withdrawal of Cuban troops from Angola.
1989	Jan.	Brazil claims not to have helped Libya build a chemical weapons factory.
		New cooperation agreements are signed with Angola during the visit of President José Eduardo dos Santos.
	Feb.	President Sarney visits Angola.

Neoliberal Period (1990–2002)

1990 Diplomatic relations are established with Namibia. Brazilian Embassy is established in Windhoek.

Sep. Speech by President Fernando Collor at the UN, in which he outlines the importance of ZOPACAS for Brazilian foreign policy, condemns apartheid and expresses the desire for an economic partnership with the Southern African Development Coordination Conference (SADCC).

1991 Formalisation of trade agreements with Cabo Verde and Zimbabwe; economic cooperation with Algeria; and scientific, technical and technological cooperation with Morocco.

May A high-level Brazilian delegation meets with UNITA leader Jonas Savimbi in Brussels amid the ceasefire agreement negotiations.

Aug. Nelson Mandela visits Brazil.

Sept. President Collor visits Angola, Zimbabwe, Mozambique and Namibia.

1992 Brazil withdraws some of the sanctions against South Africa and sends an ambassador to the country.

Oct. President Itamar Franco travels to Senegal to attend the G-15 Summit.

1994 Feb. First meeting of the foreign ministers of the Portuguese-speaking Countries in Brasília.

May Foreign Minister Celso Amorim visits South Africa.

Jun. Brazil sends troops to the UN Peace Mission in Mozambique.

Sep. Third Meeting of Peace and Cooperation in the South Atlantic, in Brasília, and the Declaration of South Atlantic Denuclearisation.

Brazil withdraws the remaining sanctions imposed on South Africa.

1995 Aug. Brazil sends troops to UN peacekeeping mission in Angola.

José Eduardo dos Santos, President of the Republic of Angola, visits Brazil

Oct. Visit of the President of the Republic of Namibia, Sam Nujoma and the Minister of Foreign Affairs of South Africa, Alfred Nzo.

Nov. Seminar in Brasília on Zumbi dos Palmares and Afro-Brazilian Relations.

1996	Jul.	Foundation of the Community of Portuguese-speaking Countries (CPLP, acronym in Portuguese) in Lisbon.
	Aug.	Prime Minister of the Republic of Mali, Ibrahim Boubacar Keita, visits Brazil.
	Nov.	President Fernando Henrique Cardoso visits South Africa and Angola.
		Signing of agreements with South Africa for cooperation and mutual assistance in combating drug production and trafficking; cooperation in the field of culture; on air services between their territories; and for exemption from visas in diplomatic, official and common passports.
1997	Jul.	President of Guinea-Bissau, General João Bernardo Vieira, visits Brazil.
1998	Jul.	Nelson Mandela visits Brazil.
		Second Meeting of Heads of State of the CPLP, in Cabo Verde. General Cooperation Agreement is signed under the CPLP.
1999	Sep.	Presidents of Zimbabwe, Robert Mugabe, and Namibia, Sam Nujoma, visit Brazil.
2000	Jul.	Third Meeting of Heads of State and Governments of the CPLP takes place in Mozambique; Agreement on the abolition of visas on diplomatic, special and service passports (under the CPLP) is signed with Cabo Verde, Guinea-Bissau, Mozambique, Angola, São Tomé and Príncipe, and Portugal.
	Dec.	President of South Africa, Thabo Mbeki, visits Brazil; Mercosur–SACU Framework Agreement is signed.
2001	Jun.	President of Mozambique, President Joaquim Chissano, visits Brazil.
	Dec.	Agreement signed on naval cooperation with Namibia.
2002	Mar.	President of Angola, José Eduardo dos Santos, meets with President Fernando Henrique Cardoso in Brasília.
	Jun.	Cooperation agreement is signed with Senegal for the establishment of a political consultation mechanism.
	Aug.	Fourth Meeting of Heads of Government and State of the CPLP.
		First Meeting of the Brazil–South Africa Joint Commission.
		The 'Education for all 2002–2005' agreement is signed with Angola.

Sep. Cooperation Protocol for the promotion of small and medium-sized enterprises and industries with Gabon.

Luiz Inácio Lula da Silva Government (2003–10)

2003 Mar. Brazil, in the exercise of the Presidency of the CPLP, promotes consultations in order to identify possible support measures for Guinea-Bissau, which is in a period of political and institutional crisis.

Brazilian Embassy is established in São Tomé and Príncipe.

May Foreign Minister Celso Amorim visits Mozambique, Zimbabwe, São Tomé and Príncipe, Angola, South Africa and Namibia.

Brazilian business mission visits South Africa.

Jun. Brazil and South Africa sign a cooperation agreement on defence.

IBSA Dialogue Forum (India–Brazil–South Africa) is set up.

President of Cabo Verde, Pedro Pires, visits Brazil.

Jul. Brazil contributes two transport planes to the United Nations Temporary Multilateral Emergency Force in Bunia, DR Congo.

Brazilian government strongly condemns and repudiates military coup in São Tomé and Príncipe.

Aug. Trilateral meeting between Ministers of Defence of Brazil, South Africa and India is held in Pretoria.

Sep. President of Burkina Faso, Blaise Compaoré, visits Brazil and signs an international cooperation programme with the Brazilian Ministry of Health.

Brazilian government condemns military coup in Guinea-Bissau.

Nov. President Lula visits South Africa, São Tomé and Príncipe, Angola, Mozambique, Namibia – Lula's first visit to Africa.

Dec. President Lula visits Egypt and Libya.

President of Angola participates as special guest of the XXV Mercosur Summit.

2004 Mar. First meeting of the IBSA Trilateral Joint Commission is held in New Delhi.

Apr. Brazilian government congratulates Guinea-Bissau for the good progress of the legislative elections, organised with the technical support of the Brazilian electoral mission.

	May	Foreign Minister Celso Amorim travels to Egypt to participate, as a special guest, in the Ministerial Meeting of the Arab League.
	Jun.	President of Uganda, Yoweri Kaguta Museveni, visits Brazil.
	Jul.	Lula visits São Tomé and Príncipe (CPLP Summit), Cabo Verde and Gabon.
	Aug.	Visit of the President of Mozambique, Joaquim Alberto Chissano to Brazil.Brazil supports UN Security Council resolution imposing embargo on international arms trade for the Darfur region of Sudan.
	Sep.	Delegation of the Southern African Customs Union (SACU) visits Brasília for trade negotiations with Mercosur.
		Brazilian embassy in Addis Ababa, Ethiopia, is reopened. It had been decommissioned in the late 1960s.
	Nov.	Vice-President of the Democratic Republic of the Congo, Arthur Z'Ahidi Ngoma, visits Brazil.
		Due to civil war in Cotê d'Ivoire, Brazilians living in Abidjan, are evacuated.
		Mining company Vale do Rio Doce wins international tender for the exploration of the Moatize coal complex in Mozambique.
		The King of Morocco, Mohammed VI, visits Brazil and talks with President Lula about bilateral business opportunities.
		Brazilian Embassy in Kinshasa, Democratic Republic of the Congo, is reopened after being decommissioned in 1997.
2005	Jan.	Foreign Minister Celso Amorim visits Cabo Verde, Guinea-Bissau, Senegal, Nigeria and Cameroon.
	Feb.	Brazilian embassy in Yaoundé, Cameroon, is reopened. It had been deactivated in 1999 due to budget constraints.
		Foreign Minister Celso Amorim visits Tunisia and Algeria.
	Mar.	Celso Amorim visits Kenya, Ethiopia, Mozambique and South Africa. In Mombasa, Kenya, he attends the WTO Mini-ministerial Meeting.
		The Second IBSA Joint Commission is opened in Cape Town.
		Democratic Republic of the Congo's Vice-President, Jean Pierre Mbemba Gombo, visits Brazil.
		Celso Amorim visits Algeria to participate in the XVII League of Arab States Summit.
		Brazil establishes diplomatic relations with Comoros.

Apr. President Lula visits Cameroon, Nigeria, Ghana, Guinea-Bissau and Senegal.

Brazil establishes Consulate General in Lagos, Nigeria.

May President of Angola, José Eduardo dos Santos, accompanied by a ministerial delegation visits Brazil. Memorandum of Understanding is signed on the granting of credits of $580 million to the Angolan government.

President of Algeria, Abdelaziz Bouteflika, visits Brazil and bilateral agreements are signed on phytosanitary measures, health, veterinary and visa exemption.

Jun. President of the Republic of the Congo, Denis Sassou Nguesso, visits Brazil.

Jul. Foreign Minister Celso Amorim visits Angola to attend the Tenth Meeting of the Council of Ministers of the CPLP.

Celso Amorim meets in London with Ministers of the G-4 and IBSA countries. The next day, a G-4 meeting takes place with Ministers of the African Union.

President of Botswana, Festus Gontebanye Mogae, visits Brazil.

Aug. President of the Gambia, Yahya Jammeh, visits Brazil accompanied by a ministerial delegation.

President of São Tomé and Príncipe, Fradique Bandeira Melo de Menezes, visits Brazil.

Prime Minister of Cabo Verde, José Maria Pereira Neves, visits Brazil.

Oct. President of Cabo Verde, Pedro Verona Rodrigues Pires, visits Brazil.

Nov. Brazil establishes embassies in Khartoum, Sudan and Malabo, Equatorial Guinea.

Celso Amorim participates in the Arusha, Tanzania meeting of the African Union Ministerial Conference on WTO negotiations.

Dec. Brazilian Embassies are reopened in Cotonou, Benin (formerly Dahomey) and in Lomé, Togo, after the closure of activities in the 1990s.

2006 Jan. Start of the joint missile construction project with South Africa.

Feb. President Lula visits Algeria, Benin, Botswana and South Africa.

	Apr.	Brazilian Air Force (FAB) aircraft makes the first flight to African capitals, with a view to establishing a regular FAB line between Brazil and Africa.
		Memorandum of Understanding is signed between Brazil and Ghana for the installation in Accra of the EMBRAPA Regional Office in Africa.
	May	Brazilian Embassies are reopened in Lusaka, Zambia (decommissioned in 1996); and established in Conakry, Republic of Guinea.
	Jun.	Brazilian Embassy in Gaborone, Botswana, is inaugurated.
	Jul.	President of Ghana, John Agyekum Kufuor, visits Brazil.
		Brazilian Embassy in Malabo, Equatorial Guinea is inaugurated.
		Brazil hosts the Second International Conference of Intellectuals of Africa and the Diaspora (CIAD), the first held outside the African continent, with the participation of heads of state or government of Botswana, Cape Verde, Ghana, Equatorial Guinea, Jamaica and Senegal, and the Chairman of the Commission of the African Union, Alpha Konaré.
	Sept.	First IBSA Summit is held in Brasília.
	Nov.	First Africa–South America Summit (ASA) is held in Abuja, Nigeria.
2007	Feb.	The Chairperson of the African Union visits Brazil.
		Technical Cooperation Agreement is signed between Brazil and the African Union.
	Mar.	Memorandum of Understanding is signed between Brazil and Republic of Congo in the Health Area and on Technical Cooperation in the Areas of Agriculture, Livestock and Fisheries.
	May	President of Senegal, Abdoulaye Wade, visits Brazil.
		Agreement signed on Air Service between Brazil and Senegal.
	Jul.	President of Mozambique, Armando Guebuza, visits Brazil.
	Aug.	President of Benin, Thomaz Boni Yayi, visits Brazil.
	Sep.	President of Mozambique, Armando Guebuza, visits Brazil.
		Memorandum of Understanding is signed between Brazil and Mozambique in the area of biofuels.
	Oct.	President Lula visits South Africa, Angola, Burkina Faso and Republic of Congo.

		Second Summit of the IBSA Dialogue Forum.
		Memorandum of Understanding between Brazil and the West African Economic and Monetary Union (WAEMU) in the field of biofuels is signed.
		Memorandum of Understanding is signed to establish a mechanism for political consultations between Brazil and Angola.
	Nov.	President of Guinea-Bissau, João Bernardo Nino Vieira, visits Brazil.
		Brazil and China begin distribution of free satellite images to Africa.
2008	Feb.	President of Equatorial Guinea, Teodoro Obiang Nguema Basongo, visits Brazil.
	Mar.	Humanitarian aid to Angola, Guinea-Bissau, Mozambique and Zambia.
	May	Foreign Minister Celso Amorim travels to São Tomé and Príncipe.
		Technical Cooperation Agreement is signed between Brazil and Sierra Leone.
	Jun.	Celso Amorim visits Cabo Verde, Algeria, Morocco and Tunisia.
	Jul.	Seventh Summit of Heads of State and Government of the CPLP in Lisbon.
	Sep.	Memorandum of Understanding to establish a mechanism for political consultations between Brazil and Namibia.
	Oct.	Third IBSA Summit.
		President Lula visits Mozambique.
		Celso Amorim visits Zimbabwe and Zambia.
		Agreement with São Tomé and Príncipe to implement a malaria prevention and control programme in the country.
2009	Jan.	Memorandum of Understanding between Brazil and São Tomé and Príncipe on cooperation in aquaculture and fisheries.
	Feb.	President of the Republic of Namibia, Hifikepunye Pohamba, visits Brazil.
	Mar.	Foreign Minister Celso Amorim travels to Egypt.
		Prime Minister of São Tomé and Príncipe, Rafael Branco, visits Brazil.

		Agreement is signed to implement the National Rural Extension Programme (PRONER) in São Tomé and Príncipe.
	Apr.	Memorandum of Understanding is signed with Cabo Verde to encourage the scientific training of Cabo Verdean students.
	May	President of Senegal, Abdoulaye Wade, visits Brazil.
	Jul.	President of Mozambique, Armando Guebuza, visits Brazil.
		President of Nigeria, Umaru Yar'Adua, visits Brazil.
		Memorandum of Understanding is signed between Brazil and Egypt to promote joint technical cooperation activities in African countries.
		Memorandum of Understanding is signed on cooperation between Brazil and Nigeria in the area of energy.
	Ago.	President of Sierra Leone, Ernest Bai Koroma, visits Brazil.
	Sep.	President of Malawi, Bingu Wa Mutharika, visits Brazil.
		Foreign Minister Celso Amorim travels to Tunisia and Morocco.
		Nigerian Ministerial delegation visits Brazil.
		Second Summit of ASA is held in Isla de Margarita, Venezuela.
	Oct.	President of South Africa, Jacob Zuma, visits Brazil.
		Prime Minister of Cabo Verde, José Maria Neves, visits Brazil.
		Celso Amorim visits Mali, Equatorial Guinea and Togo.
		Memorandum of Understanding is signed between Brazil and South Africa to promote trade and investment.
	Nov.	A business mission, made up of ninety entrepreneurs and headed by the Minister of State for Development, Industry and Foreign Trade, Miguel Jorge, arrives in Luanda.
		Agreement with Republic of Congo (2009–12) on economic, scientific, technical and cultural cooperation is signed.
	Dec.	Celso Amorim travels to Egypt.
		Memoranda of Understanding are signed between Brazil and Egypt in sport cooperation and for the Establishment of a Strategic Dialogue Mechanism.
2010	Mar.	Agreement with São Tomé and Príncipe to support programmes to combat tuberculosis and to implement the minimum wage in the country.

Apr. Fourth IBSA Summit is held in Brasília.

President of Liberia, Ellen Johnson-Sirleaf, visits Brazil.

President of Mali, Amadou Toumani Touré, visits Brazil.

Diplomatic relations established with the Central African Republic.

President of the UEMOA Commission visits Brazil.

May Brazil–Africa Dialogue on Food Security, Fighting Hunger and Rural Development.

Memorandum of Understanding between Brazil and Zimbabwe on cooperation in family agriculture and rural development.

Jun. President of Angola, José Eduardo dos Santos, visits Brazil and signs a financial cooperation protocol and a joint declaration on the establishment of strategic partnership.

Jul. Brazil–Economic Community of West African States (ECOWAS) Summit takes place in Praia, Cabo Verde.

President Lula visits Equatorial Guinea, Kenya, Tanzania, Zambia and South Africa.

Business Seminars Brazil–Kenya, Brazil–South Africa and Brazil–Tanzania.

Memorandum of Understanding is signed between Brazil and Kenya on Promotion of Trade and Investment.

Memorandum of Understanding is signed between Brazil and Algeria for the establishment of a Strategic Dialogue mechanism.

Memorandum of Understanding between Brazil and the United Nations World Food Programme for the Promotion of Triangular Technical Cooperation in Mozambique.

Seventh Conference of Heads of State and Government of the CPLP in Luanda, Angola.

Aug. Angola's Defence Minister, Candido dos Santos Van-Dúnem, visits Brazil.

President of Cameroon, Paul Biya, visits Brazil

Memorandum of Understanding is signed between Brazil and Cameroon for cooperation on Agriculture and Livestock.

President of Guinea-Bissau, Malam Bacai Sanhá, visits Brazil.

Mercosur–Egypt Free Trade Agreement is signed.

Sep. Third Meeting of the Council of Foreign Ministers of the South America–Africa Cooperation Forum.

Nov. President Lula travels to Mozambique.

Foreign Minister Celso Amorim visits the Democratic Republic of the Congo.

Cooperation to assist victims of sexual violence in DR Congo.

President of Zambia, Rupiah Banda, visits Brazil.

Agreement is signed with Sudan for the establishment of a Permanent Joint Commission for Cooperation.

Dec. Memorandum of Understanding is signed with Côte d'Ivoire and Ghana for cooperation in strengthening agriculture and food security.

NEPAD Executive Director, Ibrahim Mayaki, visits Brazil.

South Africa joins the BRIC.

Dilma Rousseff Government (2011–16)

2011 Jul. Diplomatic relations are established with the Republic of South Sudan.

Foreign Minister Antônio Patriota visits Angola to discuss the Strategic Partnership between the two countries, as well as economic issues and African policy issues.

Foreign Minister Patriota visits Guinea-Bissau. Issues such as the restructuring of the African country's security and defence areas are addressed.

Foreign Minister Patriota visits Namibia, and addresses the deepening of bilateral cooperation, mainly partnership in the naval area between Brazil and Namibia.

Foreign Minister Patriota visits South Africa.

Foreign Minister Patriota visits the Republic of Guinea.

Sep. Foreign Minister Patriota visits Morocco for a meeting with the Moroccan Foreign Minister, where they discuss trade and bilateral cooperation.

Oct. Dilma Rousseff makes first visit to Africa and participates in the Fifth Summit of the IBSA Forum in South Africa, where the Tshwane Declaration is signed.

Dilma Rousseff visits Mozambique, the largest Brazilian cooperation partner in Africa, where she meets with President Armando Guebuza and Brazilian investors in the country.

		Dilma Rousseff visits Angola, where she reiterates the priority given by Brazil to the country, one of its largest trading partners in Africa.
	Nov.	Foreign Minister Patriota attends the Fourth Ministerial Meeting of the South America–Africa (ASA) Summit in Malabo, Equatorial Guinea.
		Foreign Minister Patriota visits Ghana.
2012	Apr.	Foreign Minister Patriota participates in the 319th Meeting of the Peace and Security Council of the African Union in Ethiopia.
		Foreign Minister Patriota visits Tunisia where he discusses economic issues with the Tunisian chancellor, as well as the possibility of establishing direct flights between Brazil and Tunisia.
		Foreign Minister Patriota visits Mauritania, where he signs cooperation agreements in the areas of agriculture and aquaculture.
	Jul.	Foreign Minister Patriota meets the Minister of Agriculture of Burkina Faso, Laurent Sedogo, in Brasília, to discuss food security and agricultural development projects, as well as emergency food donation.
	Ago.	Foreign Minister Patriota visits Senegal to address the expansion of the bilateral cooperation and African affairs agenda.
		Foreign Minister Patriota visits Cabo Verde.
2013	Jan.	Foreign Minister Patriota participates in the Eighth Ministerial Meeting of the South Atlantic Peace and Cooperation Zone (ZOPACAS), in Uruguay.
	Feb.	Dilma Rousseff participates in the Third Summit of Heads of State and Government of South America–Africa (ASA) in Malabo, Equatorial Guinea.
		Dilma Rousseff visits Nigeria, where a Memorandum of Understanding is signed to develop a strategic dialogue mechanism to establish a Nigeria–Brazil Bilateral Commission.
	Mar.	Dilma Rousseff visits South Africa to attend the Fifth BRICS Summit.
	May	Dilma Rousseff participates in the Fiftieth Anniversary celebration of the African Union in Addis Ababa. She announces the formation of an international trade agency for Africa and Latin America, and Brazil's cancellation of external debt for twelve African countries.

	Jun.	Sixth IBSA Summit scheduled in New Delhi to commemorate its tenth anniversary is not held. Until 2018 no other summit takes place.
	Jul.	Eighteenth Ordinary Meeting of the Council of Ministers of the CPLP is held in Mozambique, to address the situation in Guinea-Bissau, among other matters.
		Guinea's Foreign Minister visits Brazil and talks on the revitalisation of ZOPACAS and the forgiveness of Guinea's debt with Brazil.
	Sep.	Ambassador Roberto Azevêdo assumes the position of Director-General of the WTO, having been elected in May of the same year with the support of African countries.
		Foreign Minister Figueiredo meets with foreign ministers from South Africa, India and China in Foz do Iguaçu for the XVI Ministerial Meeting of BASIC.
	Nov.	Sotuba Experimental Cotton Station (Cotton 4) is inaugurated in Mali. It works as a regional agricultural research centre, coordinated by the Brazilian Cooperation Agency (ABC) and implemented by EMBRAPA.
		Defence Minister Celso Amorim travels to Cabo Verde to strengthen security conditions in this Atlantic region, and inaugurates Brazil's permanent naval mission in Praia City to help the country's Coast Guard in its modernisation.
		First Session of the Brazil–Nigeria Strategic Dialogue Mechanism.
	Dec.	Dilma Rousseff attends the funeral of Nelson Mandela accompanied by her predecessors Lula, Fernando Henrique Cardoso, Collor de Mello and José Sarney.
2014	Mar.	The Council of the League of Arab States accredits a Special Representative of Brazil to the League of Arab States for the first time in order to strengthen the country's relations with Arab countries, including those in North Africa.
	Apr.	President of Ghana, John Mahama, visits Brazil.
	Jun.	President of Angola, José Eduardo dos Santos, visits Brazil. Dilma Rousseff expresses Brazil's support for Angola's election to a rotating seat on the UN Security Council.
	Jun./ Jul.	During the World Cup in Brazil, the country is visited by several heads of state, including Jacob Zuma, President of South Africa, Denis Sassou Nguesso, President of the Republic of Congo, and Joseph Kabila of the Democratic Republic of the Congo.

Jul. Sixth BRICS Summit in Fortaleza. The formation of the BRICS Development Bank is announced and a Contingency Fund against speculative attacks on the currencies of the countries of the bloc.

Sep. Fourth Annual Meeting between the National Standards Organisations of the IBSA, aiming to expand trade among members, and identifying, preventing and eliminating unnecessary trade barriers.

Angola signs agreement to buy seven Brazilian patrol ships.

Oct. Donation of more than $13 million in supplies for Guinea, Sierra Leone and Liberia to fight the Ebola epidemic.

2015 Mar. Foreign Minister Mauro Vieira visits Ghana, São Tomé and Príncipe, Mozambique and Angola.

Foreign Minister Mauro Vieira carries out a mission in Accra, Ghana, where he is received by President John Mahama.

Agreement is signed between Brazil and Mozambique on Cooperation and Investment Facilitation.

Apr. Foreign Minister Mauro Vieira pays official visit to Angola, where he signs the bilateral Agreement on Cooperation and Investment Facilitation.

May Seventh Ministerial Meeting of the South Atlantic Peace and Cooperation Zone – ZOPACAS takes place in Praia, Cabo Verde, aiming to promote regional cooperation and maintain peace and security in the countries of Africa and South America with coasts on the South Atlantic Ocean.

Aug. Foreign Minister Mauro Vieira visits Kinshasa, Democratic Republic of the Congo, where he meets President Joseph Kabila.

In Goma (DR Congo), Mauro Vieira has working meeting with the UN Secretary-General's Special Representative for the DRC and head of the UN Stabilisation Mission in the DRC (MONUSCO), Martin Kobler. He also meets with Brazilian General Carlos Alberto Santos Cruz, Commander of MONUSCO.

Foreign Minister Mauro Vieira visits Cameroon, where he is received by Prime Minister Philemon Yang.

Sep. Meeting of Foreign Ministers of BRICS takes place in New York on the sidelines of the Seventieth Annual Session of the UN General Assembly.

Foreign Minister Mauro Vieira visits Cabo Verde, and attends the 3rd Political Consultation Mechanism Meeting. He meets President Jorge Carlos Fonseca and Prime Minister José Maria Pereira Neves.

In Dakar, President Macky Sall and Prime Minister Mohamed Ben Abdallah Dionne receive Foreign Minister Mauro Vieira. He inaugurates the First Brazil–Senegal Business Forum.

Oct. Foreign Minister Mauro Vieira visits Algeria.

Nov. Meeting of BRICS leaders takes place in Antalya, Turkey, on the sidelines of the G20 Summit

Foreign Minister Mauro Vieira participates in the ministerial meeting and the Fourth meeting of the Summit of South American–Arab Countries – ASPA, in Riyadh.

2016 Jan. The Second Meeting of Science and Technology Development Agencies BRICS and the First Meeting of the Working Group on Financing of the BRICS Science, Technology and Innovation take place in Beijing.

Feb. The Department of Human Resources, Science and Technology of the African Union Commission holds the first School Nutrition Day of Africa in Addis Ababa. The programme resulted from a high-level mission to Brazil in 2015.

Mar. Ethiopian Prime Minister Hailemariam Desalegn receives Foreign Minister Mauro Vieira in Addis Ababa. Vieira attends the Brazil–Ethiopia business seminar and meets with the Chairperson of the African Union Commission, Nkosazana Dlamini-Zuma.

Foreign Minister Mauro Vieira visits Rabat.

Foreign Minister Mauro Vieira visits Tunis.

Apr. Mauro Vieira pays an official visit to Angola.

First Meeting of the Steering Committee of the Cotton-4 + Togo Project takes place in Brasília.

The Brazilian Government welcomes Riek Machar's appointment as First Vice-President of South Sudan.

Michel Temer Government (2016–18)

2016 Fourth South America–Africa (ASA) Summit scheduled in Quito, Ecuador, is postponed *sine die*.

May Foreign Minister José Serra visits Cabo Verde.

Jun. Seminar on Maritime Security in the South Atlantic is held in Rio de Janeiro. The International Maritime Organisation (COMCONTRAM) co-organises the seminar.

Aug. The Vice-President of Comoros, Abdou Moustadroine, makes an official visit to Brasília.

Oct. Brazilian experts participate in the 'Attracting Investment to Uganda's Mineral Exploration Sector' conference held by the African Union Commission (AUC).

An agreement is signed between Brazil and Cabo Verde on air services.

Eighth Summit of BRICS is held in Goa, India, with the theme 'Building Sensitive Solutions, Inclusive and Collective'.

Foreign Minister José Serra meets with the foreign ministers of Angola, Cabo Verde, Guinea-Bissau and Mozambique and the CPLP executive Secretary.

2017 Jan. Oil Minister of Nigeria, Emmanuel Ibe Kachikwua, visits Brasília.

Mar. Fifth Technical Meeting of the Focal Points for Science, Technology and Higher Education of the CPLP is held in Lisbon, Portugal.

May The South African Minister of International Relations and Cooperation, Maite Nkoana-Mashabane, welcomes the Minister of Foreign Affairs, Aloysio Ferreira, on his visit to Pretoria. The PTA between the Customs Union of Southern Africa and the Mercosur comes into effect.

Foreign Minister Aloysio Ferreira and South Africa's Minister for Small Business Development, Lindiwe Zulu, confirm their commitment to the Strategic Dialogue of IBSA and to the BRICS Partnership.

Foreign Minister Aloysio Nunes Ferreira visits Namibia, Botswana, Malawi, Mozambique and South Africa.

Jul. The Twenty-second Regular Meeting of Council of Ministers of CPLP is held in Brasília.

Aug. Brazilian business mission organised by the Foreign Ministry and Apex-Brazil (Brazilian Trade and Investment Promotion Agency) visits Nigeria and Ghana.

Sep. The Ninth BRICS Leaders Summit is held in Xiamen, China.

The Free Trade Agreement between Mercosur and Egypt comes into effect.

	Nov.	The CPLP Internet Governance Forum takes place in Lisbon, Portugal.
		Meeting between Mercosur and Morocco is held in Brasília to discuss the technical nature of negotiations aimed at creating a free trade area.
	Dec.	First Meeting of the Joint Committee of the Free Trade Agreement (FTA) between Mercosur and Egypt.
2018	Feb.	Foreign Minister Nuno Ferreira pays a visit to Luanda, where he promises new loans of $2 billion to finance Brazilian investments and exports.
	Apr.	Ex-president Lula da Silva begins serving a twelve-year prison term for corruption after the Supreme Court rejected his final appeal in a controversial process.
	May	The board of the New Development Bank holds third annual meeting. Loans worth $1.6 billion for six environmental and infrastructure projects in BRICS countries approved.
	Jun.	Ambassador José Viegas Filho is nominated Special Representative of the Secretary-General of the United Nations in Guinea-Bissau; Lieutenant-General Elias Rodrigues Martins Filho is nominated Force Commander of MONUSCO.
		The External Affairs Minister of India, Smt. Sushma Swaraj, The Minister of International Relations and Cooperation of South Africa, Ms Lindiwe Sisulu and the Deputy Minister of Foreign Affairs of Brazil, Mr Marcos Bezerra Abbott Galvão, meet in Pretoria on 4th June. For the occasion, the IBSA Declaration on South–South Cooperation was released.
	Jul.	Johannesburg holds the 10th BRICS Summit, under the theme 'BRICS in Africa: Collaboration for Inclusive Growth and Shared Prosperity in the 4th Industrial Revolution'.
		Cabo Verde holds the XII Conference of Heads of State and of Government of CPLP, with the presence of President Michel Temer.
	Jun.	Foreign Minister Aloysio Nunes visits Algeria, where he met with the President Abdelaziz Bouteflika, the Prime Minister Ahmed Ouyahia and the Foreign Minister Abdelkader Messahel. They discussed initiatives to expand and diversify bilateral relations.

Sep. During 73rd Session of the United Nations General Assembly, the foreign ministers of India, Brazil and South Africa met for the IBSA Dialogue Forum, releasing a Joint Communiqué.

Oct. Right-wing candidate Jair Bolsonaro wins presidential elections with 55.1% of the votes. In his victory speech he announces his intention to free Brazil's foreign policy from the ideological bias to which it had been submitted in the last years and to ensure that the country would no longer be separated from the more developed nations.

Nov. Career diplomat Ambassador Ernesto Araújo is appointed to the position of Minister of Foreign Affairs in Bolsonaro's future government.

Bibliography

A Redenção, vol. 1, January 1887 (São Paulo).

ABC – Agência Brasileira de Cooperação, '335 Entidades Brasileiras Parceiras', 2012, www.abc.gov.br/Gestao/EntidadesParceiras.

—— 'Centro de Formação Brasil-Angola', n.d., www.abc.gov.br/Projetos/CooperacaoSulSul/CentroFormacaoAngola.

—— 'África – Execução Financeira 2000–2014', 2010, www.abc.gov.br/Content/ABC/imagens/africa_financeiro.png.

—— 'Países Parceiros da Cooperação Sul-Sul Brasileira', n.d., www.abc.gov.br/Gestao/PaisesParceiros.

—— 'Projetos Estruturantes', n.d., www.abc.gov.br/Gestao/ProjetosEstruturantes.

—— Execução Orçamentária da ABC de 2015 a 2017, received 27 March 2018 through the Electronic System of the Citizen Information Service (e-SIC).

Abdenur, Adriana Erthal, 'Organisation and Politics in South-South Cooperation: Brazil's technical cooperation in Africa', *Global Society* 29:3 (2015), 321–38.

—— 'China in Africa, Viewed from Brazil', *The Journal of Asian Studies* 74: 2 (2015), 257–67.

—— 'Brazil-Africa Relations: From boom to bust?' in *Africa and the World: Bilateral and multilateral international diplomacy*, edited by Dawn Nagar and Charles Mutasa (London: Palgrave Macmillan, 2018).

Abdenur, Adriana Erthal and Danilo Marcondes de Souza Neto, 'Brazil's Development Cooperation with Africa: What role for democracy and human rights', *SUR – Revista Internacional de Direitos Humanos* 19 (2013), 17–35.

—— 'O Brasil e a cooperação em defesa: a construção de uma identidade regional no Atlântico Sul', *Revista Brasileira de Política Internacional* 57:1 (2014), 5–21.

—— *Brazil's growing relevance to Peace and security in Africa*, NOREF Norwegian Peacebuilding Resource Centre Report, March 2014.

—— 'Brazilian South-South cooperation in public health: Dilemas of the ARV factory initiative', in *Mozambique and Brazil. Forging New Partnerships or Developing Dependency?* edited by Chris Alden, Sérgio Chichava and Ana Cristina Alves (Johannesburg: Jacana Media, 2017), 173–93.

Abdenur, Adriana Erthal and João Marcos Rampini, 'A Cooperação Brasileira para o Desenvolvimento com Angola e Moçambique: Uma Visão Comparada', in *Política Externa Brasileira, Cooperação Sul – Sul e Negociações Internacionais*, edited by Haroldo Ramazini Júnior and Luis Fernando Ayerbe (São Paulo: Editora Cultura Acadêmica, Fundação Friedrich Ebert, Instituto de Estudos Econômicos e Internacionais -IEEI-UNESP, 2015).

Albuquerque, Felipe Leal Ribeiro de, 'Cooperation on Food Security with Africa as an Instrument of Brazil's Foreign Policy (2003-2010)', *Brazilian Journal of International Relations* 4:3 (2015), 559–81.

Almeida, Elga Lessa de, 'Entre o Discurso Solidário e a Ação Pragmática da Cooperação Brasileira em Moçambique: os casos dos projetos de implantação da fábrica de medicamentos antirretrovirais e o ProSavana', *Caderno CRH*, Salvador 29:76 (2016), 53–68.

Almeida, Eugénio Costa and Luís Manuel B. Bernardino, 'A Comissão do Golfo da Guiné e a Zona de Paz e Cooperação do Atlântico Sul. Organizações Interzonais para a persecução da Segurança Marítima na Bacia Meridional Atlântica', *Revista Militar* 2532 (2013). Available at: www.revistamilitar.pt/artigo.php?art_id=797.

Altemani, Henrique and Antônio Carlos Lessa, *Relações internacionais do Brasil: temas e agendas* (São Paulo: Saraiva, 2006).

Amorim, Celso, 'O Brasil na 48ª Sessão da Assembleia Geral da ONU', *Resenha de Política Exterior do Brasil* 19:73 (1993), 59–68.

—— 'Um Balanço das Relações Brasil – África', *Diálogos Africanos* 1(2015), 17–26.

Amos, Alcione Meira, *Os Que Voltaram. A história dos retornados afro-brasileiros na África Ocidental no século XIX* (Belo Horizonte: Tradição Planalto, 2007).

Ampofo, Akosua Adomako, 'Africa's Fast-Growing Pentecostal Mega Churches are Entrenching Old Injustices against Women', *QuartzAfrica*, 16 June 2017, https://qz.com/1007819/pentecostal-churches-in-ghana-and-nigeria-are-entrenching-sexist-gender-roles-for-women.

Aragon, Daniel P., 'Chancellery Sepulchers: Jânio Quadros, João Goulart and the forging of Brazilian foreign policy in Angola, Mozambique, and South Africa, 1961–1964', *Luso-Brazilian Review* 47:1 (2010), 121–49.

Arraes, Virgílio, 'Estados Unidos: um possível significado para a Quarta Frota', *Meridiano* 47: 97 (2008).

Banco Mundial and Instituto de Pesquisa Económica Aplicada (IPEA), *Ponte sobre o Atlântico. Brasil e África Subsaariana: Parceria Sul-Sul para o crescimento* (Brasília, 2011).

Barcelona Centre for International Affairs (CIDOB), *CIDOB International Yearbook 2008*. 'Country profile: Nigeria and its regional context' (Barcelona, 2008).

Barroso, José Manuel D., 'Um Portugal Atlântico ou um Portugal Europeu?', Speech 13/773, Algarve Business Forum, 5 October 2013. Available at: http://europa.eu/rapid/press-release_SPEECH-13-773_pt.htm.

Beny, Eduardo, *A nova geopolítica do petróleo: do Golfo Pérsico ao Golfo da Guiné* (Lisbon: Novo Imbondeiro, 2007).

BNDES – Banco Nacional de Desenvolvimento Econômico e Social, 'BNDES e bancos africanos de desenvolvimento assinam Memorandos de Entendimento', 21 June 2012, www.bndes.gov.br/wps/portal/site/home/imprensa/noticias/conteudo/20120621_mou.

—— 'BNDES retoma desembolsos para mais dois contratos de exportação de serviços de engenharia' 16 March 2017, www.bndes.gov.br/wps/portal/site/home/imprensa/noticias/conteudo/bndes-retoma-desembolsos-para-mais-dois-contratos-de-exportacao-de-servicos-de-engenharia.

—— 'Nota à imprensa: BNDES aciona seguro de crédito para operações com Moçambique', 24 June 2017, www.bndes.gov.br/wps/portal/site/home/imprensa/noticias/conteudo/bndes-aciona-seguro-de-credito-para-operacoes-com-mocambique.

Boadi-Siaw, Samuel Yaw, *Development of Relations between Brazil and African States, 1950–1973* (PhD dissertation, Los Angeles: University of California, 1975).

Brasil 247, 'Temer acaba com Ciência Sem Fronteiras', 2 April 2017, www.brasil247.com/pt/247/brasil/288242/Temer-acaba-com-o-Ciência-sem-Fronteiras.htm.

Bustamante, Luisa and Maria Clara Vieira, 'Vergonha Brasileira', *Veja* 50:47 (2017), 81.

Camargo Corrêa, 'Group's Business', n.d., www.camargocorrea.com.br/en/Group.html (see now also https://moverpar.com.br and http://www.camargocorreainfra.com).

Canani, Ney, *Política Externa no Governo Itamar Franco (1992-1994): continuidade e renovação de paradigma nos anos 90* (Porto Alegre: Editora UFRGS, 2004).

Cardoso, Fernando Henrique, 'Discurso do Presidente da República por ocasião da sessão solene de abertura da reunião de Cúpula da Comunidade dos Países de Língua Portuguesa, Lisboa, 17 de julho de 1996', *Resenha de Política Externa do Brasil* 23:79 (1996), 29–32.

—— 'Discurso do Presidente Fernando Henrique Cardoso, por ocasião do banquete oferecido pelo Presidente da República da África do Sul, Nelson Mandela. Pretória, 27 de novembro de 1996', *Resenha de Política Externa do Brasil* 23:79 (1996), 167–70.

Cardoso, Fernando Henrique and Mario Soares, *O mundo em português: um diálogo* (Rio de Janeiro: Paz e Terra, 1998).

CartaCapital, 'Lava Jato: 41ª fase foca em operações da Petrobras na África', 25 May 2017, www.cartacapital.com.br/politica/lava-jato-41a-fase-foca-em-operacoes-da-petrobras-na-africa.

Carvalho, José Jorge de, *Inclusão Étnica e Racial no Ensino Superior* (Brasília: Universidade de Brasília, 2003).

—— 'Inclusão Étnica e Racial no Brasil: a questão das cotas no ensino superior', *NAyA* (São Paulo: Attar Editorial, 2005).

Castillo, Lisa Earl, 'Mapping the Nineteenth-Century Brazilian Returnee Movements: Demographics, life stories and the question of slavery', *Atlantic Studies* 13:1 (2016), 25–52.

Castro, Therezinha de, *Geopolítica: princípios, meios e fins* (Rio de Janeiro: Bibliex, 1999).

Cervo, Amado, 'Um balanço da reunião da OMC em Cancún', *Meridiano 47 Journal of Global Studies* 4:38–39 (2003), 1–32.

Cervo, Amado e Clodoaldo Bueno, *História da Política Exterior do Brasil* (Brasília: Ed. UnB, 2010).

Cervo, Amado Luiz and Antônio Carlos Lessa, 'O declínio: inserção internacional do Brasil (2011–2014)', *Revista Brasileira de Política Internacional* 57:2 (2014), 133–51.

Chan, Stephen, 'The Origins of AFRICOM: The Obama administration, the Sahara-Sahel and US Militarization of Africa', Forum of the Royal Africa Society, 9 November 2009. Available at: http://concernedafricascholars.org/docs/bulletin85volman-keenan.pdf.

Citifmonline, 'GNPC Donates $4.5m for Construction of Sickle Cell Centre', 9 March 2016, http://citifmonline.com/2016/03/09/gnpc-donates-4-5m-for-construction-of-sickle-cell-centre.

Clapham, Christopher, *Africa and the International System: The politics of state survival* (Cambridge: Cambridge University Press, 1996).

Clapham, Christopher, Jeffrey Herbst and Greg Mills, eds. *Big African States: Angola, Sudan, DRC, Ethiopia, Nigeria, South Africa* (Johannesburg: Wits University Press, 2001).

Collor, Fernando, 'Presidente Fernando Collor é recebido na Casa Branca. Resposta à saudação do Presidente George Bush na cerimónia oficial de chegada, na Casa Branca, em 18 de junho de 1991', *Resenha de Política Exterior do Brasil* 17:68 (1991), 165.

Comissão Pró-Índio de São Paulo, 'Terras quilombolas em 2015: apenas 10 terras tituladas', 21 December 2015, http://comissaoproindio.blogspot.com.br/2015/12/terras-quilombolas-em-2015-apenas-9.html.

Costa, Ana Benárd da, 'Cooperação portuguesa com os PALOP ao nível superior: Impactos e Desafios', in *Formação Superior e Desenvolvimento. Estudantes Universitários Africanos em Portugal*, edited by Ana Benárd da Costa and Margarida Lima de Faria (Coimbra: Almedina, 2013), 19–38.

Costa e Silva, Alberto da, *As relações entre o Brasil e a África Negra, de 1822 à 1ª Guerra Mundial* (Luanda: Museu Nacional da Escravatura, 1996).

—— *Um Rio Chamado Atlântico. A África no Brasil e o Brasil na África* (Rio de Janeiro: Editora Nova Fronteira, 2003).

—— 'O Brasil na África Atlântica', *Revista do Património Histórico e Artístico Nacional* 34 (2012), 361–73.

Costa Leite, Iara, Bianca Suyama, Laura Trajber Waisbich, Melissa Pomeroy et al., *Brazil's Engagement in International Development Cooperation: The state of the debate*. Evidence Report no. 59 (Brighton: Institute of Development Studies, 2014).

Costa Vaz, Alcides and Daniel Flemes, *Security Policies of India, Brazil and South Africa: Regional security contexts as constraints for a common agenda*. GIGA Working Paper no. 160. (Hamburg: GIGA German Institute of Global and Area Studies, 2011).

CPLP – Comunidade dos Paises de Lingua Portuguesa, n.d., 'Segurança e Defesa', www.cplp.org/id-4271.aspx.

Cruz, Márcia Maria, 'Número de professores negros em universidades públicas gera debate', 2 March 2016, www.em.com.br/app/noticia/gerais/2016/02/03/interna_gerais,731244/numero-de-professores-negros-em-universidades-publicas-gera-debate.shtml.

Dantas, Raymundo Souza, *África Difícil* (Rio de Janeiro: Editora Leitura, 1965).

Dávila, Jerry, *Hotel Trópico: Brazil and the challenge of African decolonization, 1950–1980* (Durham and London: Duke University Press, 2010).

Defense Industry Daily, 'Super Tucano Counter-Insurgency Plane Makes Inroads in Africa', 12 April 2017, www.defenseindustrydaily.com/super-tucano-counter-insurgency-plane-makes-inroads-into-africa-07348.

Defesanet, 'ZOPACAS – Amorim propõe ações para fortalecer cooperação em Defesa', 16 January 2013. www.defesanet.com.br/geopolitica/noticia/9322/ZOPACAS---Amorim-propoe-acoes-para-fortalecer-cooperacao-em-Defesa.

Deutsche Welle, 'Corrupção: Os tentáculos da Odebrecht em Angola e Moçambique', 25 April 2017, www.dw.com/pt-002/corrupção-os-tentáculos-da-odebrecht-em-angola-e-moçambique/a-38569474.

Dnotícias, 'Comissão do Golfo da Guiné propõe órgão para questões de defesa e segurança', *dnoticias.pt*, 10 August 2013, www.dnoticias.pt/hemeroteca/400603-comissao-do-golfo-da-guine-propoe-orgao-para-questoes-de-defesa-e-seguranca-FODN400603.

Escorrega, Luís Carlos Falcão, 'Da Importância Geopolítica e Geoestratégica dos Açores no Actual Contexto Estratégico', *Revista Militar* 2497/2498 (2010), 203–39.

Esterhuyse, Abel, 'A Iraquização da África. Africom: a perspectiva sul-africana' *Air & Space Power Journal* Edição em Português 21:1(2010), 74–86.

Fernandes, Florestan, *A integração do negro na sociedade de classes*, vol. 1, 3rd ed. (São Paulo: Ática, 1978).

Fig, David, *The Political Economy of South-South Relations: The case of South Africa and Latin America* (PhD dissertation, London: Department of International Relations, London School of Economics, 1992).

Filho, Pio Penna, *O Brasil e a África do Sul. O arco atlântico da política externa brasileira (1918–2000)* (Brasília: FUNAG/CESUL, 2008).

Filho, Pio Penna and António Carlos Moraes Lessa, 'O Itamaraty e a África: as origens da política africana do Brasil', *Estudos Históricos* 39 (2007): 57–81.

Flemes, Daniel and Alcides Costa Vaz, *Regional Security Contexts as Constraints for a Common Agenda: Security policies of India, Brazil and*

South Africa GIGA Working Paper no. 160 (Hamburg: GIGA German Institute of Global and Area Studies, 2011).
Folha de São Paulo, 'Ranking Universitário Folha 2016', 2017, http://ruf.folha.uol.com.br/2016.
Freyre, Gilberto, *Casa-Grande & Senzala* (Lisbon: Livros do Brasil, 2003 [1933]).
Fundação Osvaldo Cruz, 'Relatório de Atividades Internacionais 2014–2015', Centro de Relações Internacionais em Saúde (Rio de Janeiro 2016), https://portal.fiocruz.br/sites/portal.fiocruz.br/files/documentos/fiocruz_relatorio_de_atividades_internacionais_2014-2015.pdf.
Gala, Irene Vida, *A Política Externa do Governo Lula para a África. A política externa como instrumento da ação afirmativa ...e ainda que não só*, dissertation (Brasília: Instituto Rio Branco, 2007).
García, Abel T., *La política exterior de Estados Unidos hacia el Golfo de Guinea durante la administración de W. Bush* (Buenos Aires: CLACSO, 2011).
Garcia, Eugênio Vargas, *Cronologia das Relações Internacionais do Brasil* (Rio de Janeiro: Contraponto, 2000).
Ghanaian Chronicle, '$13.66m Blood & Sickle Cell Centre for KATH', *Modern Ghana*, 29 November 2010, www.modernghana.com/news/306308/1/1366m-blood-amp-sickle-cell-centre-for-kath.html.
Góes, Francisco, 'Acordo entre BNDES e banco africano eleva potencial de exportações para o continente', *Valor Económico*, 4 December 2015, www.valor.com.br/brasil/4342050/acordo-entre-bndes-e-banco-africano-eleva-potencial-de-exportacoes-para-o-continente.
Gorender, Jacob, *O escravismo colonial*, 3rd ed. (São Paulo: Ática, 1980).
Governo do Brasil, 'Ciência sem Fronteiras já beneficiou 17,5 mil negros com bolsas de estudo no exterior', 29 November 2015, www.brasil.gov.br/educacao/2015/11/ciencia-sem-fronteiras-ja-beneficiou-17-5-mil-negros-com-bolsas-de-estudos-no-exterior.
Gregory, Shaun, *French Defense Policy into the Twenty-First Century* (Houndmills: Macmillan Press; New York: St. Martin's Press, 2000).
Guimarães, Samuel, ed. *South Africa and Brazil: Risks and opportunities in the turmoil of globalization* (Brasília: Fundação Alexandre de Gusmão/IPRI, 1996).
Guizelin, Gilberto da Silva, 'Relações Brasil – África: A Missão Niterói à Libéria', *Cadernos do Centro de História e Documentação Diplomática – CHDD* 15:28 (2016), 549–65.
Hammerstad, Anne, *South Africa's Security Engagement in the Region: Lessons for IBSA?* Documento de trabalho no. 2, Projeto Líderes Regionais e Segurança Internacional (Brasília: UnB/Ford Foundation, 2005).
Henriques, Ricardo, *Desigualdade Racial no Brasil: evolução das condições de vida na década de 90*. Texto para Discussão 807 (Brasília: Instituto de Pesquisa Econômica Aplicada – IPEA, 2001).
—— 'O custo do racismo',*Geledés*, 21 November 2014, www.geledes.org.br/o-custo-racismo-por-ricardo-henriques.

Hirst, Mónica, 'Países de renda média e a cooperação Sul-Sul: entre o conceitual e o político', in *Brasil, Índia e África do Sul: desafios e oportunidades para novas parcerias*, edited by Maria Regina Soares de Lima and Mónica Hirst (São Paulo: Paz e Terra, 2009), 207–33.

—— *Aspectos Conceituais e Práticos da Atuação do Brasil em Cooperação Sul-Sul: os Casos de Haiti, Bolívia e Guiné-Bissau*. Texto para Discussão 1687 (Brasília: Instituto de Pesquisa Econômica Aplicada – IPEA, 2012).

Hofbauer, Andreas, *Uma história de branqueamento ou o negro em questão* (PhD dissertation, Universidade de São Paulo, 1999).

Hora, Zero, 'Temer (PMDB) elimina ministério que defendia mulheres, negros e LGBT', *Enio Verri*, 13 May 2016, http://enioverri.com.br/temer-pmdb-elimina-ministerio-que-defendia-mulheres-negros-e-lgbt.

Hurrell, Andrew, 'The Politics of South Atlantic Security: A survey of proposals for a South Atlantic Treaty Organization', *International Affairs* 59:2 (1983), 179–93.

IBSA Fund, '2017 On-going Projects Reports', 2018, http://tcdc2.undp.org/IBSA/projects/projects2017.htm.Idoeta, Paula Adamo, 'Ainda como investidor pequeno, Brasil está na corrida para fincar pé na África', *BBC Brasil*, 9 May 2012, www.bbc.com/portuguese/noticias/2012/05/120504_brasil_africa_fdi_pai.

India, Brazil and South Africa Dialogue Forum (IBSA), *Brasília Declaration*, 4th IBSA Summit, Brasília (2010).

—— *Tshwane Declaration* 5th IBSA Summit, Pretoria (2011).

INEP – Instituto Nacional de Estudos e Pesquisas Educacionais, *Censo da Educação Superior 2016. Divulgação* (Brasília: Ministério de Educação, 2017).

Instituto de Pesquisa Econômica Aplicada (IPEA), *Cooperação Brasileira para o Desenvolvimento Internacional 2005–2009* (Brasília, 2010).

—— *Retrato das desigualdades de gênero e raça* (Brasília, 2011).

—— *Cooperação Brasileira para o Desenvolvimento Internacional 2010* (Brasília, 2013).

—— *Cooperação Brasileira para o Desenvolvimento Internacional 2011–2013* (Brasília, 2016).

Instituto Ethos, *Perfil Social, Racial e de Gênero de 500 maiores empresas do Brasil e as suas ações afirmativas* (São Paulo, 2016).

IPEA – Instituto de Pesquisa Econômica Aplicada, Cooperação Brasileira para o Desenvolvimento Internacional 2011–2013 (Brasília, 2016).

IRI – Instituto de Relaciones Internacionales, Luanda Final Declaration of the VIth Meeting of ZOPACAS Member States, 18–19 June 2007, www.iri.edu.ar/publicaciones_iri/anuario/CD%20Anuario%202008/Africa/Luandadeclaracion.pdf.

Jardim, Marcelo A. de M., *A Zona de Paz e Cooperação do Atlântico Sul* (dissertation, Brasília: Instituto Rio Branco, 1991).

Júnior, Alfredo, 'Camponeses querem travar o ProSavana', *Voz da América*, 24 October 2017, www.voaportugues.com/a/camponeses-querem-travar-prosavana/4084596.html.

Keenan, Jeremy, *The Dark Sahara: America's War on Terror in Africa* (London: Pluto Press, 2009).

Khanyile, Moses Bangani, *South Africa's Security Relations with the Mercosur Countries* (PhD dissertation, Pretoria: University of Pretoria, Faculty of Humanities, 2005). Available at: http://upetd.up.ac.za/thesis/available/etd-03242004-150754/.

—— 'South Africa's Post-1994 Military Relations with the Mercosur Countries: Prospects and challenges', *Strategic Review for Southern Africa* 26:2 (2004).

Kornegay, Francis, *The Geopolitics of IBSA: The South African dimension*, International Policy Center for Inclusive Growth – UNDP (Brasília, 2008). Available at www.ipc-undp.org/conference/ibsa/papers/ibsa14.pdf.

—— 'South Africa, the South Atlantic and the IBSA-BRICS Equation: The transatlantic space in transition', *Austral: Revista Brasileira de Estratégia e Relações Internacionais*, 2:3 (2013), 75–100.

—— *South Africa, the Indian Ocean and the IBSA-BRICS Equation: Reflections on geopolitical and strategic dimension*, ORF Occasional Paper (New Delhi, 2011).

Kumar, Hemanth, 'EMR Capital Buys 80% Interest in Zambia's Lubambe Copper Mine', *Mining Technology*, 15 August 2017, www.mining-technology.com/news/newsemr-capital-buys-80-interest-in-zambias-lubambe-copper-mine-5901451.

Lampreia, Luiz Felipe, 'Palavras do Ministro das Relações Exteriores, Embaixador Luiz Felipe Lampreia, por ocasião da solenidade de encerramento do Seminário sobre Zumbi e as Relações Afro-Brasileiras', *Resenha de Política Externa do Brasil 22:77* (1995), 201.

—— 'Palavras do Senhor Ministro das Relações Exteriores, Embaixador Luiz Felipe Lampreia, por ocasião da abertura da Reunião Ministerial da Comunidade de Países de Língua Portuguesa, Salvados, Bahia, 17 de julho de 1997', *Resenha de Política Exterior do Brasil*, 24:81 (1997), 15–18.

—— *O Brasil e os ventos do mundo. Memórias de cinco décadas na cena internacional* (São Paulo: Objetiva, 2010).

Lechini, Gladys, 'Is South–South Co-operation still Possible? The Case of Brazil's strategy and Argentine's impulses towards the new South Africa and Africa', in *Politics and Social Movements in an Hegemonic World: Lessons from Africa, Asia and Latin America*, edited by Atilio A. Boron and Gladys Lechini (Buenos Aires: CLACSO, 2005), 319–46.

—— 'O Brasil na África ou a África no Brasil? A construção da política africana pelo Itamaraty', *Nueva Sociedad* (2008), 55–71.

—— 'BRICS e África: a grande incógnita', *Boletim de Economia e Política Internacional* 9 (2012), 139–50.Leite, Patrícia Soares, *O Brasil e a Cooperação Sul-Sul em três momentos de política externa:os governos Jânio Quadros/João Goulart, Ernesto Geisel e Luiz Inácio Lula da Silva* (Brasília: Fundação Alexandre Gusmão, 2011).

Lima, Márcia and Paulo Ramos, *Educação e políticas de promoção da igualdade racial no Brasil de 2003 a 2014*. Análise 31 (São Paulo:

Friedrich-Ebert-Stiftung Brasil, 2017). http://library.fes.de/pdf-files/bueros/brasilien/13615.pdf.
Lima, Marco Aurélio de Andrade, *A iniciativa da Bacia do Atlântico: um risco para o Brasil?* (Rio de Janeiro: Escola Superior de Guerra, 2011).
Lima, Maria Regina Soares de Lima, 'A política externa brasileira e os desafios da Cooperação Sul-Sul', *Revista Brasileira de Política Internacional* 48:1 (2005), 24–59.
Luna, Francisco Vidal and Herbert S. Klein, *Escravismo no Brasil* (São Paulo: Imprensa Oficial do Estado de São Paulo and Editora da Universidade de São Paulo, 2010).
Macauhub, 'Governo de Moçambique negoceia reinício das obras da barragem de Moamba-Major', 8 February 2018, https://macauhub.com.mo/pt/2018/02/08/pt-governo-de-mocambique-negoceia-reinicio-das-obras-da-barragem-de-moamba-major.
Marcondes, Danilo and Emma Mawdsley, 'South–South in Retreat? The transitions from Lula to Rousseff to Temer and Brazilian development cooperation', *International Affairs* 93:3 (2017), 681–99
Marcopolo S.A., 'Resultados do Exercício em 2017', 21 February 2018, http://ri.marcopolo.com.br/ptb/3366/Relatrio%20da%20Administrao%202017.pdf.
Marshall, Jane, 'Mobility of African Students – Europe losing ground', *University World News*, 17 November 2016, www.universityworldnews.com/article.php?story=20161117045045147.
Martin, Guy, *Africa in World Politics: A pan-African perspective* (Asmara: Africa World Press, 2002).
Mello, Patrícia Campos de, 'Brasil recua e reduz projetos de cooperação e doações para a África' *Folha de São Paulo*, 22 March 2015, www1.folha.uol.com.br/mundo/2015/03/1606466-brasil-recua-e-reduz-projetos-de-cooperacao-e-doacoes-para-a-africa.shtml.
Melo, Ovídio de Andrade, 'O reconhecimento de Angola pelo Brasil em 1975', *Comunicação & Política* 7:2 (2000), 75–165.
—— *Recordações de um Removedor de mofo no Itamaraty. Relatos de política externa de 1948 à atualidade* (Brasília: Fundação Alexandre Gusmão, 2009).
Milani, Carlos R.S., *ABC 30 Anos. História e Desafios Futuros* (Brasília: Agência Brasileira de Cooperação, 2017).
Ministério da Indústria, Comércio Exterior e Serviços (MDIC), 'Balança Comercial Brasileira: Países e Blocos', www.mdic.gov.br/index.php/comercio-exterior/estatisticas-de-comercio-exterior/series-historicas.
—— 'Programa de Financiamento às Exportações – Proex', n.d. www.camex.gov.br/financiamento-e-garantia-as-exportacoes/programa-de-financiamento-as-exportacoes-proex.
Ministério da Saúde, 'Acordos Internacionais', n.d., http://portalsaude.saude.gov.br/index.php/o-ministerio/principal/leia-mais-o-ministerio/279-aisa-raiz/aisa/24941-acordos-internacionais.

Ministério de Cultura. Fundação Cultural Palmares, *Conferência Mundial contra o Racismo, Discriminação Racial, Xenofobia e Intolerância Correlata, Durban 31 de agosto a 8 de setembro de 2001* (Brasília, n.d.)

Ministério de Defesa, 'Brasil e África do Sul fortalecem cooperação na área de defesa', 21 March 2014, www.defesa.gov.br/index.php/noticias/8406-parceria-brasil-e-africa-do-sul-fortalecem-cooperacao-na-area-de-defesa.

Ministério do Desenvolvimento, Indústria e Comércio Exterior (MDIC), *Balança Comercial Brasileira: Dados Consolidados 2012* (Brasília, 2013)

MRE – Ministério das Relações Exteriores, 'Acordo entre o governo da República da Índia, o governo da República Federativa do Brasil e o governo da República da África do Sul sobre o Fundo IBAS para o alívio da pobreza e da fome', Nota 346, 17 October 2017, www.itamaraty.gov.br/pt-BR/notas-a-imprensa/17618-acordo-entre-o-governo-da-republica-da-india-o-governo-da-republica-federativa-do-brasil-e-o-governo-da-republica-da-africa-do-sul-sobre-o-fundo-ibas-para-o-alivio-da-pobreza-e-da-fome.

—— *Balanço de Política Externa 2003–2010 – África – Defesa* (Brasília, 2011).

—— 'Entrada em vigor do Acordo de Preferências Comerciais MERCOLUL-SACU', 4 April 2016, www.itamaraty.gov.br/pt-BR/notas-a-imprensa/13717-entrada-em-vigor-do-acordo-de-preferencias-comerciais-mercosul-sacu.

—— 'Exchange Program for Undergraduate Students', n.d., www.dce.mre.gov.br/EN/PEC/PECG/php.

—— 'Programa de Estudantes-Convênio Pós-Graduação', n.d., www.dce.mre.gov.br/PEC/PG/historico_Africa_3.png

—— 'Zona da Paz e Cooperação do Atlântico do Sul', n.d., www.itamaraty.gov.br/pt-BR/politica-externa/paz-e-seguranca-internacionais/151-zona-de-paz-e-cooperacao-do-atlantico-sul.

Mombassa, Aires Zarina Bonifácio and Eucidio Pimenta Arruda, 'História da Educação a Distância em Moçambique: perspectivas atuais e as contribuições do Brasil', *Práxis Educativa* 13:3 (2018), 1–18.

Montague, Dena, 'Stolen Goods: Coltan and conflict in the Democratic Republic of Congo' *SAIS Review*, 22:1 (2002), 103–18.

Mourão, Fernando Augusto Albuquerque, 'O Centro de Estudos Africanos da Universidade de São Paulo e os Trinta Anos da Revista África', *África: Revista do Centro de Estudos Africanos*. USP, São Paulo, 29–30 (2008–2010), 9–12.

Munanga, Kabengele, ed., *Estratégias e políticas de combate à discriminação racial* (São Paulo: Edusp, 1996).

—— 'Uma abordagem conceitual das noções de raça, racismo, identidade e etnia', paper presented at the 3° Seminário Nacional Relações Raciais e Educação, PENESB, Universidade Federal Fluminense, Rio de Janeiro, 5 November (São Paulo: Attar Editorial, 2003).

Ndutumu, Samuel S., *Géopolitique Maritime du Golfe de Guinée au XXIe Siècle* (Paris: L'Harmattan, 2012).

Nogueira, Danielle, 'BNDES suspende US$ 4,7 bi de desembolso a obras no exterior', *O Globo*, 11 October 2016, http://oglobo.globo.com/economia/bndes-suspende-us-47-bi-de-desembolso-obras-no-exterior-20274312.

Odebrecht, '2017 Odebrecht uma grande transformação', n.d., www.odebrecht.com/sites/default/files/relatorio_anual_2017.pdf.

OECD – Organisation for Economic Co-operation and Development, 'Brazil's Development Cooperation', n.d., www.oecd.org/dac/dac-global-relations/brazil-development-co-operation.htm.

OECD-DAC, 'Recipient Countries', 2018, https://public.tableau.com/views/OECDDACAidataglancebyrecipient_new/Recipients?:embed=y&:display_count=yes&:showTabs=y&:toolbar=no?&:showVizHome=no.

Ogwu, Joy, 'Nigeria and Brazil: A model for the emerging South-South relations?' in *South-South Relations in a Changing World Order*, edited by Jeker Arlsson (Uppsala: Scandinavian Institute of African Studies, 1982), 102–27.

OHCHR – United Nations Office of the High Commissioner Human Rights, 'International Convention on the Elimination of All Forms of Racial Discrimination', 1969, www.ohchr.org/EN/ProfessionalInterest/Pages/CERD.aspx.

Oliveira, Guilherme Ziebell de, 'Política Africana do Brasil: Mudança entre Lula e Dilma?' *Conjuntura Austral* 6:29 (2015), 33–47.

Olivo, Indira and Ernesto Navarro, 'EUA instalam novas bases militares na América do Sul', *Brasil de Fato* (30 May) 2012.

ONUBR – Nações Unidas no Brasil, 'Década Internacional de Afrodescendentes', https://nacoesunidas.org/wp-content/uploads/2016/05/WEB_BookletDecadaAfro_portugues.pdf.

ONUBR – Nações Unidas no Brasil, 'ONU e governo brasileiro iniciam planejamento da Década Internacional de Afrodescendentes', 3 March 2015, https://nacoesunidas.org/onu-e-governo-brasileiro-iniciam-planejamento-da-decada-internacional-de-afrodescendentes.

Penha, Eli Alves, *Relações Brasil-África e Geopolítica do Atlântico Sul* (Salvador: EDUFBA, 2011).

Pereira, José Nunes, 'Brasil-África no Governo Figueiredo: um balanço', *Contexto Internacional* 2 (1985), 81–104.

Pimentel, José Vicente de Sá, 'Relações entre o Brasil e a África subsaárica', *Revista Brasileira de Política Internacional* 43 (2000), 5–23.

Pinheiro, Letícia, 'Brasil, Portugal e descolonização africana (1946–60)' *Contexto Internacional* 4:9 (1989), 91–111.

—— *Política externa brasileira (1889–2002)* (Rio de Janeiro: Zahar, 2004).

Prado Júnior, Caio, *História Econômica do Brasil* (São Paulo: Brasiliense, 2006).

Preti, Oreste, 'A Universidade Aberta do Brasil em Moçambique: a experiência de um programa de cooperação internacional no continente africano', *Pesquisa de Debate em Educação* 3:1 (2013), 28–48. Available at www.revistappgp.caedufjf.net/index.php/revista1/article/view/46

Puente, Carlos Alfonso Iglesias, *A cooperação técnica horizontal brasileira como instrumento da política externa: a evolução da cooperação técnica com países em desenvolvimento – CTPD – no período 1995–2005* (Brasília: Fundação Alexandre Gusmão, 2010).

Pulitzer Center, 'Atlas of Pentecostalism' database, n.d., www.atlasofpentecostalism.net.

Queiroz Galvão, 'Construção Internacional', 14 July 2016, www.grupoqueirozgalvao.com.br/en/construcao-internacional.

Ress, Susanne, 'Racialization through "Time" in Brazil's Cooperation in Higher Education: An ethnographic case study of UNILAB', in *International Perspectives on Race (and Racism): Historical and contemporary considerations in education and society*, edited by Diane Brook Napier (Hauppauge, NY: Nova Science Publishers, 2015).

Reuters, 'Factbox: Africa bears heavy AIDS burden, hope ahead', 4 March 2011, www.reuters.com/article/us-aids-africa/factbox-africa-bears-heavy-aids-burden-hope-ahead-idUSTRE7232VJ20110304.

Ribeiro, Cláudio Oliveira, *Relações Político-Comerciais Brasil-África* (PhD dissertation, Universidade de São Paulo, 2007).

—— 'Imprensa e política africana no Brasil: uma análise dos governos Jânio Quadros e João Goulart', *África. Revista do Centro de Estudos Africanos,* USP, São Paulo 24-25-26 (2002–2005), 9–74.

Ribeiro, Matilde, 'Antigas personagens, novas cenas: mulheres negras e participação política' in *Mulher e Política. Gênero e feminismo no Partido dos Trabalhadores* edited by Ângela Borba, Nalu Faria and Tatau Godinho (São Paulo: Fundação Perseu Abramo, 1998), 189–207.

Rizzi, Kamilla Raquel, *O Grande Brasil e os pequenos PALOP. Relações do Brasil com Cabo Verde, Guiné Bissau e São Tomé e Príncipe* (Porto Alegre: Leitura XXI/CEBRAFRICA-UFRGS, 2014).

—— 'Relações Brasil – PALOP: 40 anos de cooperação para o desenvolvimento no Atlântico Sul (1974/75–2015)', *Revista Brasileira de Estudos Africanos* 1:1 (2016), 143–67.

Rockmann, Roberto, 'Infraestrutura e serviços estimulam negócios na África', *Valor Econômico*, 25 October 2013, www.valor.com.br/brasil/3316182/infraestrutura-e-servicos-estimulam-negocios-na-africa.

Rodrigues, José Honório, *Brasil e África: outro horizonte.* 1st ed. (Rio de Janeiro: Editora Civilização Brasileira, 1961).

—— *Brasil e África: outro horizonte.* 2nd ed. Rio de Janeiro (Editora Civilização Brasileira, 1964).

Rodrigues, Raimundo Nina, *As Raças Humanas e a Responsabilidade Penal no Brasil.* (Salvador: Livraria Progresso, 1957).

—— *Os Africanos no Brasil* (São Paulo: Madras Editora, 2008 [1932]).

Rosi, Bruno Gonçalves, 'As Relações Brasil-África no Regime Militar e na Atualidade', *Conjuntura Austral* 2:3–4 (2011), 31–46.

Rossi, Amanda, 'O aeroporto fantasma feito pela Odebrecht em Moçambique, que o BNDES financiou e tomou calote', *BBC Brasil*, 27 November 2017, www.bbc.com/portuguese/brasil-42074053.

Santana, Ivo de, 'Relações económicas Brasil–África: a Câmara de Comércio Afro-Brasileira e a intermediação de negócios no mercado brasileiro' *Estudos Afro-Asiáticos* 25:3 (2003), 517–55.

—— 'Notas e comentários sobre a dinâmica do comércio Brasil-África nas décadas de 1970 a 1990', *Revista Brasileira da Política Internacional* 46:2 (2003), 113–37.

Santos, Gevanilda, *Relações raciais e desigualdades no Brasil* (São Paulo: Selo Negro, 2009).

Santos, Ivair Augusto Alves dos, 'A influência militar e das industrias brasileiras de armamento na África', *Portalafro*, 14 June 2015, www.portalafro.com.br/a-influencia-militar-e-da-industria-de-armas-brasilieras-na-africa.

—— 'O movimento negro e o estado (1983–1987): o caso do Conselho de Participação e Desenvolvimento da Comunidade Negra no Governo de São Paulo' (Master's thesis, Universidade Estadual de Campinas, 2005).

Santos, Joel Rufino dos, *O que é racismo* (São Paulo: Brasiliense, 1983).

Saraiva, José Flávio Sombra, *O Lugar da África: a dimensão atlântica da política externa Brasileira de 1946 a nossos dias* (Brasília: Ed. UnB, 1996).

—— *África parceira do Brasil atlântico. Relações internacionais do Brasil e da África no início do século XXI* (Belo Horizonte: Fino Traço Editora, 2012).

Schoeman, Max, Gavin Cawthra, André du Pisani and Abillah Omari, eds. *Security and Democracy in Southern Africa* (Johannesburg: Wits University Press, 2007).

Scolese, Eduardo, 'Lula pede perdão por negros que foram escravos no Brasil', *Folha de São Paulo*, 15 April 2015, www1.folha.uol.com.br/fsp/brasil/fc1504200508.htm.

Seabra, Pedro, 'Brazil as a Security Actor in Africa: Reckoning and challenges ahead', *GIGA Focus Latin America*, 7 (2016).

SEADE – State System of Data Analysis Foundation, 'Instrução maior eleva fosso salarial entre branco e negro', 15 November 2017, www.seade.gov.br/instrucao-maior-eleva-fosso-salarial-entre-branco-e-negro.

Seibert, Gerhard, 'Brazil's Engagement with Africa', in *Africa South of the Sahara 2017*. 46th edition (London: Routledge, 2016), 42–50.

Selcher, Wayne A., *The Afro-Asian Dimension of Brazilian Foreign Policy 1956–1972* (Gainesville: The University of Florida Press, 1974).

Silva, Anaxsuell Fernando and Karen Susan Silva Pititinga Rosa, 'A Igreja Universal do Reino de Deus em Angola: faces da nova cartografia religiosa global', *Ciências Sociais Unisinos* 53:2 (2017), 234–41.

Silva, Luiz Inácio Lula da, 'Discurso do Presidente da República, Luiz Inácio Lula da Silva, por ocasião da abertura de Encontro Empresarial, durante visita à República do Congo, Brazzaville, 16 de outubro de 2007', *Resenha de Política Exterior do Brasil* 34:101 (2007), 133–4.

Stolte, Christina, *Brazil's Africa Strategy: Role conception and the drive for international status* (New York: Palgrave Macmillan, 2015).

Summit of South American-Arab Countries (ASPA), *Brasília Declaration* (Brasília, 2005).

Takahashi, Fábio, 'Brasil financiará melhoria de ensino superior na África', *Folha de São Paulo*, 6 June 2013, www1.folha.uol.com.br/educacao/2013/06/1290566-brasil-financiara-melhoria-de-ensino-superior-na-africa.shtml.

Taylor, Ian, *The International Relations of Sub-Saharan Africa* (London: The Continuum International Publishing Group, 2010).

—— *Africa Rising? BRICS – diversifying dependency* (Woodbridge, UK: James Currey, 2014).

The Economic Times, 'IBSAMAR 2016: Navies of Brazil, India and South Africa to hold exercise off Goa coast', 23 February 2016, https://economictimes.indiatimes.com/slideshows/nation-world/ibsamar-2016-navies-of-brazil-india-and-south-africa-to-hold-exercise-off-goa-coast/ibsamar-2016-joint-trilateral-naval-exercise/slideshow/51102550.cms.

Thompson, Nathan and Robert Muggah, 'The Blue Amazon: Brazil asserts its influence across the Atlantic', *Foreign Affairs*, 11 June 2015, www.foreignaffairs.com/articles/africa/2015-06-11/blue-amazon.

Tokarnia, Mariana, 'Educação reforça desigualdades entre brancos e negros, diz estudo', *Agência Brasil*, 18 November 2016, http://agenciabrasil.ebc.com.br/educacao/noticia/2016-11/educacao-reforca-desigualdades-entre-brancos-e-negros-diz-estudo.

Ukah, Asonzeh, 'African Christianities: Features, promises and problems', Working Paper 79, Department of Anthropology and African Studies (Mainz: Johannes-Gutenberg-Universität, 2007), www.ifeas.uni-mainz.de/Dateien/AP79.pdf.

Ukeje, Charles and Wullson Mvomo Ela, *African Approaches to Maritime Security – The Gulf of Guinea* (Abuja: Friedrich-Ebert-Stiftung, 2013).

UN Office for Disarmaments Affairs, 'The Arms Trade Treaty', n.d., www.un.org/disarmament/convarms/att.

UNCTAD – United Nations Conference on Trade and Development, *Economic Development in Africa Report 2010* (Geneva, 2010).

UNDP – United Nations Development Programme, 'Finances', IBSA Fund, n.d., http://tcdc2.undp.org/IBSA/finance/finances.htm.

UNESCO – United Nations Educational, Scientific and Cultural Organization, 'International Decade for People of African Descent (2015–2024)', 2015, https://en.unesco.org/decade-people-african-descent/objectives.

UNHCR-ACNUR – The UN Refugee Agency, 'Dados sobre refúgio no Brasil', 2018, www.acnur.org/portugues/recursos/estatisticas/dados-sobre-refugio-no-brasil.

UNILAB, 'Unilab em números', n.d., www.unilab.edu.br/unilab-em-numeros.

UNIOGBIS – United Nations Integrated Peacebuilding Office in Guinea-Bissau, 'Secretary-General appoints José Viegas Filho from Brazil as Special Representative for Guinea-Bissau', 7 May 2018, https://uniogbis.unmissions.org/en/secretary-general-appoints-josé-viegas-filho-brazil-special-representative-guinea-bissau.

United Nations, 'The Durban Declaration and Programme of Action', Durban Review Conference, Geneva, 20–24 April 2009, www.un.org/en/durbanreview2009/ddpa.shtml.

United Nations General Assembly. Resolution A/43/512 (1988) Annex – Zone of Peace and Cooperation of the South Atlantic. New York: 1988.

—— Resolution A/45/474 (1990) Annex – Zone of Peace and Cooperation of the South Atlantic. New York: 1990.

—— Resolution A/49/467 (1994) Annex IV – Zone of Peace and Cooperation of the South Atlantic. New York: 1994.

UNOSSC – United Nations Office for South-South Cooperation, 'Launch of the 2017 IBSA Fund Overview of Project Portfolio Report and Exhibition', 11 September 2017, www.unsouthsouth.org/2017/09/11/launch-of-the-2017-ibsa-fund-overview-of-project-portfolio-report-and-exhibition.

Veiga, Pedro da Motta and Sandra Polónia Rios, *Os investimentos brasileiros na África: características, tendências e agenda de política*. Texto CINDES 39 (Rio de Janeiro; Centro de Estudos de Integração e Desenvolvimento -CINDES, 2014).

—— *As Políticas brasileiras para a África na esfera econômica: principais características e percepções dos agentes públicos e privados*. Textos Cindes 42 (Rio de Janeiro; Centro de Estudos de Integração e Desenvolvimento – CINDES, 2015).

Verschave, François-Xavier, *De la françafrique à la mafiafrique* (Brussels: Éditions Tribord, 2004).

Vijgen, Richard, 'Pentecostalism: Massive global growth under the radar', Pulitzer Center, 9 March 2015, https://pulitzercenter.org/reporting/pentecostalism-massive-global-growth-under-radar#slideshow-8.

Visentini, Paulo Fagundes, *Relações Internacionais do Brasil: de Vargas à Lula* (São Paulo: Fundação Perseu Abramo, 2008).

—— *A Política Externa do Regime Militar Brasileiro* (Porto Alegre: Editora UFRGS, 2011).

—— *A Relação Brasil-África. Prestígio, cooperação ou negócios?* (Rio de Janeiro: Alta Books, 2016).

Visentini, Paulo Fagundes and Analúcia Danilevicz Pereira, *A política africana do governo Lula*. (Porto Alegre: Núcleo de Estratégia e Relações Internacionais, UFRGS, 2008).

Visentini, Paulo Fagundes, Luiz Dario Teixeira and Analúcia Danilevicz Pereira, *Breve História da África* (Porto Alegre: Leitura XXI, 2007).

—— *História da África e dos Africanos*, 3rd ed. (Petrópolis: Vozes, 2014).

Volman, Daniel and Jeremy Keenan, 'The Origins of AFRICOM: The Obama administration, the Sahara-Sahel and US militarization of Africa', *Concerned Africa Scholars Bulletin* 85 (2010), 84–90. Available at: http://concernedafricascholars.org/docs/bulletin85volman-keenan.pdf.

Walters, Ronald, 'O princípio da ação afirmativa e o progresso racial nos Estados Unidos', *Estudos Afro-Asiáticos* 28 (1995), 129–40.

White, Lyal, 'Understanding Brazil's New Drive for Africa'. *South African Journal of International Affairs* 17:2 (2010), 221–42.

—— 'Emerging powers in Africa: Is Brazil any different?' *South African Journal of International Affairs* 20:1 (2013), 117–36.

Williams, Paul, 'Britain and Africa after the Cold War: Beyond damage limitation?' in *Africa in International Politics: External involvement on the continent* edited by Paul Williams and Ian Taylor (London: Routledge, 2004).

World Bank and Instituto de Pesquisa Económica Aplicada (IPEA), *Bridging the Atlantic: Brazil and Sub-Saharan Africa – South-South partnering for growth* (Brasília: IPEA, 2011).

Yeomans, Jon, 'Inside Simandou: The mining project that has cursed all who come near it', *The Telegraph*, 5 June 2017, www.telegraph.co.uk/business/2017/06/05/inside-simandou-mining-project-has-cursed-come-near.

Zamparoni, Valdemir, 'A África e os Estudos Africanos no Brasil: Passado e Futuro', *Ciência e Cultura* 59:2 (2007), 46–49.

Zarpelon, Janiffer, *Cooperação para o desenvolvimento do Brasil na área da saúde com os PALOP*, Oficina do CES no. 414 (Coimbra: Centro de Estudos Sociais, 2014).

Index